CINEMA'S DOPPELGÄNGERS

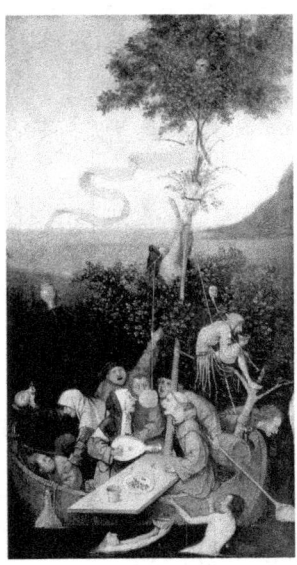

Fig. 1. Hieronymus Bosch, *Ship of Fools* (1490–1500)

First published in 2021 by punctum books, Earth, Milky Way.
https://punctumbooks.com

ISBN-13: 978-1-953035-62-2 (print)
ISBN-13: 978-1-953035-56-1 (ePDF)

DOI: 10.53288/0320.1.00

LCCN: 2021939314
Library of Congress Cataloging Data is available from the Library of Congress

Book Design: Vincent W.J. van Gerven Oei

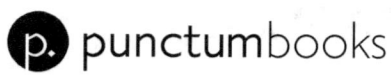 punctumbooks

spontaneous acts of scholarly combustion

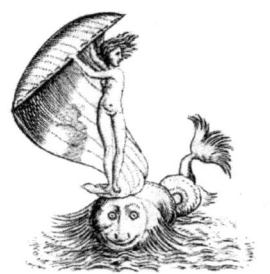

HIC SVNT MONSTRA

DOUG

CINEMA'S
DOPPELGÄNGERS

DObbEFCVИCEKS
CIИEWV2

DIBBEKИ

p.

to
The Omega Collective,
Whoever, Wherever, and Whenever They May Be

Contents

Tlön may well be a labyrinth, but it is a labyrinth forged by men,
a labyrinth destined to be deciphered by men.

— Jorge Luis Borges "Tlön, Uqbar, Orbus Tertius"

Prolegomenon on the Aesthetics of Non-linearity

Ozu Yasujiro found himself pacing through the dark. It was December 12, 1936 and it seemed that the world was shifting. The director hardly ever worried, his lead actor Ryu Chishu recalled, but that morning he looked as he if were "drifting, like a fragment of a cloud, along an ever-widening spiral,"[1] first circling around the camera, then around the dining room table where he'd arranged the shoot for that day, and finally along the perimeter of the soundstage itself, his hands clasped behind his back, head down in contemplation, no longer aware of the set he'd so painstakingly designed the night before with teacups, flowers, and sake bottles arranged methodically across the table and floor to provide a sense of depth to the image and to display his authorial style to the intellectual critics in Tokyo who'd already heralded him as the leading filmmaker of his generation.

Ozu wasn't troubled by the scene, Ryu said; he'd always planned every shot in a day's work long in advance, after all. Acting on an Ozu set was like "being a salaryman — perhaps more like working at a flower shop than a bank, but a simple job

---

1   Ryu Chishu, *I Know Nothing,* trans. Kyoko Hirano (Ann Arbor: University of Michigan Center for Japanese Studies, 2001), 101.

like any other."[2] No, the director's perambulations were unusually anxious that morning because of the meeting he'd just had with Shochiku president Kido Shiro, who'd finally confirmed what everyone at the studio had quietly expected but also quietly feared for several months. Soon after Gerhard Mannheim's *The Rhineland* premiered as the world's first all-talking picture, earning windfall profits in Germany earlier that year, Hollywood's three major studios had announced that they'd follow suit with a slate of movies recorded entirely with spoken dialogue. And that morning, Kido had finally told his favorite director the inevitable: that the company would soon be joining the American and German film industries in making the transition to a production schedule consisting entirely of recorded, synchronized sound, and that the movie that Ozu was then directing — *Tokyo Winter*, to be released in 1937 — would therefore be his final silent film.

Perhaps because the sensational crowds that thronged to the first talkies had made Ozu nervous about the future of his career, he and his screenwriting collaborator Noda Kogo had written an especially somber script that spring, obsessed with the conjoined themes of birth and death and with what Hara Tatsuki has called "Ozu's fatalistic analysis of diachronic osmosis" — that is, his concern with the past's tendency to permeate the present and the present's tendency to continually re-imagine the past.[3] And in this sense, Ozu's film can function as the quintessential emblem of the juncture between the silent and the sound eras and thus the quintessential emblem, too, of film history itself, which scholars have similarly defined by the conceptions of intertwining deaths and births, by the folding over and permeability of time.

Tokyo Winter opens in unexpectedly dramatic fashion for Ozu, with a husband leaning in to listen to his wife as she rises

---

2   Ibid., 145.

3   Hara Tatsuki, "Ozu's Anti-Chronology: *Tokyo Winter* and Time's Permeability," in *Ozu: Formalism, Ideology, Interpretation,* ed. David Desser (Cambridge: Cambridge University Press, 2004), 117.

painfully from her deathbed. He cuts from an intense close-up of the woman's whispering lips to a series of intertitles in which she admits to her husband that she'd been married once before she met him, that her first husband had died in the 1923 earthquake, that she'd been pregnant at the time, and that she'd given her baby daughter away to a childless couple because she had been too ravaged by grief to take care of her on her own. And then, when Ozu cuts back to a two-shot, revealing Ryu Chishu's blank expression, the wife lies back in bed with a heave of relief, closes her eyes, and passes away.

The movie hinges on a moment near the end when Ryu catches sight of a ragged thirteen-year-old girl wandering alone in the street, and in an extended close-up, his emotionless visage evokes a surging sense of anguish. And then, in what David Bordwell pointed out was the only flashback in his career,[4] Ozu cuts to what is demonstrably that same city street in the aftermath of the Great Kanto Earthquake thirteen years earlier, as Ryu, now a young man, stands in front of the ruins of what we understand immediately to be his family home, flames licking up against the charred timbers from pockets amid the rubble. From here, in what was certainly the most elaborate set the director ever created — with hundreds of soot-faced extras streaming through billowing smoke past heaps of bricks and twisted metal beams — Ryu wanders in a daze through a series of atypically surrealistic images for Ozu, past prostitutes smoking in the back seats of burned-out cars, dogs urinating into flowerpots, and abandoned children wearing inverted toilet bowls to ward off the rain. Finally, he comes across a lone woman cowering beneath a tarp, and as he bends down to drape her in his coat to fend off the cold, she looks up to meet his gaze, and we realize as we recognize her face that this is the moment when he first met his wife — the woman whose death thirteen years later had opened the film — huddling now in the street because her home, like his, has been destroyed. But because of the flashback struc-

---

4   David Bordwell, *Ozu and the Poetics of Cinema* (Cambridge: Harvard University Press, 1986), 53–54.

ture, we understand — in a way that Ryu won't for another thirteen years — that her husband is dead and that she is pregnant with a child whose very existence she knows instantly she'll have to hide from this man who may represent her only chance for survival.

The sequence is harrowing precisely because its oneiric character lies in such uncomfortable juxtaposition with the quotidian realism of the rest of the picture. When Ryu comes back to the present, he approaches the girl who'd caught his attention on the street, who must now be the same age as his wife's first child, and gently offers to buy her a meal. But she makes an ugly face and runs away. Ryu turns home, initially in quiet contemplation, but eventually accompanied by the visual signifiers of a silent audio barrage — close-ups of car horns whose honking we're prompted to imagine, store owners haggling with customers, women in window perches hectoring their husbands across the street — as if the environment, like memory itself, has begun to assault him. Finally, he returns to the small rooms above the noodle shop that he'd shared with his wife for the last thirteen years and kneels stiffly in the dim light in front of his single table to eat dinner. Then, his daughter, now about twelve years old herself, emerges from a back room, cradling a baby doll in the crook of her elbow, and gazes for a while at her father's back, as if trying to make sense of him by coming to terms with his bent shape, while the image slowly fades and the movie comes to an end.

Interpolation: Unmasking the Fictive

It's at this point where I, the author, feel an obligation, unusual for an academic historian, to step out from behind the curtain in order to acknowledge what many readers have already picked up on or begun to suspect: the fact that what you've just read in this book's opening section is not what most people would consider a work of history at all. That's because most of what I've written never actually took place. At least not in this world. For those readers unfamiliar with the finer points of film history, let me be clear about some of the factual issues that you've encountered so far: Ozu Yasujiro, for example, was an actual Japanese filmmaker — indeed, one of the greatest who ever lived — but he never directed a film called *Tokyo Winter,* though cinephiles intimate with his oeuvre might have chuckled knowingly since the title sounds very much like a movie he might have made. Ozu's favorite lead actor was, in fact, a man named Ryu Chishu, but Ryu never published a memoir in which he wrote the words that I've attributed to him. Nor does any film scholar named Hara Tatsuki exist, nor does his essay "Ozu's Anti-Chronology," as much as I'd like to read it. And though the scholar David Bordwell actually has written a book titled *Ozu and the Poetics of Cinema,* he points out there that the director, in fact, never once included a flashback in any of his films, which makes my reading of the fictive *Tokyo Winter* somewhat antithetical to Ozu's existing aesthetic and intellectual program.[5] Finally — and most ostentatiously — there is no film director named Gerhard Mannheim, nor was *The Rhineland* the first talking picture, since the first talkies weren't released in Germany in 1936, but in the United States in 1927 and 1928.

This being the case, I have to acknowledge that I, Doug Dibbern, am not really the author of the book that you will be reading. No, the real author of what you have read so far in the Overture and of what you will continue to read beginning with the next section and throughout the rest of the book is not me but my doppelgänger — let's call him "Doug Dibbern," for simplicity's sake — a film historian and critic very much like his twin but who writes from some alternative unfolding of historical time. The world from which he writes is much like our own, but with some notable differences. In that other dimension, for instance, neither the Bolsheviks nor the Nazis came to power, so

---

5   Ibid. Hint: Bordwell's book on Ozu, like many of the authors and books in the footnotes, is an actual author and an actual book, whereas many of the other authors and books in these footnotes do not exist — at least not in this existing unfolding of historical time.

there was, therefore, no World War II and no Holocaust. That world suffered, nevertheless, through its own catastrophes. Germany and Japan lived under the yoke of authoritarian regimes throughout most of the century, and anti-Semitic pogroms swept across Eastern Europe throughout the 1950s and 1960s. Film industries, too, evolved differently in that alternative existence. Hollywood was dominated by three major companies, for instance, rather than five, which limited the freedom of directors who worked in the studio system. It is also a world in which, because of these differences, the intelligentsia considers Kobayashi Masaki — not Ozu nor Kurosawa nor Mizoguchi — to be the greatest Japanese filmmaker, in which Alfred Hitchcock never came to Hollywood, in which Orson Welles's first film was his adaptation of Conrad's *Heart of Darkness,* whose financial failure prevented him from ever making *Citizen Kane,* and a world whose cinematic aesthetics and critical literature all evolved slightly differently because an obscure director named D.W. Griffith was killed by a speeding train in 1913, just as he'd begun preparing the script for an epic film based on Thomas Dixon's novel *The Clansmen.*

So, what's going on here, exactly? This book lays out a counterfactual history of the movies — in fact, two alternative histories of the same counterfactual world, as you're about to find out — not just to engage in a playful exercise, but because an approach like this can serve a legitimate historiographic purpose. Embracing speculative fiction as a historical methodology will necessarily highlight the arbitrary nature of the past. It can underline how the trajectory of film — more than any other art form — has been determined by political, economic, technological, and bureaucratic forces. And it can call attention to the inherently aesthetic nature of all historical writing and thus of the inherent hermeneutic nature of the reader's task. And I hope that by acknowledging the contingent nature of the past's chronological unfolding, other historians might be inspired to deploy some more adventurously intellectual strategies of their own. To address these issues, let's let my fictive alter ego speak once again. It's at this point that I, Doug Dibbern, will retreat into off-screen space and let my doppelgänger "Doug Dibbern" take up the reins once again, beginning with the very next sentence and continuing for the remainder of the book.

Causal Explanation and Counterfactual Speculation: Materialist Historiography's Aesthetic Demands

In his book *Plausible Worlds: Possibility and Understanding in History and the Social Sciences,* Geoffrey Hawthorn suggests that we should reclaim counterfactual speculation from the realm of the parlor game so that it can play an explicit and central role in the historian's project. Though most historians tend to gloss over this aspect of their mission, their explanations of why any historical event took place are intimately bound up with — and dependent upon — the plausibility of those explanations' implicit counterfactual suppositions. That is, a historian might maintain that some historical event A occurred because of preceding historical events X, Y, and Z. But, this explanation is only valid if one can argue convincingly that A would not have happened if something other than the combination of X, Y, and Z had actually taken place — and, crucially, that Not X, Not Y, and Not Z are all believable scenarios.

Take, for example, one historian's explanation of why the first talking pictures arrived in Germany in 1936 rather than in Hollywood in 1924. In his book *The Talkies: The Global Transition to Sound,* Donald Crafton argues that sound cinema didn't appear initially in the American film industry, as one might expect due to its economic clout, partly because the three major studios — Paramount, MGM, and Fox — had colluded to corner the market by buying out all their smaller competitors back in 1923. So, in 1924, when RCA first approached the Hollywood studios with its new audio technology, the Big Three saw no economic need to experiment with their product since they no longer had any viable competition. But if the majors had failed to consolidate the industry in 1923 or had done so only in 1925, Crafton suggests, one of their minor rivals that they had not yet eliminated — Universal, maybe, or Pinnacle, or Warner Bros. — most certainly would have taken the risk of trying out RCA's sound-on-film system.[6] But Crafton's reasoning is credible only to the extent that the reader accepts that these alternative scenarios are realistic. That is, Crafton's explanation about why the talkies emerged in Germany in 1936 depends in part on convincing his reader of the plausibility of a fictional course of events, in which Warner Bros. might have adopted sound technology in 1924 and thus produced the first all-talking features in, say, 1926 or 1927. As Hawthorn puts it, "the plausibility of this [historical] reasoning will turn on the counterfactuals it suggests. And if the counterfactuals themselves are not plausible, we should not give the explanation the credence we otherwise might";[7] or, as he writes elsewhere, "the force of an explanation turns on the counterfactuals it implies."[8]

Hawthorn's insight thus reveals a counterintuitive enigma in regard to historical understanding. For historians to make a compelling case as to why some event or phenomenon took place, they must delineate a series of plausible causes, but the more detailed their list becomes, the more alternative scenarios they generate. That is, because they imply that the opposite of each of the causal events they've laid out might also have taken place, when they propose an interconnected series of circumstances as the crucial factor in bringing about the current state of affairs, they are simultaneously positing that multiple combinations of interconnected actual and fictional events might also have occurred, all of which, presumably, would have led to outcomes other than what actually happened in the real world. For instance, if a historian argues that event A took place because of three causes X, Y, and Z, he is postulating eight possible combinations of preceding events, only one of which could possibly

6 Donald Crafton, *The Talkies: The Global Transition to Sound* (New York: Charles Scribner's Sons, 1998), 293.

7 Geoffrey Hawthorn, *Plausible Worlds: Possibility and Understanding in History and the Social Sciences* (Cambridge: Cambridge University Press, 1992), 16–17.

8 Ibid., 14.

have resulted in phenomenon A.[9] Thus, in his "first paradox of explanation," Hawthorn writes that "in explaining history we increase alternatives as we also reduce them."[10] Thus, the supreme irony of historians' enterprise is that the more intelligent and complex they make their case, the more deeply reliant on fictional suppositions their work becomes and thus the more like a novelist they appear. So even though Hawthorn himself doesn't quite say so explicitly, to a certain extent we judge the validity of any historical explanation by the same standards that we use in judging any novelist's imaginary creations.

Counterfactuals are especially important in understanding the history of film because its particular mode of production creates specific types of historical causes and effects. Fernand Braudel, the most articulate advocate of studying the past from a great remove, argued that historians too often focused on what he called the "history of events," investigating microscopic decisions that individuals — the so-called "great men" — had made that produced instantaneous, observable effects at a specific place and time. He became interested, instead, in macroscopic causes and effects that would have remained largely invisible as they were transpiring — especially demographic shifts whose significance we could see only centuries after the fact when we studied what he called the *longue durée*.[11]

But Lydia Bivington has argued that certain subjects, disciplines, cultures, or eras require historians to adopt what she calls a "materialist historiography" that focuses on the kind of microscopic effects that institutional forces tend to produce. Drawing on the recently renascent works of the German economic philosopher Karl Marx, she suggests that a culture's ideology is to a

---

9   In this example, there are eight possible combinations of historical events: (a) X–Y–Z; (b) X–Y–!Z; (c) X–!Y–Z; (d) X–!Y–!Z; (e) !X–Y–Z; (f) !X–Y–!Z; (g) !X–!Y–Z; and (h) !X–!Y–!Z. In the real world, of course, most historians don't conceive of causal factors in such rigidly binary terms, but this example is intended merely to serve a theoretical purpose.

10 Hawthorn, *Plausible Worlds,* 37.

11 Fernand Braudel, *On History,* trans. Alexander Friebertson (Chicago: University of Chicago Press, 1979), 28, 27, 34.

large extent determined by its economic organization. So anyone studying the aesthetics of an industrial medium, therefore, needs to examine the bureaucracies that created those artistic standards for financial gain. "Historians of fields like the motion pictures," she writes, "thus must study microscopic causes and effects in which individual figures, or more often corporations, make sudden decisions — often regarding the adoption or deployment of new technologies — that can have immediate and decisive effects on the look and feel and on the uses of their commercial products."[12] But though she doesn't explicitly say so herself, it becomes clear that because the pivotal actions that Bivington urges materialist historians to investigate always create such conspicuous counterfactuals, it logically follows that materialist historians will necessarily produce — more than other types of historians — a proliferation of alternative histories. In other words, the very volatility of the economic-aesthetic link that undergirds the qualities of screen entertainment demands that film historians, especially, propose and analyze fictional scenarios.

Film historians interested in explaining a smaller time frame — for example, why filmmakers produced the first narrative motion pictures in America in 1904 rather than in 1905 — will focus on people and institutions that made substantive decisions rather than on large-scale cultural shifts over which individual agents had little control. When Charles Musser suggests, for instance, that the Edison Manufacturing Company decided in 1903 to produce both fictional films like The Great Train Robbery and feature-length sports actualities like *Tour de France* in order to counteract the sudden downturn in film rentals in 1901 and 1902, he implies that the company would not have turned to fictional storytelling or to multi-reel movies if the popular genre of the boxing film had not been banned in

---

12 Lydia Bivington, "Materialist Historiography and the Artistic Industrial Complex," in *Art, Economics, and Culture: New Approaches*, eds. Lydia Bivington and Micaela Lorenzo (Oxford: Oxford University Press, 1992), 27. See also Lydia Bivington and Niranjan Menon, eds., *The Karl Marx Reader* (London: Routledge, 1999).

many states at the turn of the century.[13] These types of microscopic institutional decisions that a materialist historian would tend to explain are much more likely to engender plausible alternative scenarios than are the long-term demographic shifts that historians like Braudel are interested in.

Thus, some disciplines are inherently more amenable to counterfactual speculation than others because they are more beholden to specific types of real-world factors. Military historians, for instance, treat counterfactuals with more respect than social historians because the decisions that generals made in the heat of battle had more far-reaching consequences than did, for instance, the consumer choices that women in a particular nation made over the course of a decade. Civil War historians, for instance, are not embarrassed to speculate about whether the Confederacy might have won the war if the South had prevailed at Antietam or Gettysburg; if anything, they think that analyzing such what-if scenarios is one of their central intellectual functions.[14] Film historians, to my mind, have much more in common with military historians who focus on immediate structural changes than they do with historians of poetry or painting whose aesthetic shifts may have causes much more related to the *longue durée*. Because the cinema has a corporate, institutional, and economic structure linked to mass culture, it is especially contingent upon any sudden changes in society's material composition. If some company invents a new technology, such as three-strip color or stereoscopic imaging, and the film studios that dominate the existing industrial organization decide to take it up — and if audiences flock to see the new novelty — the entire course of film history can change overnight.

If materialist historians trying to explain why the art of film has taken the shape that it has have an obligation to value counterfactual speculation, they also have an obligation — and for

13 Charles Musser, "Rethinking Early Cinema: Cinema of Attractions and Narrativity," *The Yale Journal of Criticism* 7, no. 2 (1994): 203–32.
14 See James M. McPherson, *Battle Cry of Freedom: The Civil War Era* (New York: Oxford University Press, 1988).

the very same reasons — to embrace non-linear modes of writing. That is, if a historian's ultimate goal is to explicate how the dominant cinematic aesthetics came into being, he should not necessarily write a narrative that commences with the moment when Edison or the Lumieres first projected film on screen, but should instead organize his analysis around those economic, political, and institutional factors that were the most important causes of the medium's prototypical formal and narrative features. The very order in which the historian chooses to arrange his explanations would thus constitute an argument in and of itself, suggesting which actors and events were the most important in shaping the art of the screen. Historians who begin their chronological accounts in 1895 when people first projected motion pictures to an audience are thus making an implicit — and perhaps unthinking — teleological argument about the essential relationship between film's origins and its later aesthetic evolution. A historian, on the other hand, who opened his account with the invention of the talkies and concluded with Edison and the Lumières in 1895 would be making the case for the aesthetic significance of the human voice in contrast to the image itself, and he would thus also be staging a critique of those scholars who treat the spectacular visual qualities of those early single-take movies as the ontological foundation of the art form.[15]

Adopting Hawthorn's theoretical position on counterfactuality to its furthest extent could inspire a historian to delve into more unambiguously fictional modes of writing and more radically non-chronological approaches, both of which would highlight — in an intellectually productive manner — the intrinsically aesthetic nature of historical writing as a genre. The possibility of treating one's counterfactual suppositions as fact is intriguing for a number of reasons. It has the potential to liberate history from the formulaic chronologies and teleological assumptions that many readers have accepted as a given, transforming it into a vehicle that they might attend to with the same aspirations

---

15 See Wanda Strauven, ed., *The Cinema of Attractions Reloaded* (Amsterdam: Amsterdam University Press, 2006).

they bring to other art forms. Hayden White, for instance, argues that historians are not like scientists who observe the world in order to uncover the truth; rather, they are practitioners of language, and thus, "the historian performs an essentially poetic act."[16] The historical work is not a window onto a phenomenal world, but a "verbal structure in the form of a narrative prose discourse,"[17] and as such we shouldn't judge it by how accurately it represents the past. Historians organize written texts to make arguments about their characters and their interactions with the world just as novelists or playwrights do. So when we do judge historians, we should employ the same methods we use to analyze the artistic and rhetorical components of a story in any genre. In other words, White argues, "the best grounds for choosing one perspective on history rather than another are ultimately aesthetic and moral rather than epistemological."[18]

Drawing upon history's innately artistic character to write a work of fiction might also enable historians to develop more nuanced modes of intellectual argument. That is, by presenting explanations about why certain events and phenomena took place in an alternative development of time, writers would simultaneously be formulating other implicit arguments about why certain events and phenomena took place in the actual world: by positing plausible alternative scenarios, they would highlight which causes and effects in our actual world they thought were inevitable and which had been arbitrary. Thus, by inventing an alternative history, authors would prompt readers to engage in a hermeneutic process in order to understand their historical vision in the same way that artists inspire audiences to interpret their work. Returning to a previous example, an adventurous historian could write a fictional account of film history in which Hollywood's three major studios failed to take control of the American film industry in 1923 so that one of their smaller

---

16 Hayden White, *Metahistory: The Historical Imagination in Nineteenth-Century Europe* (Baltimore: The Johns Hopkins University Press, 1973), x.

17 Ibid., 2

18 Ibid., xii.

American competitors, unlike them, was willing to experiment with RCA's sound-on-film technology in 1925 as a way to compete with them. By presenting a fictive history in which Warner Bros., for instance, invented the talking cinema in Hollywood in 1927, a historian would be making a tacit argument about how the organizational structure of the film industry had more to do with the introduction of sound than did the technological inventions that comprise most accounts of the talkie revolution.

But as intellectually valuable as it might be to write such a book, historians — unfortunately, perhaps — must adhere to the facts, no matter how poetically they choose to present them. Nevertheless, materialist historians' interest in the intellectual utility of both counterfactual speculation and non-linearity will necessarily nurture questions about the organizational principles of their entire books. Once scholars accept that any historical explanation automatically gives birth to an array of alternative scenarios, none of which are the product of any inevitable evolutionary path, it seems appropriate that they should deploy an array of alternative historical methods themselves. By embracing radically dissimilar historiographic tactics within the same work, historians will shed light on the arbitrary nature of historical development, while at the same time underlining historical writing's fundamentally artistic qualities.

Hence, I've chosen to organize this book not as just one history, but as two. Parts One and Two each recount the same history of film — covering the same facts and suggesting similar arguments — but in two alternative formats. By placing them beside each other, I hope to create a collage-like effect in which each plays off the other, functioning as counterexamples — mirrors, or doppelgängers, if you will — highlighting once again the essential imperfections of all historical writing and encouraging readers to interpret history in the same way they might other artistic forms. I've organized the first section in one type of non-chronological format. There, I emphasize the aesthetic components of film history, compiling a collection of essays about what I consider to be some of the most significant movies ever made. This framework lays out the aesthetic values that give credence to the arguments about economics and politics I make throughout the book, while avoiding the pitfalls of a traditional chronological account. The second section proposes an alternative mode of conceptualizing the history of cinema as a collection of moments when certain changes in some institutional, economic, or political structure led to far-reaching effects in the products we see on screen. I've organized this section in order of those events and decisions that made the most vital changes in the medium's aesthetic trajectory. Each of these two sections points both forward and backward in time, so that this history eschews the typical model of a straight line and instead aims to resemble a lattice, a collection of nets, or a multidimensional grid.

The idea that historical understanding is essentially an aesthetic and non-chronological experience returns us finally to Ozu Yasujiro's film *Tokyo Winter*. It was probably no coincidence that Ozu used the only flashback in his career in a movie that he knew would be his last silent film, at a time when he thought — just as we do today — that the existing global order was on the verge of collapse and that the cinema itself might be on its deathbed as well. It was on the morning that Kido Shiro told him that this would be his final silent picture — as Ozu paced the set slowly, in an ever-expanding spiral — that the idea of a flashback first came to him, since the flashback is by its very nature a challenge to time's chronological development. The flashback, after all, reignites memory and revivifies the dead; it imbues the present with the weight of its antecedents, reminding us that the past never entirely disappears, since its afterglow is always visible in the present state of affairs. It reminds us that history, too, is ever-shifting, contracting and expanding, spiraling back in on itself like a dream, so that every present moment is not some terminal point on a straight line but merely an arbitrary juncture — a random fleck on a loop that keeps spinning in and out of phase, a speck we can catch a glimpse of only now and then, out of focus, like every moment that has come before and every moment that is yet to come.

PART ONE

Revising the Canon: Outline for an Alternative History of the Cinema

Many historians of the arts recount narratives that emphasize the causes and effects of the medium's evolutionary development. But this chronological methodology has aesthetic repercussions, tending to value those artists involved in vanguard movements that challenged the era's overriding formal assumptions. It thus valorizes social networks, demographic homogeneity, urban values, and the cultural centers of the wealthiest nations. Though this model may seem at first to apply mostly to histories of the high arts like painting, it's equally valid for the history of the movies, which has paid disproportionate attention to directors in Hollywood and Paris who managed to subtly reform the generic conventions of their time by working within the system. But since the evolutionary approach to the study of film makes us focus on insiders, it produces problematic consequences regarding nationality, race, and gender, among other issues. Just as important, it tends to exclude and undervalue those filmmakers who were not working in the same aesthetic registers as those insiders — either those who were happy to adhere to the standard style of the day or those who were exploring even more innovative but idiosyncratic formal experimentation on their own.

But even if historians want to disregard this storytelling mode, they can't escape the fact that they will have to organize their books — typically more implicitly than explicitly — around their own aesthetic judgments, since they must make choices about which films and which filmmakers to cover. One consequence of abandoning narrative, therefore, is that historians merely shift their artistic assessments from one organizing principle to another — often without acknowledging that their structural decisions have been dictated by issues of taste. With this in mind, I've decided to organize this section, the first of my two competing renditions of an alternative history of film — two intertwined historical doppelgängers — as an overt argument about evaluative aesthetics, a non-chronological collection of essays about what I consider to be fifty of the most significant films ever made. And since aesthetic judgments are intimately bound up with political, economic, and national issues, my selection of movies that are worthy of analysis is simultaneously an implicit assertion about which material conditions and which ideological issues have played the most significant role in shaping the art of the screen.

Given that every film historian aims to reimagine the medium's past, my selection of films does not resemble the most common canonical lists of movies. The differences and similarities between my list and the prevailing conception of the canon constitutes an argument most obviously about artistic preferences, but also more implicitly about which past structural circumstances nurtured — or constrained — the aesthetics of motion pictures. That is, because movies are the product of industrial production, one's ideas about issues that seem to be purely artistic are intimately bound up with judgments about larger political and economic forces, one of the fundamental tensions of historical writing about film that has become more self-evident today for those of us now living in a much more politicized era than even a decade ago.

That being said, if aesthetic judgments are founded upon ideological assumptions, historians' taste is always dependent upon their explanations of material causes and effects. But arguments about cause and effect, by their very nature, necessarily hint at the notion of evolutionary development. In other words, in each of these essays, I analyze films in relation to the movies of both their contemporaries and their predecessors and I explain their existence as a product of political, economic, and bureaucratic phenomena. Thus, even a mode of history writing that attempts to create a non-chronological account of the medium will always be drawn back, on some level, into the very evolutionary models it attempts to escape. So, while this book purports to embrace an anti-teleological methodology, to a certain extent it merely embraces, perhaps, a contrasting conception of development, focusing on microscopic evolutionary explanations rather than the dominant macroscopic evolutionary vision that has defined the scholarly discourse since its inception.

With that in mind, to understand the specifics of my intervention — and thus of my aesthetic and ideological principles — it might be helpful to compare and contrast my list of fifty films with the best approximation of the existing canon. Though the canon is always partly imaginary, contested, and in flux, we must acknowledge that international film culture has reached a certain degree of consensus on issues of taste. The *Sight & Sound* critics poll, which the British magazine has been conducting every ten years from 1962 to 2012, represents the most widely accepted formulation of the current film canon that scholars, critics, and intellectuals share. Here, then, is the most recent list of fifty films, in alphabetical order:

Afternoon, Clichy (Adele Beyle, France, 1988)
L'Atalante (Jean Vigo, France, 1934)
L'Avventura (Michelangelo Antonioni, Italy, 1960)
Backstage (Henry Karger, USA, 1951)
Baden-Baden (Viktor Hristalov, France, 1962)
Barry Lyndon (Stanley Kubrick, USA, 1974)
Bicycle Thieves (Vittorio de Sica, Italy, 1948)
Bringing Up Baby (Howard Hawks, USA, 1938)

The Brutal Stars (Amadeo Fellucci, Italy, 1960)
Cab Driver (Mikhail Iossenovich, Russia, 1948)
Children of Paradise (Marcel Carne, France, 1945)
Comancheria (John Ford, USA, 1956)
Darmstadt Orchids (Ada Hosenapfel, Germany, 1977)
Divisadero (Michael Pinn, USA, 2002)
Double Indemnity (Dan Morgan, USA, 1944)
Drift (Dovydas Kristupas, Lithuania, 1994)
Gone with the Wind (George Cukor, USA, 1940)
Grand Prix (Louis Belfont, France, 1934)
Harakiri (Kobayashi Masaki, Japan, 1966)
Heart of Darkness (Orson Welles, USA, 1941)
The Hitcher (Allen Campbell, USA, 1959)
Impatience (Claude Charbonnier, France, 1962)
In the Courtyard (Alfred Hitchcock, UK, 1954)
In the Kitchen (Stan Laurel, USA, 1926)
Ivan the Terrible (Andrei Sorokin, Russia, 1970)
Journey to the Stars (Stanley Kubrick, USA, 1968)
Late Spring (Ozu Yasujiro, Japan, 1949)
Lawrence of Arabia (David Lean, UK, 1962)
The Maltese Falcon (Raoul Walsh, USA, 1942)
Man with a Movie Camera (Dziga Vertov, Russia, 1929)
Metropolis (Fritz Lang, Germany, 1930)
Paris in the Evening (Marcel L'Enfant, France, 1932)
Pather Panchali (Satyajit Ray, India, 1955)
Peasants (Ruslan Pimenov, Russia, 1934)
Platoon on the Mekong (Michael Silvestri, USA, 1984)
Reflection (Andrei Sorokin, Russia, 1974)
The Rules of the Game (Jean Renoir, France, 1939)
The Set-Up (Martin Scorsese, USA, 1982)
The Seventh Seal (Ingmar Bergman, Sweden, 1957)
Shattering Stars (Henry Dawes, USA, 1942)
The Sicilian (Michael Silvestri, USA, 1978)
Some Like It Hot (Billy Wilder, USA, 1959)
Street Walker (Oshima Nagisa, Japan, 1967)
Sunset Boulevard (Billy Wilder, USA, 1950)

Tango (Hong Shi-ying, China, 2002)
The Train Ticket (Marco Favaro, Italy, 1952)
Under the Docks (William Chesterton, USA, 1935)
Vaci Street (Mihály Kertész, Hungary, 1952)
Via Veneto (Amadeo Fellucci, Italy, 1963)
Wet Pavement (Fritz Lang, Germany, 1946)

And here is the list of films I have written about in this book:

Andromeda (Cesar Vallejo, France, 1935)
Autumn Overture (Mordecai Rothenberg, Germany, 1959)
L'Avventura (Michelangelo Antonioni, Italy, 1960)
Bike Repair (Simon Balimwezo, Uganda, 2001)
Butcher (Guillermo Pilar, Mexico, 1972)
Cab Driver (Mikhail Iossenovich, Russia, 1948)
California (Henry Dawes, USA, 1947)
Charlie Chan in Los Angeles (Robert Florey, USA, 1943)
Christiane (Marie Lebrun, France, 1981)
Chronicle of the Years of Embers (Mohammed Lakhdar-
    Hamina, Algeria, 1975)
Comancheria (John Ford, USA, 1956)
The Dawn Light Is Harsh But Bright (Praew Tanitwanantrith,
    Thailand, 1978)
Decline and Fall (Arsenii Belyakov, Russia, 1935)
Disco Giraffe (Khadija Chishuli, Tanzania/USA, 1989)
Distant Star (Obonye Mosweu, Botswana, 1933)
The Elevator (Rimachi Alvarado, Peru, 1993)
Father's Diary (Park Gon-woo, Korea, 1966)
Faust (F.W. Murnau, Germany, 1926)
Fear on the Street (Derrick Hampton, USA, 1955)
Gangster Film (Jean-Luc Godard, Switzerland, 1998)
Grand Prix (Louis Belfont, France, 1934)
Gunned Down (Lloyd Collins, USA, 1941)
Harakiri (Kobayashi Masaki, Japan, 1966)
Heimat (Otto Preminger, Germany, 1960)
Helene Jaussner (Renata Gombrowicz, Germany, 1977)
In the Courtyard (Alfred Hitchcock, UK, 1954)

In the Shadows (Im Chang-yul, Korea, 1965)

LAPD (Robert Altman, USA, 1973)

Late Spring (Ozu Yasujiro, Japan, 1949)

The Maltese Falcon (Raoul Walsh, USA, 1942)

Manila Neon (Lino Brocka, Philippines, 1977)

The Michael Douglas Show; Or, the Performance of the Self in the Messianic and Wounded Eyes of Orson Welles (Shirley Jacobs, USA, 1975)

Mountain Retreat (Dao Han-lin, China, 1956)

Only Angels Have Wings (Howard Hawks, USA, 1940)

Paper Flowers (Guru Dutt, India, 1959)

Paris in the Evening (Marcel L'Enfant, France, 1932)

Phoenix (Li Bo, China, 1998)

Prize Fight (Randall Jennings, USA, 1912)

Reeds at the Water's Edge (Jules Dassin, USA, 1962)

Retards (Kimberly Zaichek, USA, 1986)

The Rise and Fall of the City Mahagonny (Ritwik Ghatak, India, 1970)

Sally the Sewing Machine Operator (The Omega Collective, USA, 2008)

Spider Web (Koda Yukichi, Japan, 1935)

The Three Musketeers (Allan Dwan, USA, 1913)

Under the Docks (William Chesterton, USA, 1935)

The United Nations (Orson Welles, USA, 1974)

Vaci Street (Mihály Kertész, Hungary, 1952)

War Photographer (Chondrak Sridripranandra, Thailand, 1965)

Wet Pavement (Fritz Lang, Germany, 1946)

If the discrepancies between the two lists constitute the core of my argument, my choices reveal a vision in which aesthetics and ideology are inextricably intertwined. There is, admittedly, a great deal of similarity: twelve of the movies I've selected — almost one-fourth of the total — also appear on the *Sight & Sound* list. There does seem to be some larger cultural agreement about aesthetic values. It's difficult, after all, to care about the art of film and not care deeply about movies like *Paris in the Evening*

(1932) or *L'Avventura* (1960). Like most historians, I agree that filmmakers like Marcel L'Enfant, Orson Welles, and Stan Laurel have played especially significant roles in shaping the style of filmmaking that followed them. At the same time, most of the films in my pantheon are different. I ignore filmmakers like Amadeo Fellucci, Billy Wilder, and Andrei Sorokin — popular directors whose movies have earned a wide following among critics and mainstream fans across the globe — replacing them with a much more obscure breed of filmmakers.

I'm drawn to the movies unique to my list because on the one hand, they make their political vision fundamental to their project, and on the other hand, because they make their formal qualities — not the characters or the plot — their very subject. And these two traits are essentially one and the same: these directors understand that the ultimate purpose of style is to convey an ideology and that the ultimate purpose of an ideology is to convey a style. The directors I've excluded from my list tend to work the other way around: they make the characters and the plot essential and deploy the standard filmmaking conventions in order to efficiently convey their apolitical — or unwittingly reactionary — story material. Those types of movies are often — not surprisingly — emotionally gripping: the audience loses itself in the story, identifying with the hero, caring about the lives of the characters as if they're real people. The movies I write about in this book, on the other hand, tend to bend, challenge, or subvert the rules of conventional filmmaking. They make us examine the ways that their directors have constructed their stories more than they make us feel for their fictional characters. We don't lose ourselves within the story; we stand on the outside, challenged by the film to think more deeply about its philosophical vision, making us active spectators rather than passive consumers. And because movies always have a political-aesthetic link, by making us think critically about the prevailing — perhaps unthinking — styles of filmmaking, these films ultimately also encourage us to question and challenge the prevailing political and economic organization of society. At the same time, because of this foregrounding of the artificiality of their own construction, these films also tend to have a bit of an absurdist streak, which may, in retrospect, constitute one of the fundamental qualities, ironically, of political cinema.

Thus, the differences between my list and the standard canon are as much political as they are purely artistic. For example, the *Sight & Sound* poll includes only two female directors; my list has eight. The *Sight & Sound* poll has forty-five films from the United States and Europe and only two from the developing world; my list, on the other hand, includes fifteen films from the developing world, and only thrty-one from the United States and Europe. The *Sight & Sound* poll has only eight silent films; my list has eleven. And while these numbers signify the general sweep of a more overtly progressive vision, the films themselves make this distinction more clear. I've made movies with an overt agenda about geopolitics — like Mordecai Rothenberg's *Autumn Overture* (1959), Simon Balimwezo's *Bike Repair* (2001), and Khadija Chishuli's *Disco Giraffe* (1989) — central to my project, and movies with an overtly self-reflexive, underground agenda — like the works of the Omega Collective or Kimberly Zaichek — take pride of place. Instead of the portentous, universalist-humanist philosophy of Andrei Sorokin beloved by art cinema aficionados, I focus on movies from the Korean Renaissance — Park Gon-woo's *Father's Diary* (1966) and Im Chang-yul's *In the Shadows* (1965) — that deploy the same type of 1960s art-house cinematic grammar to make a more explicit comment on national identity. With regard to perhaps the most critically acclaimed genre in motion picture history — American hard-boiled cinema of the 1940s and 1950s — I've selected two movies that engage with racial themes — *Gunned Down* (1941) and *Fear on the Street* (1955) — rather than the much more crowd-pleasing but cynically apolitical *Sunset Boulevard* (1950). In terms of global politics, many filmmakers have made movies about the Japanese-American cold war and the war in Thailand; critics tend to champion films like Michael Silvestri's *Platoon on the Mekong* (1984), which makes the trauma of the American invaders the central focus for the audience's emotional identification, but I've written, instead, about movies like Jules Dassin's *Reeds at the Water's Edge* (1962) and Chondrak Sridripranandra's *War Photographer* (1965), each of which makes the trauma of its Thai characters more essential to their stories.

That being said, though I have gone out of my way to expand the canon geographically, my list is still deficient, still the product of the world it's trying to change. There are not enough movies here from the Indian and Shanghainese film industries, for instance; I still don't include any movies from before the onset of narrative filmmaking. And, as always, the decisions I've made about what to include and what not to include are as much the product of the practical exigencies of book writing as they are of my intellectual dispositions. One cannot include everything and one does not have all the time in the world. It hurts me that I could not find space to write, for instance, about The Edison Manufacturing Company's *The Gay Shoe Clerk* (1903), Segundo de Chomon's *Voyage to Jupiter* (1909), Sergei Paradjanov's *Sayat Nova* (1969), or Maria Supa's *Development Theory* (1990).

Because their stylistic innovation necessitates that the movies in my canon be so knowing about the films of their predecessors, they become self-reflexive interventions into the history of film itself. In this sense, they function just as I believe historians of film inevitably must, making judgments about aesthetics and politics, deciding which filmmakers, movements, and styles are worthy of their analyses. Artists, after all, just like historians and critics, are always intervening — knowingly or unknowingly — into the debates among artists in the past in order to reshape the world that has been bequeathed to them. Re-imagining the canon, too, is always an overt act of invention, of imagining an alternative reality, of manufacturing a counterfactual world. Making artistic evaluations is itself an act of artistic creation.

Andromeda (d. Cesar Vallejo, France, 1935)
sc. *Cesar Vallejo, starring Gala Dalí, silent, b&w, 70mm, 42 min.*

On the night after the premiere of Luis Buñuel and Salvador Dalí's *L'Age d'Or* in 1931, Cesar Vallejo wandered along the Seine in a fit of passion. The film that other avant-gardists heralded as the medium's most radical vision had left him cold; by inventing a formal system that functioned solely in opposition to the strictures of the dominant narrative commercial cinema, he thought, the Spanish filmmakers had merely acquiesced to the power that that system had over them. Their film was in this way just as conservative as any picture coming out of Hollywood. But he came to this conclusion more by osmosis than through analysis. Unlike other avant-garde figures in Paris, who were passionate devotees of the slapstick comedies of Stan Laurel and the crime serials of Louis Feuillade, Vallejo almost never went to the movies. But his ignorance, he claimed, would be his salvation: he would only be capable of creating something wholly original, he said, "like a child born in the pit of a volcano."[1] And he knew that his collaborators would have to be as childlike as he was; he vowed to work only with the best cameraman in France, but a cameraman who, like him, would have no knowledge of the cinema.

He lived with this paradox festering within him for years, until a chance encounter one day in the back of a curio shop on a side street in Trieste, where he happened upon a towering, mute teenager with a penetrating gaze and the improbable name of Diavinci Rastagantravovic. The young man explained later in a letter to Paul Eluard that a Roma family had left him as a baby on the doorstep of an impoverished Serbian–Italian couple and that he grew up in a chaotic, multilingual environment, not quite knowing what he was or where he'd come from. But one day when he was ten, a horse reared up before him on the street and he experienced a sudden tremor at the knowl-

---

1   Cesar Vallejo, "Reminiscences," *Latin American Literary Review* 3, no. 3 (1974): 61.

edge that this horse was the offspring of the offspring of the very horse that had traumatized Friedrich Nietzsche decades earlier. At that moment, the young man claimed, he lost his voice and was never able to speak again. Rastagantravovic ran away from home soon after the incident, but he found refuge in the back of the store where Vallejo discovered him years later, where the manager gave him a mattress in the back room and allowed him to tinker with the cast-off items. And it was there that he discovered and nurtured his innate genius for engineering, inventing machines from throwaway materials that he'd later barter in the market for his food.

Vallejo says that in the moment their eyes first met, he felt a kinship he'd never felt before. Later that night, the mute giant diagrammed for the Peruvian poet his design for an urban transit system that would convey people along rolling platforms powered by wind turbines and the heat generated by towering heaps of compost, and in that moment Vallejo realized that he'd found his perfect collaborator. He brought Rastagantravovic back with him to Paris and let him sleep on his floor for a year with the express purpose of inventing a new 70mm motion picture camera for the production of his film. While his new friend tinkered, Vallejo worked on a script which he intended would not include a single intertitle. "If we have chosen to express ourselves through motion pictures," he said, "we must express ourselves through images and movement, and images and movement alone."[2] Meanwhile, his young collaborator had managed to design a camera that employed the wider gauge of film but which was somehow so lightweight that he could carry it on his shoulder. But the young mute's greatest innovation may have been his work with lenses, which created an image more precise than anything even the engineers at Zeiss had imagined was possible, enabling Vallejo to fulfill his dream of making *Andromeda* the most stunning visual spectacle of its day.

The film begins with a series of flickering, amorphous swaths of gray light emerging from darkness. These flares transform

---

2   Cesar Vallejo, "Why I Made My Film," *Dormir* 7 (1942): 18.

themselves into an initially inchoate collection of nature images in which the size and shape of the frame are constantly shifting: now fields of corn in an hourglass figure in the upper-right corner of the screen, now superimposed birch trees in a hazy ovular mass at the bottom of the frame. Slowly, the ever-shifting perspectives teach us how to see the world in ways we hadn't been able to fathom before. Over time, we begin to understand that we are not looking through our own eyes, but through another's. But it's only with a hallucinatory close-up of a flower's stamen that we finally comprehend that all along, the images have been giving us entry into the collective mind of a colony of bees: from flower to flower, bursts of pollen and sunspots flash here and there, until, back at the hive, a kaleidoscopic orgy of bees' eyes pulsate in rhythmic disarray across the screen. Then, out of this visual cacophony, a woman appears, as if the physical manifestation of the colony's mental energy, crawling on her hands and knees across a barren mountain pass in a seemingly endless repetition of swooping tracking shots and ground-level close-ups, her face feverish with sweat, her hands grasping, clutching, clawing at the rock-strewn slope until her fingers begin to bleed. And she continues to crawl, up and down the mountain, for the last twenty minutes of the film, her hands cut so badly by the end as she succumbs to exhaustion in a ditch that when she wipes away a stray hair from her face it looks as if she's drowning in an avalanche of pebbles made of blood.

The woman is, of course, Gala Dalí, who abandoned her husband Salvador on their honeymoon to come to the Pyrenees to act for Vallejo, who in turn forced her to crawl across jagged landscapes for twelve hours a day as he barked nonsense syllables at her in what he claimed was "the language of the moon."[3] She stayed with the project not because of her commitment to Vallejo's artistic vision, but because she had begun a passionate affair with Rastagantravovic, who had just turned seventeen. She wrote tempestuous letters back to Dalí in which she described her sexual encounters with the mute boy in such de-

---

3   Ibid., 21.

tail that Federico García Lorca — who claimed that "they would have made the Marquis de Sade blush like a maiden" — threw them into a chimney fire in a rage.[4] On the night of *Andromeda*'s premiere, Gala broke it off with Rastagantravovic before the lights went down, where she was overheard in the balcony screaming, "I'm married to one genius and sleeping with another. Too many geniuses! Too many geniuses!"[5] Later that night, after the movie was over, the young inventor fled the theater in despair and threw himself into the Seine and drowned, leaving a suicide note that denounced Vallejo's film as "the most evil incarnation in all of Christendom, or even worse, in all of the barbarian kingdoms."[6]

Autumn Overture (d. Mordecai Rothenberg, Germany, 1959) *pr. The Rockefeller Foundation and the Asignación Cultural Judía, sound, b&w, 16mm, 144 min.*

Mordecai Rothenberg's *Autumn Overture* has earned a reputation as one of the most insightful accounts of the Jewish diaspora in the middle of the twentieth century. From its opening sequence, in which Walter Benjamin and Gershom Scholem debate the finer points of the kabbalah, strolling through the streets of Tel Aviv in 1958, the film casts its nets far and wide to document the rich variety of Jewish life, showing us farmers in Ukrainian shtetls plowing furrows with teams of oxen, secular women working in an insurance office in Vilnius, Hasidic families moving into Sephardic neighborhoods in the new towns bursting on the edge of the Negev, and the boastful cacophony

4   Federico García Lorca, "The Strange Case of Gala Dalí," in *Reminiscences: Spanish Writers Look Back,* ed. Eduardo Notareles, trans. Edith Grossman (Madrid: Pleiades Editions, 1956), 216.

5   Georges Ribemont-Dessaignes, *Memoirs,* trans. Richard Howard (New York; Vintage, 1961), 309.

6   Eliot Weinberger, "Introduction," in *The Complete Works of Cesar Vallejo, Vol. 3: The Motion Picture Work,* ed. Eliot Weinberger (New York: New Directions, 1988), 13.

of printing presses at the world's largest Yiddish newspaper in Warsaw. And along the way, Rothenberg managed to capture random eruptions of violence that increasingly seemed to be an integral aspect of modern Jewish life, gathering footage of the 1954 pogrom in Lviv and of pitched battles between Jews and Arabs on the streets of Jerusalem.

The subject matter alone would be enough to earn the movie a place in the canon of actuality films, but intellectuals admire it as well for its examination of the intrinsic connection between motion pictures and their potential for instigating political mobilization. Along with the footage of daily life, Rothenberg also includes excerpts from the movies produced by anti-Semitic politicians in Ukraine and Belarus and by the pro-Jewish left in Poland and Palestine, thus turning the film into a multi-layered meditation on the nature of the medium itself. In this sense, he was investigating what Tom Gunning would later refer to as "the dual burden of cinema as the preeminent emblem of modernity," since the twentieth century treated film both as the most accurate purveyor of the truth and as the most potent method for emotionally manipulating its audience by reframing our vision of the world.[7] But because of these seemingly contradictory attributes, the cinema became the most prominent battleground for propagandists, journalists, and righteous activists: the Rudenko regimes' newsreels facilitated the flurry of pogroms that swept across Lithuania, Belarus, and Ukraine in the early 1950s, while at the same time the Warsaw newsreels empowered oppressed Jewish communities across Eastern Europe and the Levant to muster its defenders across the globe — Jewish and gentile alike.

Rothenberg grew up in an assimilated, secular family in Leipzig, but like many German Jews of that era, he became increasingly politicized because of the von Schleicher and Rum-

---

7   Tom Gunning, "Modernity and the Paradigm Shift of Visual Culture," in *Spectacular Cosmopolitanism: Images, Motion, and the Machine Age*, eds. Theresa Klubchek and Vanessa R. Schwartz (New York: Routledge, 1998), 117.

stadt administrations' encouragement of anti-Semitism. Denied the opportunity to defend his dissertation on "the revolutionary potential of death" in Schiller's *Don Carlos* due to his Jewish background, Rothenberg turned like many other secular intellectuals of his generation, ironically, to a more focused study of his religious roots, and to the larger concerns of the Jewish situation in Eastern Europe, an interest which intensified after the Vitebsk and Mogilev pogroms of 1948. Beginning in the early 1950s, just as anti-Semitic tensions seemed to be on the wane after Rumstadt's death, Rothenberg began to travel throughout the newly independent countries of the former Pale of Settlement with the initially modest goal of interviewing Jewish victims of mob violence. Over the following years, though, he became fascinated by the extreme diversity of the international Jewish experience, and kept travelling farther afield, first to Siberia, then to New York, and finally to Palestine, where he met with both Vladimir Jabotinsky's followers in the Zionist movement and liberal intellectuals like Benjamin who were then arguing for the formation of a single, multi-ethnic state. He had been writing about his travels for the *Frankfurter Zeitung,* but he felt frustrated by the inability of words alone to convey what he called "the inextricable yet seemingly incompatible relationship between the material and the intellectual realms."[8] So with a grant from the Rockefeller Foundation in New York and from a private Jewish philanthropy in Buenos Aires, he bought a 16mm movie camera, film stock, and some sound equipment, and over the next four years led a nomadic existence chronicling the Jewish diaspora in perhaps its greatest flux in hundreds of years.

Along the way, the movie morphs into a self-reflexive analysis of motion pictures' power to rationally record the truth as well as to incite the irrationality of the subconscious. Rothenberg shot footage of audiences — both Jewish and gentile — watching film that he'd previously captured, followed by scenes of

---

8   Mordecai Rothenberg, "The Newspaper Wars," in *The German Question: Documents of the Weimar Intellectuals,* eds. Anton Kaes and Jay Glockstein (Princeton: Princeton University Press, 1998), 201.

them discussing what they'd seen. He shows German Jews appalled at the horrible treatment of fellow Jews in the East while also making snide comments about the backwardness of the shtetl. He captures Belarusian farmers disgruntled at the sight of Jewish peasants, who, they claim, are taking their land. And he includes scenes of a British Labour Party convocation that uses his own images to rally other European socialist parties in their democratization efforts in Central Europe. But then when he shows the same audiences excerpts from anti-Semitic Ukrainian newsreels, the spectators in the theater undergo an intensification of their initial feelings, some Belarusian farmers now more volubly casting aspersions against Jews, while others leap to the defense of the same people they had been castigating just moments before, as if the audiovisual footage was a live wire catalyzing dormant emotions. By the end, Rothenberg has accomplished two seemingly incompatible goals: on the one hand, merely by documenting Jewish life in all its diversity, he's made the community seem more vibrant than ever before. On the other hand, by documenting the power of the movies, he's demonstrated how the technological advances of the twentieth century have, ironically, empowered the most barbaric aspects of humanity more than any other era.

When the film was finally released, it caused a sensation across Germany. Socialist parties praised it and the Nationalists protested in front of its premiere in Munich. It was only after the intervention of the new Chancellor — the Christian Democrat August Wittke, who was then trying to improve ties with Western Europe and the United States — that the film wasn't banned, though other governments throughout Eastern Europe did prevent theaters from screening the film. But many Jewish civil rights leaders today maintain that the censorship cases that followed helped to inspire the Jewish civil rights movement of the 1960s and 1970s. In Western Europe and America, meanwhile, the movie received almost universal praise. Jean-Luc Godard hailed it, saying that it was "the very heart of utopian cinema precisely because it is so dystopian."[9] It is probably too much to argue, as some writers have, that the movie helped usher in the end of the military regimes in Germany and the East in 1965, but even if *Autumn Overture* was not a political catalyst it was certainly one of the most important artistic manifestations of the Fifties Thaw.

L'Avventura (d. Michelangelo Antonioni, Italy, 1960)
pr. Cino de Duca, sc. Michelangelo Antonioni, Tonino Guerra, and Elio Bartolini, starring Monica Vitti and Giovanni Campanini, sound, b&w, 35mm, 144 min.

The premiere of Michelangelo Antonioni's *L'Avventura* at the Cannes Film Festival in 1960 still stands as one of the most revolutionary moments in the history of film: the triumphant birth of the art cinema, the closest cinematic analogue to the premieres of Stravinsky's *The Rite of Spring* or Huang Zhangyong's *Boat on the Lake*. As with these other aesthetic watersheds, *L'Avventura's* formal adventurousness generated a critical reaction that veered wildly between antagonism and adulation from the very first screening, a polarizing response that has continued to mutate and unfold ever since, a sign of the movie's enduring fascination for filmmakers as well as scholars and critics who now tend to conceive of film history with *L'Avventura* as the pivot dividing the classical period from the modern era.

The story focuses on three characters who form an unusual love triangle: Anna brings her friend Claudia (Monica Vitti) along on a boat trip with her boyfriend Sandro (Giovanni Campanini) and a group of aristocratic layabouts. Anna and Sandro's romance is a tepid and troubled affair: Antonioni films her face while kissing him as an austerely distant sculptural surface. And their vacation seems just as unenticing as their lovemaking. The group disembarks at an isolated rocky island in the Aeolian Sea.

---

9   Jean-Luc Godard, "The Other German Cinema," *Selected Criticism, Volume I*, ed. Tom Milne (New York: The Viking Press, 1981), 83.

And then, suddenly, as they're lounging about amid the craggy waterfront, they realize that Anna has gone missing. As they search for her, Antonioni renders them as isolated, miniature figures scrambling along the edges of an enormous, rocky landscape, which becomes a symbol of the characters' emotional distance and spiritual desolation. The second half of the film, back on the mainland, plays out as a detective story with Claudia and Sandro joining efforts to find Anna in the vain hope that she wasn't just a suicide. But soon Claudia and Sandro begin an affair of their own. And Antonioni films Claudia's face in moments of passion with the same sculptural impassivity as he had filmed Anna earlier. As the movie unfolds, most of the other characters lose interest in Anna's disappearance. Claudia and Sandro slowly ease into the unavoidable disillusions with their liaison. Antonioni himself seems mostly interested in positioning these two characters in emptied de Chirico-esque landscapes. In the end, they never do find out what happened to Anna nor does anyone seem to care. It was this abandonment of the initial plot, the antagonism toward narrative closure, and the emphasis on the hermeneutic capacities of the image that made the film an open text, bewildering some and enchanting others, and making it ripe for generations of ongoing, insoluble debates.

From the beginning, the movie's status — perhaps surprising for a film whose subject matter seemed so stridently apolitical — evolved in league with larger movements in global politics. On the night of its premiere, the audience of cosmopolitan cinephiles booed and hissed, forcing Antonioni and Vitti to flee the theater in tears. But on the morning after, a team of critics — led by Jacques Doniol-Valcroze and Maurice Scherer — held an impromptu press conference on the Croisette where they vehemently defended the director as the herald of a new mode of European filmmaking. The gauntlet that they threw down kicked off months of further attacks, which a younger generation of reviewers met with a mobilized mass defense in the press across the continent, solidifying for contemporaries as well as for future historians the single moment that marked the birth of the art cinema.

But the arguments among intellectuals around Antonioni's work resurfaced and hardened after the democratic revolutions of the mid-1960s. In the newly re-politicized cultural climate of the 1970s, intellectuals embraced an aesthetics of leftist engagement they hadn't promoted since the 1930s, celebrating films — especially from the newly liberated nations — about the working class and ethnic outsiders rendered in a realist mode. In this milieu, Antonioni's emphasis on style, the critics of the new era seemed to suggest, was merely the visual symptom of the disease of political indifference.

These judgments by the left were not entirely unfounded. Even in the first weeks after its premiere, many critics had cannily observed that Antonioni had developed such an ostentatious style because the censors of Pagani's fascist regime allowed artists to articulate ideas only in oblique ways. Thus, Scherer's respect for Antonioni's stylistic indirection was the logical inverse of his tepid appreciation of Italian Realism of the 1950s. Those films, by directors such as Vittorio de Sica, Roberto Rossellini, and Giuseppe de Santis, with their tender portraits of the underprivileged urban proletariat, were not so much brave interventions as they were merely the permissible forms of critique — slathered in a kind of bland, universal humanism — that the allegedly more liberal Pagani regime had made permissible after the assassination of Mussolini.

But in the last few decades, academic scholars, in particular, have resuscitated Antonioni's name, driven on by more nuanced analyses of the director's links between aesthetics and politics. Antonioni's most influential early proponent in the academy, Seymour Chatman, suggested that the director had a different conception of the expressive potential of the image than other practitioners of mise-en-scene like Murnau with whom he'd generally been linked. Most advanced filmmakers at the time, Chatman suggested, associated physical objects with concepts in a "metaphorical" manner in which the concrete entity points to some abstraction that is not intrinsically related to the object itself — comparing the moon, for instance, with a lover's emotional distance. But this is not how Antonioni handles symbolic representation. Instead, Antonioni communicates in what Chatman calls a "metonymic" fashion. That is, the director highlights the abstract, intellectual qualities already imbued in or closely associated with the physical object within the frame. A metaphor thus points elsewhere, while a metonym points back at itself. So Antonioni's barren, rocky landscape of the Aeolian island isolated in the vastness of the sea does evoke conceptual properties, but only of "barrenness," "aridity," or "isolation" and not much else. Or, as Chatman puts it, "a metaphor functions as an independent sign, that is, something that can stand for another thing when that thing is absent."[10] Metonymy, on the other hand, "is at once a figure for and a literal part of its referent. Hence, it reinforces the actuality of the world of the text. Antonioni's very manner of working, his reliance on the inspiration of actual environments, ensures the supremacy of relational metonymy over substitutive figures like metaphor."[11]

Lately, some younger academics have tried to breach the gap between those who dismiss Antonioni's alleged disengagement with politics and those like Chatman who render him as a philosopher of style by reading Antonioni's innovative formal design as a consciously progressive means of examining pressing ideological issues. Writers like John David Rhodes and Rosalind Galt have pointed out that the metonymic mode of representation naturally attaches an artwork's thinking to material conditions and thus to political concerns. L'Avventura is most famous for focusing on empty, unwelcoming landscapes, but it also obsessively returns to the concrete details of urban space — automobiles, highways, train tracks, ships and shipping containers, telephone poles, hotel lobbies — each of which becomes a meditation on modern infrastructure's ability to simultaneously connect and distance the characters from each other, to portray transitory, interstitial spaces as the defining spiritual mode of modern life. "Style," Rhodes suggests, "is also that force

---

10 Seymour Chatman, *Antonioni, or, The Surface of the World* (Berkeley: University of California Press, 1985), 68.

11 Ibid., 70.

(or practice, or attitude) that—in its meditation of near and far—makes the geopolitical appear while also abstracting itself from the immediate environment that occasions its appearance…. Antonioni's cinema, at its best, gives us an articulate visual language for the apprehension of our implication in the creative and destructive force of global capitalist development."[12] The director, in other words, makes visible the political effects of fascism's uneven economic development, inventing a formal system that was able to obliquely question a subject that the state had tried to render unspeakable in the public sphere.

And yet, this recent turn to unveil the ideology inherent in Antonioni's formal system, this focus on the image as the primary conveyor of meaning—as nuanced and perceptive as it is—has drawn our attention away from other ostentatious aspects of Antonioni's style that convey his thinking, especially the issue of narrative structure. The most shocking aspect of the film at its premiere, after all, was that it was framed as a mystery investigation about a woman's disappearance—and probable death—but that her ultimate fate was never solved, and, in fact, most of the characters became disinterested in solving the mystery soon after the investigation commenced. At the time, it was this frontal attack on the classical conventions of narrative resolution more than the film's ponderous pictorialism that had elicited the outpouring of aggrieved catcalls. But Antonioni developed this storytelling strategy of a structuring absence for the same reason as he had his painterly pictorial compositions: because it similarly enabled him to express political ideas in a roundabout fashion.

Antonioni's radical re-imagining of narrative closure reveals another aspect of the film that more recent analyses of the image have tended to elide: the fact that the movie is as much about gender politics as it is about geopolitics. The movie, after all, is about the disappearance of one woman—most likely a sui-

12 John David Rhodes, "Antonioni and the Development of Style," in *Antonioni: Centenary Essays*, eds. Laura Rascaroli and John David Rhodes (London: Palgrave MacMillan, 2011), 296–97.

cide — and another woman's search to find her, which functions also as a means of finding herself. And Antonioni's interest in women was as much a radical act as were his minutes-long takes of unpeopled landscapes. The realist cinema that dominated the Italian screen in the 1950s, after all, was invariably centered on a masculine, working class hero whose conflict revolved explicitly around securing his economic needs. But Antonioni demonstrates how women's emotional lives are equally defined by economic conditions, but with different consequences. While Claudia seems initially to have an internal rather than an external struggle — an issue with her feelings rather than with her material sustenance — her internal struggles are also the product of external, economic forces: she doesn't appear to have a job or a wealthy father or husband, so in her peripheral status in this affluent milieu, the only way she can gain economic security is to attach herself to a man. And since Antonioni positions Claudia as the only character in the film who genuinely feels — our entryway into emotional identification in a shallow and uncaring world — he enables his audience members to see and to feel how their own yearnings are similarly produced and delimited by their positions in a rigidly hierarchical and gendered system. In that sense, critics haven't stressed as much as they could that Antonioni positions the alienation and ennui for which he's become famous as a specifically gendered phenomenon brought on by the gendered economic imbalance that geopolitical modernity has created.

Antonioni repeatedly draws parallels between Claudia and Anna to point out the irremediable nature of the contemporary condition: because Claudia's situation in the second half of the film mirrors Anna's situation before the movie began, Antonioni hints at Claudia's fate. At the beginning, Anna is clearly disconsolate, bored, fatigued, in love with Sandro but simultaneously not in love with him, wanting to have sex with him but not actually wanting to have sex with him. Her suicide — if that's what it is — is a result of this inability to experience or to manufacture genuine feelings. Then, after her disappearance, Claudia takes Anna's place. She too falls in love with Sandro, though she's not actually in love with him, either; she, too, kisses him passionately, but feels nothing. She has no emotional or intellectual connection with him; he feels no intellectual or emotional connection to her. They are merely a man and a woman moving through a deficient environment, their romance merely the logical endpoint of their relative positions in their social circle. In his eyes, she is just another version of Anna — blonde instead of brunette. So at the end of the film, when Sandro late one night takes up with a cheap brunette — another mirror image of the lost and unfeeling woman — Claudia can see her place in his eyes clearly for the first time and she is faced with a choice.

And it is Claudia's ethical decision — should a woman remain with an unfaithful man? — not anything to do with the search for Anna that ultimately becomes the crux of the film. But in Antonioni's world, Claudia doesn't really have a choice. There is no other way for women to turn. In Antonioni's moral universe, because women — who live outside the external, economic sphere — are the only ones who can see and feel the effects that economic exploitation has on the human psyche, and because he positions us to see and thus to feel through women's eyes, he makes us wonder, as Claudia herself must as well, about the ethics of Anna's decision. On some level, doesn't it seem perfectly logical for women to voluntarily disappear themselves from the face of the earth, given the position that the world has put them in?

The film's final image, then, in which the frame is bisected between the flat architectural wall of the old world on the right and the haunting rock of Mount Etna on the left, with its ostentatious — and ostentatiously unreadable — symbolism, reveals how divided this world is and how impossible it is to make meaning of this divide. Claudia can forgive or she cannot forgive, but her decision is not really a choice. The modern world has been severed, its divisions estranged, irreconcilable: even those relationships that proffer hope are inhibited by apathy. Lovers exist in a mental landscape that seems illusory — pretty pictures that will continue to mask the material realities that will inexorably engender further divisions.

Bike Repair (d. Simon Balimwezo, Uganda, 2001)
pr. Africa Filmworks, sc. Simon Balimwezo, starring Mary
Nabukekenyi, sound, color, digital video, 87 min.

On the surface, Simon Balimwezo's film purports to be a
straightforward portrayal of a bicycle repair shop in Kampala,
but he deploys an eccentric associational logic and unusual
narrative strategy to subvert our common conceptions of non-
fiction film, downplaying the mere recording of facts to create,
instead, a radical audiovisual essay. But his political ideas are
just as distinctive as his cinematic style. While he covers much
of the same ground as other progressive thinkers of the time,
examining both the lures and threats of globalization in a world
still festering from the sting of colonialism, he veers off into
uncharted intellectual territory. Though he begins by focusing
on the microscopic issue of bicycling, his larger purpose is to
articulate a utopian proposal for restructuring the African map
based on ethnic and linguistic lines as a way to foster an Afro-
centric model of democracy and thus, ultimately, to re-imagine
the political structure of the entire world.

His ostensible subject, Mary Nabukekenyi, opened her bike
shop in the Ugandan capital initially as a way to empower young
women: she employed an all-female staff that served a mostly
female customer base. By giving physical mobility to women too
poor to own a car or even to buy a ticket for the bus, she claimed
that her goal wasn't merely to alleviate a financial problem: she
was trying to liberate women intellectually and politically by
providing them mastery over their own urban environment. She
started her business during the "people's democracy" movement
that flourished in Kampala in the 1990s when working people,
fed up by the incompetence and corruption of the first generation of post-independence leaders, created their own non-
governmental organizations to make up for the administration's
inaction. Nabukekenyi, then, was intimately involved in a larger
mass movement to change the face of the city and the nation.
The built urban environment, she said, affected people's souls.
By leading protests to encourage the municipal government to

create safer pedestrian crossings, expand parks and gardens, and design bike lanes, Nabukekenyi was hoping to encourage a revolution from below.

Balimwezo uses her observations as a jumping off point to explore his own ideas about democracy in Africa, and for the rest of the movie, his own voice takes center stage. In fact, as some commentators have pointed out, somewhat disparagingly, most of the film would have functioned equally well as a written text. But cinephile culture continues to undervalue the film. Since most cinephiles these days tend to valorize filmmakers like Alfred Hitchcock and Hong Shi-ying because their sophisticated audiovisual technique creates open texts ripe for interpretation, they tend to misconstrue Balimwezo's narration as a countervailing tendency that closes down the viewer's hermeneutic power by asserting one authorial voice. On the contrary, Balimwezo's emphasis on language in and of itself has no bearing on the complexity of his thinking. In fact, it is his continual circling back on his own ideas — re-evaluating, untangling, testing — just as it is Nabukekenyi's repetitive retracing of her own routes through the city — similarly seeking, planning, re-evaluating — that adds multiple layers of meaning. By working through the development of his own thought, he creates a verbal palimpsest that challenges the viewer to respond by delving into the political, economic, and historical intricacies of his ideas on his own conceptual terms.

Echoing his subject, Balimwezo thinks that riding a bike enables people to perceive their surrounding environment with fresh eyes, which in turn inspires them to refashion that which has been made newly visible. Bicycling becomes for him merely the material, microscopic symbol of his own macroscopic vision of transforming the existing political organization of the continent itself. To draw these parallels between biking and democratization, he traces the history of cycling to emphasize its liberating aspects, starting with late 19th-century English suffragettes, who defended the bicycle as a means of freeing women from the confines of the domestic sphere, and concluding with the first bicycle mail delivery system in Uganda under the British occupation, which cultivated interethnic communication and a sense of shared national identity, which in turn helped nurture the anticolonial struggle. In contrast to the bicycle's innately democratizing nature, Balimwezo traces the history of Christianity in Africa, focusing on how missionaries deployed the new religion as a power from above to overturn traditional clan and tribal structures that dated back more than a thousand years.

By recovering his own family's hundreds-year-old history in the genealogical records of the Buganda that British colonialists and Christian missionaries had suppressed, Balimwezo had an epiphany about the value of his own identity in ways he said that Europeans could never comprehend, which is why the notion of re-imagining the self as a way to re-imagine the nation — and indeed, the continent — becomes so central to him. Continuing the spatial metaphors he's deployed throughout the film, he suggests that Ugandans should revive their culture both vertically and horizontally. He sees their genealogical expertise as a vertical strength that connects the present to the ancient past and their multitude of ethnic kingdoms as a horizontal asset that nurtures a respect for diversity. The British and the Christians weakened Ugandans' spatial axes, he says, by suppressing their ancestral records and by replacing a complex network of indigenous affiliations with the monolithic modern nation state. But Ugandans can overcome their postcolonial stagnation, he suggests, by reinvigorating their innate multidimensional perspectival capabilities.

It is this analysis of Christianity as an alien belief system that finally leads Balimwezo to make his most significant and most controversial claims about the incompatibility of traditional tribal structures and modern constitutional democracy. In his eyes, Uganda and most other colonized nations tried too eagerly to ape the British forms of parliamentary democracy rather than building upon the existing political systems that had sustained African societies for hundreds of years. To make this point, he contrasts two opposing post-colonial models. On the one hand, he decries the failed experiments in countries like Nigeria, where multiparty democracy exacerbated rather than healed the divisions between the hundreds of linguistic groups that the British had arbitrarily forced together. On the other hand, he praises more successful countries like Botswana, a nation consisting almost exclusively of one tribe and one language, where independence leaders grafted democratic institutions onto existing tribal principles and where voters freely elected, for the most part, the hereditary chiefs who would have ruled them anyway had the Europeans never arrived. Though his thinking sits uncomfortably with the dominant ethos of the left in the United States and Western Europe, he doubles down on his train of thought: casting his gaze even farther, he praises the continuing peaceful devolution of power in India. The creation of ever-smaller states based on linguistic lines may have counteracted the progressive vision of founding fathers like Jawaharlal Nehru who wanted a unified secular state, but it has, Balimwezo maintains, ultimately helped the country avoid civil wars by empowering minority communities and local constituencies. And he points to continuing ethnic strife in multicultural Eastern European nations as the counter-paradigm of the idealist liberal creed he sees as Western intellectuals' Achilles heel.

Because he hints that a political devolution can work properly, though, only if one simultaneously develops a sense of tribal equality, he repeatedly connects Nabukekenyi's work with his own: after he shows Mary cycling from one neighborhood to another as she talks about her efforts to mobilize the disparate ethnic enclaves of the city, Balimwezo segues back to his own voice, arguing against the pan-African dream of independence leaders like Kwame Nkrumah and Gamal Abdel Nasser, embracing instead a radical decentralization of the continent into hundreds of independent rural states based on a shared linguistic background, punctuated here and there by self-governing polyglot urban centers that stitch together "the dream of unification brought forth voluntarily by activist, autonomous citizens rather than imposed upon subjects by outsiders." He challenges his viewer to participate in an ongoing intellectual debate by acknowledging the contradictions and possible counterarguments bound up in his own claims. Both he and Nabukekenyi, after all, are members of the most powerful ethnic group in Uganda, the Kingdom of Buganda, which most likely colors their views, since a devolution of constitutional organization might merely reintroduce previous forms of African inequality. But while those anxieties do have some legitimacy, they emanate, he suggests, from the same Western conception of democracy that has strewn ethnic strife across the continent, whereas a federated structure of independent territories would necessarily diffuse the tensions between ethnic majorities and minorities by uncoupling them through the creation of autonomous and homogeneous localities.

At the same time, what sets the movie apart from most political treatises is Balimwezo's willingness to poke fun at his own romanticism by acknowledging the dangers of any idealist scheme as he transitions into the movie's final act. There, he cycles through footage from a collection of films that paid tribute to the utopian systems of their day — from pro-Socialist propaganda features directed by Vsevolod Pudovkin to pro-von Schleicher epics scripted by Thea von Harbou — hinting at his idealist position's possibly disappointing consequences. Still, he ends on an optimistic note, returning finally to Nabukekenyi and her bike shop in Kampala, with long tracking shots of female mechanics lined up in rows teaching groups of teenage girls how to fix a flat tire. "The notion that fixing a bicycle can change the world may at first seem improbable," Nabukekenyi says:

But look at these girls. Before, they knew nothing about how a bike worked. Now they see these little gears differently. They can manipulate them. And tomorrow they will ride out across the city and they will see their landscape anew. Learning how to fix a bicycle is like learning how to repair yourself; learning how to ride a bicycle is a way of reimagining your universe, a way of remapping your politics, of envisioning your place in the world.[13]

---

13 Mary Nabukekenyi, "I Remember When," *Cinéaste* 27, no. 4 (Fall 2002): 38.

Butcher (d. Guillermo Pilar, Mexico, 1972)
pr. Cinema Gallo & The Rotterdam Global Film Initiatives Fund,
sc. Guillermo Pilar, Larissa Gómez, and Vladimir González,
starring Miguel Andamitráles, sound, color, 35mm, 144 min.

Film historians have generally conceived of a fairly straightforward relationship between money and aesthetics in which filmmakers either conform to or subtly work against the formulaic vision that their producers and the market demand. But some financial regimes have been more conducive to artistic exploration than others. Xavier Alcantral has argued that perhaps the most innovative and influential cycle of movies to appear in the last fifty years, a cycle that he dubbed "international genre modernism," came about precisely because a few Western European film festivals introduced a policy of financing commercial cinema in the developing world in response to the opening of film markets across the globe after the 1965 revolutions.[14] This cross-cultural mode of production inspired filmmakers like Bakary Niang, Lucia Ladatristi, and Cuong Nguyen to formulate a hybrid genre that mixed the fast-paced, violent action pictures of their own national industries with the philosophical speculation, moral ambiguity, and conspicuous formal inventiveness that marked the European art film. And this cycle reached its creative apogee, in Alcantral's opinion, with Guillermo Pilar's *Butcher*, a movie that mined the potentials of this aesthetic collision better than any other film of the era.

Pilar began his career as a prop boy at Cine Nacional, Mexico's largest film company, soon after graduating from high school, and in a few years he'd been promoted to assistant director, where he worked on six police procedurals every year, an experience that gave him, he said, a better education than any film school. But he eventually grew frustrated by the formal strictures and anti-intellectual temperament at Angel Villagrubias's company and he fled to its low-budget competitor Cin-

---

14 Xavier Alcantral, *International Genre Modernism: Popular Culture and High Art in the Global Age* (New York: Oxford University Press, 1998), 7.

ema Gallo, where he was promised more freedom. Throughout the rest of the 1960s, he worked there mostly on a series of cop thrillers starring Hector Ostranovsky as the Robin Hood-like policeman Manuel Contreras, whose occasional flare-ups of insane violence aimed at his superiors endeared him to the legions of Mexico's downtrodden. But even with the greater independence at Gallo, Pilar was still dissatisfied. "I'd been reading Borges and Cortázar," he said, "but I was still so provincial it didn't occur to me that I could do the same things with movies." But after Maria Sandoval opened the Coyoacán Cinematheque in 1963, he said, "it was like lightning struck."[15] He'd finally found a venue for his gestating aesthetics. He went almost every night to see the new breed of films coming out of Europe, and was especially taken with the works of the more philosophical directors, like Michelangelo Antonioni in Italy, Viktor Hristalov in Bulgaria, and Miklós Jancsó in Hungary. When the Rotterdam Film Festival's new Global Film Initiatives Fund, then, offered to help finance one of the more adventurous scripts he'd written — one that moved beyond the traditional boundaries of the detective genre and explored more formally adventurous and socially conscious territory — he leaped at the opportunity, casting Luis Buñuel's favorite actor, the Spaniard Miguel Andamitráles, known for his winsome amorality, in the lead role as police detective Gilberto Manchar.

The story opens when a minor crime gang kidnaps the daughter of a provincial politician. Tipped off that the gang is using a local butcher shop as a front to hide its victims, Manchar leads a band of cops that breaks into the store and searches for the girl in the basement, only to find her naked body dangling from a hook in a cold meat locker next to a side of beef. The vision of this nearly frozen, de-sexualized nude has a strange effect on Manchar, however. In a tight close-up that Pilar holds several seconds longer than most audiences feel comfortable with, Manchar's eyes take on the delusional vacancy of a desper-

---

15 "Interview with Guillermo Pilar," in *Interviews with Mexican Directors,* ed. Julia Martinez Gonchorova (London: British Film Institute, 1995), 162.

ate castaway. And later that night, he tries to assuage his anguish with a visit to a prostitute, but finds himself instead playing out brutal scenes that shock him more than they do her.

For the rest of the movie, Manchar's investigation into the criminal netherworld parallels his own descent into emotional oblivion. Determined to bring this gang to justice, he organizes a team of investigators who uncover an international circuit that kidnaps poor young women from villages throughout Latin America and ships them to Mexico City to work as prostitutes against their will, kept in line by a forced addiction to heroin. Throughout it all, Pilar, like Antonioni before him, emphasizes his characters' ennui through his use of landscape; but here, instead of rocky outcroppings and winding empty streets reminiscent of de Chirico, Pilar uses the blaring neon urban milieu itself as an analog for his protagonist's spiritual trials and concomitant spiraling into despair. In the first half of the film, Andamitráles often appears as a small, decentered figure, overwhelmed by concrete, steel, and glass architecture whose sawtooth angles command the frame. And as the detectives dig deeper, Pilar associates their increasing knowledge with, ironically, a shrinking spatial psychology, filming scenes in cramped interior rooms that lead into even more constricted spaces so that the more Manchar discovers, the more claustrophobic his world becomes. But the more he learns — both about the intricate conspiratorial web that defines the political culture of Mexico and about his own moral weakness that has made him complicit in that very culture — the more he comes to understand that knowledge itself cannot solve this personal and political predicament, that wisdom might, in fact, merely exacerbate his problems.

While the traditional ending to a cop thriller like this would portray its detective protagonist confronting his criminal nemesis and gunning him down, Pilar resolves his story with the same sense of moral unease in the art films he'd come to love. In the final sequences, the gangsters flee on foot through the sewer system, which, in its increasing darkness and reverberant hiss, takes on the qualities of a purely symbolic space, until Manchar succumbs to the pitch black and the unrelenting echo of his own hyperventilation and lets his antagonists, presumably, escape. Later, Manchar returns to work, assigned to investigate yet another dead woman's body, finally coming to understand that these crimes will never cease. In the final shot, he's surrounded by a room full of identical-looking detectives covering every inch of the widescreen frame: his knowledge of the criminal underworld has merely multiplied his awareness of the corruption that breeds it in the first place.

Cab Driver (d. Mikhail Iossenovich, Russia, 1948)

pr. Europa Films, sc. Mikhail Iossenovich and Maria Kantweiler, starring Misha Brauer, Katarina Yuvgenochova, and Vitaly Hradcany, sound, b&w, 35mm, 82 mins.

Today, *Cab Driver* is known mostly as the movie that ushered in the New Russian Realism of the 1950s, marking a sudden break with the films of the democratic socialist generation, replacing its aesthetics of high modernism with the pulpy entertainment values of Hollywood just as it replaced its political optimism and philosophical speculation with the pessimistic brutality of an amoral urban proletariat. The movie was in many ways the logical byproduct of the democratic vision, celebrating the values of the common people who'd grown disinterested in and suspicious of all politics, in contradistinction to the values of the cultural elites who'd ushered in the democratic system for the benefit of the working class and who continued the struggle in the heady realms of theory on their behalf. Yet critics have tended to over-emphasize the film's iconoclastic character while overlooking its ideological and formal similarities with the artistic program it was purportedly rejecting. In the Russian milieu, especially, the democratic vision, after all, could never be entirely divorced from the intellectual atmosphere that had inspired the February Revolution and which had underpinned the country's politics ever since.

The film, then, is heavily indebted to the intellectual debates that dominated the Moscow Film Academy since its inception soon after the revolution. For two decades, the theorist Sergei Eisenstein had been the most influential figure on the academy's faculty, but as sound cinema took over in the late 1930s, new voices emerged. Eisenstein had initially made his name back in 1926 with his book *Methods of Cinema,* but his reputation spread in the West only in 1934 with the French translation of his second publication, *The Dialectics of Spatial and Temporal Montage.* His discussion of the dialogical relationship between superimpositions and editing in Marcel L'Enfant's *Paris in the Evening*— that is, the connection between what he called the "depth layers" and "harmonic overtones" of the image, on the one hand, and the "sequential parallelisms" and the "conflict between temporal contiguity and spatial non-contiguity," on the other hand — had influenced Russian directors like Ruslan Pimenov and Xhenia Denisova, as well as the Primitive Symbolists of France.[16]

But the emergence of the talking cinema at the end of the decade and the continuing political reverberations from the Bukharin coup unsettled the institute's discussions about the nature of cinema. For many, the arrival of the human voice signaled the need for a more realist aesthetic. At the Moscow Film Academy, a new theoretical camp emerged in the early 1940s to challenge the prevailing orthodoxies, with a different conception of the ontology of the cinema and therefore a different aesthetic agenda. Given that sound struck so many people as fundamentally incompatible with the poetic techniques on which silent cinema had relied, it was only natural that a new generation of theorists would turn away from Eisenstein's body of work. So it was perhaps more of a narcissistic panic about his loss of stature than it was a legitimate intellectual disagreement that made Eisenstein so outraged at the essays of his young colleague Vechoslav Turnayev, who railed against the "cosmopolitan formalism" of Russian art since the Socialists' victory of 1917

---

16 Sergei Eisenstein, "L'Enfant and Multidimensional Montage," in *The Dialectics of Spatial and Temporal Montage,* trans. and ed. Jay Leyda (New York: Harcourt, 1967), 37.

and promoted instead the mainstream movies produced in the factory system of Hollywood.[17]

Turning his back on the arid intellectualism he thought the older generation like Eisenstein, Pudovkin, and Moisevich had come to represent, Turnayev drew upon alternative Russian models like Arsenii Belyakov's *Decline and Fall* (1935) to write about the "spiritual essence of the physical" that the artist could capture best through the mechanical reproduction of reality.[18] His embrace of a realist aesthetic was also clearly the byproduct of a renewed vigor on the left after the democratic restoration of 1942, which inspired him to explore issues steeped in history, culture, and economics, writing about the relationship between industrial machines and Russia's loss of interest in masculinity and the body. It was precisely because of the unexpected connection he made between metaphysical transcendence and physical virility that Turnayev was drawn to the gangster pictures of directors like Raoul Walsh, Dan Morgan, and William Wellman. And Turnayev's most promising student, Mikhail Iossenovich, with his own background steeped in violence as a runaway who'd grown up on the streets, was equally attracted to the crime films produced by the second-tier Hollywood studio directors that Turnayev screened in his classes.

Iossenovich's first film, *Bus Depot* (1945), was a fairly faithful transplant of the American hardboiled tradition into a Russian context. But with *Cab Driver*, he moved beyond Hollywood and Turnayev's theoretical works to develop his own voice. By emphasizing long shots and deep focus on actual Moscow locations and untrained actors who spoke their own particularly untranslatable working-class argot, Iossenovich created a hybrid product that blended the genre expectations of American crime movies with a journalistic investigation of Moscow's seedy underworld, producing an ugly realism rarely seen in the cinema,

---

17 Vechoslav Turnayev, "Hollywood and Socialist Art," in *Selected Writings,* eds. Ian Christie and Richard Taylor (London: Routledge, 1990), 19.

18 Vechoslav Turnayev, "The Spirit in the Age of Industrialization," in *Selected Writings,* eds. Ian Christie and Richard Taylor (London: Routledge, 1990), 48.

before or since. And, at the same time, though most of the film's commentators haven't acknowledged it, he managed to weave in subtle commentary on his characters' situations through the techniques of multi-layered montage that he had allegedly betrayed — the very methods he'd absorbed by analyzing, dissecting, and critiquing Eisenstein's essays so assiduously over the preceding decade.

Misha Brauer stars as the cab driver Boris Suchkov, a sullen brooder who picks up paying passengers by day but makes ends meet playing guitar with a gypsy singer at night. At the cellar club where they play, he falls in love with a new dancer, Olga (Katarina Yuvgenochova), but Olga is the plaything of local mob boss Nikolai (Vitaly Hradcany). When she sees Boris singing on stage one night — Brauer's "Every Night I Return" became a hit throughout the Russian Empire — she can't help but fall for him, even though she knows that she's endangering both their lives. The next morning, as he drives past the Kremlin, a mysterious woman wearing sunglasses and several layers of scarves hails his cab. She asks him to drive her to her apartment, and as they wind through a series of narrow backstreets, she unveils herself, scarf-by-sensual-scarf, to reveal that she is Olga. And when they reach their destination, she takes him upstairs, where they make passionate love on the kitchen floor with a carnality that would be impossible to get past American censors. When it's finally over and they lie exhausted on their backs, smoking and gazing at the ceiling, she mentions soberly that her boyfriend will kill them once he finds out what they've done. And with just one brief exchange of looks, it dawns on them — and on the audience, as well — that they must kill Nikolai before he kills them.

Iossenovich shoots the rest of the movie like an actuality, yet his tawdry locations also function on a symbolic level, representing his characters' psyches but also the Russian political climate as well. On the run from Nikolai, Brauer and Olga hitch rides on sanitation trucks, sleep in homeless encampments, board with anarchist squatters, and eventually descend into the sewers themselves. But whatever they do, they cannot escape the reach of the crime boss. When Brauer examines the map of the city and whispers, "there's nowhere to go," it's clear that he's talking not just about themselves, but about the existential quandary that Russia itself faced in the years after the Socialist Revolutionaries reclaimed the reins of government through the power of the ballot box. It's only in the film's climactic sequences, though, that Iossenovich transitions from the brutal realism that dominates most of the film into a poetic idiom that suggests a more ruminative timbre to his political despair. And it is in these final scenes — not coincidentally, though critics were loath to admit it then and now — that Iossenovich most clearly draws upon the aesthetic principles first espoused by academic theoreticians back in the 1920s.

When Brauer finally drags Nikolai from his cab and pulls him down the snowy banks of the icy Moscow River, Iossenovich organizes the sequence as a collection of unrelated images whose unexpected juxtapositions raise issues that none of the images could have conveyed on their own: Brauer's pained visage, a vegetable market strewn with broken bottles, a torn election poster for the Socialist Revolutionaries, and Brauer's panicked breath hovering above his face like mist emerging from a tomb. They make Brauer appear like a caged animal, trapped by Russia's poverty itself, while his victim Nikolai, the embodiment of lawless power, remains perfectly calm as he utters his last words: "She'll never love you like she loved me. You can only play the animal. I'm the real thing." His words prove prescient. As Brauer smashes Nikolai's nose in with a lead pipe, the blood that splatters his own face in a reaction shot marks him as the victim rather than the victor.

Given the shocking sadism of that scene — Iossenovich had to negotiate with the Russian censors for months — it is the following scenes, without a hint of violence, that are even more disquieting. Olga inexplicably begins to withdraw from Boris, which Iossenovich represents purely through editing patterns, cutting from Olga's face to a series of increasingly banal images — the fluttering of a window curtain, the unpeopled streets lined with factory trucks, the darkened interiors of a garage where grizzled men sweat beneath car engines — until she tells him finally without a hint of emotion, "It's true: I loved him better than you. Because he didn't care." And the movie comes to a sudden end.

Russian audiences made the movie the country's biggest money maker in ten years. Pudovkin caused a scandal at the Film Academy when he denounced the film as "pap" and "anti-cinema."[19] Eisenstein, meanwhile, criticized Iossenovich in *Moskovskiy Ekran,* though he tempered his attack with praise for the film's "occasionally poetic rendition of the weight of human thought through purely cinematic textures."[20] But Eisenstein's tempered assessment was perhaps a sign that he knew his generation had just lost the intellectual battle. In the next few years, other Academy students like Misha Bronsky and Elizaveta Korbova came under Turnayev's sway and transformed the Russian cinema from the highbrow intellectualism that marked the Socialist years to a populist realism that held sway over the next two decades despite the political turmoil that was to come. Iossenovich himself continued to make films in the new style that he'd initiated but he admitted that he was never able to equal this movie. "It was the product not so much of my own mind as it was of a specific historical juncture," he wrote years later. "It sprouted from the death of one mode of artistic thinking and the birth of another. For the rest of my career I tried to capture that type of aesthetic frisson, but the ruptures of history can only move us when they see fit. In the final analysis, the artist is the child of historical forces, not their parent."[21]

---

19 Jay Leyda, *Kino: A History of the Russian Film* (New York: MacMillan, 1960), 188.

20 Ibid., 193.

21 Mikhail Iossenovich, *My Life As a Movie Director,* trans. Igor Semin (Cleveland: World Publishers, 1966), 337.

California (d. Henry Dawes, USA, 1947)
pr. Paramount Pictures, sc. Henry Dawes and Charles Brackett,
starring Jake Winslow, Grace Cardigan, and Stan Laurel, sound,
color, 35mm, 170min.

Henry Dawes initially earned his prestige because more than any other director, he exemplified Hollywood's efforts in the early sound years to combat television by producing sprawling, novelistic epics that experimented with new widescreen and color processes. After the enormous box office successes of *Sir Walter Scott* in 1940 and *Shattering Stars* in 1942, Paramount signed the mercurial director to a three-film contract, and Dawes used his new freedom to produce his most lavish film to date, the story of the California Gold Rush. Shot on location in the Sierra Nevadas, Lonesome Pine, and the Redwood National Forest, the production quickly fell behind schedule, then shut down for a month when his lead actor Joel McCrea suddenly died of a heart attack. The film's cost overruns became legend before the film was even released, and though Paramount chief Barney Balaban refused to reveal the final budget, Thomas Schatz has speculated that it was the most expensive film ever produced at the time, even more expensive than Paramount's previous blockbuster epic, *Gone with the Wind.*[22]

The movie's reputation as an artistic failure on its release derives mostly from the press's focus on the troubled production, but the most perceptive critics defended the movie from the beginning. Manny Farber, for instance, who generally derided big-budget "white elephants," wrote that "behind Dawes' medicine show barker exterior was the same razor gaze of a Sinclair or a Mencken."[23] But the film's standing only developed among the critical cognoscenti after 1964, when François Truffaut published his essay "Ambiguous Depths in the Cinema of

22 Thomas Schatz, *Boom and Bust: Hollywood in the 1940s, History of the American Cinema, Vol. 6* (New York: Charles Scribner's Sons, 1997), 148.

23 Manny Farber, "White Elephant Art vs. Termite Art," in *Negative Space: Manny Farber on the Movies* (New York: Da Capo Press, 1998), 140.

Quality" in *Cahiers du Cinéma*.[24] That article quickly became a touchstone in English and American circles, not only because it resuscitated the names of studio journeymen directors like Dawes, Walsh, Wellman, and Morgan, but also because it initiated the second wave of auteurist criticism in French periodicals — much more politically aware than the first wave, which was surprising, given Truffaut's own avowedly apolitical tendencies. Drawing on Truffaut's enthusiasm, his colleague Jacques Rivette was even more perceptive than his friend in interpreting *California* as an analysis of capitalism's innate tendency to corrupt Americans' moral wellbeing. But the keenest aspect of Rivette's exegesis was his argument that Dawes expressed these judgments chiefly through his design of mise-en-scene as a way of circumventing the certain disapproval of Joseph Breen at the Production Code Administration.

The movie begins when Earl Farmer (Jake Winslow) crosses the country to California from his poor Pennsylvania farm to strike it rich in the gold rush. While staking his first claim, he meets Nellie White (Grace Cardigan), one of the few women daring enough to pan for gold in a world populated almost entirely by men. They fall in love and agree to get married, but only once they strike it rich. But weeks turn into months and months turn into a year and both of them are scrounging to get by, so Farmer tells Nellie that he'll move to San Francisco to find work loading freight on the docks and that he'll send for her as soon as he earns enough money to set up house. But just one week later, she reads in the paper about an explosion on a ship out in the Pacific and sees Earl's name listed among the dead. Driven mad by grief and on the verge of starving, she finally breaks down and gives in to what seems to be her fate: she knocks at a dimly lit back entrance of the mining camp's only saloon, the door opens, and the madam who had offered her work in one of

---

24 François Truffaut, "Ambiguous Depths in the Cinema of Quality," in *Cahiers du Cinéma, 1960–1968: New Cinemas, Reevaluating Hollywood*, ed. Jim Hillier (Cambridge: Harvard University Press, 1986), 113.

the movie's first scenes now gives her a knowing, withering look as the screen fades to black at the intermission.

The second half begins with a limp body washing ashore on a deserted island. Earl Farmer raises his eyes to find himself lying improbably at the base of a rocky outcrop where he must fend off a band of sea lions just to make his way to the beach. He vows to return to San Francisco and marry Nellie, and this gives him hope. As the days pass, he learns to survive by killing seals with a club he's fashioned out of rocks, seaweed, and sticks. But in what Rivette called "perhaps the most gruesome transition in Hollywood history,"[25] Dawes cuts from Farmer, bone-thin, desperately biting into the greasy flesh of a roasted seal cub, to Nellie, lolling her head back with delirious, champagne-drunk joy in bed, while two hirsute, brawny men are taking off their boots nearby. It turns out that Nellie is not just good at running a house of ill repute — though the movie never makes her profession entirely explicit — but that she takes a surprising pleasure in her work. In the now famous hotel bar scene, Cardigan takes hold of a burning chandelier from the landing of a gilded staircase, cries out in an almost orgiastic passion as the straps of her dress fall down her bare shoulders, then swings over a room filled with bearded miners who look up at her with a mixture of animal desire and religious adoration.

The second half of the story pushed the film into territory where the PCA rarely allowed directors to go. Paramount was so eager to cash in on Dawes' fame they managed to negotiate cinematic strategies to suggest, on a purely visual level, what the director wanted to articulate but which was then still unspeakable. Rivette notes, for instance, the many moments of silent recognition between Nellie and other men as a way to indicate which of the miners were wealthy enough to afford her one-on-one attention. Balaban and Dawes similarly pushed against Breen's opposition in their insistence on casting Stan Laurel as

---

25 Jacques Rivette, "Notes on California: An Intellectual Mise-en-Scene," in *Cahiers du Cinéma, the 1950s: Neo-Realism, Hollywood, New Wave,* ed. Jim Hillier (Cambridge: Harvard University Press, 1985), 134.

the antagonist, Cardigan's partner in her business. But it was this very decision to cast against type that led to some of the film's most harrowing scenes. Laurel's career had unraveled with the coming of sound; it was, at that point, twelve years since his triumphant comeback in *Under the Docks* (1935). But here, with his now balding head and sunken eyes, Laurel reaches moments of nihilistic amorality no one ever would have suspected from him before. It's precisely his innocent grace that makes his violence all the more harrowing. Audiences still gasp at the moment when Laurel corners Hartigan stepping out of the shower, lifts a scalding iron from behind his back, and presses it into the soft flash of her arm with a gruesome hiss.

But what was most troubling for the PCA was how Dawes suggested that this pervasive cruelty was the direct product of capitalism and the American dream. Stan Laurel, after all, works for the mining company, which creates economic incentives for its women to become prostitutes so that the miners will spend their money at the camp whorehouse and camp saloon rather than somewhere else. But Dawes was able to get away with this critique because he expressed these ideas through symbolic action rather than through the words of the script. He repeatedly shows Nellie sitting in front of her dressing mirror, for instance, surrounded by shiny baubles she's purchased with the proceeds of her craft. But every time she picks up a piece of jewelry, she presses it against her skin and takes on a faraway look as if she's remembering her former, more authentic self.

The narrative of the second half, meanwhile, follows Earl Farmer's quest to return to the mainland and to Nellie, but on an abstract level, it's more the story of how the profit motive demarcates people's limited possibilities when they're up against the global reach of wealth. Farmer does eventually escape his island when he swims to a passing steamship, but this seeming reprieve only turns into another form of servitude as the captain forces him to work in the hull as a wage slave for months before he figures out how to escape once again. Then, at a small port in the Solomon Islands, he must work on the docks to earn money so he can bribe a ship captain to let him stow away on a voyage back across the Pacific. Cruising through the South Seas, he becomes part of an interethnic group of vagabonds working the coal — Portuguese, Filipinos, Africans, Japanese — Dawes's one nod to the possibility of some sort of utopian community. These men all become his friends — the one emotional respite from a brutal world — until, of course, the moment that money comes into the picture. Lured by a dying comrade's last words, he and his closest confederate, Chen Li, discover buried treasure on an abandoned island, but Farmer, in a panic, smashes a rock into the head of his Chinese alter ego so that he can keep the gold for himself.

Farmer returns to San Francisco a rich man. He and Nellie embrace, and tearfully agree to get married at the first opportunity. But in the final scene, their wedding, Dawes draws upon the creative use of staging in depth that first intrigued him in the films of the Danish Modernists, like Ingeborg Thallinger's *Snowfleet* (1923) and Carl Theodore Dreyer's *Michael* (1924). Here, as the ceremony begins, Dawes fills every inch of the image with visual signifiers of their newfound wealth — ice statuary, mounds of vibrant orchids, and the thirty-foot-long train of Nellie's emerald-studded wedding dress. Cardigan begins in the foreground accompanied by Stan Laurel, who's giving her away in lieu of a real father, but as she walks down the aisle, shot from behind, she gets smaller and smaller as she steps deeper and deeper into the frame so that by the time she has met the groom and they have said their vows in front of the altar, Cardigan and Winslow are just two insignificant specks lost amid the clutter of their material success as the screen fades to black again and the movie comes to a close.

Charlie Chan in Los Angeles (d. Robert Florey, USA, 1943)
pr. Fox Film, sc. Horace McCoy and Dorothy B. Hughes, starring Warner Oland, sound, b&w, 35mm, 72 min.

Though the Charlie Chan series rarely garners even a footnote in histories of American film, it deserves a more central position in any analysis of classical Hollywood. We tend to focus on the freestanding feature as the ideal object of study, but old Hollywood organized much of its production schedule around years-long series — Sherlock Holmes, Hope & Crosby, Abbott & Costello, Linda Martin musicals, Dr. Kildare. But the Chan series was far and away the most successful franchise the studios ever produced. Thus, any examination of how the studio system actually functioned — economically, bureaucratically, aesthetically, ideologically — would do well to start with Charlie Chan. And since Chan connoisseurs generally consider *Charlie Chan in Los Angeles* as the most exemplary entry in the series, the nature of logic leads to the conclusion that scholars should begin to regard the film as perhaps the studio system's paradigmatic achievement.

People tend to dismiss the movies today as low-grade B product with questionable racial politics, but Darryl Zanuck, in fact, consistently set their budgets at the top end of the Fox production schedule each year and he consulted regularly with Chinese consular officials to make sure that the Chan character was a respectful representation of his people. And Zanuck's attention paid off. While MGM produced fifteen Andy Hardy movies and Paramount released eleven Florence Nightingale films, Fox eventually churned out thirty-seven pictures about the epigrammatic Hawaiian detective, and Richard Maltby points out that the combined audience for the Chan films far surpasses even the biggest hits of the era, including Paramount's *Gone with the Wind* and Fox's *The Grapes of Wrath*.[26] In this sense, we should not just position Charlie Chan as a significant figure in understanding the nation's uncomfortable racial past; we should instead conceive of him as the single most important character during the Golden Age of American film.

Charlie Chan has never entered the canon partly because he never fit into any dominant discourse. In the 1940s and 1950s, when critics campaigned for movies with a realist aesthetic and

---

26 Richard Maltby, *Hollywood Cinema,* 2nd edn. (Malden: Blackwell Publishing, 2003), 137.

a progressive mission, the Chan series seemed too divorced from the political struggles of the contemporary world. When an intellectual film culture finally emerged in America in the 1960s and 1970s, writers steeped in the reigning auteurist theories ignored the Chan films because they lacked a directorial vision. Later, when academic film studies moved away from the auteurist model and embraced cultural studies and identity politics, the professoriate bypassed these movies again because they didn't fit well into the prevailing tendency either to expose the conservative ideologies of cherished auteurs or to resuscitate overlooked oppositional voices. And yet, we can deploy any of these theoretical lenses to uncover the unexpectedly rich layers of the Chan universe. Surprising to contemporary audiences, many people at the time did think that Chan functioned as a political counterweight to America's racialist ethos. Shanghainese audiences, for instance, cheered Chan's presence as the most visible Chinese hero around the globe. And while it's true that Fox employed many directors on the series, the films do maintain a remarkably consistent aesthetic vision due to the reliance on Earl Derr Biggers' source novels and the charismatic personality of Warner Oland, but most of all to the hands-on role of studio head Darryl Zanuck. In fact, to the extent that the Chan series is emblematic of Hollywood as a whole, it's useful to understand it as the paradigm of the studio executive as unheralded auteur.

The Fox production records at the Margaret Herrick Library in Los Angeles reveal that Zanuck was in charge of almost every detail of *Charlie Chan in Los Angeles* from the beginning to the end. He orchestrated the writing of the screenplay, cast the film, instructed the director every morning as to camera set-ups and lighting schemes, watched rushes every night so he could order retakes the next day, oversaw the editing and scoring, and directed the publicity campaign when the movie was finally released. And despite the formulaic demands of the mystery plot, the movie does convey Zanuck's ongoing fascination with the social issues of the working class that he'd been harvesting from the headlines for movie plots over the previous dozen years. His interest in progressive causes has usually been overlooked, but his contemporaries understood it well; he was the only studio executive invited, for instance, to address the International Writers' Conference held in Los Angeles in 1943.[27] His interest in liberal causes influenced the racial politics of the Chan films as well. Though *Charlie Chan in Los Angeles* may seem somewhat backward to audiences today — due to the casting of a white man to play a Chinese character — audiences and the press at the time saw the issue quite differently. People forget that Fox originally purchased the rights to Biggers's books after the Chinese government banned Downtown Pictures' Fu Manchu series for its disrespectful ethnic representations. The State Department, in turn, approached the Association of Motion Picture Producers to create a series with positive Chinese characters as a way to curry favor with the Chiang Kai-shek administration. And at the time, the Charlie Chan movies did, in fact, fulfill that mission: though Chinese intellectuals tended to dismiss the pictures, the Shanghai press regularly praised the movies when they came out, Chinese audiences flocked to see them, and adoring crowds swarmed Warner Oland every year when he made a publicity tour in the East.

Historians could also revisit the Chan series in order to re-imagine the development of the crime film in America. Though most historians point to *The Maltese Falcon* as the beginning of Hardboiled Cinema in 1942, the Chan films prefigured that genre in many ways. Zanuck had infused the movies with dark chiaroscuro lighting and foggy urban exteriors from the beginning; the films presented a pessimistic worldview in which even the rich and powerful were always possible suspects. And Chan himself was a much more cynical observer of modern life than any other detective of the period: his famously enigmatic fortune-cookie apothegms — "rich girl's love like cobra inside lemon meringue," for instance — often expressed the same kind

27 Larry Ceplair and Steven Englund, *Revolutionary Hollywood: Politics in the Film Community, 1936–1965* (Champaign: University of Illinois Press, 1979), 312–13; and Doug Dibbern, *Hollywood Riots: Progressive Politics and the Realist Aesthetic in the 1940s* (London: Palgrave Macmillan, 2015), 34.

of poetic nihilism that made Raymond Chandler and James M. Cain darlings of both the Algonquin set and the writers of St. Germaine. When *The Maltese Falcon* had such a phenomenal success in 1942, Zanuck was wounded when reviewers praised it for inventing a style that he thought he and Warner Oland had been developing for years. Thus, it wasn't so much that Zanuck was influenced by Hardboiled Cinema when he produced *Charlie Chan in Los Angeles* — as some of even the film's most sympathetic defenders maintain[28] — but that he felt challenged to push himself even further into territory that he had already been inhabiting since the birth of the talkies.

Zanuck thus cooked up an unusual plot structure for this film, which led, in turn, to several other unorthodox aesthetic and philosophical choices. First, he instructed his screenwriting team to divide the film into two parts. In the first, they would document the crime itself and only in the second would Chan finally make a dramatic appearance to start the investigation. This approach, though intended originally to heighten the anticipation of Oland's celebrity appearance, produced disorienting, dream-logic conditions. It's no coincidence, after all, that the first person to write cogently about the film was Parker Tyler in his Surrealist-inspired magazine *View* back in 1946.[29] Because the screenwriters had to portray the perpetrator committing the crime without revealing his identity, almost all of the action in the first half takes place in off-screen space, creating an unusually expressionist quality for a Hollywood film, with random images that carry portentous significance: a mirrored image of women's hats arranged in concentric circles around a bloody glove, the gauzy reflection of a gun hovering over a row of cupcakes in a shop window, and shadows of trench-coated and one-armed figures cast against a swirling mound of butterflies at the zoo. Sound, too, takes on an unusually metaphorical quality,

---

28 See Yunte Huang, *Charlie Chan: The Untold Story of the Honorable Detective and His Rendezvous with American History* (New York: W.W. Norton & Company, 2010).

29 Parker Tyler, "Chan at Death's Door," in *The Magic and Myth of the Movies* (New York: Henry Holt and Company, 1947), 242–59.

with foghorns, clanging bells, steam whistles, and a Babel-like cacophony of languages emanating from a stevedore's cabin, all infusing the air itself with alien vibrations that evince an oneiric threat as menacing as the images themselves.

Once Warner Oland makes his entrance, though, the movie takes on even stranger hues. More convinced than ever that the masses didn't go to mysteries to participate in problem-solving rituals, Zanuck focused instead on what Adele Dessaigne later called "the ambient textures of the urban labyrinth that designate and circumscribe the hardboiled era's audiovisual imaginary."[30] Oland finds himself moving through a series of symbolic, though possibly meaningless, spaces — a basement laboratory of towering beakers, a factory of headless dolls, an aquarium comprised entirely of octopuses — where he faces off against antagonists who manifest themselves only as shadows or echoing voices. Here as well, Zanuck's newfound interest in the poetic possibilities of language comes to the fore. Telling his scriptwriters Horace McCoy and Dorothy Hughes that he wanted them to out-Chandler Chandler, Chan's pithily cryptic pronouncements here become bleak epigrams with a surrealist flair: "Murder is for the poet, not the hunter," Chan says at one point, or "Death, like butterfly, has infancy, too. But, like chrysalis, it's shrouded behind kaleidoscopic wings."

The film's bisected structure and lyrical transgressions take on a greater resonance because they create such a fruitful conflict with Zanuck's normal interest in socially engaged cinema. The film, for instance, makes the realistic urban milieu its subject much more so than any other movie in an era when almost every picture was shot on a soundstage. Zanuck chose Los Angeles for the title on a whim, but once he'd done so, he decided he'd have to escape the backlot and shoot on location instead with a hidden camera. Thus, the movie often feels much more like an actuality than a fiction film: Los Angeles and its denizens, its

---

30 Adele Dessaigne, *Hollywood's Spatial Imaginary,* trans. Hugh Tomlinson and Barbara Habberjam (Minneapolis: University of Minnesota Press, 1994), 192.

geography and architecture, its neighborhoods and ethnic strife all become as much a central character as Chan himself. During his investigation, Chan treks through the jazz cellars of Central Avenue, the opium dens of Little Tokyo, the Spanish mansions of the Hollywood hills, and even a queer dive where he bumps into an old friend from the police force and his fey companion dressed up in an elaborately feathered headdress. Given this emphasis on what a later academic called in a different context "the mutual dependence of the politics of identity and the politics of public space,"[31] it's only fitting that the final scenes take place on the steps of City Hall, where Chan subtly reveals that the murderer has been hiding in plain sight all along: the wealthy white councilman who hired him in the first place so that he could cast suspicions like a net across the city.

To the extent that Charlie Chan, then, represents Hollywood cinema at the aesthetic peak of the studio system, we can begin to see the American film industry through different eyes. Because even in its most commercial instantiations, it's not so much a system circumscribed by generic conventions, censorship codes, and a set of stylistic norms as it is an artistic practice facilitated by the constant avoidance, usurpation, and creatively poetic destruction of those very principles. As Zanuck himself said, "I usually wince when I hear people call us 'the dream factory,' because there's nothing unconscious or like an assembly-line in what we do. On the contrary, I think we're always pushing the boundaries of the audience's expectations to see what it is that they secretly want us to get away with."[32] In the final analysis, it's this productive tension between the system's rules and its simultaneous demands for their evasion — so perfectly manifested in *Charlie Chan in Los Angeles* — that makes the studio era often so much more nuanced and multilayered than the art cinema which purportedly superseded it.

---

31 Belinda Huggs, "Spatial Tension: Urban Geography, Street Life, Contested Identities," in *Hardboiled Cinema and the Spaces of Modernity,* ed. Edward Dimendberg (Cambridge: Harvard University Press, 2004), 201.

32 Quoted in George F. Custen, *A Fox in Sheep's Clothing: Darryl F. Zanuck and the Culture of Hollywood* (New York: Basic Books, 1997), 233.

Christiane (d. Marie Lebrun, France, 1981)
pr. Les Films du Losange, sc. Marie Lebrun, starring Bulle Ogier,
sound, b&w, 16mm, 328 min.

When feminism finally became a cultural force in France in the late 1960s, it took the film world by surprise. Producers, directors, screenwriters, and critics — almost all of whom considered themselves to be on the left of the political spectrum — were startled to realize that there were virtually no women working at any level in the film industry except as actresses. Hardly any female directors had helmed a major motion picture in France since the 1920s. Almost every single critic at journals like *Cinema Arts, Cahiers du Cinéma,* and *Positif* were men. And casual sexism was so common that in 1971, when Julia Timoshev published "Why are there No Female Critics? Why are there no Female Directors?"[33] — in the feminist magazine *Le Nouvelle Femme,* rather than in a film journal — the knee-jerk reaction against it seemed to be the only issue that could temporarily reunite the feuding firebrands François Truffaut and Jean-Luc Godard. One fellow cinephile claimed that he'd overheard Godard at Cannes jokingly answering Timoshev's question to his erstwhile friend, "because they belong on their backs."[34]

French producers appeased the minor protests that bubbled up in the early 1970s by allowing the first wave of female directors — Françoise Thulon, Marie-Hélène Servaine, and Lydia Miller — to make their first features. When Miller castigated the French establishment in her acceptance speech after winning the Palme d'Or in 1974, even Godard wrote an essay in which he acknowledged that the gender imbalance on the staff at *Cahiers* may have led to a masculinist approach that overvalued hardboiled auteurs, and that perhaps it was time to de-

33 Julia Timoshev, "Why Are There No Female Critics? Why Are There No Female Directors?," in *Feminist Film Theory: A Reader,* ed. Sue Thornham (New York: New York University Press, 1998), 10–27.
34 Serge Toubiana and Antoine de Baecque, *Truffaut: A Biography* (New York: Alfred A. Knopf, 1997), 233.

81

fine and pay tribute to a feminine aesthetic.[35] But while writers at the time heralded the work of this pioneering troika for its portrayal of strong women, a few more sober observers noted that these movies merely translated the heroic protagonists and narrative structures of masculine adventure films into domestic settings — now telling stories about wives who bravely overcame their husband's oppression — thereby replicating an ideological position that those filmmakers should have been dismantling.[36] It was only in the second wave of the feminist movement that some directors began to examine what a gendered aesthetic — and thus, a different vision of the cinema — might look like, and it's in films like Marie Lebrun's *Christiane* in particular that the dream of 1970s feminist theorists finally reached its fruition.

Critics have paid respect to Lebrun mostly for her nuanced portrayal of female characters, but that issue is inseparable from her more complex handling of the formal dimensions of film — especially dialogue, narrative construction, and the representation of time. "Most of what they called 'masculine cinema,'" she told the critic Maurice Scherer, "over-emphasized the role that conflict needed to play in setting up a story," suggesting that conflict was the male directors' excuse to indulge in their own adolescent interest in sensationalist violence.[37] And the unfeeling nihilism of the Chandleresque dialogue that her male colleagues treasured, she said, was merely the linguistic manifestation of a juvenile desire to escape their social responsibilities. Instead, she said, with *Christiane,* she sought to make a movie not about conflict but about consensus and cooperation, about friendship and empathy; she wanted to emphasize the poetic sensibility of the quotidian, trying to capture the ac-

---

35 Jean-Luc Godard, "Exorcising Radical Positions," in *Selected Criticism, Volume II*, ed. Tom Milne (New York: The Viking Press, 1984), 86.

36 See Adele Dessaigne, *Contested Images: Feminist Filmmaking and Feminist Criticism in France in the 70s*, trans. Hugh Tomlinson and Barbara Habberjam (Minneapolis: University of Minnesota Press, 1999), 68–86.

37 Maurice Scherer, "Interview with Marie Lebrun," in *Cahiers du Cinéma, 1973–1985: History, Ideology, Cultural Struggle*, ed. David Wilson (New York: Routledge, 1998), 127.

tual flow of human life with its boredom, its languor, and its inconsequential epiphanies. With this in mind, she shot on location with lightweight, handheld cameras, cheap film stock, and mostly untrained actresses who improvised at length about the minute details of their lives.

The story, such as it is, centers on the forty-year-old artist Christiane (Bulle Ogier) and her recollections to a pair of friends of three previous romantic affairs — one with a fellow painter, one with a married man, and one with a younger bohemian — each of which, not surprisingly, ended with her feeling dissatisfied and convinced that she'd never fall in love again. To fully explore the rich possibilities of cinematic time and of what she termed the "plotless quotidian," Lebrun thought that she needed to make a film at least twice as long as any other French movie of the time. But her conception of time was not revolutionary just because she let shots and scenes unfold much longer than her contemporaries did, but rather, because she let her characters talk on and on in an aleatory, circular style, allowing sentence fragments to drift off, unanswered, like "fallen leaves wafting on the wind," she told her actresses;[38] her scenes took on a temporal weight precisely because the dialogue seemed so incidental. This style of talking, only possible in the cinema, "encouraged the audience," wrote Sandy Loewenstein, "to seek out in the characters' silences, subtle inflections, random gestures, and verbal indirections the key to their psychology, thus turning the spectators into active participants in the meaning-making of the characters' identities."[39] At the same time, Lebrun manipulated time on a much larger scale: the conversations become fugue-like in their repetitions, folding in on themselves, developing over the course of the film so that a seemingly throwaway observation becomes, only in retrospect, the emotional peak of the drama. Scherer, who wrote about her work more incisively than anyone else at the time, praised her for her "cascade

---

38 Ibid., 131.

39 Sandy Loewenstein, *To Speak, Not to Be Seen: Feminism and the French Cinema* (Ann Arbor: University of Michigan Press 1990), 270.

of language," what he called "the film's operatic density, almost Wagnerian in its fascination with the cyclical return of leitmotifs, making Lebrun both the twin and the obverse of that other great — and unheralded — cinematic innovator of dialogue, the spare, Hemingway-esque Howard Hawks."[40]

Ironically, given Lebrun's desire to create an oppositional style to the unthinking masculine assumptions of both the commercial and the art cinema, her movie's lasting impact has been felt more among film directors in general than among women filmmakers specifically, inspiring men like Benjamin Sinsot and Maurice Pialat to explore more naturalistic styles of acting and dialogue that were more attuned to the plotless, undramatic nature of actual life. As Annabelle Jordan noted years later,

> The fact that such a surprisingly small number of other feminist filmmakers have adopted her experimental bent is a by-product of the shifts in feminist discourse over the decades.
>
> Though her gender essentialism strikes most people as anachronistic these days, it did force Lebrun to craft a style that challenged the dominant paradigms of the time. Ironically, our possibly more sophisticated anti-essentialist conception of gender today has discouraged most feminist filmmakers from examining gender differentiation; and this, in turn, has prevented them, unfortunately, from pursuing any logically concomitant aesthetic innovations as well."[41]

While Lebrun's movie has proved to be an increasingly inspiring touchstone for later generations of scholars, critics, and filmmakers, it did not inspire the audiences of its day. Not many people — not even the most ardent feminists or cinephiles, it seemed — were willing to pay money to watch a handful of middle-aged women sitting around and talking about their lives

---

40 Maurice Scherer, "Dialogue in History," in *Cahiers du Cinéma, 1973–1985,* ed. Wilson, 131.

41 Annabelle Jordan, "Reflections on 'Women's Cinema as Counter-Cinema,'" in *Feminism and Film,* ed. E. Ann Kaplan (Oxford: Oxford University Press, 2000), 152.

for more than five hours. Lebrun shrugged it off. She told her producers that she had no interest in adapting her vision to what she called the masculine profit model, so she threw the script she'd been working on into the trash. She moved, instead, to a small town in the Pyrenees, became active in the movement to foster organic farming, and published two widely praised but not particularly remunerative books — one titled *Root Vegetables* and the other *A Cultural History of Moss* — but she never made another film again.

Chronicle of the Years of Embers (d. Mohammed Lakhdar-Hamina, Algeria, 1975)
pr. National Office for the Commerce and Industry of Cinema, sc. Mohammed Lakhdar-Hamina, Rachid Boudjedra, and Tewfik Fares, starring Yorgo Vayagis, sound, color, 70mm, 175min.

Chronicle of the Years of Embers won the Palme d'Or at Cannes in 1975 and is still the only Arab-language film to have done so. Critics in the Middle East generally conceive of it — alongside Youssef Chahine's *The Land* (1967) — as one of the most significant films of the Arab world. And yet, to this day, international cinephiles tend to regard *The Battle of Algiers* (1966), directed by the Italian Gillo Pontecorvo, as the paradigmatic film about the Algerian independence struggle — even of the anti-colonial movement as a whole — while Mohammed Lakhdar-Hamina's epic remains relatively unknown to even the most ardent film enthusiasts in most parts of the world.

With a mandate from the Algerian government to commemorate the twentieth anniversary of the beginnings of the war for independence — and with a government-financed budget more than fifteen times larger than the typical film made in the country, consuming almost the entire nation's film production for three years[42] — Lakhdar-Hamina felt that he needed to

42 Roy Armes, *Postcolonial Images: Studies in North African Film* (Bloomington: Indiana University Press, 2005), 97

develop a distinctive cinematic grammar to match the revolutionary fervor of his subject. Just a few years earlier, he'd been one of the central organizers of the inaugural conference for the Cinema Committee of the Global South held in Algiers in 1973, a group that hoped to forge a united policy for filmmakers across the globe who were still fighting — in a post-colonial world — against the hegemony of both the Hollywood blockbuster and the European art film. There, established directors like Abibo Ndiaye and Carlotta Jimenez-Galt and younger filmmakers like Illary Quispe and Maria Supa had passionate conversations late into the night about the obligations of artists in the developing world. Ndiaye and Quispe — as the most celebrated non-Western directors of their respective generations at that time — ensconced themselves in a hotel suite over the conference's last few days, intending to produce a manifesto on the Committee's ideological and artistic goals, but they ultimately failed to reach common ground. Wasn't articulating a shared agenda, Quispe wondered aloud at the concluding press conference, merely another means of controlling or censoring an artist's vision just as the former colonialists had done? The failure to nurture an ongoing global community of progressive filmmakers rankled Lakhdar-Hamina, who always gravitated toward a communal vision. But the debates at the conference had nevertheless inspired him to articulate his aesthetic ideology on his own — not with a manifesto, but in the language of cinema where he felt most at home.

This goal would have remained merely aspirational if it weren't for the political climate of Algeria in the 1970s. Though filmmakers and critics on the left don't pay much attention to the fact today, the nations of North Africa in the 1960s and 1970s engaged in one of the most significant experiments in government-financed cinema the world has ever seen — decades before the European Union created a coherent cultural policy on film of its own. In those decades, when much of the Arab world was led by secular, pan-Arab progressives like Gamal Abdel Nasser and Houari Boumédiène, the Egyptian and Algerian governments each nationalized their film industries, placing the means of production in the hands of bureaucracies led by filmmakers themselves. From 1967 to 1984, the Algerian government, for instance — through its National Office for the Commerce and Industry of Cinema — held a virtual monopoly on film production, distribution, and exhibition across the country.[43] And though this experiment with socialist filmmaking was brief — waning in the late 1970s as Anwar Sadat and Chadli Bendjedid weaned their nations from the central economic planning of their predecessors — the films these nations produced in that short period are generally considered, not coincidentally, as the richest period in the history of Arab filmmaking.

That being said, government-financing of the arts cuts both ways: while it frees filmmakers from the dictates of the market, it also restricts their ability to criticize the current state of affairs. And Algeria was an authoritarian, one-party state led by the National Liberation Front, even if Boumédiène still made ostensibly leftist pronouncements on the international stage. Lakhdar-Hamina himself held a conflicted position in this new cultural labyrinth: once a committed revolutionary himself, he'd been heading up the administration's actuality film unit for more than a decade. So on the one hand, he'd managed to work within the system well enough to garner the government commission, while on the other hand, like most intellectuals at the time, he'd grown disillusioned with the country's calcified leadership.[44] A filmmaker like Lakhdar-Hamina, then, would thus have to deploy roundabout cinematic methods of criticizing his nation's post-independence political drift. On the surface, his film does follow the party's line, championing its former militants and disparaging its former opponents who sought peaceful, democratic means of seeking independence. But to express his own disenchantment with the government that was funding his film, Lakhdar-Hamina drew upon the debates about opposi-

---

43 Ibid., 7.

44 Guy Austin, *Algerian National Cinema* (Manchester: Manchester University Press, 2012), 20–32.

87

tional aesthetics that he and his fellow directors from the developing world had been wrestling with for years.

Lakhdar-Hamina focused his stylistic deviations from traditional norms in terms of both narrative construction and visual style. The story traces the political awakening of Algeria under French rule from the years 1939 to 1954, but because he wanted to make the case that it was the common people as a whole more than the heroic leadership of the National Liberation Front who led the revolution, he didn't focus on one heroic protagonist as in the typical Hollywood epic. Instead, like many Russian directors of the 1920s who made films celebrating the February Revolution, he designed his story with a collective protagonist — one representative village standing for the nation as a whole, with one character, Ahmed, functioning as the emblem of the collective, the archetypal common man. The villagers' conflict begins in the middle of a sun-cracked desert, where their smattering of mud-brick homes appears as an outgrowth of the earth, as if the people are just a minor element of the environment, mere flecks set against a remote and indifferent world. Here, their main antagonists are other peasants from nearby villages, fighting for access to the meager trickle of water in what should be a flowing river. At this point, they barely seem to know that the French even exist. It's only after they've abandoned rural life and moved into town that they can see that their true adversaries are the French occupiers. And it is this transition between one type of antagonist to another that is the source of the collective's intellectual and political evolution, the seedbed of their revolutionary consciousness that will motivate the rest of the film.

Lakhdar-Hamina designed a visual style specific to both rural and city life in order to underline this ideological division. In the countryside, he portrays the villagers as miniscule figures engulfed by imposing landscapes. In the first images of the film, a parched desert stretches to the horizon, dotted here and there with the bodies of dead sheep. The village walls — the very emblem of the idea of home — seem like an extension of this spiritual and economic desiccation. And when the villagers venture out with their flocks through the rocky hills, sandstone buttes, and jagged cliffs, the grandeur of the 70mm image overpowers them. At moments like these, the film seems more interested in the infinitely subtle variations in hues of ochre, beige, and cream than it is with the daily lives of its characters. But this is not just a fascination with color for its own sake: Lakhdar-Hamina renders nature in all its chromatic monumentality as a demonstration of his environmentally deterministic attitudes about his characters' fate; his landscapes are gorgeous and daunting: they are the bountiful, earthly paradise where the villagers yearn to return but also the very force that expels them from their embrace. He represents the villagers' stunted political imagination through their insignificance in the frame. The fact that they have not yet understood that the French are their true enemy is what makes them disappear amid the unfeeling enormity of this arid terrain. The common people have not yet achieved a politicized awareness that could free them from the environment that has diminished them.

As the film moves into the allegedly more civilized world of town, Lakhdar-Hamina devises an alternative mode of visual signification. Instead of vast exteriors, now his protagonists live in empty interiors that somehow still feel cramped, serving as the spatial metaphor of their most recent form of intellectual constriction. But then one day, a curious figure wearing a suit and hat — almost as if he's a middle-class European himself — steps off the bus. He is, they discover, a leftist intellectual from Algiers, exiled to the sleepy interior because of his anticolonial activism. And his arrival changes them. Over the next few weeks, he has tentative conversations with the men from the village, huddled together over tea. And they are eager to listen. The French arrived by the gun, he tells them, and the only way they will leave is by the gun. Now Lakhdar-Hamina designs his images as a foreshadowing of the fate of the nation to come, emphasizing the burgeoning sense of collective empowerment. Now he films his men almost exclusively in groups: handfuls or dozens of men sitting together over a newspaper, working in the blacksmith shop, drinking tea and playing cards, debating each other in the mosque. His characters proliferate and

89

expand against the edges of the frame. He peoples his images with floods of extras swirling, scattering, or surging. His men are no longer miniscule figures enfeebled by the timeless magnificence of the earth; these are men yearning to break free and claim their own liberation.

Despite this sense of communal empowerment, Lakhdar-Hamina ultimately paints a surprisingly despairing picture of the Algerian political situation. It's significant that even though he made the film a dozen years after independence, he chose not to conclude his story with the victory of revolution. Instead, he brings it to a close in 1954, just before the war for independence commenced. By the end of the film, his villagers have almost all been killed off by the French or their collaborators. All their political efforts have come to naught. It's an unusually somber way to commemorate the revolution, a not-so-veiled commentary by Lakhdar-Hamina on his own resignation at his nation's lack of development.

By 1975, the leftist dream had begun to wane. The Ben Bella and Boumédiène governments had continued to espouse progressive ideals, but had largely failed to deliver on the promise of liberation at home. The economy had stagnated; censorship had increased; the Arabic-speaking majority continued to discriminate against the Berber-speaking minority; and tensions with Islamists were already mounting. Lakhdar-Hamina managed to express his implicit criticisms of the regime by casting himself as the character of Miloud — who, like a Greek Chorus or Shakespearian Fool — wanders the stage, decrying the evils of the world. And though he's clearly speaking to the people in the diegetic world of the 1940s and 1950s, it's clear that he's speaking to the Algerian audience of 1975 as well. "More lost souls," he observes contemptuously of the villagers, the very people who are destined to lead the revolution, when they first arrive in town, "certain that they've found paradise when they're really just sinking into the sand. They think they've found the water of life when they're only sinking deeper. Here's our mirage: the city. You'll only find the water bitter." He continues these tirades throughout the film, condemning the villagers, the townspeople, and the militants themselves repeatedly for not committing themselves wholeheartedly enough to their "rendezvous with destiny." Miloud himself eventually succumbs to the fate of the nation, tortured by the authorities, dying alone in a barren wasteland, and Lakhdar-Hamina returns to the mode of visual metaphor for the film's final sequence, in which Ahmed's young son, the personification of the next generation, runs — and keeps on running and keeps on running — in one long tracking shot through more monumental, arid landscapes off toward an equally arid and imposing horizon of the future as the soundtrack reverberates with blasts of gunfire — a conclusion which a general audience might see as a hopeful vision of the nation's impending liberation, but which one might also read as a condemnation of the current political situation because more than a dozen years after independence, the true battle for freedom has yet to come.

The film won rave reviews both in Algeria and in France upon its release. But despite the accolades, neither Lakhdar-Hamina nor other Arab-language filmmakers like Youssef Chahine have ever made much of an impression on international cinephile culture. Filmmakers from that generation had careers that waxed and waned in tandem with their own nation's politics. After the first years of independence, the revolutionary fervor faded. Ahmed Ben Bella was overthrown in a coup in 1965. Nasser died from a heart attack in 1970. Both Algeria and Egypt cut back on government funding for their film industries in the 1970s and terminated their motion picture divisions in the 1980s, leaving filmmakers struggling to find funding for anything other than lighthearted commercial fare. And the dream of a liberated, socialist cinema became just a dream once again.

Comancheria (d. John Ford, USA, 1956)
pr. *C.V. Whitney Pictures, sc. Frank Nugent, starring Ricardo
Montalbán, Gilbert Roland, Natalie Wood, and Ward Bond,
sound, color, 35mm, 119 min.*

Most cinephiles now consider *Comancheria* to be Ford's greatest achievement — and thus, perhaps the apogee of the Western — because it marks the culmination of his evolution from
cheerleader of manifest destiny to its most complex critic, not
just as a filmmaker but also as a historian, a journey he'd begun in 1946 with *Tombstone* and explored further with *Custer*
in 1951. Nevertheless, despite its secure position in the canon,
the film still has a vocal cadre of naysayers, who disparage it
for embracing the very ethnic stereotyping that it purports to
be critiquing. But both the film's champions and detractors still
gloss over some of the central aspects of its achievement. While
writers tend to focus almost exclusively on Ford's position on
the multicultural frontier, the film is equally fascinating because
of his sophisticated use of purely visual means to explain nuanced political ideas about the past, reviving the language of
silent cinema to a degree rarely achieved in the era of sound
cinema. At the same time, though its backers defend it for its
thoughtful portrayal of the Mexican victims of American expansion and its opponents attack it for its crude portrayal of Native Americans, both sides fall back on binary judgments such
as these for evaluating racial representation influenced by our
contemporary politics. Ford's representational politics, though,
are much more multidimensional than this debate understands.

Ford does, in fact, deploy fairly simple positive and negative
conceptions of racial identity, but he does so precisely so that he
can turn them on their heads. That is, he subsumes the movie's
racial tensions within a secondary binary opposition — that
between the private, domestic sphere and the public, frontier
world, which he sees as a much more significant dynamic in the
development of the American West. The Mexican protagonist
played by Ricardo Montalbán and the Comanche chief Scar,
as representatives of the frontier, exhibit eerily similar charac-

teristics, while the Mexican, American, and Indian characters in the domestic world mirror each other as well. Contrary to the claims of his detractors, by setting up these interconnected Manichaean oppositions between the frontier and domestic worlds, Ford incessantly reveals the similarities — more than the differences — between the ethnic groups that comprise this milieu. And he does so in order to suggest that all three civilizations have thrived and ruptured for the same reasons. So, unlike most directors of Westerns in the 1950s, Ford did not portray ethnicities as having any innate characteristics. Instead, he saw every racial group developing the same characteristics at the same time because of the same historical and cultural forces. Ford saw the American West, as well as each of his characters, defined by the conflict between the frontier and the domestic sphere — or, between the desert and the garden, to use Peter Wollen's terms — more than by any ethnic or cultural identity.[45] And it is the brutal victories on the frontier over the decades that leave the victor's domestic world — that part that we call "civilization" — living in seeming comfort, but still riven by unspeakable racial conflict and incapable of understanding its past precisely because of the ignorance that the frontier mentality necessarily engenders.

Ford had been an avid reader of American history since he was a young man, and his bookishness had informed his films as early as *Iron Horse* in 1924. But beginning in the 1940s, he said, his interests broadened beyond just the accounts of white settlers that he'd read in the past to include more primary sources from the 19th century that covered Comanches, Apaches, the Spanish, and Mexicans as well. He told the critic Peter Bogdanovich that the idea for the film first sprouted when he realized that competing empires had been claiming the area we now call Texas for hundreds of years — first Spain, then Mexico, then the Republic of Texas, then the United States, then the Confederacy,

---

45 Peter Wollen, "The Auteur Theory," in *Signs and Meanings in the Cinema* (London: British Film Institute, 1969), 74–115.

and finally the United States once again.[46] But despite these official designations, the story was still even more complex, since the single dominant force of this multiethnic borderland throughout the 19th century had been the Comanches, who themselves had only come into existence mere decades prior to the arrival of American immigrants. Once he started poring over old maps, Ford realized that in the decades after the Mexican War, Comanches controlled territory that encompassed modern-day West Texas, New Mexico, Colorado, and Kansas, an area roughly the same size as France, Germany, and the United Kingdom combined. The struggle between Mexicans, Comanches, and Americans for dominance in the Southwest, he thought, could make a story as grandiose and compelling as Tolstoy's account of the Napoleonic Wars. But with his now more critical attitudes toward the American role in westward expansion — and with the urging of his producer C.V. Whitney, who wanted to take advantage of the recent craze for the new wave of Latin Lovers — Ford decided to tell his history of the Southwest from the point of view of the Mexicans rather than of the Americans.

The movie begins with a title card that reads, "Texas, 1868." Ricardo Montalbán then rides a dying horse over a ridge to look down on a cabin that stands alone in a desert valley beneath a pair of orange buttes that Ford filmed in Monument Valley but which is supposed to exist somewhere near a fork of the Brazos River. He's been wandering for years throughout the West — though it's initially unclear why — and now has finally come home to the ranch where he was born and raised and which his older brother, played by Gilbert Roland, has been managing for years. Roland has struggled to hold on to the property that their parents founded — in what was then the farthest reaches of the Spanish Empire — in the face of ever-increasing hostility from both white American settlers and their Comanche antagonists. Montalbán has become jaded by his sojourn through the former Mexican states that now belong to the U.S.,

---

46 Peter Bogdanovich, *John Ford* (Los Angeles: Movie Magazine Limited, 1967), 102.

a region, he tells his brother, that feels as if the Confederates had actually won. But he hasn't been away from home for years, we learn, only because of some political despair. In one of his most sophisticated scenes, Ford explains the past conflict that continues to propel the entire narrative: in just a few shots, he shows Roland's wife folding Montalbán's clothes tenderly on the night of his return, followed by Montalbán giving her a thankful kiss on the forehead so that we understand immediately — without a word of dialogue — that the reason he left home years before was that he and his brother's wife had secretly been in love.

The story proper begins after Comanches lure Montalbán and Roland out on a patrol; they then take advantage of their absence to raid the ranch, murdering Roland's wife and kidnapping his ten-year-old daughter, played by the young Natalie Wood. With a craving for vengeance and no need to tend the land anymore, Montalbán convinces his brother to join him in tracking down the young girl, leaving behind a community of friends and a woman next door who makes it clear to Roland that she'd be willing to become his new wife. But the weeks of searching turn into months and the months into years, and their quest becomes less a story about rescuing a girl and more an exploration of Montalbán's psyche as an emblem of the racial hatred that governs the West: obsessed with his niece's sexual purity to an unhealthy degree — partly, because we begin to suspect, she may not be his niece but actually his daughter, the product of the illicit affair with his brother's wife that forced him to leave home soon after she was born — he swears to Roland that when they do finally catch up with her, they must kill her in order to save her from the shame of being a Comanche warrior's bride. And the tension between the two men — one who wants to return the girl to civilization and the other who wants to murder her on the frontier — drives the rest of the film.

Ford begins to complicate his audience's racial assumptions by making the men's journey an anthropological mapping of the United States's ethnic imagination. Along the way, they meet a Swedish family that's settled along the Brazos, Mormon pioneers who've fled violent mobs to settle in the basin of the Great

Salt Lake, teams of former Chinese railroad workers starving as they make their way back to San Francisco, roaming bands of Apaches and Cheyennes who've been brutalized even more by Comanches than they have by white frontiersmen, and Federal Army regiments still riven by Yankee–Confederate tensions. And these communities' resilience against the stunning but uncaring landscapes reminds them of the neighbors they left behind. Roland begins to soften. In a rare moment by campfire at night, he admits to his brother that he has ambiguous feelings about their pursuit, recalling that they too come from a multi-ethnic heritage forged by racial brutality — one of their grandmothers was a Zapotec raped by a Spanish soldier, while the other grandfather immigrated from Germany and took a mestizo wife — so that his own sense of restoring his daughter's racial dignity is more complicated than he's been willing to acknowledge. But Montalbán's anger never falters. There is only us and them, he tells his brother. So they push on, continuing their peregrinations through scorching deserts and freezing snow, year after year. Finally, after seven long years, they get news of the girl's whereabouts at a nearby Comanche camp, and they sneak up to rescue her. But here, Ford complicates his audience's received notions yet again. Roland's daughter Natalie Wood is afraid just to set eyes upon them. She looks upon her father and her uncle as if she's seeing ghosts. She waves them away frantically from across a creek, almost hissing at them as she implores them to leave. She'd rather stay there — with "my people" — she says. She's a Comanche now. She's not their daughter anymore.

Ford continually draws parallels between Montalbán and the Comanche chief whom they've been tracking for years, the man who kidnapped his niece — and who has presumably made her his new wife — a warrior who's known only as Scar, a sobriquet that speaks of the source of his terrible resentment. Both men stew with racial animosity: they've both been wandering throughout the West for years because their families have been destroyed by their enemies. They both lead war parties for empires that are dying at the hands of the new power of the United States, they each prefer to charge recklessly into battle rather than plan out a systematic approach, and they both scalp their victims. They've each become fluent in the same three languages, Ford hints, by having sexual relationships — most likely coercive — with women from different cultures. And most importantly, Ford demonstrates that Scar and Montalbán share a paternal and quasi-sexual intimacy with Natalie Wood, emphasizing that the family bonds that are so vital in maintaining the competing communities in the West have so often been the product, ironically, of sexual predation. In this sense, Montalbán and Scar are both branded by their past, and since they see no future for themselves or for their communities, they take pleasure in wandering the deserts and the plains — just as Ahab did in wandering the seas — in a self-destructive quest to bring down the world that has already decimated their people.

While Montalbán, Scar, and the American general who's a stand-in for Custer come to represent the racial brutality — but also the courage — of the frontier, Ford creates a wholly separate domestic realm to complement each of these three frontiersmen. For Montalbán, it's the community in Monument Valley that awaits his and Roland's return. Back near the Brazos, the woman who yearns to be Roland's new fiancée waits patiently, surrounded by an extended family that includes Mexicans and white Americans, Catholics and Protestants, and even a married couple who had formerly been enslaved, while nearby an Apache encampment lives in peace. But while Ford defines the frontiersmen by both their savagery and their valor, he uniformly portrays the people in the so-called civilized world — of any ethnic stripe — as naïve caricatures. The comic actor Cantinflas plays a gap-toothed rube who courts Roland's potential new bride by proudly handing her a bag of boiled sweets, while Harry Carey, Jr., plays a neighboring rancher so unworldly that he's embarrassed to explain to a pretty girl the difference between a cow and a steer. Meanwhile, Ford draws the parallels between Montalbán and Scar yet again, surrounding the Comanche chief with his own domestic sphere comprised of toothless elders unaware of the region's politics and starry-eyed girls who are just as gullible as the women who await Montalbán and Roland's return.

Ford's film should be a touchstone not just for its rich conception of history but also for its complex handling of cinematic style. In the opening shots, for instance, when Montalbán returns home on a speared horse, Ford positions Roland on one side of the porch while his wife and daughter stand on the opposite side, already hinting that they do not constitute a real family. Later, Ford repeatedly emphasizes Montalbán's intimacy with Roland's wife and daughter by grouping the three of them together in the frame while portraying Roland only in shots by himself. And when Montalbán rides away one morning, Ford doesn't show the brother, but the wife and daughter alone to see him off. He uses similar strategies of staging to comment on the community as a whole. When a multi-ethnic group of neighbors comes to the house to celebrate Montalbán's return, Ford renders the domestic world's naïveté simply in the way he fashions the mise-en-scene, positioning the simpletons who manage the farm and home — whether Mexican or American — in the foreground, dominating the frame, while placing the former warriors shrinking in the frail light of the background of the image.

Ford reserves some of his most trenchant commentary on the American myth and some of his most sophisticated filmmaking for the final scene. When the Americans have finally massacred the niece's Comanche band, the two Mexican brothers return with her to the land where they were raised to restore their homes in what they hope will become an ethnically diverse community in the newly expanded United States. The film's detractors criticize the ending as a triumphalist nod to American exceptionalism, while the film's defenders tend to brush it aside as the necessary closure that the Hollywood system requires; but the conclusion is much more ambiguous than either side acknowledges. As Roland introduces the girl to the white Americans who gather on the porch outside Harry Carey, Jr.'s home, Ford places his camera inside the darkness of the house, situating the audience — metaphorically — in the space of the civilized but stupid domestic world that the brutality of the American army has established and protected. But as Roland carries his daughter across the threshold, the girl glances from her benefactors to the murky void of the home, and her face expresses only uneasiness and fear. Then, the doors close, with Montalbán still standing alone outside in the desert, unable to be integrated into the civilized realm that his obsessive hatred has helped create, and Ford leaves us, the audience, in the ignorant darkness that people in the domestic sphere have inhabited throughout the film, unwilling to admit today that our comfortable lives have been fashioned for us by the violent figures whom we've conveniently displaced from our communities and thus from our histories as well.

The Dawn Light Is Harsh But Bright (d. Praew Tanitwanantrith, Thailand, 1978)
pr. Prommitr International Production, sc. Praew Tanitwanantrith and Chupitra Kongpaisam, starring Anita Pawnithiprapta, sound, color, 35mm, 94min.

The Dawn Light Is Harsh But Bright entered the cinephile consciousness because Lavanya Qasoori saw it as the perfect vehicle to make the centerpiece of her groundbreaking 1986 book *Developing Celebrity*. The movie's central concerns were her own concerns as well. And its narrative development echoed her principal arguments about how women shaped their sense of self in response to their nation's narrative of its own identity through the vehicle of popular entertainment. But it was also a perfect object of study because its star had become one of the most popular celebrities in the developing world. This was the movie, after all, that catapulted Anita Pawnithiprapta to stardom — not coincidentally, just at the same time as Thailand itself was refashioning its own identity in the wake of the Japanese occupation.

Qasoori argued that scholars of film stardom had settled too easily on examples from Hollywood's classical period, focusing on luminaries like Linda Stahl, Bette Davis, and Mitch Randall.

99

She was initially interested in overturning the dominant Althus-serian model of star studies that saw celebrities as tools that cor-porations deployed in order to "interpellate subjects," but along the way she borrowed Benedict Anderson's idea of the nation as an "imagined community" to suggest that nations constructed a range of permissible celebrity identities in much the same way that an individual created a "performatively imagined self within the framework that a newly globalized economic and cultural landscape had shaped for her."[47] She used the movie, which was still virtually unknown to the outside world, to study fan communities in Thailand, Tamil Nadu, and the Pakistani enclaves of Manchester and Leeds to investigate how people in marginalized communities "actively and knowingly engage with the vibrant presence of the diegetic fiction as well as with the biographical fictions fashioned by fan magazines so that they can comprehend, reconstruct, and stage their own personas as a technique for survival — both in league with and in opposition to — a rapidly changing world."[48] By living vicariously through these celebrities' fictional performances and real-world roman-tic dramas, their fans embraced a form of what Qasoori called "cosmopolitan modernity" that both the nation state and the in-ternational political order tried to repress in order to legitimize their own existence.[49]

Qasoori focused on *The Dawn Light Is Harsh But Bright* not because she could reveal, as most scholars would, that these themes lay beneath the surface of the film unknown to its mak-ers, but precisely because Praew Tanitwanantrith, she thought, was an equally intellectual interlocutor who had been con-sciously analyzing the same issues as Qasoori herself, only in a different medium and different emotional register. By the 1970s, Praew had made an increasingly sophisticated cycle of cheap women's weepies that had cast Anita — as she was known to her

---

47 Lavanya Qasoori, *Developing Celebrity* (Minneapolis: University of Min-nesota Press, 1986), 5.

48 Ibid., 31.

49 Ibid., 33.

legion of adoring fans — as "an idealized icon of tenacious grit in the face of adversity."[50] She'd earned her renown by playing a series of outcasts in Praew's films: poor village girls, prostitutes, or Bangkok factory workers who were clawing their way through the muck of modern life to reclaim a sense of dignity for themselves. At the same time, Anita was becoming one of the country's biggest pop singers — with fervent anthems of female empowerment like "Taxi-Driving Girl" and "I Have a Vegetable Stall in the Market" — which naturally created a productive tension in her movies between the melodramatic degradation of the plots and the ameliorating vision of the songs, a tension that Qasoori describes as "the fruitfully uncomfortable tonal balance that is both a manifestation of and a necessary coping mechanism for the trauma of post-colonial drift."[51]

In *The Dawn Light Is Harsh But Bright,* Anita captures this contemporary disequilibrium perfectly, playing two roles that represent two generations of Thai women whose lives have been determined for them by their very different personal and political circumstances. At first, we see her as Noon, a naïve teenager who comes from a village to Bangkok to work as the maid for a wealthy industrialist's wife. But she also plays the role of the wife, Apinya, an aging beauty who acts imperiously, we learn, as a way to shelter herself from her own insecurities. Praew cleverly shoots most of the scenes in which the two characters appear together in a split-screen system with their faces reflected in the two mirrors of a dressing table, so that Anita-as-Noon appears on the left, combing her employer's hair, while Anita-as-Apinya appears on the right. Despite their initial discomfort, the two women begin to bond over their shared admiration for an outspoken beauty queen who was defrocked because of a sex scandal. Eventually, Apinya opens up to Noon and reveals to her that she too was once a naïve young girl from the countryside who came to Bangkok to make a better life for herself.

---

50 Ibid., 42.
51 Ibid., 55.

The movie then flashes back to the years of Apinya's youth under Japanese rule, when money flowed into the capital and people embraced a bacchanalian existence as a way to defuse the infantilizing pain of the occupation. Apinya becomes a devotee of the cinema, falling in love so deeply with the movie star Supichaya that she adapts her persona, wearing similar flower-print chenille dresses, pulling her hair back in the same artfully misshapen bun, and sporting hoop earrings almost as daringly large as her idol's. And this transformation of her identity pays off: soon, some Japanese soldiers take notice and offer her a better job as a bar hostess at the local military canteen. In this new setting, she retreats to the state of carnivalesque revelry that marked Bangkok life in the later years of the occupation. It is at the tail end of one of these soirees for Japanese officers and the wealthy Bangkok elite that she meets a handsome colonel, Iwabaki Kudai, and over the course of one long, increasingly drunken evening, Iwabaki manages to manipulate her into a back room, corner her, and force himself on her in a gruesome scene. Months later, forced out of her job because of her ensuing pregnancy, alone in a hospital ward for wayward women, she gives her daughter up for adoption.

It was only through a miracle, she tells Noon back in the present, that she eventually met and married her husband — the scion of a successful Thai family. He's a decent man, she says, but she's never truly loved him, and the tragedy of their marriage — almost as difficult to bear as having to give up her own daughter — is that her husband has always known that she would never love him, even on the night of their wedding. Apinya's emotional confession to her young employee culminates in the film's first song — a duet rendered in split-screen — "I Am from Your World," in which Baniwath Jaipur's characteristically unconventional arrangements, harmonizing oboe and bassoon with traditional Thai instruments like the *khim* and the *saw sam sai,* create an uncanny emotional juxtaposition, much like the feeling of returning to the present from a horrible but unforgettable dream.

The film's climax is not just an emotional peak, but an intellectual epiphany, in which Noon and Apinya realize how intricately the struggles of their generations are intertwined. The movie takes an unexpected turn one night at a dinner party when Apinya is introduced unwittingly to her former tormentor, Colonel Iwabaki, now a respected corporate executive in Tokyo who's returned to Bangkok on business. The next day, though, she bumps into him again while she's out shopping and he confesses that it's not a coincidence that they ran into each other, that he's followed her there, and that, in fact, he came back to Thailand for the express purpose of seeing her — not to frighten or disturb her, no, but to apologize, to beg for her mercy, and to help heal her wounds. Like so many veterans in the wake of Japan's retreat from Thailand, he tells her, he suffered through years of dislocation and misery after returning home, but eventually he was befriended by a Catholic priest who took his confession and urged him to make amends. And, not only has he come back to Bangkok to fulfill this purpose, but he also has hired a private investigator to find the young girl whom Apinya gave up for adoption. "You see," he explains to her. "She's now a young woman, just eighteen years old, who works as a maid for a wealthy family right here in the city. I've even discovered her name, in fact. Her name is Noon." The revelation stuns Apinya, and only later at home, as she gazes at herself in the mirror while Noon is combing her hair, does she realize how eerily similar Noon's face is to her own, and grabbing her daughter by the hand, she bursts into song — her second greatest hit of the decade, "The Dawn Light Is Harsh But Bright."

Qasoori regards the intertwined stories of Anita's two lives in this film as a manifestation of post-occupation Thailand's fears about its future: by drawing so many parallels between the older and younger generations in the present, the movie suggests that the post-independence generation may be doomed to relive the trauma of imperial subjection in some heretofore unrecognized form. Whereas most people cheered the movie's ostensibly happy ending, Qasoori sees the reunion of mother and daughter as "a brittle utopianism aware of its own fragility."[52] In this way, Thai audiences embraced Anita in this film "not because they were drawn like moths to the flame of her talent and beauty, but because they were consciously participating in the invention of a particularly female conception of national identity that tried to repudiate the hold that the past has upon the future precisely because they feared that it was impossible to do so."[53] Or as Anita said later in life, "we were all living through trauma in the Seventies but we weren't aware of it then because we all thought we were finally free. It was only years later that we realized that we never could be free. Praew knew it back then, but it took me another decade to catch up with her."[54]

Decline and Fall (d. Arsenii Belyakov, Russia, 1935)

pr. Moskva Films, sc. Arsenii Belyakov and Maria Volkunna, starring Maria Volkunna and Leonid Tschalgaff, silent, b&w, 35mm, 202 min.

Arsenii Belyakov had worked on propaganda pictures for the Socialist Revolutionary Party throughout the 1920s, directing a series of earnest features about peasant life that pleased both the mainstream press and the bureaucrats at the Ministry of Culture. But he felt increasingly adrift, he said. More and more, he found himself withdrawing from his youthful engagement with political filmmaking, more inspired by the films and writings of the Parisian Modernists, the essays of the professor Sergei Eisenstein, and by the example of his countryman Dziga Vertov, whose iconoclastic style in *Man with a Movie Camera* (1929) had sparked a minor controversy among leftist critics and government officials. So he peppered *Olga* in 1932 — another ennobling film about rural life — with a handful of bravura montage

---

52 Ibid., 61.

53 Ibid., 63.

54 Anita Pawnithiprapta, *Anita Speaks!* (Los Angeles: New World Publishing, 1989), 164.

sequences, which caught the eye of cineastes in Paris, who hailed him overnight as one of the most important young directors shaping a new Eastern Europe aesthetic. Then, out of the blue, he received an invitation from his hero Marcel L'Enfant to visit him in Paris. His stay at the older man's Left Bank apartment, originally scheduled for a week, turned into a month, then half a year — a meeting of minds that would prove to be emblematic of larger international convulsions in the arts over the next decade.

At first, L'Enfant lapped up the younger man's admiration; he told his wife that the young Russian was the only person he'd met who'd read his essays with the attention that they deserved. But tensions grew between the two men. Belyakov confided to the older filmmaker that he was already becoming disenchanted with the "unthinking ubiquity" of the hyperbolic montage sequences and exaggerated superimpositions that had come to define modernist cinema.[55] Though it was his refinement of this very mode of filmmaking that had garnered him esteem and the older man's approval, he thought now that he'd adopted that style not because of its own merits but because it was the only radical example out there. And the new style's increasing popularity, he had come to believe, was a sign that radical filmmakers should be experimenting in other directions. After a few tentative discussions, he finally admitted to his mentor that he was curious about exploring once again the aesthetics of realism that he thought might be the motion pictures' primal mission.

Over the next week, their friction came to a boil. Every morning, Belyakov and L'Enfant strolled through Montparnasse debating how — or whether — one could elicit a sense of the poetic out of the mere mechanical reproduction of reality, and L'Enfant took umbrage at some of the younger man's claims: hadn't the art cinema developed, after all, precisely because it had distanced itself from the simple recording function of the camera? He accused the younger man of being "mercurial." Sensing that their intellectual honeymoon had come to an end,

---

55 Arsenii Belyakov, *Years in the Furnace*, trans. Evgeny Muratov (New York: Liveright 1968), 111.

Belyakov packed his bags suddenly one night and caught a train back to Moscow, leaving a note for the older man that said simply, "The cinema is an ocean; it is vast enough for both of us."[56]

As he wandered the city anxiously on his first days back in Russia, grappling with his artistic crisis, Belyakov bumped into a young woman he'd met briefly before he'd left, a botany student and aspiring actress named Maria Volkunna, and that night they fell into a tempestuous affair that would alter the rest of their careers. When he confided to her that he felt stuck as an artist, she told him, "just start shooting and it will come to you."[57] So over the next few days, Belyakov gathered his new mistress, his cameraman Eduard Fedoseyev, and five actor friends from Nikolai Okhlopkov's theater school and set out for a friend's dacha with no script in hand, saying only, "let the winds explain to us what it is that the camera is supposed to do."[58] The next few weeks were difficult: Belyakov and Fedoseyev spent most days filming brief scenes of the director's new muse sweeping the floors, wandering aimlessly through tall grass, swimming naked in a lake, and standing over the kitchen fire slicing mushrooms into a pan. They insisted on shooting only in the hour after sunrise and the hour before sunset in order to capture the perfect light. But after six weeks, Volkunna recalled years later, they'd accomplished almost nothing cinematically, though at least, she said, she had finally managed to finish *War and Peace*.

It was Volkunna, in fact, and not the wind, who eventually provided Belyakov his creative breakthrough. One morning as he and Fedoseyev filmed her peeling a potato in the kitchen, she lashed out in frustration, yelling that if it was the "poetics of realism" they were after, they'd have to film her peeling not just a portion of one potato, but the entire bucket.[59] "It was with this shot," Belyakov later wrote, describing the seventeen min-

---

56 Kevin Brownlow, "Introduction," in *Paris in the Evening: A Reconstruction,* ed. Kevin Brownlow (New York: Alfred A. Knopf, 1980), 118.

57 Lydia Tupoleva, *Maria Volkunna: Muse as Auteur,* trans. Masha Primakova (New York: Harcourt 1977), 81.

58 Ibid., 91.

59 Ibid., 101.

ute take that would open *Decline and Fall* and go on to become one of the most influential shots in the history of cinema, "that I discovered that contrary to most film theorists' assumptions, the mechanical nature of the motion picture camera gave cinema the power to render the phenomenal world with a sumptuous, poetic flare because it facilitated a more acute mode of perception of both the visual field and the passage of time than we can possibly experience in our daily lives."[60] And it was this shot — and this realization — that set the tone of the hyperaware meditation that was to define the film's first half. In the movie's first two hours, Belyakov portrays life in the village with a sensual affection impossible to articulate in words, capturing the lyrical qualities of the natural world and of its unique tempo: seven-minute shots of a man cutting wheat with a scythe, a four-minute shot of women gathering water at a well, a five-minute shot of a man butchering a goat, and also minutes-long observations of landscapes, of sun-dappled hills, empty roads, and clouds drifting almost imperceptibly across the sky.

The film's other defining characteristic — its formal contrasts between the idylls of country life and the political unrest of the city — came about partly by chance, or as Andre Bazin argued, came to fruition precisely because the improvisatory filming methods they'd developed tended to expand expressive possibilities.[61] Belyakov and his collaborators had intended that in the second half of the film, the peasant girl would follow her Socialist boyfriend back to the city and come to realize that the regimented nature of urban life was not for her. But the very day that the crew returned to Moscow — in one of those bizarre coincidences that so often become the backbone of history — just happened to be the day that Nikolai Bukharin instigated the coup that overthrew Konstantin Chernov's Socialist government. Armed forces had taken control of the train stations and

---

60 Belyakov, *Years in the Furnace,* 171.
61 Andre Bazin, "Countervailing Trends in the Realist Mode: Belyakov, Dovzhenko, and Room," in *What Is Cinema? Vol. II,* trans. Hugh Gray (Berkeley: University of California Press, 1971), 102.

patrolled the streets everywhere they went. When they discovered on the following morning that the army had blocked the entrance gates even at Moskva Films, they thought they might never be able to finish their picture.

But after a quick conference, the group decided to keep on filming any way they could, so they threw out most of the script that Belyakov had worked up over the last few months and decided instead to improvise a new ending that would incorporate the political turmoil that was sweeping through the city. They began shooting on the streets that afternoon, with tanks and soldiers marching behind them. Thus, the story of a young peasant woman who comes to the capital to continue the summer affair she'd started with a Socialist politician took on an ugly new shading after the Party's leaders had been arrested. The two lovers were now on the run from the law, hiding out in friends' attics and moving through the city surreptitiously through the sewers. Because of their hectic new shooting method, the second half of the movie takes on a much different style than the first. Whereas the average shot length out in the country was more than a minute long, the shots in the city last just four or five seconds. And yet, as Bazin was the first to point out, the second half displays just as many signatures of a realist aesthetic as the first, creating "two competing — or complementary — modes of realism: the rural world's distance from political and intellectual life as a temporal weight, as a thickness of time, compared with the urban world's political and intellectual disruptions as the cause of a mental cacophony, a perceptual upheaval."[62] Belyakov and his team staged the final sequence — in which the two lovers wake up the morning after their wedding and the husband is gunned down by government troops in the street, all without using a single intertitle — on the last day before Bukharin finally declared himself president. On hearing the news, Belyakov, Fedoseyev and Volkunna gathered all their footage and took the train that very night, arriving in Paris a week later, where they immediately began editing the film.

---

62 Ibid., 108.

When they premiered the movie there three months later, Moscow was still in chaos and the European left was riven by turmoil over the Socialists' fate. *Decline and Fall* spoke to the times more than any movie of the day and it became a sensation across the continent — except, of course, in Germany and its Eastern satellites, where governments condemned it as leftist propaganda. In Parisian circles, many leftist critics initially attacked the film. Its fascination with the so-called realism of time, they maintained, was an example of aesthetic conservatism, a cowardly retreat from the intellectual advances of modernist aesthetic theory. But Marcel L'Enfant — whose personal break with Belyakov had by then become well-known — surprised his colleagues by coming to the film's defense. "*Decline and Fall,* more than any other film," he wrote in *Cinema Art,*

> proves that aesthetic theorization, though important, must always play a secondary role to artistic practice. Belyakov understands that to be an artist, one must observe the physical realm with the same attention to detail as the greatest painters of still lives. Only then can one withdraw from the subject and devise one's theories. Yes, *Decline and Fall* is the most realist film I have seen, but what people have failed to see is that Belyakov's realism is not the same as that of Emile Zola or of Jean Renoir or of material existence itself because his realism, like that of all true artists, comes out of his own intense devotion to humanist ethics, and it is this primary fact, an artistic practice imbued with a spiritual commitment, that enables him see the phenomenal world anew, that ultimately creates his philosophical vision.[63]

---

63 Marcel L'Enfant, "Belyakov's Vision," in *Collected Writings,* trans. Benedict Leonard and Rochelle Fleury (Cambridge: Harvard University Press, 1987), 244.

Disco Giraffe (d. Khadija Chishuli, Tanzania/USA, 1989)
pr. The Ford Foundation, sc. Khadija Chishuli, starring Khadija
Chishuli, sound, color, 16mm, 78 min.

Khadija Chishuli's disco-infused essay film investigating Tanzanian president Julius Nyerere's socialist philosophy of "Ujamaa" has become a touchstone in academic discussions of political cinema due to its nuanced progressive assessment of leftist utopianism, its complex method of intellectual argument that Kristin Thompson has dubbed "harmonic structuralist montage,"[64] and its extravagant dance numbers famous for their symmetrical designs populated by a multicultural panoply of Speedo-clad pool boys.

Chishuli was born in Tanzania, where her parents were well-connected intellectuals who'd been active supporters of Nyerere during his early years in office. But they broke with the president in the early 1970s after he signed legislation making the government's policy of collective agriculture compulsory rather than voluntary. And after their friends who worked in the administration slowly stopped inviting them out or returning their calls, they decided to leave the country, eventually settling in the Bronx, where they worked as a cab driver and cafe waitress while publishing a newsletter about politics in the Swahili-speaking region. Like many immigrant children, Chishuli felt torn between two worlds, proud of her roots and her parents' activism, but desperate to fit in with the world around her, which in that part of New York in the early 1980s was defined by the burgeoning hip-hop scene.

As a teenager, she felt that she was becoming divided into even more seemingly irreconcilable identities: during the day she was a studious achiever at a prestigious magnet school, but at night — while she told her parents she was babysitting — she worked as a flunky at downtown recording studios where she befriended and eventually sang backup for both Afrika Bambaataa

---

64 Kristin Thompson, *Webs of Dislocation: Neo-Formalist Film Analysis Revisited* (Princeton: Princeton University Press, 1993), 106.

and Grandmaster Flash. Later, as a comp lit major at Brown, she circled back to her roots, becoming interested for the first time in her family's background, inundating her parents with questions and taking her first trip with them back to the land of her birth. Then, finally inspired to immerse herself in her origins, she wrote her senior thesis as a Gérard Genette-inspired narratological analysis of Sukuma and Nyamwezi folktales. After graduation, she floundered for a few years, dropping out of one master's program in comp lit and another in creative nonfiction before she won a grant from the Ford Foundation to make an actuality on the history of Safari tourism — "you know," she told one interviewer, "the kind of shit Republicans from Maine like to watch"[65] — but from the beginning she intended to use that money instead to secretly produce the kind of movie, she said, "that Hugo Ball and Richard Huelsenbeck might have made if they'd accidentally ingested just the slightest bit of LSD."[66]

The plot — such as it is — centers around the protagonist, Her Royal Ladyship, Empress Khadija 3000, played by Chishuli herself, a cyborg from the 9th dimension who comes to planet Earth to study human conceptions of the ideal form of government. The opening sequence sets the tone for the entire film as Chishuli strides through the South Bronx on streets lined with seven-story brick apartment blocks, wearing lavender platform boots, a headdress of fluorescent tulips, and a full-length cape made of reflective aluminum foil and imitation rubies. Then, as children emerge here and there from apartment windows and from under stoops, flocking to her like delirious penitents at the sight of a minor deity, a synthesizer wails, a disco beat kicks in, and she belts out the chorus of the movie's theme song, "Robot Empress Bitch (Where the Humans At?)."

Her Royal Ladyship explores the political landscape of the South Bronx, conducting interviews on the street like a televi-

---

65 Quoted in Molly Yan, *Fanning the Flames: Interviews with Independent Women Directors* (Detroit: Wayne State University Press, 1998), 312.

66 Berenice Reynaud, "Interview with Khadija Chishuli," *Cinéaste* 19, no. 1 (Spring 1993): 34.

sion journalist with anyone willing to speak to a woman who's wearing a pink wig and foot-long fake nails. But the stories she hears — snide racial jokes at the office, electrical fires in old tenement buildings, and also a child's nightmare of a talking bear with the head of a falcon — gives her the impression that maybe she has not yet found the Earthling utopia. Then, after one woman at a playground mentions in passing the socialist vision espoused by Tanzanian president Julius Nyerere, she hops on a plane and lands the next day in Dar es Salaam. In the second section of the film, she travels by bus through a series of rural villages — now bedecked in a yellow cape with purple, elbow-length vinyl gloves — and interviews residents about the program that the government calls "African Socialism" but which some leftist detractors in the country and abroad have derided as an undemocratic land-grab in the guise of a progressive mission.

But the people she meets paint a much more complicated picture — one old woman points to the concrete home she built with the help of government subsidies for her collective, while the same woman's cousin from a neighboring village complains about the bribes she still has to pay to move her cassava harvest to market. Nevertheless, while Chishuli strives to be even-handed, the very act of presenting so many imperfections belies the utopian vision that the government has been offering up to its citizens. But despite her implicit criticisms of Nyerere's idealistic naïveté, Chishuli further complicates her analysis by criticizing her own position as well, self-consciously juxtaposing the image of a family of farmers sitting in thatched huts on dirt floors with the image of her own galactic exoticism — now wearing Egyptian sandals, glitter make-up, and a purple motorcycle helmet — emphasizing her alienness as a way to acknowledge her inadequacy at explaining what she as an outsider will never be able to fully comprehend.

Some writers attack Chishuli's penchant for vulgar humor as antithetical to her political aims. In one scene on an airplane, for instance, she wears what can only be described as a demented child's vision of a British Admiral's uniform as she aggressively rubs her breasts up against a pair of awkward businessmen in first class as she sings "I Gotsta Humpty," while in another scene, she clambers through a New York subway car dressed in a pink parrot outfit accompanied by half a dozen shirtless homeless men serving as her backup dancers as she sings "I'm Coo-Coo-Coo for Communitarianism." But Meredith Schwallenberg-Kakionides argues that she "deploys her transgressive sexuality as a tool for constructive bedazzlement, inspiring the people she meets on the streets to open themselves up and express what would normally have been taboo, while at the same time destabilizing the ideological assumptions of the educated liberals who make up the bulk of her audience."[67]

The film's reputation grew slowly, but simultaneously, in two contrasting settings, first on the underground film circuit when Takoya Michiko, lead singer of Space Faerie and the Bandits, programmed the movie continuously at her underground club, The Beaver Hatch, the central hub of Berlin's gay nightlife in the early 1990s. At the same time, the film gained traction in academic circles after Fredric Jameson devoted a few pages to it in his chapter on Kidlat Tahimik in *The Geopolitical Aesthetic*.[68] But it won its prominence among intellectuals after Chishuli published an essay in response — "The Prose of Death: Why Insane Zebras Should Feast on Fredric Jameson's Brain" — which has now become even more influential in discussions about globalized aesthetics than has the work of her professorial antagonist. Today, Chishuli's movie remains central for writers like Fatimah Tobing Rony in discussions of postcolonial cinema, Richard Dyer on queer aesthetics, and Lacy DuGarde on postfeminisms, but arguably the film should be embraced mostly for what Chishuli herself said was "its intentional emphasis on au-

---

67 Meredith Schwallenberg-Kakionides, "The Zebra's Décolletage: Negotiations of Difference in Khadija Chishuli's *Disco Giraffe*," in *Feminist Film Theory: A Reader*, ed. Sue Thornham (New York: New York University Press, 1998), 221.

68 Fredric Jameson, *The Geopolitical Aesthetic: Cinema and Space in the World System* (Bloomington: Indiana University Press, 1992), 195–203.

dacious idiocy as the only antidote to the inescapable failure of radical utopianism."[69]

Distant Star (d. Obonye Mosweu, Botswana, 1933)
sc. Obonye Mosweu and David White, starring Akanyang Marumo, silent, b&w, 8mm, 48 min.

Years later, Obonye Mosweu recalled that the idea for making *Distant Star* first germinated in 1931 when he was working as an adviser to the Tswana chief and he met the young English couple David and Florence White, who'd just arrived in Botswana as Christian missionaries. Mosweu and David White, it turned out, shared a passionate interest in machinery, and soon were spending most afternoons together taking apart radios, fixing bicycles, and constructing a rudimentary irrigation system for a nearby village. Then, one day, White received a new toy he'd ordered in the mail from London — an 8mm camera that Kodak had just introduced on the market — and he and his new friend turned all their attention to this amazing invention. Within weeks, they were hooked, designing their own editing suite and setting up their own film-processing lab in the back room of a beer distributor's warehouse in the closest town, Serowe.

Neither man had been particularly interested in the art of the cinema at first. In an interview with the South African critic Hendrik Stassen later in life, Mosweu remembered that when he started experimenting with the camera he'd seen only a few films, but he could recall only Stan Laurel's *In the Kitchen* and a movie whose plot he described as "a European princess gets enslaved by a rich man and later escapes."[70] So when Mosweu decided on a whim to make a movie of his own, he didn't feel any pressure to copy what he'd seen. Nevertheless, he bristled

---

69 Khadija Chishuli, "The Prose of Death: Why Insane Zebras Should Feast on Fredric Jameson's Brain," *Framework* 41, no. 1 (1995): 23.

70 Hendrik Stassen, "Interview with Obonye Mosweu," *The Sunday Times* (Johannesburg, South Africa), January 13, 1962, B8.

when he later heard that some supporters had referred to him as a "naïve artist": "I was in no way naïve," he said. "I knew exactly what I was doing. Even if I had never seen a single movie, I would have understood immediately every rule that every other filmmaker around the world was instinctively following, so I knew immediately every rule that I wanted to break."[71]

In order to develop his own iconoclastic storytelling style, Mosweu decided to revive some old Tswana traditions, since the indigenous ethos, he said, was so much more open-minded than the culture the British had been foisting upon them over the preceding decades. He drew inspiration especially from childhood memories of an old storyteller whom the local villagers both revered and reviled as a cantankerous old coot who was partly insane but also partly enlightened. He was a wandering mystic who made his home in a cave and often spent his days conversing with the animals and the trees, eating only insects, honey, and milk he got from a goat he kept with him at all times and which, legend had it, he sometimes dressed up in a three-piece suit he'd made from the fur of other animals. As a boy, Mosweu used to go on long expeditions into the hills in search of the man so he could sit at his feet and soak up his stories.

In his favorite, the old seer spun the tale of a spiritual being from another star who travelled to Earth and inhabited the body of a bat. But because he could not communicate with the other bats, he escaped the caves and flew on the winds to a village where he chanced upon the youngest son of the chief, who was the only person in this world who could understand his alien sounds because he alone was pure of heart. He told the boy that he came from a place far away in the sky, where the beings did not live within bodies but floated through the atmosphere as sparks of energy that collided now and then in a futile quest to create a single planetary consciousness. The boy nodded sagely and said he understood, then he led the bat out to the desert, where he conducted a ritual using the carcass of a vulture to transport his new friend back home on the far side of the stars.

---

71 Ibid., B9.

In order to fully inhabit the mystical pitch of the old man's vision, Mosweu lived alone for a month in a cavern lit only by torches he'd fashioned from fallen branches, dried grass, and the dung of a goat he'd taken as a pet. The extreme deprivation of his time in the wild seems to have stimulated the excesses of his cinematic style. The first third of the film is a disorienting collage of images. Surrounded by moist stalactites, he filmed bats only in oblique close-ups with flickering illumination, capturing here a wing, there the fluttering of a group in flight. Later, he edited this footage at a pace so frenetic he created visual collisions that would have made even Abel Gance gasp, an aesthetic mode meant to evoke the mystifying sensation of being born into an alien lifeform and looking out onto an incomprehensible land. Unwittingly, his technique also evokes the theories of radical montage espoused at the same time by French modernists like Francis Picabia and Abel Gance, but Mosweu nevertheless surpasses them in the unrelenting application of his ideas.

The meeting between the bat and the human boy that finally takes place after a blistering twenty minutes of almost pure abstraction becomes all the more powerful because Mosweu transforms the film's style so suddenly and so dramatically. Up until the moment of their first encounter, his shots range from one to four seconds, but in that instant of recognition, he holds a close-up of the boy's face for a disturbingly long three and a half minutes, a shot that has become infamous for its trance-like effects. The film continues this rigorous examination of the weight of real time as the boy leads his new friend and mentor through the barren desert landscape until the psychic breakthrough over the vulture's carcass that leads to the film's denouement. Mosweu constructs the final third of the movie around visual metaphors for the bat's experience of travelling through galactic portals back home — anticipating Kubrick's *Journey to the Stars* (1968) by several decades — by making photograms out of grass, leaves, pebbles, and sand, and — decades before Stan Brakhage — scratching swirling designs into the film strip itself.

By all accounts, the first audience of roughly a dozen people was baffled by the film at its premiere. Undaunted, Mosweu and White screened the film at perhaps a dozen village gatherings across the country over the next two years — and even once in Cape Town — but there's no written record of any responses from the 1930s. The film would have been lost forever except for a series of odd coincidences. After David White died in 1943, his wife Florence returned to London, where she was introduced to Graham Greene at a screening of Shirley Temple's *Rebecca of Sunnybrook Farm* (1938) sponsored by the Catholic Church. When she was told that he was a film critic, she mentioned in passing the movie that her husband had collaborated on years earlier in Botswana. Greene in turn wrote about this "fascinating story of a film" to his friend Henry Martin, the English novelist then stationed in Cape Town, who was just about to set off on a trip to the Botswanan capital, Gaborone.[72] Within a week, Martin had managed to track down Mosweu, then overseeing a goat farm out in the bush, who eagerly screened the deteriorating 8mm print for him. Martin, who'd written film reviews for *The London Times* back when Greene was the film critic for *The Spectator* and who'd praised the work of Cesar Vallejo and F.W. Murnau, was stunned by what he saw and convinced Mosweu to let him take the print back to Cape Town to make a 16mm copy. Six months later, he introduced the movie at the London Film Society and rapturous reviews immediately appeared in the press. Nevertheless, it still took decades for the film to enter the canon. It was only after 1959, when the Russian theorist Ludmilla Tchernokova devoted a chapter to *Distant Star* in her book *On the Unreality of Mechanical Dreamworlds* that other scholars began to write about the film as seriously as they had written about the work of L'Enfant, Jennings, or Vertov.[73]

Mosweu himself never made another movie. Instead, he operated a hotel and hunting lodge, ran a bicycle shop, and was for a few years the chief of radio news in Botswana before he

---

72 Graham Greene, *Graham Greene: A Life in Letters,* ed. Richard Greene (New York: W.W. Norton & Co, 2008), 196.

73 Ludmilla Tchernokova, *On the Unreality of Mechanical Dreamworlds,* trans. Olga Chepanskova (Cambridge: Harvard University Press, 1962).

ran afoul of the authorities and retired to the countryside as the owner of the sprawling goat farm where Martin had found him. There are only three known accounts of his thoughts on his brief filmmaking career: two pages in Florence White's memoir, Henry Martin's brief recollection of their meeting in 1943, and the long interview that Hendrick Stassen conducted with him in 1962, one year before his death. Mosweu was pleased to hear that his film was finally receiving attention, but he remained nonplussed: "Of course it is a good movie," he told Stassen. "Because it did not come from this world, but from the stars."[74]

The Elevator (d. Rimachi Alvarado, Peru, 1993)
sc. Rimachi Alvarado, starring Rimachi Alvarado, sound, color, 16mm, 59 min.

Ever since the first screening of *The Elevator*, his only film, writers have tended to associate Rimachi Alvarado with figures like Adolf Wölfli, outsider artists whose genius sprung from their mental illness rather than from their conscious intentions. Stories of his multiple incarcerations, voluminous impassioned writings, and violent attacks on prominent intellectual figures like Jacques Lacan circulated in the cinephile community, giving him the aura of an unhinged visionary not responsible for his own pronouncements. But this conception of Alvarado has done a disservice to the director and to his film; the movie's rambling structure, conspicuous shifts in tone and subject matter, and loopy sense of humor are all part of a coherent plan to challenge the modern audience's assumptions about how the logical development of thought is supposed to appear. Alvarado experimented with a mode of collage that emphasizes associational leaps, spatiotemporal disjunctions, and comic irony, making the movie a much more innovative essay film than most of its more famous predecessors in the genre.

---

74 Stassen, "Interview with Obonye Mosweu," B8.

Alvarado grew up in an educated, bourgeois family in Lima; his father was the head of anesthesiology at a local university hospital and his mother was a professor of linguistics. But his maternal grandmother, who lived with them and raised him while his parents were off at work, spoke to him mostly in Quechua and filled his head with stories of the ancient past. Thus, from his early childhood, shuttling between Incan mythology in the kitchen and French lessons at the capital's most prestigious academy, Alvarado always felt, he said, that he belonged to multiple worlds and incompatible millennia. He moved to Paris in 1962 to study at the Sorbonne, but he felt hemmed in by its traditional pedagogy and usually skipped class to study topics on his own, teaching himself to paint by copying each of the Titians in the Louvre or spending weeks learning to identify trees in the Bois de Boulogne. In later years, he said that his favorite classroom had been the Cinémathèque Française, where he saw a movie almost every day over the course of the decade, and where he became especially entranced by the modernists of the late silent period like Abel Gance and Marcel L'Enfant, who had demonstrated that film was more multifariously expressive than any other medium.

Like many of his generation, the 1965 revolutions opened his eyes to the politics of liberation, and he entered a PhD program in anthropology intending to work on a dissertation that would, he wrote, "reveal the illusory nature of the modern Peruvian subject through the lens of a traditional Andean belief system."[75] But his years in academia sparked the beginnings of both his mental breakdowns and his aesthetic breakthroughs. He abandoned his thesis at some point in the early 1970s after getting into a physical altercation with his advisor on the street. "The old man was one of those Lévi-Strauss acolytes," Alvarado explained, "and he was threatened by the first chapter I gave him because it attacked structuralist anthropology. They were all

---

75 Muriel Castillo-Bevecque, *Screaming over the Precipice: Rimachi Alvarado, In and Out of the Visible World,* trans. Lolita Brunelle (Chicago: Anti-Matter Press, 2002), 75.

wedded to these binary models of culture. But they didn't know what to do with a civilization like the Inca that was cosmologically so multidimensional."[76]

Feeling untethered without the structure of school, Alvarado drifted for a few years and felt the first pangs of emotional dislocation; he sought relief in the writings of Freud, and then Jung, which eventually inspired him to become a patient of Lacan, whose minor fame was then reaching its peak. But his trouble with authority figures surfaced yet again. After a few successful months of therapy, the situation turned for the worse, and then news came that he'd attacked his analyst one night as the older man was out walking along the Seine. Lacan apparently refused to press charges, explaining to the police that despite the presence of a blood-stained knife, theirs had been merely an intellectual discussion, not a violent episode. He didn't want this "brilliant but headstrong man to get into trouble with the law," according to the incident report, simply because "he was exploring necessary but difficult psychic avenues. The process of struggling with radical philosophy, after all, often leads to psychic ruptures that may initially be socially unacceptable to certain segments of the culture's ideological carapace."[77]

Disillusioned by the lack of revolutionary spirit in France, Alvarado returned to Peru and settled in a small Quechua-speaking village in the Andes a few hours outside of Cuzco. The few available accounts over the next several years suggest the life of an artist who was, despite his occasional outbursts, consciously pushing himself into ever-more adventurous aesthetic territory. His biographer Muriel Castillo-Bevecque travelled throughout the region for almost a year trying to track down anyone who'd had contact with him, but even his fellow villagers had little to say. A few old local priests claimed to have known him well: they said that he was always reading — usually environmental polemics or the prison notebooks of Antonio Gramsci — and that like St. Francis, he preferred the company of the

---

76 Ibid., 82.
77 Quoted in ibid., 95.

less intelligent animals. The next substantive records of his life place him back in Lima in 1980 where he distributed flyers for an organization called the Anarcho-Mutualist Front for Global Interdependence, though Castillo-Bevecque maintains that he and his then wife Hildegarde Bremen may have been the only two members. In 1981, he was sentenced to a year in prison for smuggling cigarettes, then disappeared for several more years after his release. In 1988, he emerged again in Lima as the leader of an avant-garde theater troupe that staged improvisational didactic plays and organized discussion groups with members of the local truck drivers' union that tackled the writings of Charles Fourier and Peter Kropotkin.

The production history of *The Elevator* as well points to a mind that was rationally engaged with the leading trends of modernist filmmaking of the time. Alvarado made the movie in Peru in the last year before he died. It's not clear how he raised the money or where he got the equipment, but by the early 1990s he'd seen the travelogue films of Kidlat Tahimik and Chris Marker and he'd become excited about the possibilities of cinema, he said, for the first time in twenty years. Following in the footsteps of these two predecessors of the essay film, *The Elevator* is a movie about the clash of cultures. At first glance, Alvarado's film seems much more anarchic than the work of his two paragons, but he carefully designed both the visuals and narrative in patchwork structures that have more in common with the works of Hannah Höch or Robert Rauschenberg than with the work of the typical essayist, literary or cinematic. But he created these models of associative thinking precisely because he thought they were more in tune with the non-linear processes of Andean cosmology. Developing his organizational framework from his antagonism toward structuralist anthropology, he doesn't just examine the Manichaean tensions between the Quechua and Spanish, the developing world and the West, or the traditional and the modern, but tries to evoke, instead, what he called "multivalent modes of consciousness": "there is no sense, after all," he said, "in speaking of a conflict between the traditional and the modern, as European thinkers would have us believe, because the traditional has always been just as avant-garde as the contemporary world, while contemporary industrial society is just as conservative as hunter-gatherer cultures."[78]

In making these arguments, Alvarado takes as his departure point his own fear of elevators as a particularly poetic manifestation of modernity's inherently anxious state. The film's first twenty minutes are a transcendent, hypnotic series of swirling, superimposed shots seen from the viewpoint of a glass elevator in Lima's largest shopping mall, rising up to the sky and down again to the shoppers below in a kaleidoscopic orgy of movement and color, over which Alvarado explains that his fear of elevators was born of the knowledge that he did not belong to this world but that, as his grandmother used to tell him, he had the soul of a pre-Colombian breathing in the mind of a conquistador. The movie then delves into more ruminative terrain, with Alvarado taking on the voices of various real and imaginary characters — his grandmother, his high school swimming coach, and the Inca god Pacha Kamaq, each of whom spout poetic aphorisms, which eventually blend in and bleed into one another to create an unintelligible sonic superimposition.

Alvarado treats the Spanish discovery of the Inca in the 1520s as the paradigmatic encounter of the modern world, what he calls "the viral infection that gave birth to the surrealist order," and it is this grand-historical juxtaposition of civilizations that leads him to glide, dreamlike, through a series of unexpected analogies.[79] And this form of "associational drift," he wrote to his mother, in one of his few remaining letters, felt much more true to the nature of both Andean and modernist modes of thinking.[80] He brings the film to its climax with a series of increasingly unrelated sequences in which his words bear only a tenuous relation to the visuals. He ruminates on his great grandmother's childhood as it's pictured in family photo albums, his own philosophical isolation in his years as a graduate student

---

78 Ibid., 207.
79 Ibid., 229.
80 Ibid., 236.

in Paris, the beauty of the Seine, his love of the flowers of the horse chestnut tree, his passionate hatred of Claude Lévi-Strauss and Jacques Lacan, his equally passionate love of Raymond Chandler's sentences, and his ideological disagreements with anarcho-syndicalists. These non-rational associations lead him ultimately to the film's disquieting denouement in which he offers up parthenogenesis and hermaphroditic reproduction as positive counterexamples to the innate spiritual sterility of the human sexual act. Thus, in the final scene, he emerges in Lima's largest shopping mall, dressed as a tree with the head of a condor but with pendulous, fuzzy, and disturbingly moist catkins hanging from his limbs, then rides up and down a glass elevator, chanting to his fellow befuddled passengers about his desire to pollinate the world through the power of the wind.

The Elevator had its premiere in Paris in 1993 just a month after Alvarado died of still unknown causes. It was received with quiet confusion in most quarters but was adored by a few critics on the fringe. The critical establishment to this day treats it more as a curio than a legitimate work of art, but any careful analysis will see that it's just as coherently organized — on its own idiosyncratic terms — as the much more famous films of Marker and Tahimik, and perhaps, in the final analysis, more intellectual and more playful than either of these.

Father's Diary (d. Park Gon-woo, Korea, 1966)
pr. New Seoul Films, sc. Park Gon-woo, Lee Song-gi, and Hyon Il-Song, starring Ok Jin-hyuk and Ryo Chun-ja, sound, color, 35mm, 100 min.

Released just five years after the Korean liberation, *Father's Diary* is generally recognized as one of the two cornerstones of the Korean Renaissance, the modernist twin to Im Chang-yul's more traditional *In the Shadows* (1965). Park Gon-woo knew that he wanted to make a film about the politics of the occupation, but even in the mid-1960s, the nation still hadn't found a way to talk openly about the past.

Like every other director of the independence generation, he'd worked his way up the Korean film industry during the years when the Showa's puppet government appointed the president of National Pictures, the only film company that it allowed to operate in Korea. He began as an errand boy, then worked as assistant director, and finally secured a position as screenwriter to Goy Gan-hee. But considering that Goy had been National's most successful director throughout the 1950s — perhaps because he was the most compliant, as some suggested — Park felt that he needed to move in another direction. Unlike Im — with whom he's most often compared — he was inspired by the new generation of modernist European directors like Michelangelo Antonioni and Viktor Hristalov, who'd extended, in his words, "the symbolic capabilities of the language of film." Their example, he said, offered him a model to "articulate that which was inarticulable."[81] So on the surface, *Father's Diary* tells the story of a young boy who slowly comes to understand that some members of his family had helped cover up a crime a generation earlier during the Japanese colonization. But the movie functions on a deeper level, as a philosophical meditation on the relationship between politics, public history, and private memory.

Since he was making a movie about the impossibility of knowing the facts of the past, Park knew he needed to develop methods to portray the plot's most significant events through filmic means other than the visible. In this case, he saw that any nation liberating itself from foreign rule would feel the need to construct a coherent identity for itself, most often in the form of historical narratives and myths of origins. But because one of the primary goals of colonization is to pacify its subjects by erasing their past, newly independent countries often find themselves trying to construct an identity whose foundation, ironically, is a historical absence. So one of Park's primary goals was to devise visual analogues to make this theoretical claim, deploying the non-verbal techniques of narrative ellipses, stag-

---

81 "Interview with a Korean Auteur," in *Park Gon-woo Interviews*, ed. Sanderson Kim (Jackson: University Press of Mississippi, 2011), 181.

ing in-depth and off-screen space, for instance, to point out that the politics of nation-building are predicated on an illusion. The plot is orchestrated around the discovery of the hidden past. But because the past, in Park's view, is ultimately unknowable, his characters are motivated by what Melinda Watanabe calls "an epistemic void."[82]

Park uses the opening sequences to introduce his overriding interest in the conflict between knowledge and power, and also to demonstrate to his viewers the particular cinematic language he will deploy to comment on this connection because the characters themselves cannot speak openly about it. The movie opens on a close-up of the young protagonist's hand tentatively pulling a book from beneath a pile of papers at the bottom of a trunk, then pulls back as the boy surreptitiously hides the book beneath his shirt, and then tracks backward to reveal that he's in a basement and follows him up a flight of stairs as he sneaks out onto the street, through the bustling crowds past vendor stalls and into a back alley amid a cacophony of caged chickens, where he bends down behind a garbage heap and the camera tracks in on his face — almost seven minutes after the shot began — as he begins to read.

Park then cuts to the family sitting around the dinner table later that night for an elaborate meal in honor of the boy's uncle who's visiting from Pyongyang. He places the camera in the kitchen in the foreground looking out at the dining room table in the background, obscured by the walls of the kitchen so that the family in the background — the agents of the past — can see events taking place in off-screen space to their left and right that we in the audience cannot see, while we — the embodiment of the present — can see action going on in the kitchen that they cannot see, thus suggesting through his spatial architectonics — using a motif that he will repeat throughout the film — how epistemological hierarchies determine characters'

---

82 Melinda Watanabe, "Epistemology, Depth Planes, and Off-Screen Space: Nationalism and the Politics of Style in Park Gon-woo's *Father's Diary*," *Critical Inquiry* 28, no. 3 (Spring 2002): 651.

behavior and our own ability to understand those actions today. This silent dinner table is fraught with tension. In an elegant series of wordless close-ups, the boy looks at his father, his father looks at the uncle, and the uncle looks back at the boy, and we understand that the family has buried some secret shame that has nevertheless determined its dynamics ever since; at the same time, we glean that the father and uncle are now beginning to suspect that the boy has started to question the family history himself.

Then, in a flashback, in the 1930s, we learn that the boy's father was working as a police captain in a small coastal town when local fishermen found the body of a young woman washed ashore one morning. After the coroner reported that she'd been raped and strangled, the Japanese general in charge of the district assigned the father to the case because, the father learned later, the general thought he could be easily manipulated into conducting a lackluster inspection.

Eventually, the boy begins to suspect that his father and uncle were complicit in the cover-up of the woman's murder as a way to advance their own careers. Even more disturbingly, he learns that his father met and fell in love with his mother while he was investigating the murder because, shockingly, she was the young victim's own sister. But this possible cover-up of the crime is not merely an ethical issue. Park emphasizes repeatedly how these personal conflicts are always imbued with larger political concerns. He demonstrates, relentlessly, how even in the most private occasions, his Korean characters can make decisions only according to the limited range of possibilities that their Japanese occupiers have prescribed for them. In almost every scene, his protagonists seem trapped by the image itself: they throw nervous glances to their left and to their right, where a Japanese authority figure, we are led to believe, is almost always standing just outside the edge of the frame. This formal motif reminds us that the characters' seemingly unimportant personal lives always have macroscopic reverberations. The whitewash of the murder, then, is not just an affair between a couple friends, but an analogy for Koreans' larger crime of papering over the political and psychological implications of Japanese imperialism.

In the final sequence, back in the present, Park repeats the formal strategies of the dinner scene that began the film. But now, as the boy looks at his father, who looks at his mother, who looks back at him, it's clear that he can't figure out whether his mother still doesn't know that her husband helped cover up the murder of her sister or whether she has recognized that fact for decades. Either way, Park reveals again how the private memories of one generation will forever remain a secret to historians. As the sun sets and the family continues to eat in silence in the darkening dining room, Park is suggesting — once again, without any of his characters ever actually articulating this position — that if a family or a nation can only create a better world by coming to terms with the trauma of the past, the hopes for the new, post-independence generation of Korea is necessarily quite grim.

Faust (d. F. W. Murnau, Germany, 1926)
pr. Ufa, sc. Gerhart Hauptmann and Hans Kyser, starring Gösta Ekman, Camilla Horn, and Emil Jannings, silent, b&w, 35mm, 85min.

Writing about silent cinema — more than about the talkies — tends to gravitate toward the theory of aesthetics. The absence of the human voice created an alluring, yet perhaps alarming, detachment from reality that nurtured artists' desires to express themselves in unfamiliar ways. The presiding aesthetic philosophy of the silent period has centered around the writings and films of Marcel L'Enfant, who valorized the techniques of montage and superimposition. A filmmaker's ultimate goal, he said, was to manipulate spatiotemporal reality in order to instill in the spectator an intended set of emotions and beliefs. But by valuing L'Enfant's ideas so highly, theorists have avoided grappling with the meaning-making potential of the image on its own, a philosophical blind spot that has infected critics and historians as well.

There were theorists in the silent era, though — especially in Germany — who did write about mise-en-scene more than they did about montage. But because cultural power across the globe was located in democratic France rather than in authoritarian Germany, latter-day writers have tended to ignore these theorists of the cinematic image. In Central Europe, though, the most influential film writer in the mid-century was the German perceptual psychologist and philosopher of aesthetics Rudolf Arnheim, whose 1931 book *Film as Art* crystallized the thinking of many film writers in the German sphere. Given that German filmmakers were breathing the same air as Arnheim, a re-engagement with his work may help reinvigorate both our understanding of film theory and of film history, especially of those silent directors who focused particularly on visual design — the epitome in this case being the German director Friedrich Wilhelm Murnau, whose film *Faust* represents one of the most arresting, elaborate, and intellectual manipulations of the cinematic image.

In the classical period, film theorists saw their primary goal as defending the motion picture from its detractors who claimed that film was not an art form because it was merely the mechanical reproduction of reality, and to do so, they set out to define the medium's essential characteristics. In articulating an ontology of film, though, theorists tended to adopt two competing ontological approaches, which led, in turn, to two somewhat contradictory aesthetic programs. The dominant mode, centered in Paris and echoing the ideas of Marcel L'Enfant, defended the new medium by emphasizing film's difference from the other arts. In doing so, directors in this camp tended to stress the importance of techniques like editing that enabled artists to manipulate time in ways they claimed other media had theretofore been unable to achieve. The secondary mode, centered in Berlin and echoing the ideas of Rudolf Arnheim, defended the new medium by emphasizing film's difference from the phenomenal world. In doing so, they stressed techniques like the design of mise-en-scene, which distinguished the spatial aspects of the image from the perceptual qualities of real life. Though this distinction is a bit of a simplification — Arnheim, after all, did write about editing and superimposition and L'Enfant did discuss the design of the image — the division was clear to both theorists and filmmakers at the time and has filtered down in film histories and the critical literature ever since. And F.W. Murnau's work is important to understand not because he was influenced by Arnheim but the other way around. As the most innovative German director of the silent era, Murnau's thinking about the image was a central foundation of Arnheim's philosophy; thus, *Faust* expresses — perhaps better than any other movie — the underappreciated film theory of the German intellectual sphere.

To appreciate *Faust,* then, one must come to understand the aesthetic theory it inspired. "It is worthwhile to refute thoroughly and systematically," Arnheim wrote, "the charge that photography and film are only mechanical reproductions and that they therefore have no connection with art — for this is an excellent method of getting to understand the nature of film art." In that sense, he made a distinction between the film image and the "image" of reality that constitute everyday perceptions: "It will be seen how fundamentally different the two kinds of image are; and it is just these differences that provide film with its artistic resources. We shall thus come at the same time to understand the working principles of film art."[83] He went on to delineate the differences between the film image and the perception of reality that he thought were artistically significant: two-dimensionality, the absence of color, framing, camera distance, the lack of any senses other than sight. These differences created aesthetic restrictions, but in the final analysis, these restrictions — as with poetic forms like the sonnet or sestina — didn't limit aesthetic choices, but rather honed them. Even the most basic decisions about how to photograph a simple cube, after all, would always end up representing a photographer's choices, so even the sim-

83 Rudolf Arnheim, *Film as Art* (Berkeley: University of California Press, 1957), 9.

plest mechanically produced image was always fundamentally expressive. The differences between the image and phenomenal world, then, created restrictions, but those constraints were exactly what enabled personal expression to be born.

To the extent that he is known by the filmgoing public today, Murnau is remembered mostly as one of the four directors who ushered in the talking pictures in Germany in 1936 with his film *The Teutonic Knights* — known for its moody, fog-enshrouded mountains and forests, torchlit castle interiors, and imperious armor-clad soldiers who cross the screen astride horses like sentinels from a dimension of ghosts. But most cinephiles have long preferred his earlier career. He began filmmaking in the 1910s, but by the time he made *Faust,* Murnau had already developed a reputation — along with Fritz Lang — as one of the most inventive film directors in the country. The financial success of *Nosferatu* (1923) and *The Last Laugh* (1925) had given him the cachet to make more pressing demands of his employers, so for his next picture, he convinced Ufa studio chief Erich Pommer to give him a budget as large as any of Lang's epics by promising to adapt Goethe's play along orthodox lines. But while the plot may be similar, he knew that it would be his experiments with cinematic style that would make or break the picture.

Throughout the film, Murnau expresses his ideas about Goethe's story — both amplifying and challenging the dramatist's thinking — purely through his design of the image. Though he divides the story, as Goethe did, into two halves, initially plunging Faust into the pit of despair only in order to provide a redemption in Christian faith at the end, Murnau renders both the hopes of heaven and the depths of hell, both the light of the intellect and the depravity of unbridled physical sensation, in an unrelentingly bleak mise-en-scene, suggesting a much more somber vision of the human condition than the script on its own had expressed. In the first half of the film, the aging intellectual Faust — who the title cards make clear is "God's favorite" — struggles with his twin faiths in God and science in a world torn asunder by the plague. Murnau films every scene — both in the actual world and the metaphysical — shrouded in darkness: Emil Jannings as Mephistopheles raises his wings in the heavens above medieval towns like a harrowing Expressionist painting come to life. While in the real world, Murnau fills seemingly every setting with swirling black smoke so that the characters cannot even conceive of a world of light, but only of a world defined by the subtle play of grays on darker grays, a world of chalky exhausts and billows. Murnau's image is the physical manifestation of the medieval world's ignorance and despair. He blocks off both the foreground and background with sharp, angular walls drenched in trapezoids of dark shadows cast jaggedly against gray walls. And he arranges almost every frame into multiple planes of action divided by sharp diagonals so that the paranoid mobs fleeing their dying neighbors in tight rivulets of panicked movement through the middle of the image are unable to see or even apprehend other aspects of their world. He renders Faust's rooms, too — seemingly the last refuge of educated rationalism in a world seeped in irrational mysticism — as one cramped, oblique space bleeding into other angular, constricted spaces, highlighted by teetering stacks of brightly lit scientific tomes in the foreground and gauzily lit beakers, flasks, and tubes far in the background, trapping Faust between them, bent over beneath a low-hanging roof. And after he makes a pact with Mephistopheles, selling his soul for the power presumably to save Europe from the plague, Faust's world becomes even more tightened, increasingly narrowed, devoid of even those few symbols of scientific thought that once had evoked — even in those bleak rooms — the hint of hope. There's nothing left to highlight in the foreground or the background anymore: his books and beakers have disappeared. Now, Murnau films Faust and Mephistopheles in vast, empty plains of smoke-filled swamps, layers of gray on gray.

In the second half of the film, after Faust has given up on saving humanity and has instead dedicated himself to the selfish pursuits of revitalizing his youth and falling in love with the young maiden Gretchen, Murnau designs his image with only the merest hints that Faust has extricated himself from his pinched and darkened surroundings. The now miraculously

youthful Faust and and his lover Gretchen frolic in open mead-
ows, and Murnau paints the center of the image in soft grays.
But even here, he surrounds them with an aureole of darker
gray; even the blooming trees have only the faintest glimmer
of new buds, as if the bare tree branches are struggling against
a late frost. Murnau depicts his young lovers' faces in soft, lus-
cious light; their eyes glimmer: their humanity still glows deep
within them. But even in their romantic bliss, the threat of the
metaphysical realm never entirely leaves them. Mephistopheles
is always lingering, and whenever he appears he brings with
him his shadows and his angled compositions so that an open
courtyard is suddenly overcome by black lines intersecting each
other diagonally, leaving Faust alone, huddled in the bright but
shrinking corner at the edge of the frame.

The young maiden can't escape fate, either. As the movie hur-
tles toward its fatalistic resolution, she wanders alone through
snow-swept landscapes, begging strangers to save the child
she's had with Faust, the product of their love, for which the
townspeople condemn her. But Murnau somehow manages to
portray even a world of snow as bleak and forbidding. In the
final scenes, fields of gray snow are covered with eddying black
fumes; Murnau paints even the plain where the townsfolk will
burn Gretchen at the stake as suffocatingly cramped and en-
closed as the courtyards in the opening sequences where people
lay dying in heaps from the plague. Even as Faust rushes to what
he hopes will be her rescue, he rides a black steed with Mephistopheles behind him, hurtling diagonally into a corner, speeding through an image engulfed by inky smog. In the final scene
when Faust, now an old man again, leaps onto the burning fire
to save Gretchen from eternal damnation with the power of his
love, Murnau restores light to the world, but even here the Arch-
angel — the only purely white figure in the entire film — glows
only in the middle of the frame, unable to completely eradicate
the darkness that surrounds him.

Fear on the Street (d. Derrick Hampton, USA, 1955)
pr. *American Pictures*, sc. *Chester Himes and Philip Yordan,*
starring Mark Branson and Sidney Poitier, sound, b&w, 35mm,
100min.

Fear on the Street initially earned its place in the canon because
its critical and financial success seemed to mark the end of the
overt racial segregation of American pictures — which *Variety*
had formerly arranged in two separate sections as "new releases"
and "race pictures" — making possible the first spate of movies
geared for both white and Black audiences. From this point on,
Sidney Poitier was a star, quickly followed by James Edwards,
John Steele, and Daisy Harris. African-American audiences
flocked to the film because it was, as many writers in the press
noted, the first positive portrayal of a Black hero on American
screens since Ransom Pictures' *Gunned Down* more than a decade earlier. But the truth is a little more complicated. If anything,
the film has retained its hold on the culture's consciousness not
because of its positive representation, but because it examines
issues of race — and thus of the human condition — with a more
nuanced approach than all the other socially conscious pictures
of its day, making its knowing audience uneasy rather than re-
lieved about the racial situation in America.

By the mid-1950s, as most of the other independent production companies were in the process of collapsing, American Pictures had consolidated its hold over the secondary markets that
its former competitors used to service, and studio head Michael
Feynman realized that in addition to the rural white population
that American had usually seen as its target, the company now
also had access to a captive African-American audience that
Million Dollar Pictures and its ilk had formerly entertained.
American had begun experimenting with all-Black cast movies for the race market as far back as the early 1940s and had
been quietly turning out two or three a year. For the most part,
though, they made only modest profits.

But Feynman wanted to push the genre forward as much from
his political convictions as from the possibility of exploiting

new revenue streams. He'd quit his job as one of Darryl Zanuck's underlings at Fox, after all, partly because he thought that the socially engaged pictures Zanuck was producing weren't nearly as courageous as his acolytes in the press like Bosley Crowther made them out to be. He made his indignation known most famously when he stormed out of the premiere of *Wilson* (1944) because he thought that the movie had glossed over the former president's policy of re-segregating the federal workforce. In the first decade after he took over American, his attempts to create a more progressive cinema were more successful critically than financially, and he was never able to match the financial success of Ransom's *The End of the Road* (1943) or Columbia's *Double Indemnity* (1944). But just like Harold Arlickson with *Gunned Down* in 1941, he thought that if he could find a Black actor acceptable to white audiences in the North and team him with a white actor who appealed to rural communities, he could capture the Black audience and enough of the white audience outside of the South to make a big hit.

So by 1954, after A. Philip Randolph's marches on Washington had galvanized the burgeoning civil rights movement, Feynman sketched the outlines for what he thought might make a perfect formula: like Arlickson before him, he set his sights on an apolitical genre pic about a pair of detectives — one white and one Black — investigating something uncontroversial like a bank robbery, a movie that might touch on political themes more skillfully than his past attempts precisely because the racial dynamics would play a secondary role. He finally decided to put his plan into action when he caught a matinee at the American Negro Theater in New York and realized that he'd found his leading man: Sidney Poitier was handsome, a gifted actor, and a possible role model off-screen as well. Feynman signed him to a contract within the week and flew him out to Hollywood to prepare for what he hoped would be his most important production.

To capture the critics and the civil rights crowd, he gave the film the veneer of social realism by shooting on location; in this case, he chose the streets of Detroit — in fact, Hampton and his crew started shooting in the city eight years to the day after the worst race riots of the century had catalyzed the city's slow demise. To flesh out his outline for the script — and to buy him some credibility with the Black community — he tried to hire a leading African-American novelist, asking Richard Wright, then Ralph Ellison, and then James Baldwin, but they all politely declined; finally, at Baldwin's suggestion, he hired a young writer named Chester Himes, who was then also living in exile in Paris. At the same time — and without initially informing Himes — Feynman also hired a second screenwriter, Philip Yordan, whose play *Anna Lucasta,* originally about a Polish immigrant family, had been transformed by the American Negro Theater into an all-Black cast production and had become a major hit on the New York stage.

But Feynman hadn't anticipated how much the racial differences on his liberal screenwriting team might affect its artistic vision, and the process dragged on for weeks due to seemingly insurmountable disagreements. While Yordan and Feynman wanted to create an insensitive white detective as the movie's main foil, Himes argued that by consigning all the film's bigotry to one unlikeable character they were ignoring the true sources of racism in the country. Instead, Himes wanted them to take a more aggressive stance on the causes of racial strife in Detroit, suggesting that it was not the aberrant feelings of a few individuals, but institutional structures that were the problem, including the ostensibly leftist but white-led auto unions, the majority-white police force, the almost all-white district attorney's office, and the exclusively white city council that had exacerbated ethnic tensions in the city. Whether Himes quit in the end or was fired is still unclear, but Feynman brought in the young playwright Arthur Laurents to work on final touch-ups in the weeks before production began, and the final screenplay remained closer to the Feynman-Yordan vision that it did to Himes's more nuanced appraisal.

Derrick Hampton signed on to direct only a week before filming began. Feynman had initially asked his old friend Orson Welles, but Welles turned him down because he was starring in a pair of Italian epics at the time in order to raise money so he could start filming his adaptation of *Don Quixote* later that year. Feynman took a chance in the end and gave the reins to Hampton, who'd initially come to prominence directing Shakespeare on Broadway in the 1940s and who'd recently directed a couple of low-budget gangster pictures for Universal that met with positive reviews. Hampton had a fairly typical career arc for a liberal director of his generation. He'd started out as an actor at the Group Theater in the 1930s, where Harold Clurman had taken him under his wing. He'd worked as an assistant on Welles's *Voodoo Macbeth* in Harlem, and used to pal around in New York with Elia Kazan and John Garfield before they moved to Hollywood. As a director, he was a committed progressive who gravitated toward political themes, but he was still a middle-class white man with ambitions to make a career in Hollywood, so he had a more complicated relationship with the idea of "engaged cinema" than he would care to admit. He found, he said, that the best way to make his most trenchant political arguments was not to put them in the characters' mouths, where the producers could see them and easily excise them, but to sneak them in while on set through what he called "symbolic indirection."[84] In this way, he was able to reintroduce some of the radical elements he'd seen in Himes's earlier drafts merely through his careful design of mise-en-scene.

In the opening shot, the veteran detective Mitch Taylor (Mark Branson) walks through a busy precinct office in a long tracking shot as his chief announces that he's partnering him with Eddie Payton (Sidney Poitier), who's just been promoted to detective. But even in this seemingly nondescript shot, Hampton lays out his aesthetic and political blueprint for the entire film: though the white characters talk about a Black man's promotion with monosyllabic nonchalance and Poitier himself seems more interested in finding his car keys than in analyzing the interpersonal dynamics of the department, the image itself

---

84 Quoted in Peter Bogdanovich, *Who the Devil Made It* (New York: Knopf, 1997), 711.

reveals the unspoken racial tension that demarcates the entire social system. Hampton portrays a precinct room that's filled entirely with white faces except for one Black janitor bent over in the background whose intense fascination with the methodical task of mopping evinces a strategic disregard for the white people who dominate the rest of the frame, the best survival tactic he can fashion, given his position. And by the end of this first shot — tracking through the precinct offices, down the stairs, and out into the street — Poitier demonstrates, through his equally intense preoccupation with the entries in his log book, the pressure that he feels to demonstrate his unbiased professionalism to his white peers. And by drawing this visual parallel between Poitier and the janitor, Hampton suggests that the notion that Black people have a choice about whether or not they should engage with white culture is fundamentally an illusion since in the end they can only choose which type of calculated and accommodating strategy they'll adopt to deal with the racial power structure as it exists.

Hampton's visual design, then, brings to life Himes's arguments about racial politics that are latent in the script. The heist that the detectives were initially investigating was not itself a major crime, but their work leads them to uncover a criminal network that uncomfortably parallels the world that they themselves inhabit — with a white syndicate dominating a Black criminal outfit in a competition for territory — and it slowly dawns on Poitier and Branson that this concealed realm of illegality may not just mirror but may, in fact, nurture and sustain their own domain of seemingly legal surfaces. Hampton repeatedly makes a similar connection between the unspeakable quality of racism and its very obvious visible manifestations. He likes to cut back and forth between the detectives' routine conversations in the squad car to images of the street from their point-of-view so that as they cross from the white parts to the Black parts of town, or vice versa, the city's glaring but unacknowledged racial segregation becomes the obvious driving force of the entire film.

And Hampton accentuates the similarities between the racial dynamics in the legitimate world with parallel dynamics in the underground by organizing the mise-en-scene in a few key scenes so that the white and Black characters are mirror images of each other in the frame. In what has become the movie's most memorable scene, for instance, a white roughneck manhandles an old Black woman in the background while Branson beats a Black suspect in the foreground. By repeatedly suggesting — purely on a visual level — that the cops and the criminals are moral equals, Hampton makes us empathize as much with the gangster victims as we do with the detective assailants in the final scene: as Poitier and Branson gun down their multiracial antagonists in a long tracking shot through the maze of the city's dark alleys, they are ostensibly restoring justice — while in fact, they are merely reinforcing an allegedly civilized culture whose inequality Hampton has been making evident throughout the film.

Feynman advertised the film more heavily than any other movie with a racial theme ever released, and it paid off fairly well: it did great business at Black theaters, but only middling numbers at white venues. Critics and cultural elites, though, were surprisingly mixed. Many leading Black intellectuals were taken aback by the film's seeming sympathy for Black criminality. Walter White, the president of the NAACP, chided the film for rehearsing the stereotype that African-Americans were innately drawn to the gangster lifestyle. But Manny Farber raved about the movie in *The Nation,* calling it "a whipcrack descent into the fetid illusions of the surface world" and one of the only American films to deal intelligently with racial themes since *Gunned Down* in 1941 and King Vidor's *Hallelujah* back in 1931.[85] And African-American audiences loved the film, too. The readers of *The Pittsburgh Courier,* the most influential Black newspaper in the nation, overwhelmingly chose it as the best movie of the year. Since then, its prestige has continued to grow, not just because of its complex racial ideology and its compositional intricacy, but also because it's become the paradigm of the "ad-

---

85 Manny Farber, "Films," *The Nation* 180, no. 10, March 5, 1955, 200.

venturous nihilism"[86] that marked the final years of the independent production companies in Hollywood.

Gangster Film (d. Jean-Luc Godard, Switzerland, 1998)
pr. The European Media Project, sc. Jean-Luc Godard, starring
Jean-Paul Belmondo and Mimiette Yvoux, sound, color, digital
video, 86 min.

Though Jean-Luc Godard had been both the most influential and the most controversial film critic in France from the 1950s through the 1970s, by the time he finally got the opportunity to direct his first movie in 1998, his writings hadn't played an important role in the international cinephile community for almost twenty years. If anything, he'd become invisible to everyone but the film festival elite or film theorists interested in the history of auteurism. Some film lovers, it was said, weren't even sure if he was still alive. But this neglect of an iconoclastic critic, who as much as anyone had spearheaded a re-evaluation of Hollywood studio filmmaking, made his sudden re-appearance as an experimental moviemaker all the more poignant, reminding everyone once again of the ironically intrinsic role that the classical cinema plays in formulating any modernist agenda. "*Gangster Film*," wrote Jonathan Rosenbaum,

> felt like both a disquisition on the history of film as well as an elemental rupture within that history. After all, just as *Finnegan's Wake* figuratively situates itself at some theoretical stage after the end of the English language as we know it, from a vantage point where one can look back at the 20th century and ask oneself, 'What was the English language?' Godard's film — or video, to be more precise — similarly projects itself into the future in order to ask, 'What was cinema?'[87]

---

86 James Naremore, *More Than Night: Hardboiled Cinema in Its Contexts* (Berkeley: University of California Press, 1998), 25.

87 Jonathan Rosenbaum, *Chicago Reader,* July 15, 1998, 35.

In the 1980s, after *Cahiers du Cinéma* finally folded, Godard gave up on trying to find regular work as a critic and dropped out of the Parisian film scene, retiring to the small village of Rolle in Switzerland. After a few years off, he began to intermittently self-publish a series of inscrutable pamphlets about the more esoteric aspects of film history in editions of a hundred. These essays moved away from the leftist politics he'd embraced in the 1970s into more abstruse poetic grounds, deepening his own irrelevance. His obscurity was made famous when the French Minister of Culture Olivia Lamouière mistakenly referred to him as "the late Godard" at a Cannes press conference in 1993. But though Godard may have fallen off the map, he'd never disengaged from the cinema; if anything, he'd become more experimental in the 1980s than he had been in his more famous incarnations as Hollywood auteurist of the 1960s or radical Brechtian of the 1970s.

And his long-held desire to become a filmmaker — long thought impossible, since even French producers had been unwilling to take a chance on his type of modernist experimentation — finally came to fruition only at the tail end of his career due to an unexpected confluence of events. Spurred on by the new digital video cameras and editing systems that became available at consumer prices in the 1990s and also by the European Union's leftward turn in cultural policy around the same time, Godard was able to raise government funds to make a feature-length movie, in his own estimation, for less than $30,000 — or, as he put it to an interviewer from *Le Monde,* less than 1/20th of one percent of the average Hollywood blockbuster.[88]

Gangster Film's contradictory aesthetics — at once indulging in genre tropes while at the same time deconstructing them — was the product of Godard's own evolution as a cinephile. He'd initially banded together in the 1950s with other like-minded young critics — such as François Truffaut, Jacques Rivette, and Luc Moullet — who'd staked out controversial terri-

---

88 David Sterritt, ed., *Jean-Luc Godard: Interviews* (Jackson: University of Mississippi Press, 1998), 203.

tory, crusading for unknown directors from the Hollywood studio system like Howard Hawks, Derrick Hampton, and Raoul Walsh in the pages of Andre Bazin's influential magazine *Cahiers du Cinéma*. But Godard took a radical turn after the Paris riots of 1968, inspired by the new leftist governments that had recently won elections in the Indian states of Kerala and West Bengal — and to a lesser extent by the French and Shanghainese followers of Antonio Gramsci who'd swept through academic circles in the 1960s — and staged a public break with his old colleagues by dismissing them in indelicate terms: in his famous letter to Truffaut, he excoriated his one-time best friend and alter-ego, writing "no one else will call you a liar, but I will. It's no more of an insult than 'fascist.' You say you admire films that are big trains that go along in the night, but the big trains you admire these days are like the trains that led to Birkenau."[89] He quit his day job as film reviewer for *Arte* and, living solely on a small inheritance — a fact that did not go un-noticed by the allegedly bourgeois Truffaut, who'd occasionally had to live on the streets as a teenager — he spent the next ten years re-engaging with the anthropological studies of his college years, travelling throughout the developing world, living in Bolivia, Senegal, India, and Nepal in a period that his onetime friend Claude Chabrol described archly as "self-defilement in the cause of global political fraternity."[90]

After he returned to Paris from his self-imposed exile in 1980, he tried to re-establish his career as a critic but was unable to find work in a post-Socialist milieu where even intellectuals wrote about a "film market" rather than a "film culture." Thus, he gave up in disgust and moved to Rolle, a town of two thousand on the shores of Lake Geneva, where after a few years he started working on his increasingly enigmatic books. In these, he eventually abandoned prose all together, designing instead

---

89 Claude de Givray and Gilles Jacob, eds., *François Truffaut: Correspondence, 1945-1984* (New York: Farrar, Strauss, and Giroux, 1990), 422–23.

90 Françoise Gerif, *A Garden of Mine: Conversation with Claude Chabrol*, trans. Vivienne Thevenin (New York: Random House 2002), 362.

multilayered collages of images from obscure films overlaid with orphic pronouncements arranged in crossword-puzzle patterns that Godard himself referred to as "Navajo English." These later books became so mystifying that some of his defenders felt the need to write about them in language so oblique that their interpretations took on the qualities of art itself. Others like Serge Daney defended Godard's books as a kind of vanguard cinema manifesting itself in an alternative medium: "A love of the cinema desires only cinema," he wrote about Godard's book *Cinema Archeology* (1992), "whereas passion is excessive: it wants cinema, but it also wants cinema to become something else, it even longs for the horizon where cinema risks being absorbed by dint of metamorphosis; it opens up its focus onto the unknown."[91]

In the early 1990s, the economics of film production in Europe took a decisive turn, empowering non-commercial filmmakers as they'd never been before. In 1994, the Socialists swept elections across Western Europe, and François Mitterand's government pushed its German and British allies to create a continent-wide system for subsidizing film production, enabling Godard's former colleagues Jacques Rivette and Luc Moullet to finally direct their first films despite their advanced age. At the same time, the audiovisual digital revolution was just then picking up steam. Ensconced in his lakeside villa, Godard became intrigued with the new technology, teaching himself computer editing and experimenting with digital cameras, obsessed — to the consternation of his purist cinephile peers — with the stunning variety of visual textures the new medium generated that were unavailable in film.

After he won a grant from the European Media Project, he abandoned the idea of shooting with a finished script, deciding that the affordability of digital production gave him the freedom to improvise the movie instead — in this case, mostly with a group of truck drivers he'd stumbled across in a Geneva bar. But in the starring role he cast an old friend from the 1950s,

---

91 Serge Daney, "The Godard Paradox," in *Selected Film Criticism,* ed. Lionel Franke (Berkeley: University of California Press 2011), 318.

the washed-up character actor Jean-Paul Belmondo — who allegedly agreed to act in the film without pay after losing a bet to the director over a game of bezique. The final result proved to be an outrageously uncommercial film in the guise of a hardboiled Hollywood picture from the 1950s. And yet, even its pain-inducing sequences of audiovisual collage are playful enough that the movie continues to make mainstream audiences laugh out loud on the few occasions when they get a chance to actually see it.

The film opens with Belmondo as a former crime boss with the decidedly un-French appellation of Chandler Raymond who's retired from the business and gone straight by opening — in an impishly self-reflexive but also intellectually fruitful move on Godard's part — a revival movie house in Montparnasse with his pretty coquette of a wife played by Mimiette Yvoux. But even in the opening scenes, Godard makes clear that the traditional narrative expectations of the genre will play a secondary role to his own idiosyncratically poetic ruminations on film history made possible by the formal qualities of the new audiovisual medium. After he hangs up on an ominous phone call from an old gangster friend, the hand-held camera follows Belmondo through the theater lobby — with its posters of Howard Hawks's *Rio Bravo* (1959) and William Wellman's *Billy the Kid* (1953) — up the winding staircase to the projection room, where we see through a sliver of glass a sequence from Derrick Hampton's *Fear on the Street* (1955), which Belmondo ignores so that he can lean sensually over a pinball machine shoved up incongruously against the projector. And then the image suddenly freezes, and after a few confusing moments, begins to disintegrate like a waterfall of pixels cascading into oblivion as Sidney Poitier and Mark Branson's voices echoing from the auditorium below crackle into distorted abstractions.

Godard's fascination with the painterly qualities of the digital picture and the aesthetic possibilities of sonic fuzz wasn't merely an eccentric gesture, but was in part the logical outcome of decades of theorizing about audiovisual representation. Apart from politics, the other leading cause of Godard's break with his erstwhile colleagues at *Cahiers* in the 1970s, after all, had been based on his burgeoning preference for theory instead of movie reviews. He'd become especially interested in the material conditions of the medium, influenced in part by his readings of the formalist Noël Burch and of the then-obscure Russian theorist Sergei Eisenstein, whose essays on intellectual montage received renewed interest in the 1970s. By the 1990s, Godard had come to believe that the distinct properties of pixilated sound and image could help him articulate some aspects of human character that heretofore had been inexpressible in film, but which artists like Jean Dubuffet had been able to achieve in painting. "Even the supposedly uninventive old masters like Frans Hals," Godard said, "understood the modernist notion that one might represent a fractured interior psyche by disturbing the fixed exterior of the face."[92] Thus, the digital mottling of Belmondo's wincing expression lit by the glow of the pinball machine is not just an arbitrary aesthetic choice but the physical manifestation of his anxieties about whether or not he's actually able to leave his old life behind, anxieties that Godard felt he must portray visually as an ugly dissolution of the self because the narrative must lead — this being a gangster film, after all — to the protagonist's inexorably violent death.

True to classic genre form, Belmondo's attempts to go straight can lead him only to a dead end. When he learns that an old rival has gunned down his best friend, the man he left in charge of his former outfit, Belmondo gathers a group of wizened old cronies — the same pack of W.C. Fields-look-alikes that Godard had recruited from Geneva's worst dives — and hatches a plot to seek revenge. In a funny twist that allows Godard to engage in a kind of meta-commentary on the cinema itself, Belmondo's caper consists of stealing his rival's stash of stolen diamonds, which he will then ensconce — somewhat illogically — in the hollowed-out base of a movie projector back in his own theater. But his antagonist's henchmen catch his team in the act of the

---

92 Jean-Luc Godard and Youssef Ishaghpour, *Cinema: The Archeology of Film and the Memory of a Century,* trans. John Howe (New York: Bloomsbury Academic, 2005), 100.

crime and follow them back to Belmondo's place, which enables Godard to choreograph a fifteen-minute climactic sequence inside the movie theater, in which a handful of gangsters sneak through the aisles until they end up behind the screen, where the movie that's being projected reflects across their fleshy, bemused faces, a movie which is — impossibly — an experimental actuality about the history of the cinema, replete with multiple superimpositions, exaggerated editing, and mysteriously terse texts that mimic the "Navajo English" of Godard's most recent books. And just then, as Belmondo picks up a prized diamond necklace for the first time up in the projection booth, Godard segues from the diegetic world of these gangsters into an amorphous, poetic mode, so that we are no longer watching what we thought was *Gangster Film,* but are now watching instead a radical collage-style essay that comments on how Jean-Luc Godard's *Gangster Film* intervenes into the long history of French filmmakers' adaptations of Hollywood genres, referencing, in particular, Jean-Pierre Melville's 1950s work that in turn re-imagined Hollywood's Hardboiled Cinema of the 1940s in a different cultural milieu.

In the final scene, Godard returns to the diegetic world of the movie to fashion a tragic ending that both fulfills and subverts the genre's conventions. After Belmondo escapes the movie theater on foot with the loot, an unseen rival shoots him in the back. Despite the pain, he manages to jump into the getaway car, and as it speeds away, his bleeding torso hangs out of the back window and his arms flail about, almost scraping the pavement, while all throughout, Godard has been turning the soundtrack on its head, mixing together a collage of audio snippets that includes dialogue from Howard Hawks's *The Big Sleep* (1944), Frank Callaghan's *The Long Goodbye* (1954), and his old friend Claude Chabrol's *Maigret* movies starring Jean Gabin, along with two superimposed tracks of the theme song from Robert Altman's *LAPD* (1973). The car weaves its way through the streets of Paris until the camera zooms in on Belmondo's almost-dead face, and just as the movie seems about to end, he opens his eyes, looking directly into the camera, and winks to the audience as he wipes his mouth sullenly with his thumb, turning the film's final moments into a poetically unnerving disquisition on the impossibility of paying homage to an object of adoration without disfiguring the very love that inspired the gesture in the first place.

Grand Prix (d. Louis Belfont, France, 1934)

pr. Cinemonde, sc. Louis Belfont, starring Achille Pujol and Odile Goujon, silent, b&w, 35mm, 71 min.

The critical fervor for Louis Belfont's *Grand Prix* has itself been the object of intellectuals' fascination ever since the movie was released. After all, on the surface it's just an action picture about a car race, even if its hyperkinetic visuals and dynamic audio do make for gripping viewing. But even at its first screening, when Robert Desnos was so appalled that Louis Delluc would defend this mercantile trifle that he allegedly struck the older man across the face, the movie's curious appeal has been a matter of intense debate. But now, eighty years on, the film still retains a surprising allure for the critical community: every generation that comes along finds something new in this movie that initially appears to be about nothing but speeding automobiles, innocent romance, and the thrill of victory.

Audiences loved the movie when it first came out for its gut-level entertainment values. Reviewers in the daily press praised the film for what Jean-Pic Moireaux called its "hypnotic obsession with swerving velocity and its erotic charge at the machine's ability to triumph over our human limitations."[93] But some critics sensed something deeper: a "cryptic grammar," an "audiovisual enigma," or an "encomium to the mechanical age."[94] Writers with a theoretical bent like Delluc praised the film because, they claimed, it took advantage of the medium's most productively

---

93 Jean-Pic Moireaux, "Grand Prix," in *Grand Prix: Louis Belfont, Director,* ed. Charles Affron (New Brunswick: Rutgers University Press, 1989), 165.

94 "Film Reviews," in ibid., 193–97.

contradictory characteristics. On the one hand, that is, motion pictures were the most accurate means of reproducing reality, but on the other hand, they could also reveal the phenomenal world in ways that would be impossible for the human eye on its own. And Belfont, more than any other director, made this aesthetically constructive incongruity the very subject of his film.

Evaluations and interpretations have drifted with the tides over the years. In the 1950s and 1960s, the younger generation of French cineastes re-examined the film and resuscitated Delluc's original defense. This commercial entertainment about race-car drivers, they maintained, manifested the same antagonism toward realism as had all the experimental movements of the period, especially in Paris and Tokyo, that advocated for so-called "pure cinema." At the same time, the movie had a purely functional charm. Jacques Rivette wrote in 1958 that "through his methodical organization of images, Belfont has streamlined the film into its most primal essentials, becoming cleaner, more honest, and more pure, the perfect mixture of the unadorned functionalism of American cinema that we see in Howard Hawks and Richard Fleischer and the bravura modernism in the works of aesthetes like Marcel L'Herbier and Marcel L'Enfant."[95] Then, in the 1980s, with the blossoming of Freudianism and the historicist turn in academia, scholars in the United States and England revisited Belfont's own writings from the 1920s back when he was involved in avant-garde circles. By locating his own interests in the then popular confluence of Surrealism and Sigmund Freud, some writers pointed out that despite Belfont's surface fascination with sonic and visual textures, his real interest lay in the mysteriously otherworldly aspects that the minute focus on physicality ironically engendered — or, as Beverly Kimmelman put it, the film was "an oneiricist's attempt to articulate

---

95 Jacques Rivette, "Modernism and the Late Silent Period," in *Cahiers du Cinéma, the 1950s*, ed. Hillier, 45.

the collective unconscious by manipulating the dismembered audiovisual fragments of the phenomenal world."[96]

The story follows two characters: Ricky, a working-class race car driver, and his fiancée Mirielle, the daughter of a rich industrialist who opposes their plans to get married. In the dream-like world of movie logic, they convince themselves that the only way that they can have a wedding is for Ricky to win the upcoming Monaco Grand Prix and use the prize money to elope and set up house together. The plot is intentionally shallow — Ricky and Mirielle have only five or six intertitles of dialogue each — because Belfont deployed narrative only so that he could make the racing milieu the central character of his "cinematic portrait." In the beginning, he takes us through the couple's Parisian demi-monde with sweeping tracking shots through cafes, garages, and back alleys, peopled with gruff mechanics, aristocratic drunks, and village girls who've sold themselves into prostitution. But the majority of the movie concerns the race itself, and it's in this second half that Belfont most fully embraces carnivalesque audiovisual experimentation, abandoning his earlier lush, gliding camerawork for decentered images, staccato editing, and a sonic palette of screaming crowds and exploding engine roars.

Belfont attached cameras to a dozen cars in an actual Grand Prix event, so the racing sequences in the film are arguably more of an actuality than a work of fiction. But he makes the sound mix as much the star of the film as the visual splendor. Produced entirely in the studio after the fact, the soundtrack includes revving motors, squealing tires, overheard conversations in the crowd, the voice of the radio announcer from his booth, and music from nearby PA systems that come in and out every time the drivers take a turn. And Belfont continually increases the dramatic tension — along with the speed of the editing and the volume of the audio track — as the race nears its finish in a climactic ending whose formal audacity hadn't been seen since Abel Gance's *La Roue*.

---

96 Beverly Kimmelman, *The Hyperbolic Signifier: Modernism and the Cinema in Paris, 1929–1936* (Princeton: Princeton University Press 1995), 66.

Belfont's brazen innovation with audio is essential in understanding his ultimate goal of deploying a materialist aesthetics. He began production in the years that most writers still dubiously refer to as the "late silent period" — roughly between 1932 and 1936 in the West — when many producers were experimenting with sound-on-film technology in order to create recorded musical soundtracks but still considered recording characters' spoken dialogue to be too onerous. While American studios like MGM and independent producers like David Selznick had released several pictures at this point that included a musical score, and German directors like Elke Sonnabend and Fritz Lang had filmed a few moments of dialogue as a kind of crowd-teasing novelty, Belfont thought that no one had yet explored the full potentials of audio recording. "If one believes in the tenets of pure cinema," he told Louis Delluc in an interview for *Cinema,* "one must now force a revolutionary break and emphatically embrace the fact that the motion pictures are not, as everyone has heretofore believed, primarily a visual art form, but an audiovisual one. The soundtrack must play an equal and independent — not a subordinate — role to the image. If anything, in fact, perhaps we should be subordinating the image to the sounds!"[97]

With this in mind, Belfont designed the entire movie before he filmed and recorded it, hiring a team of illustrators to lay out every shot of the film on long horizontal rolls of butcher paper so he could see the images unfolding in the semblance of time. He also worked with his composer George Antheil during pre-production to design the sounds that would accompany each image. He avoided dialogue as much as possible, since the spoken word, he said — even though it still only appeared on title cards — belonged to the novel and the theater. But what the novel could not do and what the theater rarely did at all was to treat sound effects and ambient noise as emotional and psychological aspects of the narrative. Thus the movie is awash in layers of sound — from the music halls and cafes of the opening

97 Louis Delluc, "Interview with Belfont," in *Grand Prix,* ed. Affron, 208.

scenes with their overheard bits of conversation, cacophony of silverware, and music by expatriate jazz musicians to the lively symphony of the streets with its car horns, traffic, and working-class argot. "People who say the movie has no story have obviously never listened to it," Belfont said. "Because the sounds themselves create every tension and every release in a fluid arc from the beginning to the end."[98]

But his overriding goal in recording the natural world in as accurate detail as possible, he told Delluc, was that such an intimate focus on just a few meticulously observed details forced listeners into modes of perception contrary to the ways they experienced the material world in everyday life, thus possibly unlocking the unconscious layers of the mind, just as dreams did. Many of his later admirers have been surprised to learn that before he made *Grand Prix,* Belfont spent more than a decade hovering on the fringes of various avant-garde groups in Paris. He'd been friends with many of the French Impressionist film-makers in the early 1920s, had directed two avant-garde shorts, and contributed a few reviews to Delluc's *Cinema,* but then drifted from the Parisian film scene for a few years.

When he returned to the capital in the late 1920s, though, he became more interested in poetry than in the cinema: he became friends with Georges Ribemont-Dessaignes and attended a few Surrealist meetings, but was turned off by Andre Breton's imperiousness and some of the others' dalliance with utopian socialism. Nevertheless, surrealist philosophy did play a significant role in the development of his aesthetic. Breton's enthusiasm for Freud rubbed off on him and Belfont recognized "The Surrealist Manifesto" as one of the founding documents of the age. In fact, his own response to that essay, "Against the Autonomy of the Imagination: The Industrial Word as the Universal Subconscious," functions as a kind of road map for future interpretive analyses *Grand Prix.*[99]

---

98 Ibid., 209.
99 Louis Belfont, "Against the Autonomy of the Imagination: The Phenomenal Word as the Universal Subconscious," in *French Film Theory and*

Belfont maintained that by valorizing the unfettered mind, Breton was reinforcing the superiority of the individual over the collective — an ideology that Belfont thought was responsible for the ethical and spiritual decline of the West ever since the Enlightenment. Instead, he drew upon Carl Jung's notions of the collective unconscious to counteract the Surrealist leader's theories, but he did so in an unorthodox manner, suggesting that the modern machine — with its illogically poetic formal design — was the obvious manifestation of the primal autonomous complex of the communal imagination that could only be made manifest after the Industrial Revolution released it from its millennia of slumber. So, in his thinking, technology itself was as fundamentally oneiric as the latent mental conflicts of the individual mind.

That being said, whether Belfont was actually able to portray machines as a form of liberating consciousness remains debatable, since the film struggles throughout with the tension between the feeling world of humanity and the discombobulating aural and visual onslaught of the dissected automobiles. Oftentimes, as Kimmelman points out, Belfont's theorizing might be most useful, ironically, in helping us understand the personal conflicts of the director rather than that of civilization as a whole, since the thundering engines feel more like a symbol of the characters' spiritual dissipation than of their freedom. By breaking both the automobile and the drivers into minute sections — headlights, spinning tires, eye goggles, hands clutching a wheel — he transforms both humans and machines into mere abstractions. And by cutting back and forth between crowd scenes of eager faces and these abstract parts, Belfont turns the race into a purely artistic exercise in which human consciousness dissolves into the discomfiting mechanized tumult of industrialization. As a few people have noted, though, Belfont never discussed this in print: he embarked on the film only a year after he simultaneously abandoned both his Catholic faith

---

Criticism: A History/Anthology, Volume 1: 1907–1936, ed. Richard Abel (Princeton: Princeton University Press, 1993), 464.

and his first wife. As Ricky turns his car around the corner to start the final lap, Mirielle's beaming face followed by extreme close-ups of one eye, a hand, and her mouth light up the screen. But her accompanying screams of excitement seem to be not so much emanations of her orgiastic bliss as they are a howling reaction to her own disembodiment — and thus disempowerment — at the hands of the modern world's manufactured despoliation.

Gunned Down (d. Lloyd Collins, USA, 1941)
pr. Ransom Pictures, sc. Horace McCoy, starring Grant Miller and Juano Hernandez, sound, b&w, 35mm, 72 min.

These days, most historians and critics have come to accept that it was the independent production companies during Hollywood's classical period, not the three majors, that were most responsible for the lasting appeal of the studio system. Independent productions, after all, have appeared disproportionately as Academy Award nominees and on canonical lists like the Sight & Sound critics' poll. Academic scholars, too, give pride of place to independents, whether in auteurist analyses like Peter Wollen's work on Howard Hawks or in genre histories like James Naremore's history of hardboiled cinema. Taking up the popular assumption that origins determine essences, many historians thus tend to seek out the first film in a movement in order to define that movement's fundamental characteristics. The standard narrative generally regards Ransom Pictures' *Gunned Down* as an ur-text since it was the movie that first made the success of the independent studios possible because it challenged the moral standards of the majors, thus appealing to audiences eager for more adventurously uncouth entertainment.

Historians champion the independents partly because they assume that they functioned differently than the three major studios — Paramount, Fox, and MGM, known as the Big Three — being less beholden to the dictates of an unrefined central producer, and thus more willing to give their directors the freedom to express themselves. But these unthinking assumptions need to be revised, because in fact, the independent companies that became most successful — Ransom, Columbia, American, for instance — succeeded precisely because they replicated the institutional structures of the majors more than their independent competitors did. Ransom had a central producer in Harold Arlickson, Columbia in Harry Cohn, and American in Michael Feynman, and the films of these outsiders are just as much the product of a collaboration between studio executives, screenwriters, and directors as are the big budget movies produced by the majors.

But just as academics and cinephiles have undervalued the role of the independent executive at the top end of the filmmaking hierarchy, they have also underestimated the role that audiences and exhibition venues played at the bottom end in inspiring the outsiders' mode of production. Because the three major studios were each struggling to beat the other two to capture about 25% of the market, they felt compelled to appeal to as broad a demographic as possible. Thus, regardless of their personal tastes, the executives at the majors like Darryl Zanuck, Barney Balaban, and Louis B. Mayer would, as a matter of course, have to produce movies that would appeal to both men and women of all ages from every region of the country. But since the outsider companies were each competing for only about 5% of the market, they found that they could be most successful when targeting a niche audience that the majors had overlooked. The reason that *Gunned Down,* then, became the first production to propel the independents to prominence was not so much that Lloyd Collins had an innovative auteurist vision but because Harold Arlickson was the first executive, from a big company or small, to successfully appeal to a marginal audience — in this case, Southern men, both white and Black, whose dreams had previously been excluded from American cinema by the homogenizing forces of the mainstream market.

At the time of the *Publix Theaters* decision in 1936, Harold Arlickson owned the Inter-Continental chain of theaters that spread across Texas and Oklahoma. The Supreme Court had found in that case that the three major studios had violated anti-trust laws and ordered them to divorce their production companies from their theater chains. But with a decisive lack of prognosticative aptitude, the court had made no ruling in regard to the legality of any smaller theater chains creating their own production companies. Realizing sooner than his competitors the opportunities the case provided for independents to expand, Arlickson bought out the small Hanson and Reliable chains, and found himself by the end of the year with the second-largest theater circuit in the South after *Publix* itself. As a Texan born and bred, Arlickson understood his audience in a way that the major theater executives with offices in Times Square never could, and he moved aggressively to solicit movies designed specifically for Southern sensibilities that he could screen in his theaters. But when he couldn't get adequate product fast enough, he did what the original studio heads had done decades before and went into the business of movie production on his own, founding Ransom Pictures to supply movies for his type of audience. With the goal of shaping a regional voice, he went out and hired the most talented Southerners who'd worked for the Big Three, screenwriters like William Faulkner and Horace McCoy and directors like King Vidor and Clarence Brown.

The idea for *Gunned Down* originated with conversations between Arlickson and his contract director Lloyd Collins. Collins was born and raised in Tennessee and came to California in the 1930s, where he initially got into the business as an assistant to Brian Foy, the head of the B unit at Paramount. But after befriending so many of the leftist playwrights from New York who'd come to Los Angeles with the coming of the talkies, Collins yearned to make movies with more social and political significance, especially about racial problems in the South. Arlickson was sympathetic but nervous about Collins's attitudes: after all, every single theater he owned was racially segregated by state law. But after the box office success of some of the race pictures that American Pictures had started to churn out for African-American theaters in 1940, Johnson decided to give Collins the greenlight for a screenplay he'd cooked up with his fellow Tennessean Horace McCoy about an unlikely friendship between a white man and a Black man in Memphis who'd teamed up as petty criminals to make ends meet. That being said, Arlickson hedged his bets just like any of the major executives would, insisting that Collins tone down the "racial angle" as much as possible so as to avoid any controversies.

The film opens on a tight two-shot of Jack Reed (Grant Miller) and Tom Stoddard (Juano Hernandez), a white man and a Black man whose faces are unidentifiable because they're wearing masks. They brandish a pair of shotguns and bellow that this is a hold-up: they're standing in a gas station somewhere in the boondocks, and the cowering, threadbare elderly woman behind the counter spits at them, "You boys know you can't make any money stealing from the poor." Later, the two men drive home, still volubly high from the thrill of the crime, finishing each other's jokes and breaking into impromptu songs, but when they get back to Reed's house to split up their bounty, they discover that their take amounts to only $23.13 each, which sends Miller's wife into howls of pitiless laughter and which remains a running gag and source of shame throughout the movie. When Stoddard reluctantly admits that maybe it's true that crime doesn't pay, their spouses indignantly confront them about the high cost of baby formula, drapes, and shoes for the kids, and Collins's camera lingers over the visual signifiers of their poverty — torn sofa cushions, patched overalls, a kitchen sink filled with tin cups and spoons. So at their wives' insistence, the men decide to abandon their penny-ante holdups and plan instead one major heist before they call it quits.

The majority of the movie, then, is a step-by-step procedural about their rehearsals to rob the payroll from the local mill, one of Memphis's biggest companies. In its meticulous handling of the minute details of the crime, the film takes a subversive disinterest in passing ethical judgment on the men's behavior. If anything, the movie presents robbery as perhaps the only ethical option left for men to raise their families in a society that's so indifferent to their wellbeing. The protagonists are, after all — as they say repeatedly in some of their most eloquently drunken pontifications — just doing it all for the sake of the wife and kids.

Given that Collins focuses on the sociocultural background of crime rather than on its cinematic thrills, it's appropriate that his portrayal of the holdup itself, shot in real time, takes only about fifty seconds, with the two men entering a bank, forcing the manager to open the vault, then fleeing with the money. And the movie's resolution has justifiably cemented its place in history as the foundation of the independent companies' more free-wheeling style in that it overturns Hollywood's typical demand for closure: while the censor Joseph Breen required Hollywood movies to follow the rule of "compensating moral values" — that is, characters were allowed to engage in immoral behavior so long as they were punished in the end — Arlickson decided to risk foregoing Breen's complaints and released the film without PCA approval. So here, the moral lesson that Reed and Stoddard learn is that crime can, in fact, pay — and quite well. In the final shot, one wife feeds her newborn in the foreground while the other wife hangs new curtains in the background, and through the window we see their sons running around in spiffy new cowboy hats, brandishing toy guns, and staging a mock hold-up. But even here, Collins hints obliquely at a darker resolution he wouldn't make explicit, since the final image is one that echoes their fathers' joyful memories of their escapades but also one that foreshadows what must be — given the inescapable inequalities of capitalism — their sons' fate.

But just as this movie shaped the future of the independent studios, the reaction of its audiences played an equally important — though unheralded — role in crafting the trajectory of independent companies' aesthetics and politics for decades to come. The movie received surprisingly positive reviews from both the Southern white press and African-American newspapers across the country. And yet, a backlash soon reared its ugly head. So-called citizens' councils sprouted up here and there across the South — instigated, historians later discovered, by white supremacist politicians coordinated secretly by Mississippi senator Theodore Bilbo. Initially, they wrote letters to the editor, but eventually they came out to picket in front of theaters screening the film. While their numbers were fairly small, Arlickson and other executives could see where the wind was blowing and let it be known that their experiments with multiracial casting would be put on hold for the time being.

In ensuing years, admirers of the film have struggled how to judge it due to its ostentatious avoidance of the issue of race. Given that the characters never mention the topic and that everyone in the film behaves as if the protagonists' very obvious skin color is surprisingly not visible to them, most critics have tended to defend the film as the bravest possible small step forward given the politics of the time. But Jeanine Brinkema make a different point. "The irony," she writes,

> is that by making one type of critique — about America's racial segregation — impermissible, the system can merely strengthen another type critique — in this case, about economic inequality. By focusing on the film's weakness in one area, then, writers too often ignore the film's truly radical conceit: because by eliding the divisive issue of race, Collins and McCoy implicitly make quite a subversive claim: that the two races will help themselves only by ignoring their differences and joining together instead to combat their true and mutual enemy, which is the capitalist system itself.[100]

Harakiri (d. Kobayashi Masaki, Japan, 1966)

pr. Shochiku, sc. Hashimoto Shinobu, starring Nakadai Tatsuya, sound, b&w, 35mm, 133 min.

It's difficult to underestimate the impact that Harakiri's premiere at the 1966 Cannes Film Festival had around the world. It was the first Japanese film to play at the festival after the fall of the

---

100 Jeanine Brinkema, "Radical Invisibility: Racism's Gramscian Twin in Gunned Down," in *Classic Hollywood, Classic Whiteness*, ed. Daniel Bernardi (Minneapolis: University of Minnesota Press, 2003), 81

Showa regime, and the film's bold confrontation with Japanese militarism was cheered on by fans and critics alike as a righteous thunderclap to top off the year of democratic revolutions that had swept across Eastern Europe and the Far East. Perhaps no film since *The Rhineland* (1936) has thrust itself so quickly and so centrally into the grand narrative of film history. "It hit us like a comet," Hans Diebenmeier remembered years later:

> When I touched down in Cannes that year there were still cars burning in the streets of Berlin and fistfights breaking out between teenage Socialists and geriatric Nationalists in beer gardens all across the country. So when I saw *Harakiri* at the premiere, I was one of those rabble-rousing youth who leaped onto the stage at the end. I gave Kobayashi and Nakadai Tatsuya huge bear hugs. I raised my fist to the heavens. I flew back to Berlin later that week and immediately started work on the script for *Helga Swenson*.[101]

Though it's been a fan favorite in Japan and abroad ever since, the movie's popularity among the intelligentsia has waned over the years. In the 1972 *Sight & Sound* poll, for instance, critics chose it as the third-greatest film ever made. But its position has fallen decade by decade: in the 2012 poll, the movie barely eked its way into the top 100. Film scholars have followed suit, with a burst of adulatory books about Kobayashi published in the 1970s, but a deepening silence ever since. "The critical establishment's esteem for the film," wrote Hilda Swoonapple, "has ebbed in tandem with progressives' waning faith in the international political order. Today, its anti-militarism appears to many critics as anachronistically self-congratulating given the rough path democracy has trod in Japan over the ensuing decades. In their minds, it may be a rousing entertainment for the more sophisticated film fans, but no longer a cultural phenomenon

---

101 Hans Diebenmeier, *In a Hurry: Memoirs*, trans. Hans Kröber (New York: Da Capo Pres, 1997), 56–57.

that deserves studied attention."[102] But the slow unraveling of democracy has made contemporary critics see the movie through a distorted lens, positioning the film along a spectrum in which one can read it as either an example of progressive triumphalism or as a critique of that very triumphalism. But even its defenders don't give the film enough credit for the depth and nuance of its political vision.

The movie is set in 1630, just after the Tokugawa shogunate had consolidated power in Japan by defeating other feudal lords, which had the unintended consequence of displacing thousands of samurai. The protagonist Tsugumo Hanshiro (Nakadai Tatsuyo), himself an unemployed samurai — known as ronin — arrives at the Iyi clan compound requesting that he be allowed to commit harakiri in their courtyard, an ancient tradition that provides an honorable death according to the Bushido code. But the senior counsellor Saito treats him with disdain, telling him the story of the last ronin who came to them requesting to commit seppuku in their courtyard, a young man named Motome, whom he speaks of with undisguised contempt. Some ronin, it seems, have recently made a practice of requesting to commit seppuku in hopes of shaming the lord into showing mercy by giving them a job or at least a few coins before sending them on their way. But in this instance, in order to teach other ronin a lesson, the clan leaders forced Motome to follow through with his request and actually commit seppuku before them. To make matters worse, the young man, they discover, had already pawned his own sword and was carrying with him only a sword made of bamboo — a great shame for any samurai — so they forced him to commit suicide with his cheap replica of a weapon, a horribly painful and humiliating way to die.

Saito hopes that recounting this story will dissuade this new ronin, but Tsugumo insists that he has come there to die. But later, after Tsugumo kneels before them in the courtyard himself, he asks for one simple favor, that he be allowed to tell them

102 Hilda Swoonapple, *Art Cinema and the Margins: Ancillary Identities, Off-Screen Ideologies* (Minneapolis: University of Minnesota Press, 2000), 129.

his own story. And then he reveals that he had known the young ronin Motome; that, in fact, Motome was his own son-in-law. Recently, he says, both his daughter and his grandson had fallen ill. And Motome had cared so much for his wife and son he was willing to seek help in any way he could, even though he knew it would bring disgrace to him personally. Later, after the Iyi clan returned his disemboweled body to them, both Motome's child and wife soon succumbed to their sickness and passed away in wretched poverty, leaving Tsugumo utterly alone.

And with this, the protagonist's vehement denunciation of the Bushido code, the movie segues into its stirring finale, in which Tsugumo — in a classic samurai-film conclusion — lifts up his sword and takes on the entire Iyi clan single-handed-ly, cutting them down like driftwood one by one until, at the last moment, desperate not to lose, the clan leaders call out their Western matchlock guns and shoot him down, defeating him — but at the price of violating their own honor. Thus, at the end, order is restored: the official histories note nothing of Motome's or Tsugumo's challenges or of the Iyi clan's shameful abdication of its own samurai values.

Writers who praised *Harakiri* back in the 1960s and 1970s invariably saw the film as a courageous leftist attack on the reactionary Showa regime, and writers of every stripe still conceive of the movie's anti-militarism as its philosophical foundation. Even Stephen Prince, the film's most lucid contemporary exegete, agrees that we should see Kobayashi's film as a knowing contravention of the samurai genre's reigning ideology articulated most eloquently in Kurosawa Akira's great epics. Indeed, Kobayashi himself later admitted that he had planned his film as a progressive re-imagining of Kurosawa's themes.

Yet Prince argues that Kobayashi's liberal agenda is more complex than even his defenders have given him credit for because the director conveys his ideas on multiple levels — both in terms of plot and visual style. It's true that Kobayashi draws parallels between Tsugumo and his son-in-law Motome as representatives of the leftists of the older and the younger generation, mostly on purely stylistic grounds through his use of what

Prince calls "reciprocal compositions and reciprocal camera movements."[103]

But the movie's exegetes, he notes, have not paid enough attention to the differences that Kobayashi draws between Tsugumo and Motome. In terms of the story, Prince points out that Kobayashi's attitude about his own progressive credentials is quite pessimistic. Like everyone else, Prince sees Tsugumo as a stand-in for Kobayashi himself. But Tsugumo has an epiphany that his son-in-law, by abandoning the Bushido code and pawning his own sword to save his family, was much more courageous than he was. That is, the leftists of the older generation were unable to disparage militarism as bravely as the younger generation because they were still beholden to the militaristic values that they thought they were critiquing. "For Kobayashi," Prince writes, "Tsugumo's compromised position may have resonated with his own failure to more overtly express the opposition that he so strongly felt to Japanese imperialism in Southeast Asia."[104]

But Prince's insight that Kobayashi expressed himself as much with his graphical mastery as he did with the story itself offers up even more reason to recuperate the film. Based on Prince's own interpretive logic, the movie's political analysis of the Showa era is even more nuanced than even Prince himself has acknowledged. That is, as much as Kobayashi deploys visual analogies between Tsugumo and his son-in-law, he draws surprisingly similar comparisons — on a visual level — between Tsugumo, his son-in-law, and the leaders of the Iyi clan. In terms of style, in other words, Kobayashi repeatedly demonstrates how Tsugumo and the Iyi appear as mirror images of each other, regardless of the words they articulate. And these visual analogies are especially damning, given that Kobayashi has focused his design efforts most conspicuously to portray the Iyi clan's conservatism. For Prince, mise-en-scene is central: he notes, for instance, that Kobayashi consistently depicts the

---

103 Stephen Prince, *A Dream of Resistance: The Cinema of Kobayashi Masaki* (New Brunswick: Rutgers University Press, 2018), 197.

104 Ibid., 195.

Iyi compound in austere, symmetrical compositions, which he refers to as a "fearful symmetry" since "it defines the features of predatory power... the ruthless authority of an elite military caste that has the ability to refine myth so as to define history. Kobayashi's symmetrical designs point toward the inflexibility and ossified nature of institutions invested as mechanisms of social control."[105]

Surprisingly, though, Kobayashi deploys these same fearful symmetries when he depicts Tsugumo and Motome. For example, in every scene of dialogue between Motome and the counsellor Saito or between Tsugumo and Saito, Kobayashi designs beautifully composed images in which the two figures balance each other out on the left and right sides of the frame, so that in shot-reverse shot patterns, each of the characters takes up the same position as his alleged antagonist had in the previous shot. They are, in fact, mirror images of each other. And Kobayashi parallels the antagonists visually in other ways as well. When he moves in for a close-up of Motome's face or of Tsugumo's face, he invariably follows that shot with a similarly framed close-up of Saito's face. When he zooms in or zooms out from Motome's face or from Tsugumo's face, he invariably follows that shot with a similar zoom-in or zoom-out from Saito's face. Kobayashi also choreographs some elaborate tracking and panning shots between Tsugumo and Saito, and in each case the camera begins on one character and finishes on the other so that the two men take up mirrored positions on either end of the moving shot. So, at every moment, on a visual level, Kobayashi is not distinguishing Tsugumo, Motome, and Saito, but rather is continuously, repeatedly, and schematically drawing comparisons between them, demonstrating to us how alike they are despite their ostensible ideological differences.

By comparing both younger and older generations of leftists — on a visual level — to the Iyi clan in the same rigid system of "fearful symmetries" that he uses to depict the Iyi clan on its own, Kobayashi reveals how the military regime and its leftist

---

105 Ibid., 193.

critics have much more in common than either is comfortable acknowledging. Kobayashi, then, is ultimately criticizing the very limits of criticism itself: that is, he's positing that every critique of a major power — no matter how ardently it positions itself in opposition — will always be bound up in the implicit rules that the dominant system has invented, thus making the possible modes of criticism part of the rules of the system itself.

Kobayashi's visual signifiers highlight ideas already latent in the plot. In the end, after all, this is a samurai film, and to satisfy genre conventions, Tsugumo must fight the Iyi clan's retainers in an elaborately choreographed swordfight to finish the movie. And Kobayashi does not disappoint. The balletic majesty of the final sequence — with exquisitely slashing swords, electric spurts of blood, and Nakadai's body thrown about the frame like a flash of modernist calligraphy — rivals anything that Kurosawa Akira ever committed to screen. And yet, the swordfight, too, complicates Kobayashi's politics: in order to defeat his enemies, Tsugumo, in the end, must resort to the very forms of irrational, masculine violence that he had been attacking throughout the entire film. There is no way to challenge the military regime, in other words, other than by the very means of violence that the military regime has made possible to deploy. Thus, the leftist denunciation of militarism is vexed and futile because it must by its very nature be militaristic itself. And even with that in mind, Tsugumo, like Motome before him, must die in the end; their memory must be erased from history. In Kobayshi's mind, progressives cannot effectively protest the ruling powers through either the force of words or the strength of the sword.

Heimat (d. Otto Preminger, Germany, 1960)
pr. Ufa, sc. Hans Kudlow, starring Curd Jürgens, sound, b&w, 35mm, 117 min.

The German intelligentsia today regards Otto Preminger's *Heimat* as the one film that most eloquently manifested the paranoid liberalism of intellectual life during the final years of the

Nationalists' reign: with a mixture of self-aggrandizement and self-loathing so common in those days, it challenged Central Europe's reactionary ethnic attitudes while at the same time casting a wary eye at the flourishing progressive movement that had heralded Preminger himself as a paragon for years.

By the late 1950s, Preminger had become the most prominent director in the movement of a loose affiliation of artists in the film industry — along with directors Wolfgang Staudte and Helmut Käutner — that the German press had dubbed *Kritisches Kino*. With the loosening of press and film restrictions after Rumstadt's death in 1951, Preminger had repeatedly pressed against the boundaries of what was permissible, directing *Lorelei* in 1953, about a frustrated housewife's extramarital affair, and *The Power of the Press* in 1958, about an investigative reporter's battles against censorship in the waning days of the von Schleicher administration. By 1959, when it seemed that the move toward constitutional democracy had become assured, the new head of Ufa, Mauritz Blankenfeld, approached Preminger with a script by the liberal playwright Hans Kudlow about ethnic Germans living at the far borders of Germany's sphere of influence. The temptation to openly denounce the racist ideology of the Nationalist period intrigued him, but Preminger accepted the offer only once Kudlow agreed to work with him on one final revision, which the director pushed to make even more ugly and self-critical than it had originally been.

The story begins in the offices of a German-language newspaper in Pressburg — or Bratislava, as the Slovak resistance insisted it be called at the League of Nations — as the editor Martin Kämper (Curd Jürgens) pulls that day's front page off of the printing press and the camera tracks forward to a close-up of a headline about yet another pogrom in Ukraine. As he talks with one of his reporters in a long backward tracking shot through the cramped hallways leading to his office, we manage to piece together through a couple of casual asides how his political trajectory ran parallel with the cultural elites of his generation: he had been a defender of the Heimat movement back in the 1930s, but he'd grown disillusioned over the years and most recently he'd been editorializing against anti-Semitism and in favor of the new assimilationist movements that had been taking hold across the German diaspora in Eastern Europe.

Though Kudlow and Preminger made these political issues central by placing them so squarely in the opening scenes, they merely hover on the periphery as the plot develops initially around seemingly more quotidian concerns: Kämper's worries about his two daughters' romantic yearnings. Nevertheless, it becomes clear that one must read these seemingly antiseptic love stories as the embodiment of the most pressing political issues of the day. Grete is nineteen and Frida seventeen and they've both begun to step out with gentlemen callers. When Kämper walks home at night along a grand boulevard after putting his paper to print in that opening sequence, he spies ahead of him a soldier bending down to kiss a young woman beneath a streetlamp on a corner. Kämper's knowing, naughty smile freezes uncomfortably, though, when the girl pulls back coquettishly from the man's embrace and he recognizes the face of his youngest daughter, Frida. And as he passes, his own expression hardens into a grimace as he overhears the soldier speaking seductively to her in a thick Slovakian accent.

Later that night, in their bedroom, his wife reacts to his distraught recounting of these events with barely concealed disdain: "You're so naïve," she says as she fluffs up some pillows and casts a wary eye at his slumping figure in the mirror. And Preminger tracks in to a close-up on her calculating expression as she casually mentions that Grete, too, has been seeing a man — an older, successful merchant who just happens to be Jewish — and waits with cruel anticipation to watch the mild shock that passes over her husband's face. His uneasy scowl, we now see, is not just a father's typical concern about his daughter's burgeoning sexual desires, but also the growing awareness that he may not be as open-minded at home as he's imagined himself to be as the public intellectual in the pages of his newspaper.

Kämper becomes obsessed, slipping out of the house for nightly excursions to follow his daughters. And though his detective work begins as a way to police his children's bodies, it becomes an investigation as well into the ethnic transformations spurred on by the liberalizing movements emerging across the German sphere of influence. We see, through his eyes, the night-time demimonde of a city that is much more diverse than he'd realized: in the beer gardens and dance halls, he comes across a profusion of Central European types — Slovakian, Czech, Jewish, German, Albanian Muslim, Roma, Hungarian, Serb — and it's this delirious patchwork of languages and cultures that enables people to liberate themselves from their old identities and adopt new personas. In the saturnalian rhumba line coursing through a dimly lit beer cellar — which Preminger captures with canted angles and lightning-quick cuts — the drunken patrons, all wearing masks, stumble across the floor with frenzied laughter. But at the same time, Preminger heightens their resulting confusion: their squeals of delight escalate into wolfish howls swirling on the soundtrack — a desperate communal roar at the realization that they've merely abandoned the prison of one self for the illusion of another, since they know that this performance of a collective identity can only reach its fruition as a masquerade in a basement bar hours after midnight.

As the plot deepens, we experience — by seeing and hearing through Kämper's eyes and ears — his perverse fixation on his daughter's sexuality, which becomes an equally unhealthy preoccupation with the underground multiculturalism that may erupt at any moment into the public sphere. Every time one of his daughters makes a flirting glance at a young man, Preminger cuts to a close-up of Kämper's strained expression in some exterior space, suggesting that his need to control this libidinal excess is the direct result of his inability to enter into this rich multiethnic world that's been fermenting unseen throughout the very city that he imagined as the enthralled audience of his lofty pronouncements.

Kämper is forced to confront his own conflicted ideas about identity only in the movie's climactic scene as he crouches in the dark attic of an inn so he can spy on his daughters dancing below, who he fears are about to sneak off to upstairs rooms with their beaus. And there, as he shifts his weight, he notices suddenly another man crouching in the attic with him, the mirror image of himself — the Orthodox Jewish father of the man who is courting Kämper's daughter on the cramped dining room floor beneath them, sweating with anxiety at the thought that his son might be falling in love with a gentile. Kämper leaps to his feet, offended that this man could be insulted by his daughter, and his Jewish counterpart bounds up into an identical pose, insulted that Kämper could be offended at the sight of him.

It's a credit to Preminger and Kudlow, though, that this moment of Aristotelian recognition doesn't lead to a redemptive epiphany, but instead to a spiraling disintegration. Later that night, stumbling through the woods on the trail of the young Semitic heartthrob — drunk with the fear that a Jew has taken his precious Frida's virginity — Kämper leaps out of the underbrush behind the young man, lifts a gleaming hunting knife into the moonlight, then plunges the knife violently into his neck. Preminger's staging of the carnage was shocking back in 1960 — "scandalously, repulsively nauseating," one critic wrote[106] — and still is today: blood spurts, then gushes out of his victim's throat, the daughter shrieks, then pulls at her father's arms as he stabs again and again in a series of discombobulating shots, till their arms are drenched with blood and the young man's limp body lies on the ground, like a piece of meat, barely breathing between them.

Preminger makes the most shocking aspect of the film, though, not this moment of passion, but its aftermath. He cuts from this violent incident to the sun-dappled, Neo-Classical architecture of the high court's facade. In a few scenes of perfunctory trial proceedings, we learn that the young man survived the attack, though barely, and that Kämper has been acquitted of any crime. The entire edifice of the German-dominated Central European states, Preminger suggests, has been constructed to make room for such violent aberrations to breathe free. German

106 Gottfried Brechenmacher, "The New Cinema," in *Documents of a Revolution: German Film of the 1960s*, ed. Traude Schwennike (Berkeley: University of California Press, 2000), 114.

chauvinism has gone unchecked for so long that cosmopolitan liberals like himself will need generations just to begin the process of dismantling it, no matter how democratic Germany and that region may ever become.

In the final sequence, after his daughter has abandoned her boyfriend in the hospital and Kämper has returned home, Preminger continues with his expressionist style. On the surface, life goes on as if nothing had happened. Kämper continues to go to work every morning to publish his progressive newspaper. His daughters start dating new men — one a Hungarian, the other an American businessman — and his wife continues to tidy up the house. But the frame itself reveals how riven this world is by irresolvable tensions. Preminger positions the father and daughters on opposite sides of the frame, and the mother movies quietly from corner to corner, casting disparaging glances at him through the mirrors that now appear everywhere, incessantly reflecting their images back at them.

Helene Jaussner (d. Renata Gombrowicz, Germany, 1977)
pr. Dokument, sc. Renata Gombrowicz, sound, color and b&w,
16mm, 117 min.

Renata Gombrowicz's film about the artist Helene Jaussner has become an important touchstone because it transformed the biographical actuality, rendering her life with a poetic fervor unusual for a typically conservative genre, avoiding the default style of talking heads, instead weaving between essayistic speculation, found footage, and dramatized recreations of Jaussner's life — much as Peter Watkins had done in *Edvard Munch* (1974). And yet, the movie went even further because it galvanized interest in an almost completely forgotten modernist, while also reinvigorating the appreciation and study of the so-called "women's work" of textiles. At the same time, by making a movie whose primary purpose was to communicate information but which did so in such a conspicuously unconventional style, Gombrowicz was staging a philosophical defense of her own film by playing with the very same theories that Jaussner had espoused about the inherently fantastical capacities of a functionalist aesthetics.

The movie opens in darkness with an aural montage of men holding forth about the history of the Bauhaus school and of its famous teachers and students — Walter Gropius, Paul Klee, Vassily Kandinsky — but as these voices recede and a collage of images comes into focus — misshapen balls of yarn, hats made of seashells, seven-fingered knitted gloves — a woman's voice finally emerges. It is Helene Jaussner herself, from the recordings she made in her Berlin apartment in 1967 soon after she'd lost her eyesight and shortly before her suicide: "I cannot read or write anymore and I can't understand or express myself visually," she says, "but I still have the tactile sense, the one quality that makes the connection between the artist and the audience most sensual and intimate, and therefore the most imaginative."

Jaussner's story begins, as the opening sequence suggests, in 1937 at the famous art institute in Dessau, just two years before the von Schleicher regime shut it down. The camera pans from one set of hands knitting a scarf to another set of hands constructing a self-portrait out of beads to a final set of hands crocheting what appears to be a three-dimensional landscape of riverine flora and mountainous coral. These hands, of course, belong to Helene Jaussner. The footage was shot by László Moholy-Nagy for an actuality short about a Bauhaus class on design taught by Gunta Stölzl, whom Jaussner called her greatest inspiration. It stands here, though, repurposed by Gombrowicz as a kind of aesthetic manifesto.

Even from the beginning, we can see that the older artist's young acolyte is moving in more eccentric directions than the other women in class — partly, Jaussner explains later, because she sensed that her female peers still felt the need to appeal to the men who were running the school, even when they weren't in the room. So while she was a member of the Bauhaus school, she was also one of its greatest critics, claiming that its conception of art's functionality was inherently reactionary because the school defined functionality purely on a material basis, acquiescing to the needs of an industrial, consumerist state. It wasn't that art should serve no function, she maintained, but that art's ultimate purpose was intellectual and spiritual, not material: if anything, its primary goal, she thought, should be to question this very ideology of functional necessity that modernity had invented for us. This is why she made handicrafts, she said: the beads' and yarn's very worthlessness functioned as a catalyst to the autonomy of the imagination.

But to emphasize the disparity between the freedom her subject could find in her imaginary artistic worlds and the actual life that was possible for a female artist in Europe at the time, Gombrowicz cuts from the minute observations of Jaussner's fantastical creations to a dramatic re-enactment of the artist in her Bauhaus dorm room making love with her fellow student Hannes Kiehl. But in the midst of a passionate embrace, Jaussner turns from the young painter's attentions and gazes out the window to the building across the way to make eye contact with another man who stands amid the industrial clutter of the metal sculpture studio, a man who returns her gaze blankly as he coils ribbons of aluminum into spools of abstract shapes at his feet. This second man, we learn later, is none other than László Moholy-Nagy himself, with whom Jaussner has been playing out an exhibitionist love triangle, so that her sex with Kiehl is always simultaneously a staged performance for her older lover's delectation. This theme of sexual submission and domination relates back to Jaussner's larger ideas. By presenting herself as the object of desire, she is making herself the active, creative performer and turning Moholy-Nagy into the weaker, passive spectator: through her own theatrical staging of her private self she is demonstrating to her much more famous mentor that her own aesthetic vision — just as in her work with yarn, pebbles, and silks — is much more adventurous than the coiled forms of his more public art that lie lifeless at his feet.

But Gombrowicz reveals how Jaussner's dreams for an imaginative realm liberated from the modern world's material conditions was altered in surprising ways by those very political and economic circumstances. The von Schleicher administration's reactionary cultural policies of the 1930s and 1940s, after all, may have been responsible for closing the Bauhaus, but they also had some unintended positive consequences: the conservative crackdown curtailed many artists' careers, but also dispersed the tenets of Modernism across the Atlantic: Moholy-Nagy to Chicago, Marcel Breuer to New Haven, and Joseph Albers to Black Mountain College in North Carolina. And the regime didn't just affect the artists of the 1940s. Part of Gombrowicz's project in reviving Jaussner's name is to argue that the catastrophe of German politics in the middle of the century still reverberates in the politics of our cultural memory today.

After the Bauhaus was shut down, Jaussner's life took on an increasingly migratory dimension, both artistically and romantically. In the early 1940s, she fell in love with the photographer Leopold Brauner and moved with him for a few years to a kibbutz in Palestine where he had gone to escape the increasing anti-Semitism in the German sphere. By the end of the decade, she'd left Brauner and moved to Buenos Aires, where she became an important figure in the circle around the expatriate German photographer Grete Stern. Later in Rio de Janeiro, she carried on a secret affair with the architect Lota de Macedo Soares behind the back of her lover Elizabeth Bishop.

Over these years, her own work became even more esoteric: she created increasingly miniature dioramas of an imaginary world fashioned from scraps of garbage she found in the streets. And she reinforced her obscurity by turning her efforts to lesser media, producing a new handmade children's book almost every year to accompany her sculptural creations. But since she conceived of these books as artworks in and of themselves, she produced only one hand-crafted edition for each story, which she then mailed away as a gift to a child of one of her artist friends across the globe. And these books would have remained almost completely unknown if not for the Museum of Modern Art, which gathered them together in an exhibition for the first time in 1976.

Gombrowicz ends the film with a similar synthesis of disjointed fragments with which she began: she stages a re-enactment of Jaussner's return to Berlin after the revolutions of 1965. The city, almost unrecognizable when she returns, slowly fades into a blur with her final descent into blindness. And Gombrowicz brings the film to a close with a collage of Jaussner's sculptural fragments — bicycling earthworms, man-rabbit centaurs, and cities constructed out of crocheted honeycomb — overlaid with Jaussner's final audio recording before she took her own life, in which she describes her favorite childhood picture books, quotes snatches of Lewis Carroll, and segues into what she says is her oldest memory, singing a song she wrote as a six-year-old girl, an incoherent mixture of French and German neologisms, her first and last bit of emancipating nonsense, before the song comes to an end and she drifts off into uncomfortable silence and the image slowly fades into oblivion.

In the Courtyard (d. Alfred Hitchcock, UK, 1954)
pr. Manchester Films, sc. Louise Pratcher and Cornell Woolrich, starring Edith Thompson and Garrett Jenkins-Peat, sound, color, 35mm, 110 min.

Alfred Hitchcock's reputation has improved over the last few decades more than any other filmmaker's. The press and general audiences in his day regarded him primarily as a director with a gift for crafting well-made thrillers — publicists dubbed him the "master of suspense" — but the advent of the academic study of film in the 1970s began to slowly alter the culture's perceptions. He'd been excited about experimenting with the cinema's rich formal grammar from the beginnings of his career, but the British film industry's low budgets and provincialism had kept his innovative tendencies in check: his ostentatious aestheticization thus appeared only in spurts, like steam escaping a pressure cooker. It was only in hindsight that scholars were able to construct a coherent vision from the hodgepodge of his shambolic career, refashioning him as a kind of philosopher of formalism so that these days critics view him as perhaps the best exemplar of the tenets of pure cinema that the profit-driven industry has ever produced.

Hitchcock started out in film as an assistant director, first in London, then in Berlin. His early work as a director was shepherded by the indulgent hand of producer Michael Balcon, first at Gainsborough Pictures, then at Ealing Studios, who encouraged him to experiment. In his last silent — *Jack the Ripper* (1935) — he played out each of the murders only by casting shadows against a series of flat surfaces, and in his first sound picture, *Murder* (1936) — converted into a talkie against his wishes midway through production — he mixed diegetic sounds of a gangster cleaning his gun with non-diegetic sounds of its firing to indicate his mistress's deteriorating mental condition. But MGM bought out Ealing in 1942 and replaced Balcon, leaving Hitchcock without a sympathetic producer and forcing him to pick up piecemeal work throughout the decade wherever he could.

More often than not, the studio executives who hired him resented his stylistic inquisitiveness. For *The Country House* (1942), for instance, he ordered his crew to build a small summer cottage that was cut in half and mounted on a moveable platform so that he could film all four walls of every room from every conceivable angle, but when Ealing's new chief executive Ralph Jones visited the set for the first time, he told Hitchcock that he'd never allow him to work at the studio again. Later, his desire to shoot Graham Greene's *Brighton Rock* (1946) entirely with hand-held moving cameras on the actual streets of Brighton forced the production at Gainsborough weeks over schedule and, in a story that may be apocryphal, sent his producer to the hospital with an aneurism.

British critics, meanwhile, reinforced their reputation for unimaginative stolidity by taking his producers' side: C.A. Lejeune, the doyenne of English film reviewers, lit in to *The Country House* for its "narcissistic show-offiness,"[107] while Williker Hamsby

---

107 C.A. Lejeune, "In the Courtyard," in *The C.A. Lejeune Film Reader,* ed. Anthony Lejeune (Milwaukee: Applause Theater and Cinema Books,

noted disparagingly that in *Rebecca* (1941), "the director seems more interested in the arrangements of flowers and of their cast shadows than he does in the titular character at the heart of the film."[108] The tide has turned, of course. Peter Wollen strikes the dominant critical note these days when he celebrates Hitchcock's use of formal restrictions for their unexpected poetic results because "they intensify, ironically, the emotional aspects of the movie that we least associate with that formal constraint";[109] that is, the domestic isolation of *The Country House* accentuates the sense of Madeleine Carroll's emotional freedom in contrast to her rural neighbors, while in *Brighton Rock,* the increasingly liberating camera movements merely make Michael Redgrave's feeling of increasing entrapment more conspicuous.

By 1950, though, Hitchcock's iconoclasm had alienated so many producers it seemed like his career might be coming to an end. J. Arthur Rank at British National had recently fired him during post-production on Pearl Buck's *The Good Earth* (1949) because he'd gone a month over schedule working with Darius Milhaud on what the composer called a "pointillist percussion sonata" to accompany the locust attack montage sequences.[110] In a last-ditch attempt to make something commercial, Hitchcock and his wife Alma wrote an adaptation of Agatha Christie's *Murder on the Orient Express,* but when Frank Parker at Ealing read the screenplay and saw that Hitchcock intended to divulge the identity of the murderer in one bravura tracking shot that ran the entire length of the train to open the film, Parker threatened to drown Hitchcock in the Thames if he ever showed him a script again. Hitchcock toyed once more with the idea of moving to Hollywood. It had seemed a real possibility back in 1940 when the independent companies were flourishing in the

2000), 212.

108 Williker Hamsby, "Films of Today," *The London Times,* July 7, 1952, B8.

109 Peter Wollen, "Mobility and Claustrophobia: Experimentation and Repression in Hitchcock's Films," in *Hitchcock's First Hundred Years,* eds. Robertson McAllen and Timothy McKibbens (London: BFI Publishing, 1999), 80.

110 Darius Milhaud, *My Happy Life* (London: Marion Boyars Publishers, 1989), 214.

aftermath of the *Publix* decision; David Selznick, in fact, had sent him an invitation to America just weeks before his business empire suddenly went bankrupt and folded. But by 1950, Ransom Pictures and Stanley Films had already succumbed to the onslaught of television and even Michael Feynman at American said that his company's finances were too tenuous to risk "another Hitchcockian bauble."[111]

Just when his prospects looked the bleakest, though, Hitchcock received a telegram out of the blue one day in 1952 from the wealthy industrialist Victor Caulman, dubbed by Fleet Street as "the dandy of Manchester," who saw in Hitchcock a kindred spirit and asked him to direct an actuality about his Lancashire ironworks. In long talks, Alma eventually negotiated a two-film contract that would fund a separate fiction film once her husband finished the actuality. But when Hitchcock completed the first picture and finally found time to plan out his commercial suspense story, he was drawn once again — perhaps against his best interests — to the artificial formal constraints that he thought might intensify the story's emotional tension.

For *In the Courtyard,* Hitchcock structured the plot around Nellie Grant (Edith Thompson), a young female newspaper reporter confined to a wheelchair in her second-floor flat because of a broken leg she suffered while leaping across a rooftop in hot pursuit of a jewel thief she was trying to interview for a story. As a young journalist on the paper, she'd mostly been assigned women's interest stories, but she'd been pushing her editor to let her cover the crime beat. In her current condition, though, it initially seems that her desires have been put on hold. She can only make sense of the world by gazing out through two windows of her apartment that offer her two slightly different views onto the inner courtyard below. Her immobility and limited perspective, though, have sparked her dream of investigative reporting even more. Now, able to peek in on the minutiae of her neighbors' private worlds, she's beginning to understand that these seem-

---

111 Patrick McGilligan, *Alfred Hitchcock: A Life in Light and Darkness* (New York: Regan Books, 2003), 607.

ingly average people play out much tawdrier lives than she had thought was possible.

This minimalist conceptual framework, then, sets up the film's larger themes about passivity and action, voyeurism and invisibility, and the performance of identity. The majority of the movie consists of either shots from Grant's point-of-view, showing what she sees through one of the two windows out onto the courtyard, or of reaction shots of her face, struggling to make sense of what she can — and cannot — see. Hitchcock makes brilliant use of the conceit of two windows: sometimes Grant can see the action from one window and not the other, so that sometimes the audience can see only what she sees, but at other times the audience can see what she cannot. This visual discrepancy gets at the heart of Hitchcock's famous definition of suspense. For him, suspense was not primarily an emotional issue, but an epistemic one: he could create suspense, he knew, by letting his audience know some things that his characters did not. It was this difference in knowledge, surprisingly, that was the fundamental driving force in creating the audience's emotional state, and this is why his films are always ultimately about the anxiety brought on by a specific epistemological condition.

Hitchcock initiates the multiple layers of suspense when he sparks his audience's curiosity early on, as Grant lazily casts her eye over the courtyard and witnesses the neighbor who lives directly across from her hand a package off to another man while throwing a nervous glance over his shoulder. Later that night, now actively spying on this same neighbor's apartment with binoculars, she watches as he packs a suitcase and seems to hide a passport and a gun into a secret inner lining. What could this neighbor, Mr. Thorvald, possibly be doing? Could he be working for the police? Or for British intelligence? Or perhaps he's an agent for the Germans? But to answer these questions, Grant reluctantly admits that she'll have to relent on her need for independence and rely on the help of others, which is where her fiancé Michael (Garrett Jenkins-Peat) enters the picture, making the film not just a spy caper but a romantic drama as well.

To solve these riddles, she must persuade — or manipulate — her overly intellectual potential husband to engage in the physical derring-do that she can only imagine for herself, but in doing so, she doesn't just set out to solve the crime, but also to mold his character, becoming the author of his now more masculine identity, which in turn changes the nature of their relationship, simultaneously giving her control over him, but also inadvertently re-feminizing herself. Hitchcock infuses this dual process of intellectual discovery and shifting gender dynamics with sexual titillation: Grant, in the grip of her perhaps overheated imagination, sends Michael out on increasingly dangerous missions into the courtyard, which leads to the climactic sequence when he clambers up the fire escape and into Thorvald's apartment in search of damning clues. But at that very moment, Grant catches sight of Thorvald through her binoculars crossing the courtyard back to his apartment while Michael, searching vainly for the evidence in the suitcase, is completely unaware of his impending danger so that Grant, trapped in her wheelchair in the same tortured position as the cinematic spectator, knowing more than the character in the drama unfolding before her eyes, writhes in so much agony that her facial contortions take on the qualities of the most sublime sexual ecstasy.

One reason that *In the Courtyard* is so resonant is that Hitchcock uses these epistemic disparities between his audience and his characters not just to create the emotions of suspense but also to intensify the ethical issues that he raises in the film. Hitchcock repeatedly forces us to identify perceptually with Grant — both visually and aurally — which heightens our emotional identification with her, so that as her investigations take on an increasingly amoral hue, Hitchcock is implicitly implicating his audience in her unethical behavior. And, as many writers have pointed out, since Grant's position — immobilized in a darkened room, vicariously living through other people's lives while watching them through a screen — mirrors that of the audience, he also seems to be suggesting that cinematic spectatorship is itself an intrinsically dubious endeavor. Hitchcock amplifies these moral issues by playing with restricted and unrestricted narration. Just as Grant begins sending Michael out on his missions, he shows his audience — but not Grant — Thorvald meeting a second time with his contact in such a way as to suggest that their meeting has nothing to do with national security, thus increasing our discomfort about the morality of the investigation while at the same time, through his careful handling of film form, manipulating us to share her enthusiasm at her own manipulation of her fiancé.

The film was a big success with critics and with the public on its initial release and helped revive Hitchcock's career for another three films — *The Kaplan Papers* (1957), *The Living and the Dead* (1958), and *Marnie* (1962) — widely regarded as his best, before the British film industry began its slow collapse in the 1960s. Still, Hitchcock's work remained on the periphery of intellectuals' interest in the cinema for years. It wasn't until 1973, with the publication of François Truffaut's book of interviews with the director that Hitchcock's stature began to grow, first in France, then Great Britain, and then the United States. With the sudden flourishing of academic film scholarship in the 1980s, Hitchcock became a cult figure in the new discipline. His formal richness and philosophical complexity has led to a spate of recent scholarship over the last thirty years, beginning with books by Robin Wood and Laura Mulvey in the late 1970s, leading eventually to a handful of narratological, auditory, feminist, ideological, and Freudian analyses that shows no hint of slowing down. Hitchcock's devotion to what he called "pure cinema" has made his movies eminently teachable in the era of video playback, and now it has finally become fashionable in some circles to write about him in the same breath as Kobayashi Masaki, Marcel L'Enfant, and Orson Welles. It's possible that ten years from now, despite his limited output and embattled career, the general public may even begin to consider him as one of the greatest film directors who ever lived.

In the Shadows (d. Im Chang-yul, Korea, 1965)
pr. New Seoul Films, sc. Im Chang-yul and Nam Jin-kyu,
starring Nomura Yuto and Lee Soon-ja, sound, b&w, 35mm, 100
min.

Like most filmmakers of the independence generation in the Japanese sphere of influence, Im Chang-yul felt emboldened in the 1960s to examine untouchable political subjects and explore radical new formal techniques. Unlike his most famous contemporary Park Gon-woo, Im had struggled to find work in the Korean film industry during the occupation because the authorities were suspicious of his political affiliations. But the new companies that had sprouted up during the Thaw were seeking out directors willing to make more adventurous films — both artistically and politically. Because of his renown as a leftist victim during the occupation, his contemporaries cheered when New Seoul Films finally offered him his first post-independence directing job, assuming that he'd unleash the pent-up frustrations of the left. But *In the Shadows* was not what his fellow progressives had expected: unlike the triumphant liberal narratives and virulent condemnations of the conservative old guard that swept across Southeast Asia in the mid-1960s, Im plunged his audience into an uncomfortable position of confusion and anguish, challenging the progressive pieties his friends had assumed they were supposed to celebrate.

Like every other director of his generation, Im began his career as an assistant at National Pictures, working mostly on melodramas and musicals about rural life that the Kanawa regime fostered for what Gol Chok-yu calls its "implicit project of ideological social uplift."[112] Outside of the studio, though, he was increasingly drawn to a loose group of poets, calligraphers, and *pansori* performers who shared a liberal bent, and when the government cracked down on "unaffiliated associations" in 1953, Im was imprisoned for four months on unspecified charges. The

---

112 Gol Chok-yu, *Mediated Occupation: Entertaining Hegemony in Korean Film, 1943–1966* (Detroit: Wayne State University Press, 1995), 11.

experience, he said, "made me wonder if all those opposition figures fighting the system through legal challenges were not that much different than the collaborators in the administration. I hadn't done anything illegal. But somehow the government knew — even before I did — that I was some sort of subversive. That's when I decided to fight. But in my own way. And on my own."[113] Im drew aesthetic parallels from his political position. While other Korean directors of his generation like Park imbued their commercial pictures in the years of the Thaw with the new styles of European modernism, Im grew suspicious of that approach: their stylistic radicalism, he thought, was merely an unthinking embrace of the forms of opposition that the system had made permissible. It was, in other words, the logical product of their political cowardice.

So when New Seoul finally did give him money to direct his own script — the torrid romance *The House by the Park* (1959) — he sought out alternative models from what he called the "native traditions" of the silent period, studying the films of Ko Chong-yol religiously, which led him to emphasize long takes, a distant camera, and the careful choreography of figures and objects in the frame, because, he said, that kind of technique would make "the trendy alienation" of his peers' work impossible since it would force him instead to focus on "people sweating and crying, people trapped within the frame, just as we had felt locked up in the real world."[114]

Im's anti-modernist experimentalism was made possible by the political and economic conditions of the occupation's final years. During the Nakajima Thaw, following the slogan "political alienation stems from economic alienation," Japan finally broke up the monopolistic industries that had dominated Korea for decades. The Korean film industry in the late 1950s thus experienced an unexpected confluence of events that empowered young directors: smaller film companies sprouted left and

---

113 Im Chang-yul, *Reflections,* trans. Jordan Ha (Berkeley: University of California Press, 2009), 82.
114 Ibid., 111.

right to challenge National Pictures' dominance, the censorship board eased up on its restrictions, and the Japanese government poured money into the country as a way to placate the population, creating an inflated commercial demand for the new film companies that became the natural breeding grounds for oppositional voices. Thus, the Korean film industry in the late 1950s and early 1960s, ironically, had more artistic freedom than it did in the years immediately after independence.

In the Shadows opens with the sound of a drum beat and a *pansori* singer introducing the protagonist, a young woman, Yong-mi (Lee Soon-ja), who barely scrapes together a living as a bar hostess in the red-light district of Seoul. Initially, we learn about her past only through subtle cues — overheard snippets of conversation, a family picture on her nightstand — but eventually she bares all to a friend in a stylized emotional outburst that counterpoints the staid dramaturgy of the *pansori* itself: her parents, she cries, were killed by Japanese forces when she was twelve because they worked for the underground, and because she was suddenly an orphan, she had to make ends meet as a comfort girl after she left school. But after years of struggle, she has managed to forge a more decent life for herself, working all night in a cocktail bar serving drunken gangsters and Japanese soldiers so that she can retreat during the day to an alternative, serene world that she's fashioned for herself in a small one-room apartment, decorated with framed images of Polynesian masks. We sense from the opening moments, though, that her carefully constructed oasis must eventually be threatened by the outside world. But this threat comes about, surprisingly, not from the occupying army but from her own romantic yearnings.

The problem is that the man she's romantically involved with is himself a Japanese soldier. Taki (Nomura Yuto) is a captain who comes to the bar regularly but who never gets drunk and never makes advances on any of the women. Yong-mi's friendship with him changes over a couple of weeks as Taki comes to trust her, dropping hints that he'd like to return home and work to overthrow the military regime. In one impeccably crafted shot after he whispers this announcement, Yong-mi lifts her eyes to meet his and the sound of the bar fades slowly into silence, and their mesmerizing, immobile fixation on each other demonstrates to the audience — and to them as well — that they have suddenly fallen in love.

What Yong-mi hasn't anticipated is that people in the underground, emboldened by the liberalizing atmosphere of the Thaw, have started to target women who sleep with the enemy. She and Taki knew that they would have to hide their love from his superiors, but now they have to hide it from her friends and co-workers as well, so that this love affair between two people in favor of Korean independence can exist, ironically, only in the urban spaces that outcasts call their own. Im designs the mise-en-scene during their most intimate moments to make an uncomfortable commentary on Korea's yearning for liberation. They sneak out at night for assignations in railyards, wharfs, and homeless encampments beneath bridges. With these late-night peregrinations, Im shows that their relationship is doomed from the start: they make frenzied, animalistic love for the first time beneath a rocky outcropping in a public park where they roll over fallen needles and pine cones in the dirt. Later, on the way home, Im shrouds the streets in inky blackness, and when lightning flashes, it doesn't illuminate a shimmering pool of water as in the hardboiled films of the 1940s, but instead lights up the twisted steel of a discarded machine, bent into oblique angles like the bony refuse of a field of war.

In one sign that Im was indeed more politically nuanced than his peers, he drew repeated parallels between the Japanese occupiers and the Korean underground throughout the film, staging scenes so that soldiers and insurgents occupy the same parts of the frame, cross the screen with the same hesitant stride, and even make the same facial gestures as they stare out a window spying on their antagonists. Im's visual parallelisms reach their fruition in the climactic sequence when their friends in the underground imprison Yong-mi and Taki in a darkened basement, where the director portrays the Korean resistance during their interrogation just as other filmmakers were then portraying the Japanese. In order to make the revolutionaries' sadism as sympathetic as he could, Im cast Philip Ahn — the son of the independence activist Ahn Chang-ho, who'd been acting in Hollywood for years — as the rebels' chief enforcer of discipline. With his trembling fingers and self-consciously pained leer, Ahn captures the psychological torture of a man who must punish a woman he knows has done nothing wrong, casting a mindless eye over her naked back before he brings the whip down and cringes at her desperate attempts to muffle her shrieks. In this final scene, whenever Ahn strikes Yong-mi across the face, her grimaces of pain are just as erotic as are his facial gestures at meting out this punishment, bringing to light the unsettling pleasure that people can take in their own victimization — Im's metaphorical reflection on the sadomasochistic psychology that defines any community struggling against the yoke of oppression.

Korean audiences in 1965, though, weren't interested in interpreting Im's sophisticated appraisal of the resistance movement. The left criticized the film as a self-hating attack on the Korean independence coalition and the right lambasted it as an incendiary socialist propaganda piece. Audiences found the film too dark. New Seoul withdrew it from theaters after only two weeks. The only major figure who defended the film, ironically, was the one man whom Im had assumed was his artistic antagonists, Park Gon-woo. In the longest essay he had yet written, Park wrote that

> more astutely than the rest of us, Im Chang-yul has crafted a cinema that speaks with a personal voice, and in doing so, he's been able to explore topics that no one else has been courageous enough to touch. Watching *In the Shadows* the first time was a challenging experience. It was like when your wife tells you something you don't want to hear and only years later do you realize that she was right. It's only now I see that my initial anger at the movie was a sign of its power.[115]

---

115 Park Gon-woo, "The New Cinema," trans. Howard Baker, *East Asian Film Journal* 15, no. 3 (2006): 35.

LAPD (d. Robert Altman, USA, 1973)
pr. *Paramount Pictures, sc. Leigh Brackett, starring Elliott Gould,*
sound, color, 35mm, 112 min.

LAPD became a cause célèbre upon its release as the subject of a
famously ill-tempered debate between two of America's foremost
movie critics — Pauline Kael of *The New Yorker,* who penned an
eight-thousand-word essay praising the movie for its "verve and
wit and slapdash fun," and Dwight Macdonald of *Esquire,* who
lambasted the film for its "masturbatory middle-brow faux-
modernism."[116] But these days, the movie that was once considered just a low-budget curio has staked out a firm position in the
canon, while the war of words that initially brought it to people's
attention has now been largely forgotten. Historians now regard
it as the film that kickstarted the movement that Brian Urquhart dubbed "Hollywood Modernism," that brief period in the
1970s when the disintegrating American studios took a chance
by producing a cycle of films — Dennis Hopper's *The Last Movie*
(1971), Melinda Nicholson's *Pole Dancer* (1974), and Melvin van
Peebles's *Prison Break* (1973), among others — that mixed commercial genre entertainment with a dash of a bohemian, European art film sensibility, hoping to cash in on the thriving youth
market.[117]

Altman's unruly aesthetics were made possible only by the
zigzagging economics of the film industry. After a long career in
television, he crossed over to film in the 1960s, directing a few
low-budget features for American International, but he finally
found a degree of artistic freedom in the early 1970s, ironically,
only after he went to work for the Hollywood studios, which
were then undergoing the most seismic management shifts
since the *Publix* decision of 1936. In the story that most historians have told, this structural confusion created surprising new

---

116 Pauline Kael, "LAPD," *The New Yorker,* September 13, 1973, 68; Dwight
Macdonald, "Middle-Brow Modernism," *Esquire,* October 28, 1973, 103.
117 Brian Urquhart, "Hollywood Modernism," *Film Comment,* October 1978:
15–28.

opportunities for intrepid auteurs. After two decades of falling attendance, each of the Big Three had been sold off at the end of the 1960s to international conglomerates that had no experience manufacturing films. Thus, these new managers initially deferred to the young directors on their payroll in a way that no previous generation had before.

Paramount, for instance, was purchased by General Electric in 1968, and its new studio head, Ted Dambrewski, came from GE's electronic appliance division, so he was at first enamored with and intimidated by the company's young filmmakers. And, after the unexpected financial success of countercultural youth movies like *Bonnie and Clyde* (1969), *Drug Bust* (1969), and *Hell's Angels* (1970), he was willing to let the younger generation take chances that would have been impossible just a few years earlier. But most historians have overlooked the ways that the Big Three were simultaneously transforming themselves into impersonal, market-driven corporate behemoths, which brought about other surprising artistic consequences — not all of which were as conservative as one might expect. The MBAs and marketing executives that Dambrewski brought in, for instance, realized that actualities cost less than half as much to produce as fictional films, so they encouraged their young staff to take up non-fiction filmmaking, which had been in decline for the last twenty years. Altman, who felt emboldened by the new regime's lax oversight of this new auxiliary endeavor, decided to take advantage of his new freedom by directing what called a "French actuality" based on a true crime police procedural he'd recently read about in *Los Angeles Magazine*.

The movie was clearly the product of the 1970s counterculture. While he'd been churning out workmanlike low-budget action fare during the 1960s, Altman had also been dabbling in New Age lifestyles — growing his hair long, experimenting with psychedelics, and wearing bead necklaces — as well as developing an interest in the theoretical writings from France that were beginning to appear in translation. Like most American directors and critics, he'd first become aware of these modernist trends only after seeing Pierre Clementi's *Into the Mouth of*

Hell (1968) and Philippe Garrel's *La Cicatrice Intérieure* (1970). And though Altman liked to portray himself as a cantankerous, hard-drinking anti-intellectual, his biographer Patrick McGilligan found copies of several influential theoretical articles of the period in the director's papers marked up with his own hand, including Peter Wollen's Gramscian analysis of Garrel's work and Jean-Luc Godard's essay "Brecht and the Soundtrack," whose publication had rankled his friendship with François Truffaut.[118]

One of the main reasons that LAPD remains such a touchstone today is that Altman destabilized the formal parameters of classical cinema in more playfully creative yet emotionally troubling ways than other Hollywood Modernists. The one formal decision Altman made that offended Macdonald and his ilk the most was his addition of fictional elements into what seemed to be a nonfictional film, a move that Macdonald saw as unethical. About twenty minutes into the movie, the two actual police detectives — who have until that moment seemed to be the subjects of the movie — are joined, for no apparent reason, by a private detective, the then-unknown actor Elliott Gould, who introduces himself to them as "Philip Marlowe," but Gould's hammy asides clearly mark him instantly as an actor performing a role. As the policemen gamely continue to pursue their investigation, Marlowe talks over the scene in post-sync improvisatory mumblings in which he opines at length about everything from tantric meditation to his pet cat's favorite brand of canned food. Altman deploys these self-referential hijinks to counteract our normal expectations of the non-fiction genre, bringing them to the fore in those moments when the actual criminal investigation begins to seem most serious. It's at the seemingly climactic moment, for instance, when the cops arrest their main suspect and bring him in for questioning that Gould inexplicably invites himself to sit in on the interrogation, and then suddenly picks up a tin of shoe polish from the table, does himself up in blackface, and bursts into a rendition of "Swanee,"

---

118 Patrick McGilligan, *Robert Altman: Jumping Off the Cliff* (New York: St. Martin's Press, 1989), 302.

dancing around the room and leaping onto the table to finish his song.

Gould's presence is also a sign of Altman's wild tonal shifts. In the same film that includes the actor's defamiliarizing antics, Altman also portrays horrifically realistic violence and genuine despair. In one scene, a petty mobster in polyester slacks smashes his girlfriend's face in with a Coke bottle and Gould — obviously no longer acting — cries out loud as blood gushes from her face. And later, when Gould accompanies the detectives to question another suspect at his beach house, we can see the older, Hemingway-esque bear of a man — played by the then washed-up Ricardo Montalbán — sneak away as his wife fixes cocktails only to re-appear a minute later in the far background where he swims out into the turbulent ocean waves in what clearly has become a suicide attempt.

Altman also experiments with music more creatively than his contemporaries. In the opening scene, as the two detectives leave the building and get into their car and the theme song erupts onto the soundtrack, then disappears mid-phrase, then inexplicably comes on again, Altman makes clear that it's his stylistic choices — not the quotidian details of police life — that are the true subject of the film. Taking Godard's ideas to heart, Altman hired the then unknown composer John Williams and the old hand Johnny Mercer to write just one song that he would play repeatedly — but only in fragments — throughout the movie. Mercer says he came up with the lyrics for "The Long Goodbye" after Altman told him that Chandler's novel was going to be his inspiration for the film (Altman later claimed that he liked their song so much he almost renamed the movie in its honor). As the detectives' murder investigation proceeds in stops and starts, the song returns in various forms with four different vocalists and one jazz instrumental version. Sometimes Altman plays only a snippet, sometimes he lets it play for almost two minutes at a time as we look out the passenger-side window of a car meandering through a Malibu beach community or the Hollywood hills, though he never once lets the song play out in its entirety. Sometimes it's diegetic, sometimes it's non-diegetic.

Sometimes, the volume goes up and down wildly in the same scene for no apparent reason. The soundtrack, in other words, did not just serve the typical "adjectival function," as Godard had called it, but instead occasionally took on the central focus normally reserved for fictional protagonists in most feature films.[119]

Altman's formal innovations, his transformation of genre tropes, and his unusually stark mixture of comedy and tragedy won over European critics of the 1970s. In *Ekran,* the editor Dmitri Markov hailed LAPD because it "brought modernism to the 1970s in the same way that Howard Hawks had when he adapted Raymond Chandler's *The Big Sleep* back in 1944."[120] And that opinion, though a minority at the time, has slowly been taking hold, though the critical consensus — as it does with most things — unfortunately still hews closer to Dwight Macdonald than it does to Dmitri Markov.

Late Spring (d. Ozu Yasujiro, Japan, 1949)
pr. Shochiku, sc. Ozu Yasujiro and Noda Kogo, starring Hara Setsuko and Ryu Chishu, sound, b&w, 35mm, 108 min.

Because his plots are so simple and his style so unusual, Ozu Yasujiro can function as an especially useful example to analyze auteurism. In *Late Spring,* widely regarded as one of his best films both in Japan and abroad, the conflicts seem quite mundane — at least on the surface. A widower lives alone with his daughter, and his sister urges him to begin arranging a marriage for her: at the age of 27, she's on the verge of becoming an old maid. But the daughter resists, saying that she'd worry about her father living alone. Eventually, though, after a few meetings with

---

119 Jean-Luc Godard, "Brecht and the Soundtrack," in *Cahiers du Cinéma, 1969–1972: The Politics of Representation,* eds. Jim Hillier and Nick Browne (Cambridge: Harvard University Press, 1989), 25.

120 Dmitri Markov, "Altman and Neo-Brechtianism," in *Reinvigorating Criticism: The Selected Writings of Dmitri Markov,* ed. and trans. Anna Petrova (London: I.B. Tauris, 2000), 38.

potential suitors, she reluctantly agrees to get married. And yet, with this simple template, Ozu managed to craft a film that has nurtured an abundance of interpretive analyses for decades.

The scholarly conversations around Ozu have hewed closely to larger discussions about auteurist theory and hermeneutics. One leading strand of thought, for instance, holds that film directors are the product of industries while auteurs are the product of critical discourse. But critical discourse itself has been shaped by the same material forces that have influenced these industries, so Ozu's shifting position has followed the main trends in the history of film criticism, which have followed the main trends in political discourse. Before the democratic revolutions of 1965, Ozu was revered in Japan: his films had won more *Kinema Junpo* awards than those of any other filmmaker, and the executives at Shochiku generally treated him as the company's premiere director. But critics and filmmakers in the West had rarely been able to see his films. The first wave of European critics after the revolutions was initially charmed by the director, but then, in the heady years after liberation, a rigid aesthetic divide set in. Japanese progressives embraced an aesthetic program that was a direct result of the new political landscape, celebrating the politically active and formally daring cinema of directors like Kobayashi Masaki, Oshima Nagisa, and Imamura Shohei. For that generation, Ozu became the epitome of the conservative Showa regime house director, the "most Japanese of all Japanese filmmakers," a designation that had functioned — within Japan — as the ultimate compliment a decade earlier but which now had become a suspect moniker to be avoided at all costs. Western critics enthralled by the new wave of radical stylists coming out of Japan fell in line with the revolutionary fervor of the East, and Ozu's films — and his defenders — were ignored as old-fashioned apologists for the former government.

The last few decades, though, have seen a gradual metamorphosis. As the political intoxication of the Sixties eventually dissipated and the new democratic administrations stumbled, predictably, with problems of their own, the canon developed in tandem: the reputations of Liberation-era favorites like Kobayashi have fallen, while the reputations of classical directors like Ozu, Kurosawa, Mizoguchi, and Naruse have risen to meet — or even surpass — them. With the cooling off of revolutionary fervor, critics and scholars no longer felt the obligation to read older films as ideological signposts. Economic changes, too, had an effect on the critical establishment. The dismantling of trade barriers gave cinephiles access to hundreds of previously unavailable films. And the opening of the archives influenced scholars, too, who now reformulated their conception of how the Japanese film industry had functioned; newer historical studies now revealed the relative autonomy that directors had at Shochiku, Toho, and Nikkatsu, helping to frame the contemporary view of classical filmmakers as individualist artists beyond the reach of the propaganda efforts of the regime.

More important than being able to chart the development of their reputations, though, the historical shifts have enabled us to see these films differently. The first major re-evaluation in the West was kicked off by the publication of David Bordwell's *Ozu and the Poetics of Cinema* in 1986, which sparked the formalist period in academic studies of the director. In that book, Bordwell eschewed the type of ideological interpretation he felt had come to unhealthily dominate the field of film studies. By analyzing the seemingly minor decisions that Ozu made as a filmmaker, Bordwell assumed that he might liberate him as an artist from the standard view of him as a conservative. Conversely, a director seen as a traditionalist, he felt, might be the perfect example to legitimize his own purely formal concerns. In that book, he mapped out Ozu's distinctive aesthetic system: his abandonment of the 180-degree rule in favor of a 360-degree arrangement of concentric circles, shot-reverse-shot patterns in which characters face the camera directly, his camera placement near the floor, his tendency to design the image with objects like sake bottles marking off multiple depth planes, his typical transition between scenes comprised of rhyming patterns of three shots of three unrelated objects, and his narrative structure that avoids conflict and character development and is organized instead around the repetition of insignificant events over the changing of the seasons.[121] Merely by performing such a rigorous analysis — almost entirely sidestepping the content of the films — Bordwell breathed fresh air into the study of the director, liberating Ozu from rote ideological analysis, freeing writers to reconceive of his work during the Showa era with fresh eyes and a variety of methodologies.

The most recent wave of critics, both in Japan and America, has drawn on this new formalist methodology to make bolder interpretive claims, linking Ozu's unique style back to the type of ideological interpretation that Bordwell had tried to avoid. But given the current leftist disillusion with contemporary Japanese politics, many contemporary writers who valorize Ozu's work come, surprisingly, from the same leftist camp as those who earlier had denigrated him. As a leading director in the Japanese New Wave himself, Yoshida Yoshishige, for instance, may seem like the last type of figure to lionize the old master. He'd been one of the preeminent vanguard filmmakers of the post-revolutionary era, after all, directing such new classics of radical cinema as *Eros Plus Massacre* (1969) and *Heroic Purgatory* (1970). Swept up in the Brechtian attitudes popular at the time in the intellectual centers of Paris, Shanghai, and Calcutta, Yoshida and his peers thought that artists who embraced a radical politics must also embrace an aesthetic program that challenged the dominant norms of commercial cinema. So in writing about Ozu, Yoshida brought his own generation's interests to bear on a subject that seemed initially to be wholly divorced from his revolutionary concerns. Yet he articulates an understanding of Ozu that's surprisingly in league with current academic trends by reframing the director with the same self-reflexive framework that had inspired him in his frenzied youth.

In retrospect, deploying Brechtian language to analyze Ozu isn't as counterintuitive as it initially seems: Ozu emphatically disavows the standard modes of narrative filmmaking on almost

---

121 David Bordwell, *Ozu and the Poetics of Cinema* (Princeton: Princeton University Press, 1986).

every formal level, after all, a manifestation of his strident individualism, even if he cloaks his conspicuous unconventionality to seem almost invisible. In *Late Spring*, Yoshida wrote, Ozu "tried to problematize the utterly peaceful relationship between the father and the daughter by offending the grammar of motion pictures and prohibiting them from gazing at each other."[122] The relationship between father and daughter, Yoshida hinted, harbored unspeakable qualities that were just as inimical to cultural norms as was Ozu's style itself.

Throughout his examination of the director, Yoshida returns again and again to the themes of "playfulness" and "artificiality." In clear echoes of the aesthetic philosophy he soaked up as a young activist, he suggests repeatedly that Ozu disrupts received formal norms, heightening the artificiality of the film in order to challenge viewers to think about what they're watching. "These images," he writes, "can be called playful, which is to say that they are simply meant to disperse the linear storyline and reveal the artificiality of the film narrative." But this playfulness induces viewer responses, he says, that run counter to what most viewers assume that they're feeling about Ozu's movies: "The audience's anxiety and irritation," he writes, for instance, "are the result of Ozu-san's playful way of positioning his camera."[123] Feelings of angst and aggravation may strike some fans as antithetical to Ozu's quiet domestic dramas, but a closer look at *Late Spring* — and indeed, his entire oeuvre — offers up many examples to back up this claim.

Yoshida makes his case by discussing the issue that is writ large over the entire film but which no character can utter out loud: the story's central intellectual conflict, the taboo topic of incest. The problem throughout the film has been obvious: the daughter loves her father too much. Her feelings are too intense, too clingy. But what is the exact nature of this intensity? This

---

122 Yoshida Kiju (a.k.a. Yoshida Yoshishige), *Ozu's Anti-Cinema*, trans. Daisuke Miyao and Kyoko Hirano (1998; rpt. Ann Arbor: University of Michigan, Center for Japanese Studies, 2003), 66.

123 Ibid., 62, 64.

being an Ozu film, it's never entirely explicit. In the climactic scene, Yoshida points out that father and daughter sleep side by side in the same room while on vacation together at a Kyoto inn, a scene, he says, "that could imply unexpected sensual meanings.... [And] this kind of ambivalence forms the climactic moment of the playfulness in Ozu-san's films."[124] Ozu, not surprisingly, emphasizes the unspeakably taboo subject of the climax with one of his typically enigmatic formal decisions. Just at the moment when the daughter voices her feelings, the one moment that could possibly be read in the most uncomfortable way — the thought of her father remarrying, she says elliptically, is "distasteful," as she glances yearningly his way — Ozu cuts to a close-up of a vase for no immediately apparent reason. "When viewers look at the shot of the vase abruptly inserted into the scene," Yoshida writes, "they cannot help staring at it. They are forced to think about the meaning of the vase and interpret it."[125] But then — as if he's anxious about his own analysis of the anxiety that Ozu evokes — Yoshida retreats from the logic of his argument, suggesting in the end that Ozu "did not want the viewers to think of incest between the two. In order to calm down the dangerously immoral passion between the characters, the image of the vase was indispensable."[126]

But if one does follow Yoshida's argument to its natural conclusion, one would have to acknowledge that the vase is a pronounced violation of even Ozu's own distinctive formal rules and that Ozu inserts this impenetrable symbol in order to "lead the viewers to interpret the meaning" of the image, because, as Yoshida himself claims, Ozu "wanted to leave them [his symbols] ambiguous."[127] So Yoshida's eventual reading of the vase as an emblem of the daughter's purity is definitely credible, but unnecessarily limiting. Because Ozu's objects are — as Yoshida himself argues — so intentionally open and multifaceted, the

---

124 Ibid., 80.
125 Ibid.
126 Ibid., 81
127 Ibid., 79.

vase must simultaneously suggest other complementary and contrary meanings. Ozu's symbol is so opaque it inspires us to mull over the multiple possibilities of its inexpressible referent, but one of the intended plausible meanings is certainly the inexpressible theme of incest that's quietly subtended the entire film.

In retrospect, this countervailing contemporary interpretation should not be that surprising given the recurring themes of Ozu's career. Anyone who's watched his films closely can see that Ozu's families are always on the cusp of disintegration, eaten away by their own transgressions. In *The Only Son* (1937), for instance, a mother sacrifices everything to pay for her son's education only to see his life amount to little more than struggle; in *A Hen in the Wind* (1948), a desperately poor wife prostitutes herself to make ends meet and when her husband finds out he beats her viciously; in *Tokyo Story* (1953), an elderly couple comes to realize that their children don't care for them; in *Early Spring* (1956), a husband has an extramarital affair; in *Tokyo Twilight* (1957), the daughters in a family struggle with divorce, out-of-wedlock pregnancy, abortion, and a strained reunion with the absent mother who had abandoned them decades earlier.

Even if the majority of Ozu's characters decide to repair their troubled marriages in the end, the films typically conclude with a sense of resignation rather than a sense of hope. Ozu's families are always alienated, distorted, and disrupted. In the final analysis, his films are never a celebration of traditional family or of Japanese values. If anything, they repeatedly demonstrate how the ideals of the family and the nation are merely facades; his movies delve beneath the culture's surfaces to reveal its complicated underbelly. And this is why Ozu had to invent his own unconventional visual and narrative strategies. His style is just as alienated, distorted, and disrupted as his families are. If his stories condemn the contemporary world, his aesthetics, too, must similarly confront the dominant formal systems. He is, then, an ideal Brechtian — just as Yoshida unexpectedly sees him — but with one significant difference: while Brecht advocated an ostentatious display of artificiality in order to waken the drowsing masses, Ozu's challenge to formal and ideological conventions is so unobtrusive, it requires — unlike with Brecht — a highly intelligent and sophisticated viewer to make sense of it.

The Maltese Falcon (d. Raoul Walsh, USA, 1942)
pr. American Pictures, sc. A.I. Bezzerides, John Huston, and John Wexley, starring Nick Alton, sound, b&w, 35mm, 100 min.

Historians have generally credited Raoul Walsh's adaptation of Dashiell Hammett's *The Maltese Falcon* as the movie that kindled the genre that American critics later came to call Hard-boiled Cinema — and what the Parisian critics dubbed *Serie Noir* — those crime films of the 1940s and 1950s defined by dark chiaroscuro lighting, alluringly dangerous women, and grizzled detectives with a penchant for Hemingwayesque poeticisms who evince the same disregard for traditional morality as their criminal antagonists.

Two of the major studios had already adapted Hammett's book: Fox's silent edition in 1932 and Paramount's talkie from 1937 had both followed the novel fairly closely, but neither caught on with the public and neither registers in the critical literature today. American Pictures' equally faithful adaptation, meanwhile, became a commercial hit overnight and has remained an important benchmark in the history of American cinema. The screenplay — penned by, in the words of studio head Michael Feynman, "any writer who happened to pass by my open door" — followed the novel almost scene by scene just as the previous adaptations had, including the majority of Hammett's dialogue word for word.[128] The script itself, then, had little to do with the movie's success, so the qualities that made this version a classic shed light on some of the most fundamental aspects of film as an art form.

First, the cinematographer Nicholas Musuraca understood the relationship between technology and poetics more than

---

128 Rudy Behlmer, ed., *Memo from Michael Feynman* (New York: The Viking Press, 1972), 405.

most of his contemporaries: he took advantage of Kodak's new, faster film stocks, suffusing the movie with a dramatic high-contrast lighting whose inky, depthless blacks suffused the film with a mood of nihilistic despair, which then became — more than the characters or the plot — the essential subject of the hardboiled era. Second, Walsh's decision to cast the then-little-known Nick Alton in the role of Sam Spade demonstrated once again the inverse relationship that theatrically mimetic acting skills have with cinematic performance. Alton was pure presence. His oversized, jutting chin, and his perpetually unshaven indifference to the vicissitudes of life turned him into a new kind of American icon. When the French critics François Truffaut and Jean-Luc Godard debated fifteen years later whether Alton was "the first existentialist" or "the last Romantic rebel," they were talking about hardboiled cinema as much as they were about the actor in question.[129]

In the opening scene, the seductive young bombshell Ruth Wonderley comes to the offices of private detective Sam Spade and asks him to look for her missing sister, but the central mystery begins to develop only the next morning after his partner is found murdered. When the police question him as a suspect in the case, Spade starts to investigate the crime himself — more to save his own neck than out of any concern for his erstwhile friend — and soon finds himself mixed up with a group of shady characters who've descended upon San Francisco in search of a black statuette they all believe must be worth a fortune. The eponymous Mediterranean bird is, of course, what the British director Alfred Hitchcock would later call a MacGuffin, the object that's insignificant in and of itself, but which inspires the characters to play out the generic expectations of a Hollywood plot. The meaninglessness of this narrative catalyst is precisely what enables directors to express their more philosophical concerns — which in this case, is not the search for the titular bird of prey, but an examination of the ubiquity of evil and thus of humanity's indifference to it. Spade, like the genre he helped create,

---

129 "Serie Noire," in *Cahiers du Cinéma, the 1950s*, ed. Hillier, 51–52.

inhabits a world that exists only at night, governed by no laws, no political institutions, and no social networks; instead, this shadow-world protagonist is what Gérard Genette called a "desultory monad," a drifter with no past and no future, an isolated animal only out for himself, whose actions are dictated by forces beyond his control, but who still strives to retain his dignity, if nothing else, since dignity may be the only thing a man can claim in a world that's permeated by banks of fog so thick that half-lit neon bar signs are the only vestige of civilization that he might ever hope to glimpse.[130]

In this sense, Nick Alton himself, as much as the darkness, embodies the hard-edged spirit of the times; his incongruously masculine sibilance is the conflicted voice of the genre. After he'd been discovered selling tickets for a circus out in Long Beach, where he learned, he said, that "guys who talked loud got punched but guys who talked soft got the girl" — he'd worked as a B-movie tough on dozens of films throughout the 1930s for the smaller outfits in town like Sunset, Gower, and Universal.[131] But the talkies made him a new type of star. He wasn't attractive. His big ears, baggy eyes, and sputtering lisp all gave him the indefinably cinematic quality that producers back in the silent era used to call "It." His dissolute iconoclasm made him the perfect emblem for those who felt uprooted by the modern world. And his cinematic image assuaged the anxieties of the dispossessed for the next twenty years. After *The Maltese Falcon* made him the surprise star of the year, Alton solidified his position as the paradigmatic figure of Hardboiled Cinema by starring later as the genre's other great icon, Raymond Chandler's Philip Marlowe, in Howard Hawks's *The Big Sleep* (1944) and Frank Callaghan's *The Long Goodbye* (1954) — perhaps the greatest of all hardboiled films.

---

130 Gerard Genette, "The Protagonist Typology in the Narrative System," in *Narratology: A Science or a Poetics?*, ed. Jonathan Culler (Ithaca: Cornell University Press, 1988), 141.

131 Nick Alton, *Tough City* (New York: E.P. Dutton, 1956), 35.

The actor's and cinematographer's defining contributions to the genre's first entry sheds light on why *Serie Noir* has been so difficult to define in any language. While so many other genres are recognized by plot structures and settings, Musuraca and Alton were chiefly responsible for defining a mood, or a sensibility. This is one reason why James Naremore, in his book *More Than Night: Hardboiled Cinema in Its Contexts,* argues that we shouldn't think of it as a genre but as "the history of an idea," which he traces backward from the first wave of auteurist American critics in the 1960s to their Parisian and Lyonnaise antecedents in the 1950s to the writings of pop existentialists like Boris Vian in the 1940s and finally to Andre Breton's Surrealist manifesto of 1924.[132] The genre remains an area of fascination for the cinephile community, he suggests, precisely because its inexplicability gives birth to hermeneutic possibilities. In this sense, *The Maltese Falcon* functions perfectly as the genre's foundational object. Alton's stolid visage and Musuraca's rain-drenched, pitch-black streets were both freighted with meaning and yet still mysterious enough to serve as blank canvases on which other filmmakers and other intellectuals could explore the darker corners of their waking dreams.

Manila Neon (d. Lino Brocka, Philippines, 1977)
pr. Showtime Banking International, sc. Lino Brocka and Mario O'Hara, starring Tiefolo Sanchez, sound, color, 35mm, 126 mins.

Lino Brocka's hothouse epic about a young cockfighter who comes to Manila to seek vengeance on his enemies has been overlooked since its release, partly because the movie's melodramatic tone didn't jibe with the dominant ethos of the *cinéma engagé* and partly because the Delgado administration's censorship drive almost succeeded in wiping the film from the face of the Earth. It was only a dozen years later that the Belgian Film Archive managed to reconstruct the movie from the few remain-

---

132 Naremore, *More Than Night,* 9–39.

ing prints scattered across the globe. A new generation — more open to embracing *outré* aesthetics and to understanding sexuality as inherently political — has now come to extol the film as one of the most mordant commentaries of the decade.

The movie opens with one long, hypnotic tracking shot, flecked and haloed with the iridescent sunbursts of the camera lens, as Tiefolo Sanchez wakes, drags a hand through his unkempt hair, climbs out of bed, saunters naked out into the yard, and turns on a hose to give himself a cold shower. The camera lingers on his statuesque body until the rising sun behind him turns him into a mere silhouette, a black outline against a blazing sky. In this wordless introductory scene, Brocka hints at both the film's major themes and its plot trajectory: an aestheticized erotics that will lead inexorably to death.

Sanchez's character grew up in a rural backwater but managed to achieve some prominence by running the local cockfights. The movie's conflict begins when a group of young toughs sent by a Manila gang lord arrive unannounced in town one night, drag Sanchez into an alley, and beat him up with a lead pipe. It's that easy to take over his business. The next morning, bandaged and bruised, he escapes by hitching a ride to the capital, where he hopes he might take revenge on the city's crime bosses who've begun to corrupt the countryside. Wandering the streets at night, homeless and without a job, he ends up sleeping in the only place he can afford, renting a cot in the back of a shantytown barbershop. And here, by portraying Sanchez surrounded by piles of garbage, homes constructed out of cinder blocks and sheet metal, and human refuse streaming through the streets, Brocka transforms his story from a commercial melodrama into an exposé of the American-sponsored crony capitalism that was turning the island into a spiritual dumping ground. The rotting excrescence that is the contemporary Philippines forces Sanchez to humiliate himself in a quest for money, thereby replicating on a personal level the degradations of the nation. To make a new life for himself among the urban poor, Sanchez earns money first by selling recycled bottles from the garbage dump, then by selling drugs, and finally by selling his own body to the jaded wives of millionaires who flock to the downtown discotheques looking for amphetamines and sex.

What makes the film more than just a gritty genre pic from the low-budget Filipino scene is Brocka's baroque use of cinematic tools to make a recurring connection between the political economy of the Philippines, the corruption of urban life, and the abasement of the body. Brocka returns repeatedly to an obsessive meditation on Sanchez's nude figure, but whenever he does, he frames him to draw parallels with the larger world: in the background of the image in the shantytowns, women give their children baths with a hose in front of a pigpen, bands of teenagers face off against each other with broken Coke bottles, and bored prostitutes hang out in alleyways in the middle of the afternoon, adjusting their nylons and smoking cigarettes. Brocka returns to this visual analogy between sexuality and the country's degeneration so often that it becomes the logical development of the narrative as well. It is Sanchez's discovery that he can make more money by selling his own body, after all, that leads to his spiraling humiliation and ineluctable demise.

And ironically for a gay director, Brocka portrays Sanchez's final ruination as a descent into queer sexuality. He begins by sleeping with the bored housewives of the country's politically connected nouveau riche, but near the end, in a sequence that hints at the film's ugly resolution, Brocka frames Sanchez getting a blow job from the effeminate son of a local politician as he leans against a Dumpster in an alley with the young man's Mercedes-Benz parked in the background. As Brocka moves in for a close-up, Sanchez's face contorts in a grimace, half pleasure and half pain, just at the moment of orgasm. Unable to confront squarely his own desires and his own identity, Sanchez eventually meets the same fate as the nation — and for the same reason. As the film barrels toward its denouement, Sanchez's affair with his gay femme pickup turns increasingly passionate, but increasingly out of control: Brocka films their sex in a cramped basement storeroom with a swinging ceiling-light like two animals trapped in a pen. In the penultimate scene, after an unexpectedly rough encounter, the fey rich kid turns on him, spits his way, and knifes him in the groin. And in the final shot, Brocka tracks in on Sanchez's naked body discarded atop a trash heap in a back alley where his boyfriend has left him to die.

After critics raved about the movie at its Manila premiere and news spread about its scathing portrayal of the political class, the Filipino domestic security apparatus wheeled into action and rounded up and burned every print it could get its hands on. But by then the distributor had already shipped a few copies to Hong Kong and Singapore, and just to be safe, Brocka managed to have his favorite actress, Lina Belmonte, smuggle another print out of the country when she traveled to Macao — ironically, on a publicity tour for her biopic about President Delgado's wife. Just one month later, the government arrested both Brocka and Sanchez on tax charges that most people saw as a thinly veiled attack on their film. Both were released after just a few months, but by planting scurrilous rumors in the press and blacklisting them at the major film companies, Delgado managed to hobble both their careers without resorting to an outright ban that might have troubled his American sponsors. Brocka was unable to direct a movie for another eleven years and then could work only on a series of low-budget musicals, while Sanchez eventually ended up working as a used car salesman in Quezon City. Both men had died by the time the film was restored and had its triumphant screening at the Rotterdam Film Festival in 1991, where Françoise Bergeron called it "more searing than any of the films of the so-called 'engaged cinema' of the period because its fervent tone makes its realist aesthetics more vividly human and thus more politically acute."[133]

---

133 Françoise Bergeron, *The Next Generation: Engaged Cinema in the Global Age*, trans. Beatrice Howard (Palo Alto: Stanford University Press, 2003), 96.

The Michael Douglas Show; Or, the Performance of the Self in
the Messianic and Wounded Eyes of Orson Welles (d. Shirley
Jacobs, USA, 1975)
pr. *The Corporation for Public Broadcasting and* WGBH-Boston,
sound, color, 35mm, 113 min.

Shirley Jacobs had originally planned on making an essay film
about the sociologist Erving Goffman's theories on the inherently performative nature of the self. Her goal had been to focus
on the celebrities who appeared on Michael Douglas's daytime
talk show as the contemporary paradigms of self-consciously
fashioned identities. But on the first day of shooting — after Orson Welles impetuously commandeered the stage to perform a
wedding between two Bolivian midget circus performers, and
then, with a sudden sweep of his magician's cape, made the
tiny couple disappear before a stupefied roster that included
Carol Channing and the bandleader Xavier Cugat — she began
to question herself. After the commercial break, when Welles
spoke wistfully to Douglas about the second film he'd wanted to
make in Hollywood — the modernist biopic about the newspaper tycoon William Randolph Hearst, which studio executives
infamously axed midway through production — she decided on
the spot to embark upon a much more poetic project, an actuality instead about the once famous film director, movie star, and
failed political candidate and his decades-long litany of unfinished, destroyed, and unfilmable projects.

The movie opens with the magic trick that first inspired her,
and the sequence ends on a freeze frame of Channing's bewildered face as the soundtrack erupts with screams and explosive
blasts, punctuated by Welles's booming voice from the 1939 radio
broadcast of *The War of the Worlds* that first made him famous.
Then Jacobs dissolves into the hauntingly sinuous first-person
tracking shot that Welles intended as the opening sequence of
his first Hollywood production — his controversial adaptation
of Joseph Conrad's *Heart of Darkness* (1941) — the same shot,
Welles reminds us in an audiotaped interview with his biog-

rapher Peter Bogdanovich,[134] that Stanley Films executives cut from the release print over his heated objections.[135] The camera begins on a tight close-up of an indignant African slave in the hull of a steamship, glides past a line of Black men chained to benches, and comes to a stop on the face of Canada Lee in the role of chief Iwakube — a Welles invention, he said, to counter the Eurocentric focus of the Conrad narrative — then follows him as he sneaks through the machine-laden underbelly of the boat and finally comes to rest three minutes later on deck as Lee looks out over the river to see here and there amid the jungle trees the curved bows that hint at the hail of arrows that will soon fall from the sky like a horde of locusts just at the moment that the credits begin to roll.

From these first moments, Jacobs's design plan is clear: rather than a chronological account of the tragic rise and fall of a washed-up talent, she instead fashions a collage-like meditation in which she repeatedly frames Welles's adventurous, baroque aesthetics as the source of his lifelong tension between corporate persecution and artistic self-annihilation. As the *Heart of Darkness* credits continue to scroll, she dampens Bernard Herrmann's score to let Welles's voice come through once again — this time an excerpt from another of his unfinished films, his 1972 version of *Moby Dick,* in which he radically refashioned Melville's words as a monologue that speaks as much about Ahab as it does about himself: "Tied up, twisted, eyes like coals still glowing in the ashes of a ruin, Ahab lifts up to the clearness of the morn his splintered helmet of a brow." Ahab, now defeated, whom Jacobs makes the stand-in for Welles gazing over the ruin of his own career, casts his eyes over the vast, impenetrable ocean into which he knows his monstrous but pearlescent nemesis will inevitably drag him, the boundlessness of his own artistry intent on swallowing him whole.

---

134 Peter Bogdanovich and Orson Welles, *This Is Orson Welles,* eds. Peter Bogdanovich and Jonathan Rosenbaum (New York: Harper Collins, 1992), 59.

135 Robert Carringer, *Orson Welles's Heart of Darkness: A Reconstruction* (Berkeley: University of California Press, 1993), 51.

Continuing in this poetic mode of assemblage, Jacobs highlights her linked themes of acting and identity, art and futility by cutting from the Welles material to grainy 8mm home movies of Erving Goffman and his family in the 1950s as we hear the sociologist reading aloud from his book *The Presentation of Self in Everyday Life*.[136] Jacobs herself tells us that she first became interested in Goffman's work because she saw his sociological analyses as merely aesthetic theories in another garb. Thus, she uses footage of Goffman throughout the movie acting out the same roles — puffed-up machismo, inveterate chicanery, wounded genius — that she'd previously shown Welles unwittingly performing on TV, which leads her in turn to explore Goffman's little-known years working in actuality filmmaking with John Grierson at the National Film Board of Canada. Goffman had initially been attracted to actualities because of what he assumed was the motion pictures' scientific potential for objectively capturing human behavior, but he quit in frustration after only a few years when he began to realize how deeply the filming process influenced the behavior of the observed subject. Paraphrasing Goffman, Jacobs wonders aloud, is there some fundamental aspect of the mechanical means of capturing and reproducing reality that intensifies our awareness of the quintessentially fictive nature of everyday life? And doesn't the indisputably affirmative answer to that question, she continues, suggest that the goal of fashioning a plausible, fictional cinematic universe — that is, the primary aim of film as an art form — is ultimately futile because the performer is trying to represent a reality that is already, by its very nature, unreal?

Jacobs lets this question hang in the air over the modernist funhouse mirror finale of *The Lady from Shanghai* (1947), then weaves between scenes of Welles's own home movies — in Los Angeles in the 1970s making peanut butter sandwiches for Bogdanovich, ice skating with his oldest daughter in Central Park in the 1950s, offering a champagne toast to Pablo Casals in

---

136 Erving Goffman, *The Presentation of Self in Everyday Life* (Garden City: Doubleday, 1959).

Cordoba in 1963 — and footage from his failed campaign for the Senate in 1954 against the then little-known congressmen from Whittier, Richard Nixon. In the presumably unrehearsed and thus "natural" footage at home, Welles clearly adapts a different persona for each of his audiences, though the same themes continually reappear: despite the outsized persona that he projects, we can always detect traces of a small and frightened creature misunderstood and tormented by the world. But he transforms the sheltered timorousness of his private personality into a tool to use for his own public glorification: in his campaign speeches, from ornate San Francisco ballrooms to the farm towns of the Central Valley, Welles returns again and again to the theme of the little man beset by larger, inhuman powers on all sides, culminating in his now famously impassioned concession speech at the Biltmore Hotel in Los Angeles in which he denounces "the forces arrayed against the common man like the constellations that control our lives but which are impossible to wipe from the sky."[137]

Jacobs transitions into the final act with a bravura montage sequence, intercutting footage of Welles's appearances on *The Michael Douglas Show* with clips from the unfinished *Moby Dick* project he continued to work on till the end of his life. Alone in his living room, sitting before a blank backdrop with deep chiaroscuro lighting, Welles looks into the camera with piercing eyes and reads aloud his reimagined version of Melville's text — "This winsome sky at last seems almost to dissolve the canker-wrinkle beating in his heart, and the cruel, stepmother world now throws affectionate arms around that stubborn neck" — then Jacobs cuts to Welles spinning tales to Douglas about the time he set Charlton Heston's beard on fire, about the time he and Ricardo Montalbán got so drunk in Guadalajara they somehow ended up as matadors in a bullring, and about the time he finally met Jorge Luis Borges at a writers' conference in Buenos Aires and wanted to punch him out for his negative

---

137 Simon Callow, *Orson Welles, Vol. 2: Hello Americans* (New York: Penguin, 2007), 463.

review of *Heart of Darkness* but instead won the older man over by acting out on the spot an improvised filmic adaptation of the author's short story "Pierre Menard: Author of Don Quixote."

And then, the final sequence: the afternoon appearance when Michael Douglas finally gathers the courage to ask Welles about his infamous failed follow-up to *Heart of Darkness,* the aborted movie about Hearst that Welles himself claimed "would have been the best movie I ever made." Welles takes Carol Channing's hand with a naughty avuncularity as he begins the story of that film — about a reporter's investigation of the dead newspaper mogul's mysterious last word, about his life revealed from multiple clashing perspectives, about the innovative techniques he'd planned with an optical printer to create the illusion of deep space as a means of signifying the growing emotional distance not just between this man and the people he loved most, but between him and his own forgotten progressive ambitions. And then, as Welles comes to the climax of the movie's narrative, his eyes suddenly fixate on an invisible object just out of reach and he transforms himself into the role of the film's protagonist that he had intended to play himself. He rises from his chair and, as himself, subtly orchestrates the camera crew in the studio and the director up in the booth with the fingers of one hand, while simultaneously, embodying the fictionalized Hearst-like character, he acts out — perhaps, for the first time in three decades — the moment when his mistress Susan, whom he'd built up from nothing into an enormous Hollywood star, announces that she's leaving him and he falls back in anguish, reeling through their bedroom with crazed hypnotic eyes, smashing flower vases, tearing paintings from the wall, and sweeping books from their shelves until he totters in an exhausted spiral and collapses onto the studio floor, grasping in one hand the mysterious object that had so transfixed him from the first moments of the scene, whispering to the studio audience that this was the snow globe he'd held as he'd spoken that final mysterious word on his deathbed in the opening sequence of the film, the same snow globe that was sitting on Susan's piano the first night they met, the very symbol of his lost innocence he tried to recapture through her, and Jacobs freezes on her film's final image, the moment that Welles lifts the imaginary bauble before him and raises his eyes to search in the vast darkness of the rafters not just for Hearst's lost virtue, but his own, as his disembodied, reverb-heavy *basso profundo* voice intones that mysterious first and final word of what he'd hoped would have been his greatest film: "Rosebud."

Mountain Retreat (d. Dao Han-lin, China, 1956)

pr. Shanghai Film Studios, sc. Dao Han-lin and Wu Lin, starring Zhao Xiu-lan, sound, color, 35mm, 101 min.

The Shanghai intelligentsia ignored *Mountain Retreat* on its initial release. The film's lush sensuality, its epic scope, and its focus on a female protagonist and her coterie of urbane male aesthetes did not sit well with the tenets of leftist realism that had dominated Chinese critical circles since the revolutionary fervor of the 1920s. But ensuing generations of critics, increasingly disillusioned with the rightward drift and corruption of the Guomindang regime, felt free to re-examine their predecessors' assumptions about the acceptable formal parameters of an "engaged cinema." Writers in the 1970s returned to *Mountain Retreat* with fresh eyes: now, the movie's orchestration of mise-en-scene, its infatuation with saturated color and the delicate textural surfaces of objects no longer seemed the stuff of trifling melodrama. On the contrary, younger critics now understood style as a more canny vehicle with which to examine the contemporary political mood than the glum authenticity of the more overtly progressive films of that era.

Ever since the May Fourth Movement in 1919, Chinese intellectual life had been dominated by progressive nationalists who took it for granted that they should use art as a weapon to shine a light on the lives of peasants and the working class in order to help forge a communal identity for a country still struggling to assert itself on the international stage. Since the silent period, then, critics had supported earnest films about the valorous endeavors of the common man. By the 1950s, though, the cultural elites' commitment had waned: decades of economic stagnation and government corruption, increasing censorship of the press, and the ongoing encirclement by Japanese forces in Manchuria and Taiwan had eroded their aesthetic as much as their ideological vision. Critics at the time felt an intense affinity for brooding pessimism, writing fervently about films produced by the liberal-leaning Lianhua Film Company like Cai Chusheng's *The Cigarette Girl* (1949) and Sun Yu's *The Shop Assistant* (1951). These movies, with their economic fatalism and their existential anomie — the cigarette girl, for instance, drowns herself in the same well where she had earlier witnessed an impoverished mother murder her newborn and the shop assistant ends up dragging her body, bleeding from a self-inflicted knife wound, across the floor of the department store where she works — appealed to the educated class's current political cynicism but also to its continuing commitment to an aesthetics of realism.

The shifting critical attitude toward commercial melodramas like *Mountain Retreat* was also shaped by economic and institutional changes over the years. After Lianhua finally folded in 1952, the only film studios able to survive were those like Shanghai Film Studios and the Xinhua Film Company, who'd both accepted co-ownership deals with Japanese industrialists tied to the Showa government, and their new leadership teams insisted that their movies adhere to an apolitical line, bringing about a sudden evolution in the look and feel of the nation's screen entertainment. And as Bei Mao and Francisco Callenbach have argued, after the Guomindang embraced a more modern form of capitalism in the wake of Chiang Kai-shek's downfall, the flourishing economy over the next decades made the leftist pessimism of the late republican generation seem dated.[138] And thus, the more capacious hermeneutic interests of film critics in the

138 Bei Mao and Francisco Callenbach, *The Great Tidal Wave: Capitalism and the Art of Emotions in the Late Guomindang Period* (Hong Kong: Hong Kong University Press, 2002).

1970s were as much the product of economic conditions as were the aesthetic commitments of their forefathers' era.

In writing about the legitimate arts like painting, modern choreography, and the novel, Mary Wong has argued that the 1950s were defined by an environment of "post-utopian disquiet," an overwhelming sense of lassitude and ennui that artists expressed in terms of form rather than content by stretching and expanding upon the "viscous weight of time" and by making visible and extending "the barren vacancies of space."[139] These "new spatiotemporal modes of representation," she argued, were the aesthetic manifestations of the culture's transformed political landscape, "its only available methods of enunciating a political critique at a time when government and institutional censorship made overt political subject matter impossible. Artists' insistent discombobulation of the visual field at a time when the whole culture seemed tossed about in the vortex of a tidal pool," she continued, "spoke more to the era's mindset than could the plots of any novel."[140] And though she didn't write about lower forms of popular culture like the movies, Wong's conception of 1950s aesthetics finds one of its greatest practitioners in Dao Han-lin.

In the opening scenes, Yu Bin (Zhao Xiu-lan), the wife of a minor warlord in the middle of the nineteenth century, meanders through her home in one long tracking shot, casting her gaze over each sparsely but elegantly decorated room with the eye of a connoisseur, re-arranging a vase of peonies, judiciously trimming the branch of a plum tree, and finally coming to an uneasy halt as she steps out onto the edge of the courtyard where her husband's retainers are practicing hand-to-hand combat. The film then erupts in a sudden montage of clashing swords and close-ups of the sweaty and agonized faces of men. From these first few minutes, Dao Han-lin makes a clear distinction between the spatiotemporal experience of the feminine domestic space and the masculine public spheres of art and war.

---

139 Mary Wong, *The Chronotope of the Postlapsarian: Art in China after the Coup* (Cambridge: Harvard University Press, 1991), 12.
140 Ibid., 18.

Madam Yu — as she's referred to in the most common English translation — was born into a prominent land-owning family in the provinces and was married off to a minor warlord just before the Taiping Rebellion gets under way. But Dao demonstrates the couple's incompatibility mostly through mise-en-scene: while Yu's rooms are austere and serenely empty, her husband's spaces are crammed floor to ceiling with swords and helmets, furs and silks, and furniture covered with unused bowls and plates and piles of coins. Luckily for her, he's often travelling, keeping tabs on his domain, so she begins to fashion a life of her own, welcoming gatherings of poets, painters, and musicians to her sprawling estate. And as one year turns to the next, she earns herself a reputation as the host of the most sophisticated salon in the region. Then, once she begins to write her own poetry — odes to nature tinged with an erotic anguish — her peers' attachment to her deepens, which Dao reveals to us by filming a phalanx of gentle, epicene youths — writers of both sexes — casting longing glances her way in discreet over-the-shoulder close-ups.

This idyll begins its painful dissolution late one evening as Yu hosts a gathering of friends in her garden. In the flickering lamplight beneath a deep purple sky, a handsome young dandy stands in front of a line of blossoming cherry trees reciting to a group of louche aesthetes a poem about the tender ache of the tree's first flowers in spring, and just at that moment, the husband appears on the edge of the frame, a mere outline emerging from the shadows so slowly and so hauntingly it feels as if he makes time itself expand. Then, in a sequence that echoes the film's opening, Dao cuts quickly to the husband leaping into the center of the image in a jealous rage, breaking the poet's jaw with one punch, then ripping the trunk of a cherry tree in half with his bare hands. Later that night, in a harrowing scene in the couple's bedroom shot almost entirely in darkness, he strikes his wife across the face and drags her across the floor to the foot of the bed, so that we can see nothing but an impenetrably black screen, hearing nothing but his animalistic grunts and her muffled, indistinct cries in a three-minute-long take that feels as if it will never end.

The second half of the film begins the next morning when a courier rushes into their bedroom, waking them up by announcing that troops of an enemy warlord are pouring in over the nearest mountain pass. Though she doesn't know it yet, the Taiping Rebellion — a metaphorical stand-in for the contemporary Guomindang's internecine squabbles — has finally begun. Over the next few sequences, Yu's gracefully spartan rooms are overrun in turn by the soldiers of the opposing warlord, merchants from the coast, then the soldiers of yet another warlord. But the movie takes an unusual tack for a war film, focusing not on warriors in battle but on the intellectual upheavals in Yu's community of artists. In one scene, the troops of an antagonist drag Yu's handsome young poet friend out into her garden lined with now-bare cherry trees and execute him unsentimentally by firing squad. In another, a young dancer friend huddles with her newborn under a low bridge crossing a stream as soldiers march above her head, desperately trying to breastfeed her baby as a way of preventing him from crying out loud. But some of Yu's intellectual friends, surprising to her, seem to enjoy the war. She visits one of her closest friends, a flamboyantly imperious judge of taste, only to discover him in his studio — in an image with uncomfortable echoes of her husband's rooms earlier — surrounded from floor to ceiling by the same kind of ceramic pottery he once derided, and he admits he's making a fortune selling these cheap knock-offs of authentic culture to the British traders in the treaty ports. When she visits another protege, Dao films his studio walls covered with grandiose landscape paintings, as if the trauma of war has inflamed a latent megalomania that he misconstrues as inspired vision.

Rumors of violence in the region wax and wane over the next few months until, one night, she wakes to see the darkness of her bedroom pierced by moonlight, a gang of ragged men hovering above her. They pull her husband from their bed and throw him across the floor, then drag him, kicking and screaming, down the hall. Meanwhile, Yu breaks free to her garden and watches in a series of painfully long takes as the soldiers set fire to their estate, and then, in a series of widescreen shots, a haunting inverse of the landscape paintings we'd seen earlier, she watches as the buildings burn to the ground. With the fires still smoldering, she sneaks away to a nearby village, dresses herself up as a peasant, and escapes on horseback through the tawny night.

For weeks, she rides deeper and deeper into the interior through forests and twisting canyons and river valleys blanketed with mist. And it's only then, after Yu has escaped civilization, that Dao presents her most audaciously pictorial landscape images suffused with saturated earth tones — as if bringing to the surface Yu's dawning realization about the sublimity of nature in contrast with the aesthetic limits of her former cultured world. As one sequence follows another, she shrinks ever smaller into the frame. Then, after weeks of travelling, she pushes over a ridge and gazes down over a narrow valley, home to a remote mountain village, which has become, rumor has it, a refuge for artists from across the country.

Here, the film once again takes on surprising tones for a war film. In this new makeshift community, the now scruffy and world-weary artists spend their days lounging about in thatched huts, totally disinterested in the fate of the country, drinking tea and any homemade beverage they can figure out how to ferment, and spend their nights arguing — in compositions that emphasize their miniscule irrelevance among the craggy mountains and fog-drenched woods — about color theory, the appropriate textures for the sculpted surfaces of vases and tea cups, or various techniques for daubing paint with brushes made from the fur of weasels or sable. Nevertheless, despite their seeming obsession with pure form, their aesthetic position, too, has evolved — and continues to evolve — because of the nation's political situation. The landscape painters become enamored with the mountains. But now, Yu is surprised to discover, they produce canvases even more grandiose than their seemingly conservative colleagues who'd remained behind, now populating their images with rocky cliffs and violent waterfalls even more melodramatic than those of their former friends whom they now refer to derisively as "collaborators." When Dao films Madame Yu observing these paintings, she cuts back and forth jarringly between her point-of-view shots, which can take in only a small portion of the paintings, and her reaction shots in tight close-ups, her face pinched in confusion. Now as she walks through her friends' ersatz studios in their humble bamboo shacks, she casts a withering eye over their oversized canvases, saying nothing. At night, she retreats to her own hut and sits quietly alone with only one flickering candle.

Then, inevitably, the war comes again. One night, as Yu sits alone reading poetry, crickets chirping around her, she hears a distant echo, then the far-off clamor of horses coming down through the ravine. She steps outside and stands amid the moonlight haze in a widescreen frame alive with the various possibilities of purples and blacks. And suddenly, soldiers on horseback are swirling around her. In the distance, at the far edges of the frame, other soldiers are dragging her friends from their homes and setting fire to their huts, so that the image becomes one giant conflagration of orange flame licking up at the starless sky, an obvious echo of the image of her home aflame earlier in the film — Dao's subtle commentary on the inevitable circularity of fate. In a tight close-up, Yu glances left, then right: she doesn't recognize these men, she can't place their accents, she doesn't know which warlord they belong to, if any. The soldiers run pell-mell through the village on a drunken spree, stomping their feet gleefully through porcelain vases and throwing canvases into the roaring flames. When she notices her captors mesmerized by the bonfires, Yu wrestles free and sneaks out of the village and into the woods, which become ever darker and more silent the further she proceeds, the soundtrack nothing other than her heavy breathing, until finally, once she's reached the top of a peak, in the film's final shot, she turns back and gazes out over the village, which appears now like a landscape painting of a world erupting in on itself, nature's grandeur no longer there, with miniscule stick figures staggering amid the carnage that once represented her artist friends' dream of a utopian community, an alternative to the political world.

Only Angels Have Wings (d. Howard Hawks, USA, 1940)
pr. *Columbia Pictures, sc. Jules Furthman, starring Cary Grant
and Jean Arthur, sound, b&w, 35mm, 121 min.*

Though Howard Hawks's position in the canon became secure
for a time thanks to the French auteurist critics of the 1950s and
1960s, his centrality to critical discussions has diminished over
the years. Film scholars, in particular, have come to value more
than anything else a director's dexterity at visual signification,
most likely because focusing on those optical formal qualities
eases both the hermeneutic and pedagogic function of their careers. Writers on film rarely focus on the issues that animated
Hawks's stylistic vision: the screenplay's construction, iconic
performance, and especially the flair for crisply and obliquely
sophisticated dialogue and for its sonic textures. Critics who
revere auteurs like Hitchcock and Antonioni who express themselves chiefly through montage and mise-en-scene often treat
such visual facility as the ideal end result in and of itself; but
those formal strategies are just some of many available tools a
director might use to convey a nuanced worldview. If the complexity of one's philosophical vision is the ultimate goal, though,
it shouldn't matter whether a filmmaker expresses that vision
through the image or through words. And yet, even those scholars who've been more inclined to elucidate an auteurist credo
than to identify a set of visual fingerprints have still miscon-
strued the nature of Hawks's intellectual convictions.

Most of Hawks's prominent exegetes writing in the 1970s, for
instance — including Robin Wood and Gerald Mast — have portrayed him as an artist with an ameliorating, humanist vision.
Wood writes that *Only Angels Have Wings* is structured around
the characters' struggles between responsible self-respect and
irresponsibility, and he sees the achievement of an adult self-
esteem as a kind of moral victory. "By the end of *Only Angels
Have Wings,*" he writes, "almost every character has undergone
a process of improvement.... [Hawks] is able convincingly to
portray creative relationships in which the characters help each

other, and through which they develop toward a greater maturity, self-reliance, and balance."[141]

There's certainly an element of truth in these writers' accounts — Hawks's all-male groups do cultivate a sense of communal allegiance, after all — but even his advocates ignore his most intriguing qualities, especially the recurring touch of amorality essential to his work. Though even his most lucid defenders rarely acknowledge the fact, it is his astute and distinctive strain of nihilism that makes Hawks such a compelling artist, a thinker in the same echelon as Schopenhauer or Nietzsche. His obsession with suicide as the best antidote to the meaninglessness of life is surprisingly joyful and exuberant, never defeatist, a nuanced and counterintuitive vision of despair.

We can examine Hawks's intellectual stance by studying his endings. In any storytelling form, after all, the notion of character development is intrinsically related to narrative closure because it is the story's resolution that determines what evolution — if any — the characters have undergone, and also what attitude the filmmaker has about the intellectual conflicts that propelled his story in the first place. But contrary to most critics' claims, in many of Hawks's films, his protagonists are actively opposed to their own moral improvement, ending the movie in the same problematic situation that they were in before the movie began, a type of conclusion that might best be understood as the closure of irresolvable circularity.

Hawks uses this type of circular ending repeatedly throughout the first half of his career, including comedies like *His Girl Friday* (1940), but it appears most emphatically in his movies about war and aviation in the 1930s, including *Dawn Patrol* (1931), *Road to Glory* (1937), and *Ceiling Zero* (1938), all of which have remarkably similar conclusions in which the protagonists embrace a passive form of suicide. Hawks does not portray these suicidal tendencies, though, as depressing. In *Only Angels Have Wings,* his pilots are rambunctious and free-spirited, gathering around a piano to belt out tunes together. Cary Grant perfect-

---

141 Robin Wood, *Howard Hawks* (Garden City: Doubleday, 1968), 24.

ly embodies their joie-de-vivre. If anything, Hawks makes his characters' decisions about their own deaths seem honorable. It is this patina of dignity in Hawks's unresolved conclusions that makes some of his advocates stress a sense of moral ameliora- tion while overlooking the nihilism — an idealistic nihilism, ad- mittedly — that is the essence of these endings.

The conclusion of *Only Angels Have Wings* leaves much of the protagonists' psychological and emotional conflicts un- resolved, leaving them in the same state of instability that has defined them for as long as we can imagine them. In the film's final scene, Bonnie Lee (Jean Arthur) comes in to say goodbye to Geoff Carter (Cary Grant). Geoff is a pilot, running an air- line that delivers the mail over a dangerous pass from a South American outpost called Barranca. Bonnie Lee is a woman who considers herself one step up from a chorus girl — she says she does a "specialty" — who just got off the boat when the movie began. They've fallen for each other, but they're both too hard- boiled to admit it.

Throughout the movie, they've both maintained that they would never ask anyone else to make a sacrifice on their behalf. Now, in the final scene, Bonnie obviously wants to stay with Geoff, but she doesn't want to ask him and she's afraid that he will never ask her. Just at that moment, the sound of the lookout station from up in the mountain pass comes over the wireless. The storm has cleared. If Geoff's outfit makes just one more de- livery, he and his business partner Dutchy will get a contract for another year. But the last attempt to make this very delivery ended in the death of his best friend, Kid. Inspired rather than intimidated by this danger, Geoff strides around the room excit- edly, shouts orders at his men, puts on his raincoat, and comes back to kiss Bonnie perfunctorily as he heads out the door.

The last time he'd tried to go up in the air, earlier that even- ing, Bonnie had shot him in the arm in a vain attempt to keep him safely on the ground with her, and they're both aware that Kid may have died instead of Geoff because of what she did, just as they're both aware that a pilot named Joe may have died in the beginning of the movie because of her as well. Now, as he's almost out the door, he hands her a coin. "Tails you go, heads you stay." He flips it and it comes up heads. But she won't stay that way, giving him one of the lines that pops up more than once in a Hawks film — "I'm hard to get, Geoff. All you have to do is ask me" — but he refuses to ask, handing her the coin and striding out the door. It's only then that she examines the coin and realizes that it's two-headed, Geoff's roundabout way of assuring that she'd stay. Her eyes brighten, the string section on the soundtrack swells, and she runs to the door, where she looks out into the rain as Geoff prepares for takeoff once more. The movie ends there, though, before we learn whether or not he returns safely or whether Geoff and Bonnie will ever develop into the kind of mature adults who are able to express their feelings for each other directly.

Though no one uses the word itself, the idea of suicide plays as significant a role in *Only Angels Have Wings* as it had in other Hawks films of the 1930s. The whole movie is organized around the possibility that Geoff is using flight as a means of taking his own life. This is why Bonnie pulls the gun on him that final night. "I won't let you go," she tells him. "I won't let you kill yourself." Geoff doesn't dispute the fact that suicide seems inevitable or that he's even opposed to the idea. "So you're going to do it to keep me from doing it," he says. In fact, the whole movie is pervaded by the concept of suicide. Every single pilot knows the chance that he will die in a plane crash is quite high. Why are they there, then? They don't get paid particularly well, given the extraordinary risks. Their living conditions are dingy. Barranca itself is a backwater, a metaphorical space for the characters' collectively embraced spiritual isolation. Joseph Walker's lighting is uncharacteristically dark for a Hawks film; his emphasis on chiaroscuro effects actualizes Hawks's nihilism. Every scene shot outside is suffused with inky blacks; Dutchy's restaurant-saloon-airplane lobby-hotel is lit almost exclusively with low hanging lanterns, and Geoff's small back office materializes his ennui with slanted shadows from his window blinds. Geoff is not the only one who embraces flight as a form of suicide. Kid, too, wants to go up in the air at the end of the film precisely because its perilousness augurs his own demise. Just before the final night of the film, Geoff has told Kid that he can't fly anymore because he's losing his eyesight. But Kid cannot imagine himself in a world in which he can't fly. For Kid, the choice to die in a plane at the end of the movie is not a sacrifice made so that others may live, but a decision to live by the creed of idealistic nihilism that he shares with Geoff or not to live at all.

As Bonnie gazes out at Geoff in the final sequence, the movie may be over, but their relationship — if, in fact, that is even what it is — has only just begun. They have started another cycle of conflict that they have both lived through before. Geoff will continue to live out his screwy ideal, convincing himself that he's living only in the present, without any burdens from the past or constraints from the future. He will be content with this philosophy, lost in the fog, playing games of chance with fate; Bonnie, too, will continue to convince herself of the beauty of his creed, as she waits, night after night, for Geoff to return once again.

Hawks's vision of a continuous circular return may have an unexpected silver lining when considering his own reputation. When he was at the height of his career, there was no film culture in America to speak of. Only when he was in the final years of his working life did critics in Paris, then London, then New York begin to take notice of him and write about him as if he were on par with the likes of Molière and Corneille.[142] But in the last couple of decades, as critics and theorists have returned once again to emphasize an aesthetics of visual design — a remnant of the theories of cinematic specificity that defined the late silent period — his star has faded and his work languishes on the margins of the discipline once again. But if Hawks's philosophical vision has any merit, we'll see that the critical pendulum will inevitably circle back around again so that someday in the future, perhaps the near future, writers will treat Hawks's films once again with the scrutiny that they deserve.

---

142 Jacques Rivette, "The Genius of Howard Hawks," in *Cahiers du Cinéma, the 1950s,* ed. Hillier, 126–31.

Paper Flowers (d. Guru Dutt, India, 1959)
pr. Guru Dutt Films, sc. Abrar Alvi, starring Guru Dutt and
Waheeda Rehman, sound, b&w, 35mm, 119 min.

India has been producing more feature films than the United States or any European nation for more than fifty years, yet its films still play a surprisingly peripheral role in cinephile culture in the West. This critical neglect is largely the product of international exhibition practices: for decades, film festivals — more than distribution companies, theater owners, or cultural ministries — have played the leading role in defining the contours of what we call "foreign film." Ever since Mussolini's fascist government organized the first film festival in Venice in 1936, these annual tourist pilgrimages among the faithful have functioned as the primary venue where Western critics introduce themselves to movies outside of the European and North American context. When they return home, they become the most influential voices spreading this notion that "international cinema" necessarily equals "art cinema." Surprisingly, the advent of new exhibition technologies over the years has done little to change this perception. Even in the era of BETA tapes, DVDs, and new streaming services, companies tend to purchase the distribution rights to those foreign films that have already created a buzz for themselves — and the festival circuit remains the primary site where a movie can build a transnational reputation.

Thus, cinephile culture has developed an oddly bifurcated relationship between the concepts of nation and genre in that critics tend to valorize genre pictures from Hollywood and France but not from the developing world. Americans and Europeans rarely write about Kung-fu masters like Gordon Liu or Mexican auteurs of hothouse melodrama like Emilio Fernández. Instead, they focus on directors who make films about serious social issues that adhere to a conventional realist aesthetic. Thus, when even sophisticated critics in the West hear the term "Indian cinema," the name of Satyajit Ray is almost always the first to come to mind — and even in that case, most people know him only for his Apu trilogy. *Pather Panchali* (1955) was not the first Indian film to appear at a European film festival, but it took hold of the critical consciousness when the British critic Lindsay Anderson wrote a series of rave reviews after its screening at Cannes in 1956, which inspired a few small distributors to pick up its rights, which led, in turn, to a series of unexpectedly long engagements at art house cinemas in London and Manhattan, transforming the movie into the paragon of art cinema from the developing world, a position it has held ever since — as much due to international distribution and exhibition practices as to its indisputable excellence.

In the Golden Age of Hindi cinema, meanwhile, most of the greatest directors — men like Raj Kapoor, Bimal Roy, and Mehboob Khan — built their careers and reputations by working in the popular idiom, turning out melodramatic musicals on relatively big budgets: movies about the intense yearning of unrequited or impossible love, usually with protagonists from the impoverished classes struggling to survive in an uncaring world. Films like these, though, were almost never invited to European festivals and thus were never distributed theatrically in the cultural centers of the West; not surprisingly, then, directors like Kapoor, Roy, and Khan are still not very well known to critics in Paris and New York. In the same vein, other Indian directors who worked within the system but who refashioned or challenged the conventions of popular film — the developing world analogues of directors like Hitchcock and Hawks — have similarly been ignored. And in the classical Hindi cinema, the one director who may best represent the figure of the populist intellectual is the director Guru Dutt, especially in his film *Paper Flowers*.

Dutt began his career as an actor in the 1940s and after he graduated to the director's chair, he released a series of small films throughout the early 1950s, each one slightly more successful than its predecessor, until his film *Pyaasa* (1957) — the story of a struggling young poet living on the fringes of society — became a huge box office success and solidified his status as one of the country's major stars. Now able to finance the biggest budget of his career — and with the artistic freedom from running his own production company — Dutt challenged himself to produce an even darker and more complex work of art with his next picture, *Paper Flowers*. From the beginning of the production process, Dutt made cinematography central to his vision, becoming the first Indian director to shoot in Cinemascope so that he could experiment with the expressive possibilities of mise-en-scene more than ever before. And he encouraged his cinematographer V.K. Murthy to make the image as dark as possible — as moodily nihilistic as the hardboiled crime films from Hollywood that he'd been screening obsessively over the last several years. Then, emboldened by his collaborators' openness about venturing into ever-darker territory with him, he decided on the night before shooting commenced to cut out a thirty-minute subplot featuring his regular comedic sidekick Johnny Walker in order to focus exclusively on the tragic aspects of a film director bewitched by his muse.

The result was an unusually philosophical examination of the intrinsic power — both seductive and destructive — of the cinema as an art form. Years before Fellucci in *Via Veneto* (1963), Fassbinder in *Beware of a Holy Whore* (1971), and Diebenmeier in *Desolation* (1972), years before Bertolt Brecht became the rage among leftist intellectuals in Paris, Shanghai, and Calcutta, and years before Ritwik Ghatak's own experimental, self-reflexive adaptation of Brecht's *The Rise and Fall of the City Mahagonny* (1970), Guru Dutt was already investigating the nature of cinematic artifice in *Paper Flowers,* an unusual hybrid of melodramatic musical, romantic tragedy, and introspective exploration of an artist's unhealthy obsession with the source of his own creativity.

From the opening scene, when Dutt positions us with the protagonist, a haggard old man — played, of course, by Dutt himself — locked out of the gates of a motion picture studio, he makes clear that the enticing but dangerous force of the movies will be the film's guiding thematic conflict. After the man manages to enter the compound, he stands at the foot of a giant statue — humbled beneath the towering symbol of the cinema — and the credits roll so that the name of Guru Dutt Films mirrors the name of the studio in the diegetic world of the film, a not-so-subtle hint that the flashback that's about to unfold will explain how the motion pictures' innate power has destroyed the life of the artist who is making the very film that we have just begun watching. But by positioning us with him from the opening scene, Dutt reminds us that being a cinematic spectator — surrendering ourselves to the iconic expressivity of the screen — is ultimately just as self-destructive a process as art-making itself.

Guru Dutt stars as the Guru Dutt-like director Suresh Sinha, who's just begun production on a searing melodrama of doomed love, a story quite similar to his previous movie *Pyaasa* (1957). Making the film is painful, though, because he's having a difficult time casting an actress in the lead. Late one night, when he's out wandering, he gets caught in a sudden rainstorm and takes refuge under a tree; there, he sees a young woman (Waheeda Rehman) shivering from the cold and lends her his coat. When that same naïve young woman, Shanti, arrives the next day at the studio to return his coat, she accidentally steps out onto the soundstage just as Suresh and his crew are filming a scene, thus inadvertently transforming herself into an aspect of the cinematic image, which will, in turn, inadvertently transform Suresh as well. When he watches the day's rushes later that night and sees Shanti as a larger-than-life, iconic face on screen, he leaps to his feet: "She's the one! That's the face!" he exclaims: she is the very image he needs for his starring role.

Dutt has thus laid bare the central intellectual conflict that propels the narrative's rise and fall: the artist is inspired by his muse, yes, but the filmic muse is merely a two-dimensional image, not a three-dimensional human being. At the heart of the cinematic enterprise, then, lies an irresolvable tension for the filmmaker, the star, and the audience as well: the cinematic image has the capacity — more than any other art form — to transform the quotidian into the sublime, and yet it can only express this sublimity as a mere surface, a simple physical exterior that provides only hints at a metaphysical interior, the shallow source of film's enigmatic power. And this insuperable tension between superficiality and depth defines their romantic relationship as much as it does the medium. That is, because the director and his muse must, by the inexorable logic of storytelling, eventually fall in love with each other — in real life as well as on screen — the artistic inspiration and the romantic love that the muse engenders must both necessarily be doomed from the start.

Dutt draws repeated connections between these themes of visual perception, artistic inspiration, and the impossibility of romantic love. From the beginning, he consistently portrays Shanti as an image that both intrigues and haunts him, a face that he can read — and transform — more acutely than anyone else. When she arrives for her screen test, she steps out onto a cavernously empty and dark soundstage — the physical manifestation of his brooding artistic soul — and steps directly into a beam of heavenly light. He removes his glasses, astonished, as if her appearance has finally given him the power of sight: "Forever my eyes have been searching," he says, "for this vision, this naïveté, this innocence." He is an artist in the field of film precisely because he has exceptionally discerning imaginative faculties, a capability that manifests itself perceptually — the proficiency to detect, as others cannot, the luminary potential hidden within the human figure. But at the same time, this capability ironically circumscribes his powers of imagination because he can only perceive his muse in the simplified, iconic mode of the motion pictures. The cinematic artist, then, is inevitably trapped in a double-bind because film gives one the ability to see more powerfully than any other art form, and yet, this perceptual power is founded upon a two-dimensional illusion. And it is this insurmountable dichotomy, Dutt suggests, that will inevitably destroy both the artist and his muse. But on an even deeper level, because the audience can see only what the director has decided to reveal, the audience, too, is ultimately trapped within the same self-destructive spiral as is the artist.

Dutt brings these ideas to life in a climactic scene in which Suresh and Shanti meet, presumably to finally declare their love for one another, a scene that Dutt situates, fittingly, on the same soundstage. The setting is vast and empty, a metaphorical space, with just two chairs and a few light stands strewn across an almost tar-black, artificial interior bisected by narrow swaths of light so that the whole thing feels like an especially austere production of *Waiting for Godot*. When the scene's tension has reached the point when the protagonists must turn and face each other to finally give voice to their feelings, a sudden silence falls, neither character capable any more of speech, and then, after a heartbeat suffused with anticipation, the music swells. But it is not the characters' voices we hear singing. No, the song — and the voices on the soundtrack — seem to emanate from some ethereal dimension. Suresh and Shanti can no longer express themselves through language: they can only gaze achingly into each other's eyes — no longer characters, but mere images, incarnations of romantic yearning pained by the force of love. The lyrics speak of the incompatibility between actual life and an aesthetic vision of self-immolating bliss: "Life brings us to such sweet pleasure of pain. Your self, you are no more. My self, I am no more."

Dutt's cinematic style — like the music itself — expresses more than words could on their own. The camera begins on a close-up of Waheeda Rehman's iconic visage and tracks back quickly, as if her soul — the core of her sensual desire — is being pulled from her body, connecting her to her soul mate across the bleak void, that hauntingly shadowed space. And as they stand across from each other in the frame, two miniscule figures overwhelmed by the detritus of movie-making technology, a light from above — presumably a cinematic spotlight, but perhaps more accurately, a shaft of searing illumination issuing from the heavens, from the source of eternal rapture — falls down in one perfect beam between them. Then in a parallel movement, the camera tracks forward just as quickly to a close-up of Guru Dutt as we hear the same lyrics repeated, the two stars connected by their desire to abandon this unruly existence and transform themselves into some incorporeal form. In the next shot, the doomed lovers stand on opposite sides of the widescreen image, the spectral beam of light dividing the picture in two.

Then, suddenly, their ghostly outlines — the immaterial perfection of their longing — step out of their bodies and walk forward to unite in the middle of the blinding light that descends from above. This spiritual union — made possible only by the magic of the movies — inspires their actual selves to act, so that their physical bodies now step forward as well. But as they approach, some invisible force — the knowledge that they must not allow themselves this cinematographic euphoria — holds them back. They cannot bring themselves to touch, to embrace, to kiss in the actual world. They cannot articulate their wishes with their own voices; they must rely on the power of the non-diegetic song. As they stare into each other's eyes, immobilized, the camera tracks in a slow circle behind them until they become just two darkened silhouettes against an abstract background of pure light, the inverse image of their perfected abstract selves, a minimalist and meaningless void, the visual analogy of the impossibility of their love. Then, without explanation, Suresh and Shanti turn from each other and walk away. And the darkness of the soundstage seems to heave and surge, filling the width and depth of the frame once again. The two figures shrink into the bleak atmosphere, standing at opposite edges of the frame, bisected once again by the blinding light which repels as much as it tempts them.

The film failed at the box office upon its initial release. It was too hopeless — or perhaps too intellectual — for film fans at the time. Guru Dutt died just a few years later at the age of 39, most likely a suicide. To this day, few critics have grappled with the film in English. But Guru Dutt's mysterious images invite us to speak back to them: it's time to treat *Paper Flowers* — and the work of its author — with the same attention we've begun to afford genre filmmakers from other countries and other traditions over the last few decades.

Paris in the Evening (d. Marcel L'Enfant, France, 1932)
pr. Rooster Films, sc. Nellie Lamoreaux and Marcel L'Enfant,
starring Adrienne Bontemps and Jean Le Couvriere, silent, b&w,
35mm, 132 min.

For decades now, intellectual critics and academic scholars alike
have cast Marcel L'Enfant more than any other figure as the
paradigmatic theorist-filmmaker of modernism, an aesthetic
martyr to the cause of pure cinema vanquished by the coming
of sound. In his previous features, *Monsieur Charles* (1928) and
L'Arlésienne (1930), L'Enfant had already experimented with film
form, drawing on the works of the Russian theorist Sergei Eisenstein to explore the expressive limits of editing, becoming
the darling of Parisian literary circles, one of the few figures admired by Surrealists, monarchists, and Catholics alike.

Nevertheless, L'Enfant wasn't entirely satisfied with the aesthetic philosophy that had inspired his earlier cinematic efforts.
"The Russian writers inspired by the montage techniques of
men like Jennings and Dwan," he wrote,

> were operating exclusively within a horizontal register of se-
> quential unfurling. Analyzing how an earlier filmmaker had
> organized images one after another would always limit us to
> move in only one direction through time. But I became curi-
> ous about whether we could use the techniques of the cin-
> ema to explore more multidimensional modes of expression.
> That's what drew me to the technique of superimposition: it
> offered a means of building a vertical axis upon the horizon-
> tal layer of editing in order to create a richer spatial lexicon
> of human thought.[143]

In *Paris in the Evening,* then, L'Enfant pushed the boundaries
of the cinema even further than he had before, bringing the

---

143 Marcel L'Enfant, "The Russian Montage Theorists and the Concept of
   Multidimensionality," in *Collected Writings,* trans. Benedict Leonard and
   Rochelle Fleury (Cambridge: Harvard University Press, 1987), 98–99.

techniques of editing and superimposition to their artistic and philosophical pinnacle to create what remains the aesthetic touchstone of the late silent period.

Like many French filmmakers of the 1920s and 1930s, L'Enfant began his career as a critic, founding the journal *Le Cinéma Moderne* in 1921 with Louis Delluc and Yvette Couqot in order to advocate a modernist style in what most intellectuals still considered to be a new medium despite almost three decades of artistic experimentation. Over the course of the 1920s, though, the editorial board split over the role that narrative should play in the cinema. Couqot, influenced by her then lover Louis Aragon's newfound interest in the work of Sigmund Freud, broke with her two male colleagues in 1929, declaring that "the ultimate goal of the cinema was the exploration of heretofore inarticulable desires through the symbolic power of pure abstraction."[144] L'Enfant was initially cool to the new theories of mind coursing through Parisian intellectual circles, and though he wasn't particularly enamored with the movies that Couqot had made to explore these theories — in particular, the twenty three minutes of dissolving shades of gray that she called *Symphonie* (1929) — her work did help him articulate what he saw as the necessary relationship between narrative conflict and the rendering of subconscious states. "Her limited palette and the shallowness of her textures," he wrote to a friend, "are the direct result of the Surrealists' narrow focus on the causes of mental agitation. Storytelling, after all, is predicated upon interpersonal conflict, which plays a much more important role than a therapeutic analysis of childhood trauma does in releasing complex, repressive mental structures."[145]

Nevertheless, despite these differences that most historians concentrate on today, more often than not L'Enfant positioned himself within the intellectual territory that Couqot had initial-

144 Yvette Couqot, "The Filmic as the Sign of the Unconscious," in *French Film Theory and Criticism, Volume 1: 1907–1936*, ed. Richard Abel (Princeton: Princeton University Press, 1993), 452.

145 Marcel L'Enfant, Letter to Georges Ribemont-Dessaignes, July 7, 1928, in *Collected Writings*, 410.

ly staked out. In his essay "The Multiple Layers of the Cinematic Psyche," he paralleled her concerns by arguing, contrary to most contemporaneous critics, that the cinema had a greater capacity to represent the depths of subconsciousness than the novel. But it was in his follow-up to that essay, "Superimpositions and Revolutionary Consciousness in Esther Summerson's *Seagulls*," published in 1930, immediately after his split with Couqot, that he most cogently laid out his arguments about how filmmakers could express the complex nature of mental life through the use of superimpositions.[146]

In fifty hallucinatory pages, L'Enfant examined Summerson's use of montage and superimposition in the already famous climactic sequence in which she crosscut between two lovers consummating their affair at the beach and a young boy who wanders out onto the eight-floor ledge of an office building. In a shot-by-shot analysis, L'Enfant made suggestions about how the director might have more skillfully portrayed the mental universe of her protagonist. "Summerson creates a sense of emotional anxiety in her audience," he wrote,

> by creating parallel storylines that follow each other in cinematic time while occurring simultaneously in the fictional world. We can call this the 'horizontal axis.' She punctuates this sequence emotionally with one superimposition which is supposed to represent the protagonist's thoughts. We can call this the 'vertical axis.' But Summerson joins this vertical mode with the horizontal only at the precise moment when the two storylines converge at the same location. But she could instead have cut back and forth between each of the spaces she had previously introduced and each of the time periods she'd shown from the past in order to render the multilayered nature of the hero's conscious mental activity on a horizontal plane, while at the same time creating multiple juxtapositions via superimposition to portray the con-

---

146 Marcel L'Enfant, "The Multiple Layers of the Cinematic Psyche," in *Collected Writings*, 114–26.

flicting modes of the unconscious on the vertical plane. Such a method could demonstrate the way that multidimensional spatiotemporal coordinates of the phenomenal world interact with the multidimensional spatiotemporal coordinates of the metaphysical, thus attempting to faithfully render the magnitude of the human experience.[147]

L'Enfant's essay caused a sensation in both Paris and Moscow, and it remains one of the central theoretical texts on film to this day because by offering not only a prognosis but an alternative, L'Enfant thrust film criticism into the realm of artistic production, a region where it has, unfortunately, rarely ventured since.

L'Enfant's theoretical speculations would have remained just that if not for the producer Pierre Boudin, who offered to finance L'Enfant's next feature through his company Rooster Films on the condition that he make a story for the masses, offering up a script by the commercially successful romance novelist Nellie Lamoreaux, and given his interest in narrative, L'Enfant was eager to accept the offer. The story follows the innocent dreamer Nicolette (Adrienne Bontemps), a nineteen-year-old orphan who sells flowers in Les Halles to support her younger brothers and her blind aunt who helped raise them. One morning, a dashing young man (Jean Le Couvriere) comes running down the street and hides behind the irises in her stall. His name is Ferdinand, he tells her, and he's been framed for a murder he didn't commit. When the police arrive and ask her about an escaped convict, she instinctively points them in the other direction. Later, as she takes her trash out in a back alley, she sees the same young man in a knife fight with a soot-faced, bear-like hoodlum, surrounded by a gang of criminals who are cheering on the older man. When the gangster cuts Ferdinand across the face, Nicolette impulsively rushes forward into the melee, distracting his attacker, and Ferdinand takes advantage of the moment to plunge his knife into his antagonist's chest.

147 Marcel L'Enfant, "Superimpositions and Revolutionary Consciousness in Esther Summerson's *Seagulls* (1922)," in *Collected Writings*, 75–76.

The man instantly falls dead at his feet. The band of hoodlums falls back, shocked. Ferdinand instinctively takes Nicolette by the arm to escape around the corner, where he opens a manhole cover and pulls her down with him into the safety of the sewers.

Only later, after he's taken her to his hideout in the secret catacombs beneath the city does Ferdinand explain his story: he too was orphaned as a child and grew up alone on the streets. But recently, he discovered that the man who'd murdered his parents was none other than Giuseppe, the leader of Paris's most vicious criminal enterprise, the man he's just killed in the alley overhead. Then, over the next few weeks, brought together by the fear of revenge from Giuseppe's comrades, Ferdinand and Nicolette build a life for themselves as outcasts in the maze of caverns that spread, like a network of ghostly veins, beneath the city. And it is there in this mysterious alternative world amid the dancing candle-lit shadows of the cave walls that they begin to fall in love.

Desperate for money and imbued with a vengeful resentment toward the bourgeoisie who rule the world above, Ferdinand lets Nicolette in on his plan to get even. She immediately assents, and the young lovers begin to carry out a series of burglaries. Crime, they discover, makes them feel vibrant and carefree. Soon they're supporting themselves as jewel thieves, targeting the most corrupt members of the city's wealthy industrial class. In an homage to the serials of Louis Feuillade, Nicolette designs skin-tight outfits with masks and capes, all in black, that they wear when they pull off their heists, and the newspapers soon make them famous, referring to them in headlines as "The Dark Lovers of the Rooftops." And it is here in the film's second act that L'Enfant pushes his experiments with film form, transforming a romantic tale in the mode of Alexandre Dumas into a picture more avant-garde than even the films of Abel Gance.

L'Enfant had given the audience glimpses of Nicolette's subconscious through his use of superimpositions from the film's very first sequence, when he layered images of her mother in the past over her face in the present, segueing into other images in which she cares for her younger brothers in the present, which then leads into yet another layer of superimpositions of her landlord demanding her overdue rent. From this opening, L'Enfant deploys the superimposition in two contrasting modes: giving the audience access to Nicolette's subconscious while at the same time providing his own omniscient commentary, which stresses throughout that money is the primary force that determines the fate of every character, whether she or he ever becomes aware of this universal fact.

It is only when Nicolette and Ferdinand delve into the most dangerous aspects of their life of crime that L'Enfant begins to experiment most creatively with his theories about superimpositions. His style becomes more baroque and more intellectually stimulating as the movie progresses. Building on his own theoretical work, he begins to add superimposed layers of other characters' stories of which his protagonists are unaware, emphasizing that their increasing anxiety is the product of their lack of knowledge about their own situation. L'Enfant makes the interplay between these affective and epistemological forms of superimposition intertwine more and more throughout the film, like a Bach fugue, until the climactic sequence in which Nicolette and Ferdinand have planned their ultimate caper, the heist that will make them wealthy forever, the plan to break into the Rothschild Bank, the most notoriously well-guarded institution in all of Europe.

At this point, L'Enfant layers the images of Nicolette's anxious imagination (of Ferdinand falling amid a hail of fire from the police) with images of Ferdinand's worried mind (of Nicolette leaping from the rooftop to her death) and cuts back and forth between these superimpositions and a third series of images that he overlaps with a fourth — the police charging into the building through the front door, while Giuseppe's henchmen enter the basement through the catacombs, apparently trying to rob the bank, coincidentally, at that very same moment, unaware that their criminal antagonists have beaten them at their own game. L'Enfant plays out the intricate connections of this sequence for more than twenty minutes, adding layers upon layers of images so that at some points there are six or seven storylines superimposed together on screen at the same time.

At the most exhilarating moments of this climactic sequence, some images escape the phenomenal world and take on a purely poetic, metaphorical existence. At the moment that Nicolette first touches the famed White Diamonds of Zanzibar, for instance, we see superimposed pictures of the police commissioner breaking into the hall behind her in the upper left corner of the screen paralleled by superimposed images of Giuseppe's gang breaking into the room beneath her in the lower right. But at that very moment, L'Enfant moves beyond the narrative with sudden bursts of a memory of Ferdinand handing Nicolette a basket of wildflowers, which leads in turn to visions of rain, thunderclouds, the moon, stars, and what appears to be swirls of galaxies. And it is this aesthetic epiphany, this cinematic eruption of purely abstract bliss that seems, more than any storytelling logic, to be the cause of Nicolette and Ferdinand's miraculous escape from their pursuers to the nighttime rooftops of Paris.

Noël Burch and Hortense Lemieux have carried on the most heated discussions about this final sequence, arguing over the extent to which L'Enfant is a material determinist, to what extent he believes in free will, and to what extent he is a fatalistic nihilist. Burch argues, for instance, that with his superimpositions, L'Enfant was tracing the cause-and-effect relationship between consciousness and fate. That is, while L'Enfant demonstrates on the one hand that the powers of institutions, historical circumstances, and money rob people of their free will, at the same time he teases his audience with the option that people can escape their fates merely through their own determination. Nevertheless, since his character's mental lives — both conscious and subconscious — are molded from the start by economic circumstances, L'Enfant's superimpositions, in the end, reveal him to be "an ironic nihilist in that the very means of escape from the material conditions that control us are themselves materially determined, thus creating the mere illusion of free will, which is simultaneously tragic and comic."[148]

Lemieux, on the other hand, emphasizes the multiplicity of readings that L'Enfant's superimpositions offer up. "The very idea of the superimposition," she writes,

> laid down both in his critical writings and in the Rothschild sequence, is that characters face a variety of choices, both in understanding their pasts and in envisioning their futures. But the very arbitrariness of L'Enfant's images in the climactic moments of the film suggest that he is the very opposite of a material determinist. His stylistic use of superimpositions points out — as does the plot of the movie itself — that behind every negative possibility, a thousand impossibly poetic and optimistic alternatives exist, and that there is no rhyme or reason as to which of these manifold occurrences might eventually unfold. This cornucopia of randomness suggests the very opposite of the notion of inevitability to which Burch and his ilk are so irrationally wedded.[149]

L'Enfant, of course, never weighed in on these conflicting interpretations. The years-long process of making the movie, he said, had exhausted him, and after the film's release, he retreated with his wife and daughter to a small farm in Provence, where after a few years of rest, he commenced work on his next project, a sweeping tale of the 1830 July Revolution. But the coming of sound derailed his plans. Eventually, he did manage to direct two more films in the talking period, but "the way that dialogue tyrannized spatiotemporal reality into merely one dimension," he said, "left me unable to think anymore along the avenues that I had been exploring in my final years of the silent era."[150] So

---

148 Noël Burch, *Film at a Distance: Observations from a Second Space,* trans. Christopher King (Bloomington: Indiana University Press, 1987), 164.

149 Hortense Lemieux, *Spatiotemporal Interpretation: Superimposition and Montage in Modern Cinema,* trans. Hugh Blackley-Coake (New York: Columbia University Press, 1992), 42.

150 Marcel L'Enfant, "My Life: In Retrospect," in *Collected Writings,* 391.

he retreated once again to his farm, where he worked on his memoirs, which he left unfinished when he died in 1948 at the age of 54.

Phoenix (d. Li Bo, China, 1998)

pr. Shanghai Film Studios, sc. Li Bo, starring Gong Xiao-li, Vindrikimurtha, and Titilayo Abiola, sound, color, 35mm, 149 min.

In the early 1990s, the president of Shanghai Film Studios, Xin Hao-tzu, decided that it was time to challenge Hollywood on its own turf for the first time by producing science fiction block-busters with competitive budgets. Financially, his plan was a success; critically, the company's films made no dent on either side of the Pacific. Of all the directors he hired throughout the decade, only one, Li Bo, earned the praise of the critical establishment. "Everyone else," Li said, "thought that if you wanted to compete with the American film industry you had to make movies just like them: bigger spaceships, brighter colors, bigger explosions. But the only reason I've had any success is that I was the only director in Shanghai who went the other way. I didn't think that outer space was bigger and brighter. I imagined the future as silent and monochromatic. As fraught. As diseased."[151] So while most of his peers tried to outdo Hollywood in terms of the splendor of their visual effects, Li earned a lasting fame because he re-imagined the goal of science fiction, using the genre to examine the politics of race, nationalism, and the new global order of the 21st century.

Many Shanghainese sci-fi filmmakers had already begun to tweak Hollywood's racial imagination — which had always unthinkingly projected America's current ethnic demographics onto the future and into outer space — by producing movies with one Chinese and one American protagonist. But Li wanted to make a movie that overturned the ethnic and gender dynam-

---

151 "Interview with Li Bo," *Cinéaste* 26, no. 1 (Spring 2000): 52.

ics of the global future, so he made a film about three female scientists on the first colony on Mars — one Chinese (Gong Xiao-li), one Indian (Vindrikimurtha), and one Nigerian (Titi-layo Abiola) — who are leading the first promising archeological investigations into the fossil record of the primitive flora and fauna that flourished on the planet millions of years ago. At the same time, while most sci-fi films imagine an apolitical future governed by an idealized, rational, and peaceful one-world state, Li assumed that since ethnic, religious, and national strife had always inflamed wars at every point throughout history, it would continue to do so in the future as well. Thus, while the movie ostensibly deals with a scientific survey of the red plan-et, it is equally concerned with the political situation on Earth, which is, as with almost every science fiction movie, a thinly veiled commentary on the politics of the present day.

The film opens with sweeping widescreen shots of the rock-strewn, orange landscape of Mars, where a white glint of met-al flashes in the distance, the solitary human intervention on the desolate surface: the League of Nations' permanent scien-tific station, part ultra-modernist architectural chic, and part post-industrial garbage heap. Li introduces us to his three pro-tagonists not with close-ups of their faces, as we'd expect, but through a montage of S-wave sub-surface images that they're studying — the squiggles and dots that are the fossilized traces of microscopic life — associating all three women with their ob-ject of study, the ancient alien plant life they find more intrigu-ing than their fellow human beings with whom they live. They are working furiously, and from these first moments, their fur-rowed brows, expectant glances over their shoulders, and their anxiety about the physical proximity of other research teams in the lab hints that they are onto something — a discovery, we suspect, that frightens as much as it excites them. And then Vin-drikimurtha, bent over a three-dimensional projection at her desk, heaves out a gasp, and Gong and Abiola, with a pretend nonchalance, step over and bend down to gaze deep into the projection, sharing her fascination. Through their viewfinders, accompanied now by an atonal surge of pizzicato bursts on the soundtrack, we no longer see mere blotches and specks as we had with previous fossilized remains, but now long, perfectly straight lines that run parallel with each other, joining to form grids, and eventually patterns, like architectural blueprints, the unmistakable evidence of intelligent design.

As the women walk back through the narrow hallway of the station, they are giddily tense and silent with each other, afraid to dare articulate what they each know the others are thinking as well, but as they step into the main communal lounge, they come upon a circle of colleagues gathered around a live 3-D news feed from Earth that's reporting on the deteriorating political situation along the McMahon Line that defines the Chinese–Indian border, a dispute that looks increasingly like it might lead to global war. As the camera tracks forward slowly toward the three scientists standing on the edge of the circle, the green glow of the 3-D projection colors their faces to heighten the sense of alarm as Gong whispers, "Did you see what I saw?" And it's not entirely clear if she's referring to the visible evidence of intelligent life they'd each just witnessed back in the lab or to the news report they're now witnessing about intelligent life on their own planet possibly on the verge of destroying itself.

The plot, then, unfolds along two interconnected paths: the deepening archeological investigations of Mars and the march toward what could turn out to be the first global conflict back on Earth since the Great War of the 1910s. The three scientists commence their new round of excavations furtively, anxious at what they might find, afraid to let their colleagues know what they are up to, coordinating an array of brontosaurus-sized robotic digging machines to penetrate into the base of a nearby mountain where they expect to find a cave system. As the political tension escalates back home, these colossal engines dig up out of the planet mounds of red rock and dirt that grow ever larger, looming on the horizon, a towering orange mountain formed out of the planet's geological past, Li's Antonioniesque symbol of both the beauty and futility of all modern endeavors. At the same time, the scientists who once sat together in a tight, collegial circle as equals now snap at each other, gathering on opposite sides of the frame. Li arranges live news broadcasts from home in the background of every scene. Back on Earth, the tenuous political stand-off between China and India is breaking apart: a dispute over mining rights for rare metals off the coast of Madagascar has escalated amid a flurry of confused submarine battles and outbreaks of mysterious plagues that appear to be the result of chemical attacks, threatening to bring the two nations to all-out war. And now, in the dining halls and conference rooms of the colony on Mars, the teams of scientists, who'd originally appeared to have few discernible national traits, huddle together with their ethnic factions, planning to defend themselves with any rudimentary weapon they can get their hands on.

As with any classical story, Li makes his parallel narratives hurtle toward a simultaneous resolution. Just as war explodes on Earth — in Li's conception, no longer as a battle between human soldiers or even nuclear bombs, but between roving nanotechnology armies that hover above Beijing and New Delhi like pulsating swarms of insects — the Martian colony, too, erupts with bands of Chinese and Indian scientists hunting each other down in the halls of the station with lead pipes, makeshift clubs, and knives. Meanwhile, the three protagonists have left the colony behind, driving a buggy across the orange expanse, encased in body suits, their heavy breathing filling the soundtrack, finally reaching the mouth of a cave a hundred meters below the surface, where their readings have led them to believe there might be the million-year-old ruins of an alien city. As they step into the pitch blackness, their footsteps echoing in the cavern, the soundtrack now dominated by their labored breathing, we see through their eyes, through their visors, as they descend even deeper, following the minute beams of their lamps. After a few minutes of vertiginous stumbling in the dark, the first structures come into view: skinny wavering columns like ocean waves frozen in time, reaching from their feet up past the horizon of their sight to where they assume a ceiling must exist somewhere far above, here and there in the distance a latticework of hexagons that curves back into the distance like the painterly folds of silk fabric. As they step forward cautiously, more fragmentary visions appear: the floor littered with minute, glassy spheres filled with a milky, flowing liquid, undulating webs of a glowing wispy fur-like material floating in and out of view above them. And then they come to a stop in front of a flat wall covered with curlicue inscriptions of what could only be a language, and beside that, some delicate etchings of mountains, rivers, trees, and two moons.

In the hushed, epiphanic darkness, the three scientists make their way methodically back to the surface. But as they emerge from the cave, gazing across the vast red expanse of rocky soil beneath an endless and starry sky, they are too dazed to register their new shock at what they now see: in the distance, where once the League of Nations station stood, a riot of mangled metal structures — the detritus of walls and ceilings, industrial machinery, conference tables and lab equipment and chairs — slowly floats in the sky, away from what must have been the epicenter of an explosion. After a few moments, gazing at the surreal beauty of the dissolution of all they have ever known on this planet, a silent resignation sets in. The sound of their breathing slowly returns, then eventually engulfs the soundtrack. With only a brief exchange of glances, they turn back into the mouth of the cave. Once again, they work their way down through crawl spaces into the black depths of the alien crypt, where they wander, enthralled, through the ruins of the ancient city, the architectural structures wavering amid their feeble and flickering lamplight, pulsating, heaving, almost as if they are living organisms themselves. Finally, the sound of their breathing slows and diminishes as they realize they're running out of oxygen. They sit down, their backs against the cave walls, exhausted, casting their eyes over the majesty of the forms twining and twisting above them, knowing that they will be the only humans ever to witness the only evidence of other intelligent life in the galaxy, a race that appears to have annihilated itself just as humans now seem destined to replicate back on Earth.

Prize Fight (d. Randall Jennings, USA, 1912)
pr. Picador Films, silent, b&w, 16mm & 35mm, 50 min.

When it was first released, the American press hailed Randall Jennings's *Prize Fight* as the first actuality — and perhaps the first movie of any kind — that they considered a work of art, and decades later, historians still regard it as one of the foundational texts in the study of the non-fiction film and in the development of film grammar. At a time when virtually every American movie was still a two-reeler in which each scene consisted of one shot that mimicked a theatrical tableau, Jennings cut back and forth at a breakneck pace between a multitude of angles that showed the boxers so close that some people thought the men on screen might start bloodying the audience there in the movie theater. "Never before have I felt such excitement," Teddy Roosevelt claimed. "It was like watching a strike of lightning. Not even charging up San Juan Hill comes close."[152]

After the blockbuster triumph of the *Corbett–Fitzsimmons Fight* in 1897, boxing films had become the biggest draw for vaudeville theaters in the United States, just as the novelty of the first Edison and Lumiere exhibitions seemed to be wearing off. But the commercial success of that film and its predecessors was a double-edged sword: it inspired religious and women's groups to campaign against them and within a few years, they'd convinced a dozen states to ban the screening of boxing films. At the same time, it inspired Edison and the owners of the Keith-Albee theater chain to support a counter-campaign. So throughout the first decade of the twentieth century, boxing films became a central locus of cultural debate, banned in the majority of states, but still quite popular where they were still legal. But by the time Jennings made his own picture of a prize fight in 1912, audience interest in boxing had begun to wane, largely due, of course, to the politics of race. By 1910, Jack Johnson had become the first

152 Teddy Roosevelt, "An Evening's Entertainment," in *Prize Fight: A Film by Randall Jennings,* ed. Richard Turnborough (New Brunswick: Rutgers University Press, 1988), 238.

Black heavyweight champion of the world, and as hopes that a white boxer might regain the heavyweight championship faded, interest in boxing films had diminished as well.

Picador Films had been the leading producer of boxing movies since the turn of the century, but its president, Hiram T. Bingham, worried by the early teens that his business was doomed to failure. So when a cameraman named Randall Jennings approached him with new ideas about how to film boxing matches, Bingham was ready to listen. Up until that time, every boxing film had been shot with just one stationary camera placed far enough away so that the members of the audience could see the entire ring in the frame, giving them the illusion that they were sitting in the stands themselves at the event. But Jennings had been a fight enthusiast from a young age and he loved to sit as close as he could. As a kid, he said, he knew he'd witnessed a good fight only if he came home sore from craning his neck to look up at the giants in the ring.

Jennings had also been an avid amateur inventor. He first formulated his new ideas for the cinema, in fact, one afternoon in 1910 after he'd perfected a machine that would carry a hot pot of coffee on a conveyor belt on a circular route from his kitchen out onto his front porch, then back inside where it would automatically get refilled. Why not, he wondered, build something similar for a motion picture camera to circle the boxing ring from above? After some trial and effort, Jennings developed a system to capture several angles of a boxing match by deploying ten cameras at a time around the perimeter of the ring: with four cameramen stationed on the corners and four along the sides, plus one camera hanging from metal girders above and another that rotated along the perimeter of the ring — the last two controlled remotely from an operating booth a dozen yards away.

Nevertheless, though most commentators at the time — and most scholars since — have praised the film because it created new angles and thus new modes of perception, Jennings was right to argue from the beginning that the most important aspect of the film's success was not this new photographic system but his expressive methods of editing his shots together. In what was perhaps a more important decision than where to place his cameras, Jennings had hired Allan Dwan's leading editor, Mabel Howard, to work with him. And thanks to Trinity Beveridge's book on the film's production, we now know that Howard took on many uncredited duties during pre-production in addition to her role as cutter. Jennings only invented his tripods' rotating heads, for example, to satisfy Howard's suggestions about how to capture the best camera angles. Beveridge argues, in fact, that the film's final design probably owes as much to Mabel Howard's aesthetics as it does to Randall Jennings's.[153]

Two other decisions by Jennings's collaborators contributed to the movie's artistic success, while at the same time making this seemingly apolitical film, in retrospect, perhaps the most famous cinematic emblem of the era's racism. Because she knew that the movie would be financially successful or not, primarily because of its filmic rendering, not because of the historical significance of the fight itself, Mabel Howard convinced Jennings that they shouldn't just settle for the next heavyweight championship fight that came along. Rather, she told him, they should shoot as many fights as possible until they captured one that unfolded, by chance, with a dramatic narrative structure. In other words, she wanted a match that began with some emotional tension between two handsome men and climaxed with a dramatic knockout — not too short and not too long, and hopefully with a decent amount of blood.

At the same time, given his enormous financial investment in this most technically complex of any actuality yet made, Hiram Bingham insisted that in order to draw as large an audience as possible, his filmmakers could record either a fight between two white boxers or one in which a white boxer defeated a Black champion. With these strictures in place, Howard and Jennings bypassed the fights between Jack Johnson and Sam Langford — the two Black men then competing for the world heavyweight championship — and finally got lucky on the fourth fight

---

153 Trinity Beveridge, *Prize Fight: The Making of the Film* (New Brunswick: Rutgers University Press, 1995).

their team photographed, the prize fight between two white middleweights Stanley Ketchel and Frank Klaus. Virtually no one at the time seemed to think it was the least bit remarkable to release a film of two white middleweight boxers rather than the Johnson-Langford fight, but over the last several decades, scholars have re-imagined the film not just as the forerunner of modern cinematic grammar but also, as Whitney Ketchings claims, as "the prime example of how the politics of race became the structuring absence not just of this era, but of American film in general."[154]

But in 1912, white movie fans clearly didn't care about such things: *Prize Fight* became an overnight sensation upon its release, with crowds lining up outside theaters in every state where it was allowed to be screened. They couldn't believe the intimacy of the close-ups, the constantly moving camera, and the fastest editing that anyone had ever seen, which made spectators — as almost every writer observed — viscerally experience the fight as if they were actually standing in the ring themselves. "I was taken aback when I first saw blood," wrote Mary Heaton Vorse, "but I'm not ashamed to say that I would see it again. There was something primal about it, like happening upon two stags smashing their antlers in some dark glade in the middle of the night."[155]

The movie's stylistic flourishes electrified its audiences. Jennings' average shot length is just four seconds long at a time when the majority of films still didn't include a single cut in a ten-minute reel, and he framed the fighters in almost every shot from the waist up or even closer at a time when most films still depicted actors with their entire bodies in the frame. When most directors still never moved the camera at all, Jennings's camera panned and tilted to capture the action in almost every single shot, following the boxers as they danced and ducked and

154 Whitney Ketchings, *The Racial Blot: Blackness and the Imaginary in American Film* (Durham: Duke University Press, 1998), 45.

155 Mary Heaton Vorse, "A Woman Attends the Prize Fight," in *Women's Writing on Cinema*, ed. Edith Cloud (New Brunswick: Rutgers University Press, 1997), 147.

lunged around the ring. And the aerial shots seemed to hover above the men, as the poet H. D. said, "like an angel observing men committing sin."[156] The close-ups of fists pummeling bloody faces shocked and titillated people across the country. In the third round, when blood first shot out of Klaus's forehead, audiences were said to have screamed; President Taft's daughter Helen was only one of dozens of women who reportedly fainted before the movie reached its end; and in Kalamazoo, Michigan, it was said that a boy fled the theater and ran to the nearest police station where he dutifully reported that he had just witnessed a murder.

The movie was so shocking, in fact, that the nationwide attempt to ban boxing films, which had dissipated over the last decade, suddenly picked up steam again. Bingham had hoped that by focusing on two "great white hopes," he might arouse such positive passions that he could overcome the lingering cultural anxiety surrounding the boxing film. And for the most part he was right; the movie broke attendance records everywhere it played. But this very success, ironically, created a backlash that proved to be even more powerful in the long run. The spectacle of realistic violence proved too much for many contemporary observers, especially religious leaders and women's groups, which soon formed coalitions across the country to protest both the sport of boxing and the movies that portrayed it. Indeed, most historians take it for granted today that this second wave of campaigns against prize fight pictures was instrumental in mobilizing the same groups of women who eventually fought for both suffrage and Prohibition. Surprising everyone, the movement spread almost as quickly as the film, and within three years, every state had finally outlawed the exhibition of boxing films. H.L. Mencken later observed that the sudden theatrical success of the movie followed by the equally sudden success of its antagonists at banning it demonstrated "a rupture in

---

156 H.D., "Prize Fight," in *Close-Up: Cinema and Modernism, 1927–1933*, eds. James Donald, Anne Friedberg, and Laura Marcus (Princeton: Princeton University Press, 1999), 123.

the American psyche so illogical it would make even a Viennese doctor conversant in the new mental quackery scratch his head in consternation."[157]

Because of these state bans, *Prize Fight* remained the only artistically significant of all the silent boxing actualities, but its influence was legendary. By 1912, companies were producing mostly fiction films, but now that an actuality had earned more money than any movie ever made, the pendulum began to sway. The success of *Prize Fight* reinvigorated nonfiction filmmaking at the same time that it brought a modernist sensibility to the cinema for the first time. The movie kicked off both the "Actuality Rage" and the "New School of Motion Pictures" that dominated American moviemaking for the rest of the 1910s, and today it remains one of the cornerstones of the academic study of film, the movie that Serge Daney called, "the ideal father of cinematic grammar in that like any mythic creator, it combines qualities that are both believable and fantastical. And like any good myth, it belongs to the past — because we can see how everything that followed derived from its example — but also to the future — because even now, almost eighty years hence, we are still striving to surpass its example."[158]

Reeds at the Water's Edge (d. Jules Dassin, USA, 1962)
pr. The California Anti-War Alliance, sc. Jules Dassin, Rod
Taylor, and Suleeporn Apinyapong, starring Rod Taylor and
Suleeporn Apinyapong, sound, b&w, 16mm, 86 min.

The most successful politically engaged art sometimes comes forth only in the direst circumstances. These days, historians tend to think of Jules Dassin's *Reeds at the Water's Edge* as the most impressive film produced by the loosely affiliated group

---

157 H.L. Mencken, "The Alleged Art of the Motion Pictures," in *A Mencken Chrestomathy: His Own Selection of His Choicest Writings* (New York: Vintage, 1982), 568.

158 Serge Daney, "Before the Picture Show," in *Selected Film Criticism*, ed. Lionel Franke (Berkeley: University of California Press 2011), 205.

known as the Hollywood Realists. But he was only able to direct the film because Thailand had just entered the most violent period of its war, which inspired Dassin to sharpen his critique of American policy. But he was able to raise funds for the production from unusual sources only because financing for independent pictures was just then drying up. So in order to finance the film, he thought that he'd have to appeal to as wide an audience as possible by crafting a story with a traditional narrative arc that intertwined both romance and adventure. But this melodramatic approach, paradoxically, only heightened the acuity of his political cynicism, turning what might have been merely a forgettable leftist screed that preached to the choir into a film that tested its own progressive assumptions.

Dassin arrived in Bangkok just weeks after he'd wrapped up production on Steinbeck's *Cannery Row* (1961), fired up to make a courageous anti-war picture that shed light on American atrocities abroad. But he arrived just days after the Khon Kaen offensive appeared to have finally turned the tide for the US. His original plan had been to shoot a straightforward story about an American GI who becomes disillusioned with the war, who challenges his superiors, and then abandons the field of battle to declare himself a conscientious objector. He envisioned a simple shooting schedule to match his simple story, bringing along just a three-man crew and one actor, his star Rod Taylor. But the shifting tides of war — and his growing sense that he actually would prefer to see the Americans defeat the Japanese — forced him to re-assess his script. What was it, after all, that he was really opposed to in Thailand? American intervention? Japanese colonization? An opposition to all war in and of itself, he was beginning to wonder, might be an intellectually dishonest opinion. Questions like these eventually led the film to its final form, as much a theoretical examination of ideas about fidelity and ethnicity as it is a piece of agitprop filmmaking.

Dassin had been one of the leading figures of the Hollywood Realists, a loosely affiliated group that included Abraham Polonsky, Cy Endfield, Dalton Trumbo, and Joseph Losey, among others, men who'd been active in organizations that supported the Henry Wallace wing of the Democratic Party and who'd found a hospitable environment at Michael Feynman's American Pictures, where they'd been able to produce socially conscious films throughout the late 1940s and early 1950s. But the audience decline that began in the early 1940s with the rise of television eventually took a greater toll on the independent companies than it did on the three majors: Feynman's company had struggled to break even every year since its inception and finally ceased production in 1958. The economic boom of the Dewey years, meanwhile, had softened the political edges of the Depression so that many of the Hollywood Realists had retreated from their ideological commitments and were by the late 1950s producing apolitical commercial entertainments. But the spiraling troubles of the American intervention in Thailand and the younger generation's increasingly passionate protests against the war, Dassin said, inspired him, unlike most of his erstwhile progressive peers, to re-commit himself once again to political filmmaking. Riled up by the results of the 1960 election, Dassin wrote the first draft of the script in one feverish week, got a commitment from his friend Taylor, then cobbled together a small budget from a surprising source — a group of progressive California businessmen who'd helped found Veterans Against the War.

That being said, when a Japanese mortar shell landed near his hotel on his first night in the country, Dassin wondered if he'd made the right decision. The region wasn't nearly as calm as the American press had led him to believe. With artillery fire echoing on the edge of town, he and Taylor knew that they wouldn't be able to film as openly out in the streets as they'd planned. So the two men threw out the screenplay they'd brought with them and retreated to their rooms, where they hashed out a new story together in all-night sessions fueled by Scotch whisky and Cuban cigars. Over the next few weeks, they came to know the hotel's owner, a young woman named Suleeporn Apinyapong, who insists they call her "May." As they got to know each other better, she confided to them eventually that she was a member of the Seri Thai, the underground resistance that was then organizing

a shadow government in anticipation of the coming withdraw-
al of both the Americans and the Japanese. Intrigued, Dassin
asked her to read what they'd written so far, but after she told
them politely that they'd gotten their Thai characters all wrong,
he asked her if she'd be willing to join them in their nightly bull
sessions. So, over the next three weeks, May sat with Dassin and
Taylor night after night amid the thunderous bombardment
coming from both sides to revise the screenplay to reflect more
of the experience of the local population. But then, when they
were finally done, Dassin pulled a surprise, asking May out of
the blue to act opposite Taylor in the film; her inexperience, he
insisted, would give the film the sense of unrehearsed natural-
ness that he'd been aiming for ever since he first directed theater
on the New York stage back in the 1930s.

The story, then, consists of two intersecting plots. In the first,
Rod Taylor plays a young sergeant whose unit burned a Thai
village to the ground, which turns him against his superiors and
the war. Arriving in Khon Kaen on a week-long R&R, he vows to
anyone who'll listen that he's about to go AWOL and never return.
In the second story, a young woman who was forced from her
home first by the Japanese and then by the Americans has found
refuge as a waitress in a bar where she meets Taylor and agrees
to help him hide from the military police. While the original
script had included a love story in which the American fell for
an elusive Thai girl, in the final film, May rejects Taylor's advances, offended that he assumes she'll be smitten with him just
because he's an American. But after she gets to know him, she
agrees to bring him along to some meetings with her friends
in the underground. There, in a restaurant's storage room, surrounded by boxes of produce and cages of live chickens, Taylor
listens to men and women swap stories of their humiliation at
the hands of their own corrupt government, the invading Japanese forces, and their purported American liberators as well.

Eventually, the two flee from the city when the Japanese
bombing intensifies, crouching in the back of a truck amid a
litter of piglets, and they go into hiding in the village where May
was raised. But even there they cannot escape the war. First,

Japanese soldiers arrive, sweeping through the village, barking commands at the elders, stealing pigs, and carting off bags of rice on their shoulders; and then just weeks later, American forces fight them back, taking up position at the perimeter of the settlement, launching shells left and right, and burning down the thatched houses of people they suspect have been sympathetic to the Japanese. Dassin and his crew improvised these battle scenes on the spot as the war flared up again just one month after the signing of the Shanghai Agreement. So while they staged the sequences of Japanese soldiers pouring into the village, the scenes of American soldiers torching people's homes was, in fact, actuality footage, which reviewers praised at the time because its jittery hand-held camera work and first-person point-of-view shots broke with traditional Hollywood codes in a way that intensified the sense of realism.

Though May and Taylor manage to escape the shelling and find their way back to the city, the cessation of hostilities doesn't afford them any peaceful resolution. The intensity of their experience out in the country only deepens their connection. One night as they crouch together in a bank of reeds and American soldiers prowl on a bank above them, they give in to their feelings that had been building since the first scenes, embracing frenziedly, almost gasping for air as they kiss, as if the fate of the war depended on the intensity of their touch. Dassin shot the scene without dialogue or music, he said, so that the unrelenting hiss of the reeds rustling above would create a sense of unease just at that moment when their romance would have, in a typical movie, signaled the coming of the happy conclusion. But Dassin troubles his audience's expectations: in the final scenes, the characters' anxiety grows rather than diminishes. Taylor's relationship with May parallels the fate of their nations. They return to their lives at the bar, but May acts as if their night among the reeds never happened. Instead, she grows more distant day by day, shying from his touch and avoiding his gaze. Dassin films her as if she's disappearing into the darkening corners of the frame. Then one night, the American military police walk in through the door and an ominous silence falls over the room.

They tell her they know that Taylor's been hiding there. May hesitates, knowing that Taylor can see her through the thatched blinds of the supply closet, but after a charged moment in which she seems frozen in time, she finally turns and nods her head in his direction. The police break down the door, and as they drag him across the floor, he calls out her name, but she refuses even to look in his direction. Dassin again challenges our expectations, shooting the entire climactic sequence in a recurring pattern of May's POV shot followed by her reaction shot in order to heighten the viewer's identification more closely with her emotional perspective than with his, making us feel a sense of justice more than we do a sense of tragedy.

Because Dassin produced the film independently, he wasn't sure if any of the majors would be willing to distribute it or if any independently owned theaters would be willing to book it. After all, by 1962, all of the independent companies had collapsed and only the three major distributors were left. Indeed, Dassin's fears proved to be correct. The film's premiere in Los Angeles created a firestorm, with California governor Drew Davies attacking it as "a pro-Jap propaganda piece straight out of Berkeley,"[159] while liberal critics like Manny Farber and Dwight Macdonald rushed to its defense — the latter praising it for its "incisive needling of middlebrow assumptions about the war, the Thai people, and the requisite style for the non-fiction film."[160] Dassin's backers eventually formed their own distribution company and screened it mostly at college campuses and the small art house theaters that were popping up in a few cities across the country. But the film did have longer-lasting practical effects. After it was banned in Memphis, the resulting Supreme Court decision, *Majestic Theater v. Binford* (1964), became the most significant First Amendment case of its era, overturning the court's previous ruling in the *Mutual* decision of 1915 to state unequivocally that the

---

159 Larry Ceplair, and Steven Englund, *Revolutionary Hollywood: Politics in the Film Community, 1936–1965* (Champaign: University of Illinois Press, 1979), 393.

160 Dwight Macdonald, "Leftists in the Reeds," in *On Movies* (New York: Da Capo Press, 1983), 180.

motion pictures deserved the same free speech protections as any other form of artistic expression.

By the time of the ruling, though, Dassin was exhausted by the furor and had settled in Provence for what he called an "extended vacation." Earlier that year, he'd met and quickly married the Greek singer Melina Mercouri; they later moved to Athens, where he took up filmmaking again in the late 1960s, though by that time, his interest in politics had finally waned, and for the rest of his career he directed just four more films — each pleasant but uninspired genre pictures starring his wife that earned them enough money to spend a comfortable retirement with homes in Paris and the island of Mykonos.

Retards (d. Kimberly Zaichek, USA, 1986)

pr. Comatose Pictures, sc. Kimberly Zaichek, starring Nathalie Richards and Kendra Wiggan-Knight, sound, color, 16mm, 96 mins.

The historian Xi Wei-hua points to Kimberly Zaichek's *Retards* — its title as intentionally offensive then as it is today — as the founding text of The Cinema of Subversion because of its deft integration of the experimental bloc's contradictory impulses. The American underground of the 1980s, she argues, was marked by two competing philosophies: first, there was the "poetic humanist element of the radical left whose rendering of the atrocity of modern life served a therapeutic function by enabling us to connect with the suffering of other outcasts like us"; and second, there was "the anarchic nihilists of the L.A. Underground, who presented their own drug-fueled hopelessness as an antagonistic attack on an audience that falsely believes it can identify with the characters on screen."[161] But Zaichek's film, in her view, became influential precisely because it was

---

161 Xi Wei-hua, *Aesthetics on the Edge of the Volcano: Underground Cinema, Apocalypse, and the Return of Repressed Classicism* (Durham: Duke University Press, 2008), 147.

able to express — like Fassbinder, with whom she's often compared — both of these positions simultaneously, demonstrating that the seemingly incompatible modes were not in opposition, but were, in fact, "mutually interdependent conditions that gave birth to the particular affective quality of contemporary leftist alienation."[162]

Zaichek had, by her own account, an unremarkable childhood in the suburbs of Southern California. But after she moved to L.A. in the late 1970s she met Zinonia Friedman and Jenny Zhang — often crashing at their apartment at Sunset & Vine — and became a part of the city's underground music scene, appearing on some of the early recordings by Volcano and the Wave Canyons (she plays tablas on "Die Gotterdammerung" and an instrument referred to as "wind-towers" on "Threnody for the Forest Dryads"). She eventually made her tempestuous love affairs with Friedman and Zhang the inspiration for her first film, *I Die Every Sunset* (1980), in which she portrayed the emotional peaks and troughs of those relationships with hand-held swish-pans, seven-minute brooding close-ups lit only by strobe lights, and a sonic collage composed by her former lovers comprised entirely of creaking doors and Geiger-counter static. Some writers have suggested that her aesthetic evolution may have resulted as much from these tumultuous romances as it did from the nation's political upheavals.

With *Retards*, Zaichek made a decisive break with the underground art movement in Los Angeles and put into practice some of the ideas that she'd been working through for a few years. In her essay "Against Manifestos," she railed against the unthinking leftist positions of her fellow low-budget filmmakers during a period of political retrenchment. Most of her friends, she said, thought that artists who weren't "hurling grenades into the prison yards of the American psyche were complicit with the wardens in their own subjugation," but it was this very desire to launch weapons, she thought, that demonstrated how thoroughly the militaristic attitudes of the ruling elite had co-opted

---

162 Ibid., 153.

the ideology of its opposition. "When I see my friends embracing violence," she wrote, "all I see are the exact forms of rebellion that the system has designed to be permissible for us." Rather than fighting the system on its own terms,

> we should be inventing new forms of political resistance, oppositional practices that might disturb the system through methods the ruling class is unable to comprehend: a radical idiom of intentional vexation, of willful obfuscation, that may scramble the culture's governing consciousness — perhaps our only hope left to inspire in the audience new aspects of desire, replacing violence with love, anger with sex.[163]

When she finally finished her low-budget magnum opus, its stridently obnoxious title and ostensibly apolitical subject matter led most writers to dismiss it out of hand. Zaichek's progressive colleagues denounced it as blatantly offensive: the story, after all, follows two women who pretend that they are mentally and physically disabled — walking spastically into doors, drooling as they stare off into space, urinating on themselves in the middle of the street — for reasons that remain incomprehensible to their family and friends, to the audience, and possibly even to themselves.

Retards begins as mysteriously as it will end. In the opening sequence, the two teenage protagonists — Alina (Nathalie Richards) and Ondoleh (Kendra Wiggan-Knight) — are walking home from school one day when one of them looks at the other and suddenly begins stuttering uncontrollably for no apparent reason, only to have the other immediately fall into the same inexplicable trance-like state herself. The next day, the two girls are making violent, spasmodic gestures in the middle of the school cafeteria. Within a week, they're staring off into space,

163 Kimberly Zaichek, "Against Manifestos," in *Underground Cinema, Documents of the Revolution: Sex, Death, and the Avant-Garde,* eds. Eric Schaefer and Julia Smoogleton (Durham: Duke University Press, 2009), 343.

unresponsive for hours at a time. Their regression is painful to watch, not just because of the physical details of their deterioration, but because in one brief moment early on, the two girls share a knowing smirk, revealing to us that they are — most likely, though it's never entirely clear — just putting on an act. Other people, too, suspect them, but can never bring the girls out of their shells. In the most gruesome scene, their mothers confront the girls at the hospital, yelling that they know they they're just acting out, that their medical condition isn't real. The two older women fall to their knees, sobbing, pleading with their daughters to return to a normal life, to no avail. The girls just continue staring blankly off into space. Finally, Alina's mother becomes so desperate she puts a kitchen knife to her throat, screaming that she'll kill herself if Alina doesn't snap out of it. But even after she draws blood, and nurses rush in to save her, her daughter just stares off into space, mouth hanging open, and the mother crumples to the floor, a broken woman.

Giving up on their ability to communicate with their daughters, the families turn to a series of authority figures — school counsellors, psychiatrists, doctors, hospital administrators — and the rest of the film plays out as a pointed commentary on the role that hierarchical organizations play in controlling those citizen-subjects who cannot or will not meet society's expectations. Thus begins a circular adventure in which the girls are shuttled from one institution to another, and after the doctors or therapists fail in their attempt to cure them, they are shunted off to yet another facility. The two girls' spiraling debilitation is made all the more harrowing when, in a few rare moments when they're alone together, they won't even look each other in the eye, refusing to acknowledge anymore the nature of their performance — that is, if they have been performing at all. In the final sequence, when their nurses have strapped them in to receive electro-shock therapy for the first time, their continuing vacuousness just when we expect them to finally absolve themselves in a cinematic epiphany intensifies our own anguish at the senselessness and cruelty of their decisions.

The response to the film upon its release was so over-whelmingly negative that Zaichek — already alienated from her peers — quit filmmaking and music and moved to Montana, where she shuffled between jobs for years, first opening a jewelry store, then trying to raise goats, before finally moving permanently to a Buddhist retreat. But during the years of her seclusion, the critical consensus slowly took on a new dimension, spurred on by Zaichek's own theoretical exegeses, so that writers today embrace its shock value as a prescient *cri de coeur* against the stultifying politeness of the political class — the un-willingness to speak out — that has facilitated our current reactionary environment. Now critics tend to see the protagonists' behavior along Zaichek's lines, seeing futility and regression as perhaps the only option left for staging a liberal protest in a system that has closed off so many avenues for permissible opposition. Surprisingly, though, Zaichek herself has come to agree with her earlier detractors. "It was an ugly movie made in an ugly time," she said, "and I thought that the only way to counteract that noxious culture was to force ourselves deeper into the filth."[164] And yet her own commentary reveals the complexity of her film's position: she admitted that once she found peace in her spiritual seclusion, she never felt the need to pursue artistic work again, and that it was only when she was delving into the muck that she was able to most astutely portray the fundamental suffering of the human condition.

---

164 Kimberly Zaichek, "Interview with Michael Flanagan," in *Underground Cinema, Documents of the Revolution,* eds. Schaefer and Smoogleton, 363.

The Rise and Fall of the City Mahagonny (d. Ritwik Ghatak, India, 1970)
pr. *The Ministry of Culture of Bengal and the Ministry of Culture of Kerala, sc. Ritwik Ghatak and Bertolt Brecht, starring Bikash Dasgupta, Trishna Kurup, and Ritwik Ghatak, sound, color, 35mm, 111 min.*

Ritwik Ghatak's career had withered, surprisingly, since the release of *Cloud-Capped Star* in 1962, which had been met with almost universal acclaim. He'd assumed that the success of that film would enable him to explore a more poetic and adventurous style in his next projects, but Calcutta Films International was just then in the process of monopolizing the Bengali film industry and was embracing populist entertainment more than ever before to shore up its hold on its withering revenue streams. After CFI rejected a few of his scripts in 1963 and 1964, Ghatak took a job teaching film production at the University of Calcutta, disgruntled about his prospects. But to his surprise, the academic environment inspired him. "I felt exhilarated by politics again for the first time in years," he said. "Everyone was talking about Gramsci. And everyone was reading the theorists coming out of Paris and Shanghai."[165] So Ghatak was ecstatic when the Bengali Farmers and Workers Party won state elections in 1969 just three years after its sister party had come to power in Kerala. He became even more enthusiastic when, in an unexpected move, the new Bengali Minister of Culture, Devadan Dass, announced that the state would set aside funds to produce a few feature films. And sure enough, knowing of the famous director's socialist sympathies, Dass reached out to Ghatak, telling him that he was the perfect candidate to direct the government's first foray into film production.

The resulting film, though, laid bare the cultural rift between India's political and intellectual left: though most of Ghatak's friends in the film world defended the movie after its premiere,

---

165 Ritwik Ghatak, "Gramsci and Film," in *Cinema & I* (Calcutta: Ritwik Memorial Trust, 1987), 98.

party leaders quickly denounced it, attacking it as "painfully incomprehensible," leading Dass to announce changes to the state's cultural policy, now requiring ministry review of scripts before production could commence.[166] The response of the political class was not surprising, in retrospect. Ghatak had not produced, after all, the panegyric that party leaders assumed they had funded. Instead, he'd created an idiosyncratic art film that both its opponents and defenders agreed was more interested in philosophical issues than it was in pushing a particular ideological agenda.

Inspired by the intellectual currents of the Indian academic milieu over the preceding decade, Ghatak assembled a script about a university theater company putting on a production of Bertolt Brecht's *The Rise and Fall of the City Mahagonny*. And to placate Dass, who'd been forging a relationship with the Ministry of Culture of Kerala, Ghatak cast a young Bengali man and a young Malayali woman as the two leads. But while rehearsing the project over the course of a couple months, he became more intrigued by the interpersonal dynamics of his cast than he was in Brecht's characters, so he transformed his original script into a modernist hybrid — both a presentation of the play and an actuality of the rehearsals of the play, so that each of his stars inhabited dual roles, both fictional and real. This bifurcated structure, he thought, was more capable of capturing what he referred to as "the innate hybridity of contemporary Indian cosmopolitanism." But this duality also revealed Ghatak's own inner conflicts: while his desire for a utopian aesthetics seemed genuine at the start of the project, his new, self-reflexive approach that highlighted what he called "India's repressed tensions" ultimately laid bare his feelings about the inherent futility of any idealistic project — whether artistic or ideological.[167]

---

166 Lydia Ng, *The Gramscian Wave: Political Philosophy and Modernism in International Film, 1965–1974* (Chicago: University of Chicago Press, 2004), 182.

167 Ghatak, "Gramsci and Film," 102, 105.

Ghatak critiques his own utopian thinking partly through his multi-layered interrogation of his own filmmaking. Though the plot drifts from its Brechtian origins from the very beginning, Ghatak adapts many of the German theorist's ideas about epic theater all along. Instead of seeing through a fourth wall as if we're voyeuristically witnessing reality unfold before our eyes, Ghatak uses multiple cameras to capture the action from every possible angle, completely disregarding the 180-degree rule, occasionally capturing himself and his crew working behind the scenes, so that we end up witnessing not just an actuality of a theater troupe rehearsing a Brecht play, but also an actuality of Ghatak making a movie about that theater troupe rehearsing the Brecht play. From early on in the process, we witness the actors grappling with, then coming to terms with the fact that it was Ghatak's documentation of their rehearsal process — not the Brecht play that they were purportedly working through over and over for hours every day — that was becoming the primary subject of the film. And this awareness leads them to act out and talk back, to rebel. In the final analysis, it's Ghatak's antipathy to aesthetic coherence — matched with his actors' antipathy toward him — that evinces his attitudes about the possibilities of creating a political utopia.

The artistic tension that flared between the cast and its director similarly let loose a network of antagonisms that had been simmering between the leading actors. During the course of rehearsals, the male and female leads, initially exuberant about the project, become disillusioned, making cracks about Ghatak behind his back and snide comments about the new Bengali and Keralite administrations. As their disagreements evolve from the political to the personal, their increasingly open bickering emboldens the play's third leading actor, a Muslim student from Gujarat playing the role of the stage manager, who senses slights from the rest of the cast that they vehemently deny. And they all become increasingly suspicious of their director, so that in a climactic scene when his actors confront him about his duplicity, yelling and thrusting threatening fingers into his face, it's hard for the audience to figure out whether or not Ghatak has been manipulating his actors to achieve a scene like this from the very beginning.

Ghatak's larger point, then, it becomes clear, even to the bureaucrats at the Ministry of Culture, was that the process of creating art — which is, after all, an attempt to create a utopian world — necessarily unleashes pent-up, insuperable conflicts. And in this sense, we can see Ghatak as a theoretician critical of the collectivist dream despite his Gramscian pedigree, suggesting that hierarchies of power will inevitably disrupt any attempt to design a more perfect world, but also that the imposition of hierarchies is a necessary check on the anarchic turmoil that is always the end product of revolutionary thinking.

In an ironic twist that Brecht himself would have appreciated, the Bengali Ministry of Culture ran out of money — or at least stopped providing funds to the production — as Ghatak's rehearsals went months over schedule. Most journalists at the time described the final film, then, as unfinished: the movie cuts to black abruptly during the middle of an argument about the aims of rehearsal that day — one reason it received such middling reviews: "two hours of yammering," one critic succinctly described it, "and we didn't even get to see the play."[168] But most people who've written about the film now believe — and Ghatak has hinted so himself — that he had always intended the film to have the feel of a messy improvisation; he had always intended for the film to end in an uncontrollable oblivion since that was the nature of the political revolution of which the film was always a reflection.

---

168 Jagdish Bose, *Bengali Cinema: A History* (Lanham: Rowan & Littlefield, 2000), 225.

Sally the Sewing Machine Operator (d. The Omega Collective, USA, 2008)
pr. *The New York State Council of the Arts, sc. The Omega Collective, starring Isolde Kaganovich and Jenny Yu, sound, color, digital video, 140 min.*

In spite of its prolific cinematic and literary output, the Omega Collective came to be known initially more for the mystery that surrounded its identity than it did for the work it had produced. Despite twenty-three movies and eleven publications — including pamphlets comprised entirely of esoteric lists ("Nineteen Greatest Drunk Scenes of the 1930s"), fervent manifestos defending acting styles of the 1910s, and book-length interviews with the directors Nellie Falqenquist, Claire Denis, and Tishumbusa Ndjeje — the names of the group's members remain officially unknown to this day, even if pundits have gravitated toward an unofficial unanimity about the most likely possibilities. That being said, while this guessing game ignores what should be the more obviously central concerns of the work itself, the collective's playful eccentricity in masking themselves reveals an essential quality of their mission: they consistently combine an analytical approach with a comic sensibility as a means of highlighting larger philosophical issues — in this case, ideas about authorship in the cinema. With this in mind, critics have finally come to accept what should have been obvious from the beginning — that is, that the collective's body of work represents one of the most cogent and inventive applications of film theory since the films of Marcel L'Enfant half a century earlier.

The collective's first movies — shot on videotape, 8mm, and a host of new digital video formats that were transforming motion pictures across the globe — popped up here and there at European festivals in the early 1990s. But it wasn't until 1997 at the Rotterdam Film Festival when they distributed their first manifesto — "The Cinema, like the Pterodactylus antiquus, Must Die So That It May Be Born Again in the Skies" — that the film community first took notice of them. Their movies were by that time appearing in a mad profusion — three or four a year — and though a lot of critics dismissed them for their grainy visuals, aberrant sound quality, and slapdash construction, many others eventually came around to accept the collective's own claims that the jarring shifts in subject and tone manifested a coherent aesthetic program intended to nurture random moments of beauty that would sprout now and then from the soil of this premeditated disorder.

The collective railed against the art cinema as a product of bourgeois ideology and argued, therefore, that the artist's goal should be to produce "fruitful disjunctions and daring fiascos because only by failing miserably can we get in touch with that aspect of the human condition that is its honest kernel, unadorned by defenses." The deployment of technical proficiency, they maintained, "is a means of covering up our pain. Only by openly indulging our ugliness and imbecility can we look at ourselves squarely and thus challenge, rather than absorb, both the mainstream audience's unexamined desire for pleasure and the avant-garde audience's unthinking Brechtian assumptions."[169] Their insouciant approach, they suggested, was a way of pushing viewers away from the deliberate detachment that marked most award-winners on the film-festival circuit, thus enabling them to see through those films' calculatedly inauthentic nihilism. Instead, the collective aimed to lace its despair with a joyful exuberance that was always indebted — however crazily — to the real-life concerns of actual people who, like them, were living precariously on the fringes of society — in particular, in the avant-garde theater world of New York in the 1990s.

Based on the movies' subject matter and setting, most critics assumed that the group consisted of two or maybe three young women who'd gone to art school or done graduate work, who lived in Brooklyn, and who supported themselves with office jobs in Manhattan. They were widely versed in the history of cinema, since their movies often made reference to obscure

---

169 The Omega Collective, "The Cinema, Like the Pterodactylus antiquus, Must Die So That It May Be Born Again in the Skies," in *The Omega Collective Manifestos* (Brooklyn: Shame Spiral Press, 2010), 12.

films, actors, and directors, and their catholic tastes had clearly inspired their diverse output. Their movies included an improvised musical about office politics in a data entry department, a quiet chamber drama about a woman suffering from postpartum depression, a prison escape film that consisted entirely of two fledgling screenwriters researching and then designing and then rehearsing exhaustively the perfect getaway, an actuality about the economics of waste management in New York, a vampire film about struggling actresses on the Lower East Side who get sustenance from the blood of masochistic volunteers from Wall Street, a fiction-actuality hybrid about a public access TV host who stages a run for the New York City council dressed as a lumberjack in a fake beard, and its sequel, a musical essay about the making of that lumberjack-candidate movie in which every song is comprised of the same melody.

At the beginning of the 21st century, the collective's output thinned and their movies became a bit more polished, less iconoclastic and absurd, and more emotionally resonant. For *Sally the Sewing Machine Operator,* their final film, they finally received outside funding for the first time — from the New York State Council of the Arts — enabling them to produce their most professional product. It was clearly intended as a kind of summation of their entire career, encapsulating all of their main themes, focusing on the travails of two young actresses directing an amateur theater company in Brooklyn, struggling — and failing — to create a work of art that is emotionally and politically engaged without any hint of the irony that marred so much of the work of their peers in the avant-garde.

Sally follows two friends, Maura and Jun — played by first-time actors Isolde Kaganovich and Jenny Yu — who are staging a 19th-century melodrama called *Sally the Sewing Machine Operator,* based loosely on an actual play, Charles Foster's *Bertha, the Sewing Machine Girl* (1871).[170] The two women also hold down day jobs, and the movie gives equal time — and surprisingly

---

170 Charles Foster, *Bertha, the Sewing Machine Girl: or, Death at the Wheel* (Rhinebeck: Victoria Theatre Books, 1998).

equal significance — to their seemingly unimportant work at the office: Maura is a technical writer working on programming specs for a cellular phone company's new database system, while Jun manages a small team of software testers at a company that produces educational applications. Rather than treating their jobs with disdain, the film shows how important — if ultimately unsatisfying — their workdays are for them, with scenes of passionate arguments among co-workers about the intricate details of software design. But the film reserves its greatest attention to their lives outside of the office, focusing on — unusually for the cinema — an intense friendship between two women that has nothing to do with their romances with men.

Four nights a week after work, the two friends gather with a handful of actors in a dimly lit theater to rehearse a play about girls who work in a textile factory, and though the film never shows the play in its entirety, it does show the troupe working through a few pivotal scenes over and over again, so that the constant repetition of aesthetic labor becomes a haunting echo of the machinists' drudgery that is the subject of the play and also of the actors' real-world lives. While the play's wildly melodramatic dialogue may sound disturbingly unrealistic to contemporary ears, its very artificiality intensifies the emotional stakes of the play's politics. *Sally*'s leftist critique of the dehumanizing effects that the Industrial Revolution has on the lives of working-class women produces uncanny parallels with the lives of the two actresses in the present day, making the seeming "artificiality" of the play a pointed commentary on the alleged "reality" of the contemporary world.

The two women, who co-direct as well as act in the play, explain to their cast on a dimly lit rehearsal stage that they are all engaged in a philosophical mission, suggesting that their contemporaries' subliminal acceptance of trendy academic theorists has led artists working in experimental styles to an unhealthy disavowal of emotional identification as a political tool. They urge their actors, instead, to understand the purposes of melodrama through the lens of Peter Brooks's writings on French theater of the 1830s. Brooks wrote that melodrama as an artistic mode arose in France in the early 19th century as a direct reaction to the overthrow of clerical power during the French Revolution. Religion, he argued, had always been the institution that satisfied the innate human yearning to see — and thus understand — virtue. But in a newly secular age that had deprived the church of its function to fulfill that role, art subsequently took up the task of meeting this most basic need. Thus the drama featuring innocent women victimized by evil men dressed in black that flourished at the time was not, as its detractors claimed, a primitive entertainment made for pre-Freudian simpletons, but instead the necessary articulation of humanity's most important spiritual longings. And to defend to the skeptical elites that such binary ethics and excessive emotionalism actually undergirds all artistic practice, Brooks demonstrated how the melodramatic mode manifests itself even in works we consider to be the most elevated of the high arts, such as the novels of Tolstoy, George Eliot, and Henry James.[171]

The film stages for its audience, then, this exact conflict between low-art and high-art conceptions of the melodramatic. On the one hand, the play represents the more primitive idea of the genre, explicitly pitting evil against virtuous innocence: the sweatshop owner Roderic Bream taunts Sally and her friends as he pushes them to work their sewing machines ever faster, comparing them unfavorably to horses, dogs, and sheep, until Sally succumbs to fatigue one day, feels a needle go through her finger, crumples down on stage, then lifts her head to address the audience with her soliloquy, "Cruel Chariot of Destiny." On the other hand, the actors' lives in the present day — also the story of women struggling for autonomy against the dehumanizing demands of a labor market — represent a more complex version of the same themes. Alone in her office, Maura rehearses a pitch she plans to make to her boss about why they should consolidate a handful of pop-up windows into one in order to improve the user's experience, but when she finally gets a chance

---

171 Peter Brooks, *The Melodramatic Imagination: Balzac, Henry James, Melodrama, and the Mode of Excess* (New Haven: Yale University Press, 1995).

to present her case at a meeting, he rebuffs her out of hand because of what "the quality control team in Connecticut" might think. Jun, meanwhile, produces reams of elaborately designed color-coded charts for her team to fill out as they test a new application, but when the computers in their lab repeatedly break down, she's forced to generate an entirely different set of color-coded diagrams to explain to her bosses why her team was unable to complete the initial collection of charts. The evil antagonist is no longer one man, as it is in the play, with Sally facing off against the sweatshop owner Roderic Bream. Now the enemy is more diffuse: it is the abstraction of bureaucracy itself — what Andripradath Gannucci refers to as "capitalism's calculated inducement of torpor as a strategy of dissimulation about its own aims"[172] — so that what the Collective ultimately points out is that the 21st century's inability to point to a specific visible antagonist, the byproduct of intellectuals' embrace of realism in place of the melodramatic mode, may be the root cause of this generation's particular style of spiritual degradation.

Meanwhile, back at their rehearsal space, where their hearts lie, the ceaselessly banal tasks of their office environments find their uncomfortable analogues in their work on stage: the endless rehearsals of the most emotionally wrenching scenes don't transport them into realms of liberating bliss; instead, they merely prove how impossible it is to wall off their artistic world from their quotidian struggles in the marketplace. At first, Maura and Jun had rationalized to each other that the practical benefits of their day jobs made that labor innately political, but the more repetitive their day-to-day activities at the office become, the more abstract — and less pragmatic — their labor seems. At the same time, as their artistic practice — which had initially seemed like a reprieve from the travails of the real world — increasingly takes on the workplace's repetitive drudgery, the life of the artist no longer revolves around issues of aesthetics and more closely resembles the office worlds they thought that they'd

172 Andipradath Gannucci, *Emotional Grids: Post-Brechtian Aesthetics, Capitalism's Masquerade* (Durham: Duke University Press, 2011), 4.

been escaping. Thus, their rehearsals continue to deteriorate, culminating in a harrowing final scene: Jun and Maura stand alone, bent over on a darkened stage, sweating and exhausted near the end of another long night. But then, with a grim nod of recognition, they gather their energy and pick up where they left off, practicing once again, crossing the stage in a series of ballet-ic steps in absolute silence — for their own benefit because there is no audience watching them — then retracing their way back to their original positions, where, without pause, they pick up where they began, moving through the same abstract gestures again and again with machine-like precision, until the screen finally and mercifully dissolves into darkness.

Five years after the film's release, the Museum of Modern Art in New York held a series of panel discussions about the Omega Collective's work, and on the final panel, in perhaps a subtle, posthumous acknowledgement of the leading roles that they had played in the group, the two stars of *Sally the Sewing Machine Operator* — Isolde Kaganovich and Jenny Yu — agreed to talk about the film, though even on that night, they were cagey, joking that they themselves were merely paid stand-ins for the real members of the collective, who, they claimed, were "just a couple of gay drunks we know who like to watch sports."[173] Most of the audience took these jokes as further strategic dissembling, since the pair spoke so knowingly and eloquently about the collective's large body of work. Yu said she was happy that *Sally the Sewing Machine Operator* marked the group's final film since its themes of aesthetic futility now seemed so prescient. The movie had played exclusively at international film festivals in its first few years and never had a commercial release; and the digital revolution, surprisingly, hadn't changed much. Despite its accessibility in a variety of electronic formats online, she estimated that even by that time, fewer than five thousand people had ever seen the movie. Yu herself had retired to the Catskills, where she was raising a daughter and making a living raising

---

173 Interview with Isolde Kaganovich and Jenny Yu, *Cinéaste* 38, no. 3 (Summer 2013): 25.

goats. Kaganovich, too, had fled the city and was now working, she said, as a teacher of freshman writing at the State University of New York at New Paltz. But she too said that she was happy with the way things turned out: "The Omega Collective was never really an artistic group at all. If anything, we always imagined it more like a spore. But like a spore, we thought it'd just keep wafting along on the wind. Ideally, we wanted to see it spread over the face of the Earth. But I'm not sure that that day will ever come — or even, in retrospect, that it should."[174]

Spider Web (d. Koda Yukichi, Japan, 1935)
sc. Koda Yukichi, starring Watanabe Kanjuro, silent, b&w, 35mm, 68 min.

For decades, historians considered Koda Yukichi's *Spider Web* to be one of the most important lost films, and a rich literature sprung up in which critics parsed the fragmentary evidence that remained. In a series of letters published simultaneously in *Positif* and *Ekran* in 1967, for instance, Françoise Segher and Leonid Kagan engaged in a heated discussion about the intended meaning of one of the movie's few published film stills. Then miraculously, out of the blue one day in 1973, the Japan Film Foundation announced the discovery of a pristine print. Ironically, though, the movie's sudden availability didn't resolve any of the ongoing debates: Segher and Kagan published a second series of letters in 1974 only to deepen their disagreements with fresh evidentiary ammunition.[175] If anything, being able to finally see the legendary film only spurred further irreconcilable arguments. There's something about *Spider Web*, it seems, that engenders analysis and conversation: these days, many historians point to the movie as the best example of the kind of hermeneutic com-

---

174 Ibid., 29.
175 Letters of Françoise Segher and Leonid Kagan, *French Film Theory and Criticism: A History/Anthology, Volume 3: 1960–1980*, ed. Ginette Dupont (Princeton: Princeton University Press, 2001), 216–27.

plexity that was possible only in the silent period—especially in Japan.

Film scholars regarded Koda's work for years as the mythic embodiment of cinematic modernism in Japan even though no prints of any of his four films survived the transition to sound. Critics knew of him only through film reviews, a handful of published film stills, and the recollections of his peers, who wrote of him as one of the most inspiring but elusive figures of the time. It was the film historian Hondo Yasujimi who came across an old 16mm print of *Spider Web* while rummaging through the back of a used manga shop in Osaka. Hondo had been seeking out people with collections of 16mm prints for years—Donald Richie credits him with rediscovering nineteen feature films—and Koda's work had always been at the top of his list. Since this discovery, though, the director's legend for mystery has only continued to grow. None of his other films—*Flowering Agony* (1929), *Lunar Eclipse over Water* (1931), or *Village of Weeds* (1932)—has yet been recovered and most people assume that they are lost forever. Koda's notoriety as a misunderstood genius along the lines of Orson Welles or Abubakar Salim, though, has sometimes dissuaded people from studying his work itself with as much analytical rigor as it deserves. If one does study the movie, one comes into contact with one of the most groundbreaking cinematic thinkers of his time. Indeed, *Spider Web* functions as an intellectual challenge to the most noted aesthetic theorists of the era—expanding upon the critical thought of Marcel L'Enfant in more complex ways than any theorist in the literary field who's followed in their wake.

Koda had been a central figure in overlapping avant-garde circles in the 1920s. He grew up poor—his mother died when he was four and his father worked as a janitor at a noodle shop near the red-light district—but somehow he came to know Matsuoka Ryusei and became a member of the Floating Cloud movement, the most experimental group of Japanese poets in the 1910s. There, as in later film circles, Koda was a charismatic but curious figure, admired as much he was scorned. Yamaguchi Ito, for instance, was only half joking when he wrote that Koda was "the greatest poet in Japan because he had no poems for anyone to say anything negative about."[176] Indeed, he may have earned his reputation as a singular genius precisely because he intentionally destroyed so much of his own work. None of his poetry survives, and we know of it now, as we do with his three lost movies, mostly through the recollections of his contemporaries.

In his autobiography, Matsuoka claimed that the Floating Cloud poets generally regarded Koda as the most innovative among them, even though his entire body of work consisted of only five or six poems. In his poetry, just as in his movies, Koda emphasized the expressive aspects of the image more than he did its communicative potential. For each poem, he handcrafted a book in an edition of nineteen, a number that he claimed had mystical significance: one poem-book was smaller than his hand, while another was three-feet wide, with each word drawn painstakingly in Koda's own moody calligraphy, arranged in spirals and waves across the pages so that the words could be read in multiple arrangements. Then in the spring of 1927, Koda suddenly announced to friends that he'd retired from poetry. Uncharacteristically forthright for such a private person, he told them he couldn't write anymore because he was tortured by the end of a love affair. His friends then and historians since have speculated about the identity of this former lover. In his meticulously researched biography, Hondo finally suggested that his romantic interest was most likely the teenage son of a navy admiral who'd recently taken his own life by leaping off the tallest building in Osaka. Koda left Tokyo soon after this traumatic event and travelled across the country for months, buying back every copy of his poem-books that he could find. And at the end of the year, in an impromptu ceremony he devised based on Buddhist traditions, he burned them all in a bonfire at sunset on a beach overlooking the Sea of Japan.

---

176 Keiko McDonald, *Reading a Japanese Film: Cinema in Context* (Honolulu: University of Hawai'i Press, 2005), 26.

After the ritual burning of his books, Koda published an essay in the avant-garde journal *Tonga* renouncing poetry because, he said, language was incapable of expressing the "multifarious emptiness" at the core of experience. Soon he'd joined the filmmakers and intellectuals involved in the Pure Film Movement and was issuing manifestos in their small magazines. Echoing the theories of cinematic specificity articulated by Europeans like Marcel L'Enfant, Rudolf Arnheim, and Béla Balázs — of whom they were most likely still unaware — Koda and his coterie argued that film must emphasize those qualities that differentiated it from the other arts because only those formal aspects were capable of manifesting the ethos of the machine age. The Pure Film directors thus made poetic use of chiaroscuro lighting and staging in depth, just as their European contemporaries did. But if the Europeans — under the influence of L'Enfant — emphasized the expressive possibilities of superimposition, the Japanese — under the influence of their chief theoretician Kinugasa Teinosuke, whose films *A Page of Madness* (1926) and *Crossroads* (1928) have been lost — emphasized the hermeneutic richness available to Japanese directors because of the collaborative role of the *benshi,* a figure endemic to Japan who stood in the theater performing his own improvised narration, unique for every screening.

The plot of *Spider Web* is difficult to recount — and intentionally so for two reasons. On the one hand, as a modernist, Koda wanted to challenge the central role that cause-and-effect narration had come to play due to the influence of Hollywood; on the other hand, like most other Japanese filmmakers of the period, he intentionally infused the film with willful ambiguities, knowing that various *benshi* would invariably alter the meanings of the movie with their own extemporaneous commentaries. Much of our understanding of the movie's plot, then, doesn't come from the recovered footage itself, but from Hondo Yasujimi's reconstruction of what he thought might be a historically accurate *benshi* narration, which he recorded — against the advice of many of his peers — for the soundtrack of the 1973 release. Many other experts on the subject objected, since Hondo's recording created the false impression that there was one correct narration, whereas Koda had intentionally designed the film with an elliptical structure precisely because he wanted it to inspire a multitude of possible *benshi* narrations and thus of possible interpretations.

The more we ignore Hondo's recording, the more multifaceted the story becomes. Most critics believe that the plot follows two identical twins, one a poet and the other a salaryman (though some insist that there is only one protagonist and that the poet's story line is the dream of the salaryman). In the opening sequence, the two men bump into each other while walking in a forest of towering pines, where they soon encounter a ghost-like woman who hovers over — or is perhaps the spiritual manifestation of — a large wooden boat covered by a seemingly sentient mound of moss. After this meeting inspires nights of fitful, elusive dreams, they return to their daily lives back in the city. But each becomes increasingly alienated from his family and colleagues over the next few days as the visual style of their waking lives — now punctuated by superimpositions here and there — begins to take on the style of their dreams.

At a drunken party, the poet denounces his friends, jumping atop a table and dancing spastically like a mechanical monkey as sunbursts suddenly and inexplicably flash across the screen. Meanwhile, the salaryman quits his job in a huff, and on the way home leaps onto the top of a moving train. The two protagonists then converge again — just as fortuitously this time around — as the poet, fleeing his friends, boards that very train. But as the train speeds off — in a series of perplexing canted angles that disrupt our ordinary conceptions of space and time — the salaryman is cut in two by a low-hanging wire, while the poet, by trying to save him, falls off the speeding locomotive into the depths of a gorge. The film's ending is equally mysterious. The two men, who are now both ghosts — or who now exist in some alternative space-time — visit the small village home of an old woman who may or may not be the forest ghost they had met earlier in the film. The woman serves them tea, and they fall into a deep sleep, which many people have interpreted as the symbolic death of the poetic imagination and which others have interpreted as the beginning of the dream which comprises the entirety of the film. Finally, Koda brings the movie to an end with a minutes-long collage of impressionistic superimpositions: coiled snakes and zebras, waterfalls and whirlpools, fields of ferns waving in the breeze, each of which dissolves and fades until they become unrecognizable, mutating white shapes on a black background.

While the film's opacity has frustrated many viewers — including some of Koda's closest avant-garde contemporaries and a minority contingent of modern critics — it is its very hermeneutic flexibility that continues to make it one of the central objects of study in all of Japanese cinema. This openness is the conscious product of the design decisions that Koda made. He parallels the multiplicity of possible narratives with an equally ambidextrous style: in some sequences he cuts rapidly between arbitrary angles; in others he covers all the action in just one long tracking shot. At some points, the superimpositions represent the subconscious workings of the characters' minds; at other points, the superimpositions work on a metaphorical level, expressing the artist's commentary on the action unfolding on screen. The sets and costumes, too, mix realist and expressionist styles. In every formal as well as narrative aspect, Koda challenged both the traditional and avant-garde assumptions of what the medium should be able to accomplish, creating a multidimensional grid of possible interpretations in a way that the coming of sound would render impossible for future generations.

In 1996, the critic Shinoda Noga arranged a series of screenings in Tokyo, Shanghai, Paris, and New York that returned the film to the forefront of cinephile discourse. Shinoda worked with three *benshi* to craft radically incompatible narrations for the film, which were simultaneously translated into the language of the exhibition city. The results were riveting. In Shanghai, Xai Jin-wan called the film "the acme of the modernist experiment,"[177] and in New York, Susan Sontag, who'd just recently published her essay "The Death of Cinema," heralded the sold-out screenings as proof that cinephilia was not as dormant as she'd feared.[178] Over the last several years, Shinoda has revived these screenings now and then at film festivals across the globe, attracting a new generation of young admirers, who find in this old movie a much more adventurous spirit than their own technologically advanced age seems able to produce.

The Three Musketeers (d. Allan Dwan, USA, 1913)

pr. Atlantic Productions, sc. Sally Potter, starring Terrence McGuire, Bettina Quick, Landon Hawthorne, Rodger Dahl, and Guy Lafleur, silent, b&w, 35mm, 98 min.

The Three Musketeers has long held an eminent position in film history for accomplishing in fiction what Randall Jennings had achieved for actualities in *Prize Fight* (1912), becoming the first narrative feature to integrate the formal experimentation that had been percolating throughout the early 1910s into an organic work of art and successful commercial entertainment. And ever since Allan Dwan took out full-page ads in the trade press extolling his own central role in developing these formal innovations, critics and historians have referred to him as "the father of film grammar." Now, more than a century later, *The Three Musketeers'* popularity has fallen and risen again. Historians today tend to downplay its revolutionary character, pointing to many other films that were inching in the same direction. And auteurist critics now give scenarist Sally Potter as much credit for the movie's aesthetic innovations. Nevertheless, after all these years, *The Three Musketeers* and Allan Dwan remain central to any analysis of the evolution of the art form.

---

177 Xai Jin-wan, "A Page of Madness Torn from History," *Film Comment* (Sept/ Oct 1996): 70.

178 Susan Sontag, "A Riposte: The Death of Cinephilia?," *New York Times Magazine*, September 25, 1996, 35.

The story of *The Three Musketeers* will always be intertwined, not surprisingly, with the story of *Prize Fight*. After crowds thronged to see that radically inventive actuality in the fall of 1912, the man who owned the biggest circuit of vaudeville theaters on the Eastern seaboard — Mordecai Brauner — hatched a plot to compete with the producers' cartel that Thomas Edison had created. By that point, the Edison Trust, as it was called, had corralled more than ¾th of the production companies in the country to work in conjunction according to Edison's plan for market domination. The Trust had instituted a factory-like regimen in which each of the companies released two-reelers exclusively. But Brauner was intrigued by the huge ticket sales he'd seen at his houses where he'd booked the Jennings film as well as a few longer fictional movies that he'd imported from Italy and Denmark.

Some independent producers as well as theater owners were also searching for ways to beat the Trust: besides Hiram Bingham, who was producing more long-form sports actualities in the wake of his success with Jennings, Carl Laemmle had invented the concept of the movie star by aggressively promoting the actresses Florence Windsor and Gloria Knight in a pair of six-reelers. With these models in mind, Brauner chose his favorite novel from childhood, Alexandre Dumas's *The Three Musketeers,* as the basis for his first multi-reel production. He was not a writer or director himself, though, so he went searching for the best talent he could find. To adapt the book, he first approached Frances Hodgson Burnett, whose novel *The Secret Garden* had just appeared in serial form, but when she turned him down, she suggested a young acolyte of hers named Sally Potter who'd just published her first short stories in *Harper's Weekly* and *The Saturday Evening Post,* and who would, unexpectedly, become as much a driving force behind the film as its much more lionized director.

At Brauner's urging, Potter watched and re-watched *Prize Fight* and some of the new Danish and Italian epics on an editing table, designing rigorously detailed charts that recorded statistics and notes on every shot — charts which now, housed at the Margaret Herrick Library in Los Angeles, have become what Kristin Thompson calls "the Rosetta Stone for cinematic narratologists."[179] Until those charts were re-discovered in the 1980s, everyone wrote about the movie as the product of one lone genius, "the father of cinema" Allan Dwan. But Trinity Beveridge's research on the film's production turned the tables, demonstrating that even before Dwan was hired, Sally Potter had already written into the scenario many of the aesthetic innovations that writers had attributed to the director for decades — especially the film's weaving together of multiple plotlines through parallel editing without the use of explanatory intertitles.[180] And she was especially responsible for the emphasis on montage, for breaking down scenes into discrete shots that advanced filmmakers' options for representing spatiotemporal continuity.

Dwan, who'd already earned a name for himself as an innovator at Bison Films over the last few years, was only hired the week before production started, after the script and casting had been finalized. Brauner had originally had his eye on a slightly more experienced man, D.W. Griffith, who'd directed many pioneering shorts for Biograph over the preceding few years, but Griffith turned him down since he was trying to raise money for his own first feature, *Judith of Bethulia.* Unfortunately for the development of cinematic narrative, Griffith died suddenly before he was able to make that film; in an ironic twist, given his recurring motif of speeding trains, he was killed in a gruesome train accident himself. Scholars like Tom Gunning and Andre Gaudreault, though, have speculated how different *The Three Musketeers,* and perhaps the entire history of film, might have been had Griffith accepted the assignment, since his movies from the early 1910s — re-introduced to the world only at an academic conference in Brighton in the late 1970s — proved to

---

179 Kristin Thompson, *Webs of Dislocation: Neo-Formalist Film Analysis Revisited* (Princeton: Princeton University Press, 1993), 48.

180 Trinity Beveridge, ed. *The Three Musketeers: From Script to Screen* (New York: Da Capo Press, 1992).

be much more formally adventurous than Dwan's work from the same period.

That being said, while acknowledging these other scholars' claims, Dwan was, in fact, responsible for many of the most inventive formal techniques that critics have praised in the film. While he never created much of a visual signature for himself in his later career in the studio system, the generally experimental nature of the early 1910s infected him as much as it did everyone else working at the time, and he became especially interested in the potentials of the moving camera and the long take. As early as 1911, inspired by the films he saw coming out of Biograph, he'd placed his camera on the backs of moving trucks to capture the heady excitement of racing horses and rushing trains in long, uninterrupted takes, and he insisted that Potter stitch together a few of her smaller scenes into larger units so that he could include as many extended takes with a moving camera as possible, which he argued gave the audience the feel of the 17th century's particular conception of time. Potter's and Dwan's contrasting formal aspirations, then, define the film's overall structure, switching back and forth between sequences on the one hand, in which the meandering camera gives one a sense of the luxurious unfolding of court life, and action sequences, on the other hand, in which the hyperbolic editing of non-naturalistic camera angles conveys the exultation that the men of the king's guard experience whenever they're confronted by danger and violence.

Dwan and Potter, in fact, make this tension between disruptive violence and indolent opulence one of the film's central themes, and it was the wide variety of aesthetic registers produced by this conceptual conflict that led critics like Lewis Jacobs to praise the film decades after its release as "one of the most richly imagined formal experiments ever made."[181] Potter followed the novel fairly faithfully. The young D'Artagnan comes to court and meets his three companions, Athos, Porthos, and Aramis, and the four men band together to defend the country

---

181 Lewis Jacobs, *The Rise of the American Film: A Critical History* (New York: Harcourt, Brace and Company, 1939), 83.

from the intrigues of Cardinal Richelieu. For the scenes in Versailles, Dwan follows the king in one flowing take through one hallway after another past a hundred costumed extras, while in the scenes where the musketeers practice their swordsmanship in a muddy courtyard, we see only body parts, glaring eyes, and the tips of crossed blades in shots that average three to four seconds apiece.

Potter made many significant decisions on her own: she dispensed with most of the romantic story, for instance, to focus instead on the adventurous quest to recover the diamond necklace stolen from the Queen. But it's telling that the movie's most famous set sequences are the product of the director and scenario writer's collaboration. The few moments where Potter took the most creative license with the source material were those scenes when D'Artagnan reaches London because Dwan told her of his ambitious plans for the climactic sequence. When D'Artagnan sneaks in to Buckingham Palace to recover the queen's purloined jewels, Dwan wanted to cut back and forth between horizontal tracking shots and vertical crane shots to heighten the audience's anxiety. And it was Potter's decision to punctuate the sequence with a series of eerie close-ups of eye-line matches and disembodied objects that gave the sequence its air of mystery, inspiring Jonathan Keller to write that "it's exactly this admixture of styles — partly intentional and partly not — that created such interpretive fecundity, a matrix of meanings that later generations of filmmakers, with their more rigid adherence to classical style, rarely ventured to attempt again."[182]

Movie fans flocked to the film and critics raved. It quickly became the most popular fiction film yet made, and it inspired other independent producers to experiment with long-form fictions just as multi-reel sports actualities inspired by Jennings's *Prize Fight* were becoming popular again. The fact that fiction films eventually did take the leading role in American and global cinema, though, had little to do with the personnel most re-

---

182 Jonathan Keller, *The Proto-Montage Practitioners: Film Directors before L'Enfant* (New York: Columbia University Press, 2008), 59.

sponsible for making *The Three Musketeers*. Potter abandoned screenwriting to write novels, and though Dwan had a long career in Hollywood, he never again matched his work here commercially or artistically. Brauner only financed one more movie before he was forced to sell his theater chain — to his rival Marcus Loewe — in order to cover losses from a mining company he'd set up in Montana. But *The Three Musketeers* remains today the paradigmatic instance of radical stylistic innovation that is the product of its time more than it is of its makers, and is one example of why filmmaking of the 1910s is still the most underappreciated and unexamined topic in the history of the cinema.

Under the Docks (d. William Chesterton, USA, 1935)
pr. MGM, sc. Ben Hecht and Charles MacArthur, starring Stan Laurel, Betsey Drew, and Charlie Chaplin, silent, b&w, 35mm, 122 min.

It's one of the great ironies of film history that Stan Laurel is remembered today mostly for his later films like *Under the Docks* and *California* (1947), which seem so antithetical to the movies of his earlier career that first made him famous. He was universally acclaimed as the greatest silent clown, but his character here is at odds with his beloved screen persona. He became a star in the Teens for his humor, of course, but also for his childlike naiveté, his blank-faced curiosity, and his constant emasculation by the forces around him, all of which elicited a nurturing sympathy from his audience. It is exactly these expectations that made his role in *Under the Docks* so riveting: his blankness now alienating, his emasculation now a source of potential vengeance. "The whole endeavor," Kenneth Tynan wrote of the film decades later, "is blanketed by the emotional pallet of a gray winter sleet. What we remember most at the end is not our laughter, but the charcoal-blank eyes piercing out from Laurel's calcified face, a silent cry for help. His somber, ashen visage, which had seemed like the surface of a more genteel, Victorian age, has been transmogrified here into the icon of modern existential malaise."[183]

After his initial burst of stardom in 1916 when he became an overnight sensation, immediately a more recognizable figure than the president of the United States, Laurel made a series of shorts and features that made him the darling of both the ticket-buying public in America and the modernist salons of Paris. But things changed after 1928's *Circus Clown*. The burden of fame had gotten to him, it seemed. A pall of mystery had fallen over his life. People didn't see him out anymore at his old haunts. He'd retreated from the world without explanation, secluding himself in his Bel Air mansion. It may have been the death of his mistress Arlene Trevont from an overdose of morphine, his biographer David Robinson suggests, that was the catalyst; whatever the case, he stopped making films, and over the next six years, he rarely ventured out of the house, except, they say, for the occasional trip on his yacht *Cristabelle*, where, it was reported, he'd sit on deck alone gazing out at the ocean for days on end.[184]

But Robinson revealed a more complicated figure than just a man in mourning. It was at night below deck, he says, that Laurel started reading; the man who'd had only a few years of schooling in London now read Tolstoy, Turgenev, and Dostoevsky. In the last of these three, especially, he discovered an aspect of his personality he hadn't known existed. "I suddenly saw all those gamblers and anarchists and religious seekers like a distorted image of myself," he later wrote, "but they were all somehow more real than the image of myself I held in my mind."[185] Finally, after five years of brooding in his mansion and out on the open seas, he began working on a new script. Given his new temperament, though, he abandoned his old collaborators and hired in their place two young newspapermen-turned-playwrights from Chicago, Ben Hecht and Charles MacArthur, who'd recently had

183 Kenneth Tynan, *Show People: Profiles in Entertainment* (New York: Simon & Schuster, 1980), 66.

184 David Robinson, *Stan Laurel: His Life and Art* (New York: McGraw Hill, 1985), 400.

185 Stan Laurel, *My Autobiography* (New York: Simon & Schuster, 1964), 110.

a huge Broadway success with their cynical account of the news-paper business, *The Front Page*. Despite the heady enthusiasm of his new confederates, though, the screenplay took almost a year to complete as Laurel kept pushing them to explore ever darker themes. Finally, he took the project to Irving Thalberg, his old boss at MGM, who reluctantly agreed to produce the film, hoping that the star's return to the screen would overcome the box office poison of such a dismal story.

Laurel stars as Archibald McLean, a happy-go-lucky owner of a hat shop in Chelsea whose wife and mother fall sick in the 1918 flu epidemic and who both die within hours of each other. He's so stricken with grief he's unable to get out of bed, and in just a few months, his hat shop goes out of business, forcing him and his six-year-old daughter to move in to a poor house, where they live on handouts. The final sequence of the first act, in which the once jovial prankster cowers with his child on a cold embankment of the Thames, staring into the rippling waters with a face as lifeless as a Roman statue, remains a touchstone in the study of silent film language. It's earned its reputation primarily because of the way that Laurel tells his story — and manipulates his audience's feelings — through his creative assemblage of disparate images, but also because of his innovative use of recorded music in that brief period before the introduction of recorded dialogue. As he and his daughter are bending down at opposite ends of the dock to study themselves in the water, Laurel cuts back and forth between their shimmering reflections until the girl leans forward just a little too far and suddenly falls into the wavering image of her own face, as Laurel, unaware, continues to study his own distorted visage nearby. Laurel then intensifies the parallel editing between his own stony expression reflected in the undulating surface and his daughter's head, then arms, then hands, disappearing into the water as George Antheil's score accentuates a rhythmic conflagration between piccolos, trumpets, and woodblocks. The sequence reaches its unexpected climax when a third figure enters the scene. An odd, diminutive man dressed as a dandyish hobo turns the corner twirling a walking stick, and jumps up in shock because he can see what Laurel cannot. Then, as the editing becomes increasingly hyperbolic, the tramp leaps into the water, pulls the girl out of the depths, and with the help of Laurel, now frantic with worry, pulls her to safety back up on the dock.

For the role of the beggar, Laurel cast an old music hall acquaintance, Charlie Chaplin, who, ironically, had initially been scheduled to join him on his first trip to the United States with the Fred Karno players back in 1911, back when Laurel first caught the eye of the executives at the Mutual film corporation. Some film historians, enamored with Chaplin's unusual gift for mixing comedy with pathos in some small, but significant roles in British productions like *War Veteran* (1926) and *This Bum's Life* (1931), have even speculated that had Chaplin not caught the flu and had instead ventured out on that tour with Karno's troupe, it would have been him and not Laurel who would have become the world's biggest star. Though it's impossible to speculate about historical counterfactuals, the evidence from this famous sequence is clear: it is not the world's most famous silent clown, Stan Laurel, but Charlie Chaplin who commands the viewer's attention from the moment he first enters the screen.

The charismatic competition between the two men propels the film forward. After Chaplin saves the girl, he and Laurel become fast friends, moving into an abandoned shack near a junkyard and turning it into a home for the new family of three. And yet they can't help themselves from vying with each other for the girl's affections: in rhyming scenes, we see each man stealing flowers from the same street vendor every morning to take home as gifts for her. After a couple weeks, when they're low on funds and desperate for food, Chaplin sheepishly admits to Laurel that he's sometimes made a living as a pickpocket, and when his friend seems intrigued, Chaplin agrees to teach him his techniques. Since the wealthy have such a financial incentive to safeguard their assets, he explains in an intertitle, it's much safer and more efficient to steal from the poor. So, in a few virtuoso pantomime scenes set in a funeral home lobby, a hospital waiting room, and a playground at a school for blind children, Chaplin demonstrates his pilfering skills with such nonchalant finesse it becomes clear why some critics believe that he might have been the greater talent. But soon after Laurel has mimicked, then perfected Chaplin's tactics, he convinces his friend to work against his principles on some more elaborate and remunerative schemes: first they snatch purses in a movie palace lobby, then they swipe handbags at a high-end department store, and finally, in one beautifully choreographed five-minute-long tracking shot, they sneak themselves through three floors of a shipping magnate's mansion to rob the capitalist of both his wife's and his mistress's diamond necklaces.

The movie reaches its logical peak when the two men make elaborate plans for and then execute — in what has become another master class in silent film narrative technique — the largest bank heist in the history of Britain. Their undertaking begins with a collage of blueprints, scale models, and life-sized replicas of lobbies and vaults, then segues into rehearsals of improvised and unpredictable scenarios, which through their unrelenting repetition, unintentionally echo the performance style of experimental theater. Eventually, after weeks of planning, the two friends enact a scheme that involves baby strollers, an organ-grinder monkey, an elderly somnambulist, a train wreck in Scotland, and an explosion at a nearby wig factory. Their heist culminates when they drag their bags of gold to the bank's rooftop, where — in a not-so-subtle reference to how the film's title reminds us where the partners began — they load their booty into the basket of a hot air balloon and sail over the city, where they gaze down upon the muddy banks of the Thames and celebrate their freedom, the happiest of all happy endings.

But as is so often the case, our heroes realize that a happy ending can offer no resolution. Stan Laurel's face, as always, functions as an emblem — in this case, for the ultimate futility of ambition itself. In the final scene, one year later, Chaplin comes to visit his old sidekick at his new mansion in Chelsea. Now the owner of the ritziest hat shop in all of London, Laurel should be happy, but he sits with his friend — in a room whose grandeur engulfs them — with nothing to say. His daughter now prefers to spend her time outside of the house with her friends.

What is all this money for, after all? While Laurel had played out his legendary style of pantomime during the heist itself, now he evokes an acting style more reminiscent of the films of Carl Theodore Dreyer. After Chaplin says his farewells, his daughter has gone off to school with her chauffeur, and the maids and butlers have cleared his breakfast table, Laurel sits alone, staring off into space, and the camera tracks forward, achingly slowly, to end the movie on a lingering close-up of his enigmatic, porcelain expression.

The United Nations (d. Orson Welles, 1974, USA)
sc. Orson Welles, starring Orson Welles and Oja Kodar, sound, color, 35mm, 120 min.

Middlebrow pundits had long derided Welles's late career for its litany of unfinished projects, but his infamy as a squandered talent has finally, fortunately, begun to fade. Nevertheless, though many people now praise The United Nations as one of the most groundbreaking essay films in the canon, they still fail to see the movie on its own terms, overlooking its most revolutionary aspects. When they do come to its defense, they emphasize its connections with other modernist essay films of the 1970s — particularly the works of Chris Marker, Kidlat Tahimik, and Tabitha Williams. In this view, The United Nations' value lies in the fact that unlike the actualities of the previous seven decades, it doesn't try to persuade its audience to understand any particular truth; it's structured not as a linear argument but as a poetic rumination, spiraling through time, zig-zagging between characters and locations according to an eccentric Wellesian logic that combines intellectual rigor with playful irreverence. And to make this point, these critics have latched on to the print that premiered at the Biarritz Film Festival in 1974 as the definitive version in order to defend Welles from the frequent pseudo-Freudian charges that his tendency to work on projects for decades was a moral failure stemming from some "fear of completion."[186]

But this defensive strategy has blinded us to Welles's truly radical vision: as equally important as his pioneering aesthetics is his philosophical challenge to our assumptions about the nature of the medium itself. Because by constantly revising the film and presenting fundamentally different versions over the years, he was questioning the very notion of what a film might be. Drawing on his early years in theater and radio, Welles became the first — and still only — filmmaker to espouse the idea that we should not treat film as a static text, but should instead, as we do with these other media, embrace its intrinsic qualities as an evanescent performance. His enthusiasm for improvising like a stage magician — at times like a Paganiniesque virtuoso — inspired him to create not one official version of the film, but multiple renditions, making us in the end question whether we should even refer to *The United Nations* as a "film" at all. The title turns out to be nothing more than a placeholder, pointing to a constellation of diverse manifestations of the platonic kernel of a movie. Maybe we should refer to the movie instead as a "conceptual machine," an "aesthetic catalyzer," or a "seedbed of the imagination." Welles's most radical innovation was that he was proposing an alternative conception of the ontology of film, which necessarily hints at an entirely different historical trajectory for the medium — just as he was, not coincidentally, proposing an alternative conception of a global governing system.

The general contours of the movie are clear: it examines the decades-long efforts by activists and intellectuals across the globe to create a one-world government. It focuses especially on the movement's most prominent leaders, including Watanabe Kotaro, Mike Norris, and Abdurrahman Walid, tracing its course from its origins with the League of Nations, to its rejuvenation in post-colonial centers like New Delhi and Cairo, and finally to its glittering but ineffectual present-day incarnation

---

186 Charles Higham, *The Films of Orson Welles* (Berkeley: University of California Press, 1970), 190.

among academic theorists and millionaire free-traders on the fringes of conferences in global hotspots like Aspen and Davos. While his sympathies are clearly with the one-worlders, Welles also meets up with a range of politicians and thinkers who are frightened by the possibly stultifying uniformity of a globalized system: he has dinner over roast boar and a jeroboam of Burgundy with anarchist economists leery of any imperialist hierarchy, he plays table tennis — and loses gracefully — to the former League of Nations president U Myint, and rides trains, buses, and donkey carts with his companion Oja Kodar through the recently formed Indian states of Manipur, Meghalaya, and Tripura, where he witnesses throngs of crowds celebrating the devolution of existing states into smaller but more linguistically cohesive political units.

The initial version of the film was met with rapturous reviews at its premiere. But by 1974, his reputation was in such tatters that even the Biarritz success couldn't secure him a distributor — either in the United States or in Europe. As was so often the case with Welles, though, this seeming setback was a blessing in disguise, inspiring him to tinker with the movie yet again, making him realize that he enjoyed his own film best when he could treat it just as he did his magic act and theater productions, expanding and refining it every time he gave a new performance. "It's been the most liberating feeling," he told his friend Zsa-Zsa Gabor, "to just make a movie like child's play again, like you're improvising a puppet theater show for your chums at school."[187]

Welles began screening different cuts of the movie throughout the summer of 1974 at a series of dinner parties in Paris and Majorca. Most of our knowledge of these early versions still depends upon interviews that Jonathan Rosenbaum and Joseph McBride have conducted with Welles's friends over the years. Paloma Picasso, for instance — who hosted a screening at her home in Aix-en-Provence — remembered vividly that the movie began with a dizzying montage of ping pong balls and

---

187 Zsa-Zsa Gabor, "A Weekend on the Riviera with My Friend Orson Welles," *Vanity Fair* 40, no. 7 (July 1977): 111.

rackets and that it culminated with U Myint defeating Welles in straight sets, while Jeanne Moreau and James Baldwin, on the other hand — who saw the movie at Yves Montand's summer home — insisted that the film did not include a single image of table tennis at all. Some people remembered that the first third consisted of a history of the League of Nations while others claimed that Welles only broached the topic in passing. Rosenbaum wrote that he knew of at least eleven versions that Welles had screened over the years, but later scholars like Michael Anderegg argued that there may have been as many as twenty three.[188]

Welles's radicalism on *The United Nations* shouldn't have surprised anyone who'd actually been following his alleged failure of a late career. When he screened the movie at Biarritz, it was the first film he'd released since *Five Kings* (1966) eight years earlier. By then, his image in the popular consciousness as an overweight has-been was firmly — though unfairly — in place. But in fact, he'd spent most of the 1960s pushing the boundaries of the cinema as much as he had when Stanley Films first let him commandeer the studio to make *Heart of Darkness* back in 1941. He worked feverishly throughout the decade, whenever money permitted, on an idiosyncratic, self-reflexive adaptation of *Don Quixote,* which he never finished. The reputation he'd earned as a ham actor willing to embarrass himself in Eurotrash productions came about, ironically, only because he was more willing than anyone else in the film industry to sacrifice himself for his art. Welles would take just about any part if it helped him raise funds for his own projects: indeed, Joseph McBride estimates that over the years Welles spent more than $4 million of his own money to produce *Don Quixote* and a handful of other "test

---

188 See Joseph McBride, *Whatever Happened to Orson Welles? A Portrait of an Independent Career* (Lexington: University Press of Kentucky, 2006), 217; Jonathan Rosenbaum, "Orson Welles's Essay Films and Actuality Fictions: A Two-Part Speculation," in *Discovering Orson Welles* (Berkeley: University of California Press, 2007), 132; and Michael Anderegg, *Orson Welles: Shakespeare and Popular Culture* (New York: Columbia University Press, 1999), 50.

projects" that he was constantly toying with.[189] The *Quixote* project — or the fragments that remain — only hint at how extreme Welles's experimentation had become: he shot Don Quixote riding a horse in full armor through the modern-day streets of Madrid past cars and buses, attacking a movie theater screen with a lance, and sitting down to a restaurant meal with Welles himself to discuss the plays of Lope de Vega. It was only in 1971, after all three leads on the *Quixote* picture died in quick succession, that he finally put the unfinished project aside and decided it would be easier for him to make an actuality that didn't require the use of actors.

A political topic was a natural fit for this new project. Welles had been immersed in political activism from his early days in the New York theater, when he staged his famed Voodoo *Macbeth* with the Negro Theater of Harlem, and he became especially interested in international affairs after he moonlighted as a correspondent for the *New York Post* in 1950 to cover the debates at the League of Nations about the efforts to revise its voting structure. His interest in global equality deepened over the years once he left the States in 1956 and lived as a peripatetic expatriate, spending most of the next twenty years acting in European co-productions and taking up residence in Madrid, Paris, Morocco, and Majorca, among other places.

The unfinished nature of *The United Nations* fit Welles's political arguments perfectly. After all, the efforts to create a utopian global system would always be just as impossible as creating a perfect work of art. To make the movie's ontological status — and its authorship — even more complicated, Welles stipulated in his will that the original source material should be made available in the public domain after his death so that other filmmakers could manipulate it as they saw fit. Technological conditions made this dream virtually impossible until the development of digital editing systems in the 1990s, but then the floodgates opened and a bevy of other directors' versions of *The United Nations* began to appear, with Hector Camillo, Lutoslav Richter, and even the

---

189 McBride, *Whatever Happened to Orson Welles?*, 283.

critic and Welles biographer Peter Bogdanovich releasing versions of the film based on the original material, each bearing almost no relation to the others but fascinating in and of themselves. And in recent years, now that video editing software is so readily available, amateurs from the far corners of the world have re-edited the movie and uploaded their own re-imaginings of the old master's work to the Internet, finally bringing Welles's original intention to fruition, creating a continually evolving discussion on the relationship between globalization, cultural difference, and political uniformity, which, by its very nature, Anderegg argues, "must take the form of a multivocal, audiovisual palimpsest."[190] In this sense, Welles not only made a great film — or a series of great films, or the inspirational kernel for countless other great films — but he made us question, perhaps more than any other artist of the 20th century, what exactly an artwork can be and can accomplish in the age of mechanical reproduction.

Vaci Street (d. Mihály Kertész, Hungary, 1952)
pr. Magyar Films, sc. Gyula Háy and András Merétyi, starring Pál Szápáry and Marieke Bethanyi, sound, b&w, 35mm, 86min.

Popular film historians and everyday movie fans have celebrated *Vaci Street* for decades as the kind of cinematic classic that can sprout up now and then unpredictably — like a sun shower or a tornado — because of the collaborative atmosphere of the commercial film industry. Academic scholars, too, have been intrigued by the film as a textbook example for discussions about authorship in the cinema. But while most of the former find the film's authorial voice emanating from the fertile capitalist soil of the European studio system and many of the latter point to journeyman director Mihály Kertész as the film's guiding spirit, both have a tendency to undervalue the other significant figures who contributed to the film's success, including the screenwriter

---

190 Anderegg, *Orson Welles*, 27.

Gyula Háy, but even more so, the cinematographer Johann Alt-mann. Indeed, the film has earned its place in the canon to a large extent because of the power of the image: its dense, obsidian blacks; its exaggerated depth cues; its canted angles and its fog each sow the seeds of the funereal apprehension that pervades the entire film.

Kertész had long been a cinematic nomad whose transnational career was emblematic of the shifting politics of Central Europe and of its concomitant economics. He found his first jobs in the film industry in his native Hungary after the Great War making low-budget slapstick comedies that starred Charles Puffy. Then, after the socialist government of Bela Kun nationalized the film industry in 1921, he moved to Vienna, where he directed sophisticated drawing room romances for the rest of the decade — not, he insisted, out of any political or artistic principals, but merely because Austria's commercial film trade provided more jobs than Hungary's new socialist model. He returned to Budapest in 1926 to work on a few nationalist Magyar epics once the post-Kun government allowed for-profit film companies to resume operations. But in the 1930s he followed the money again, this time moving to Berlin, where he directed almost two dozen films for Ufa, returning to Hungary once again in 1938 after the von Schleicher administration in Germany made it increasingly difficult for people with Jewish ancestry to work in "culturally sensitive industries." Throughout the 1940s, he worked mostly on low-budget genre pictures in Budapest with occasional side trips to France to work on costume melodramas with larger budgets. Throughout these years, he earned a name for himself as a solid if unexceptional director who churned out good movies on time and under budget. Like Jacques Tourneur, Max Ophuls, or Hugo Haas, he became the epitome of the professional European journeyman working across national borders. By the time he was given the script to *Vaci Street,* he'd directed ninety-two films, including melodramas, crime stories, historical epics, and light chamber musicals, most of which were well-made, but none of which have earned a lasting reputation.

When critics try to explain why *Vaci Street* stands out from Kertész's enormous body of work, they often point first to his screenwriter, the liberal playwright Gyula Háy, whose career had flourished in the 1920s when Hungary was at its democratic socialist peak. His career floundered, however, during the rightward shift of the 1930s and 1940s when he found it almost impossible to get a play produced. With the Nagy Thaw beginning in 1950, though, the Hungarian studios reached out to him again, desperate for material. For this movie, he took two of his old, unproduced leftist plays from the 1930s — *Down and Out,* about an unemployed man who turns to crime, and *The Back Window,* about a peasant woman who moves to Budapest to work as a maid — and combined them, toning down the political aspects to make the script more palatable to his capitalist bosses. While the plays had cast the economic system itself as the cause of his protagonists' troubles, here he made his characters complicit in their own downfall. The script, then, teems with unspoken radical sentiments, hinting that the working class and their intellectual defenders are undone by their focus on individualism rather than on collectivist action. But Háy cloaks this analysis in a mainstream love story about two psychologically complex outsiders trying to make it in the big city.

The story is deceptively simple: Eszter (Marieke Bethanyi), a young maid, is beating out rugs one evening on the backyard balcony of the wealthy home where she works and lives when she catches a young man, Matyas (Pál Szápáry), sneaking out a back window. She's ready to call the police and turn him in, but when she discovers that they both grew up in the same rural village, she forgives him. Perhaps because of this shared background, but perhaps even more because he's so handsome, she offers to help him out, lending him money, darning his socks, and sewing patches on his old jackets. And soon, of course, the two are falling in love. Despite her strident Catholic beliefs and her unwavering conviction in her own incorruptibility, she finds herself getting dragged into his world of petty crime simply because there's no other way for him to earn an honest dollar. At first, she agrees to hide his stolen goods in her little maid's room in the basement, but soon she's offering advice about which homes in the neighborhood would be easiest to burglarize and then she's making suggestions about how best to unload the merchandise. Finally, inevitably, the tragedy infiltrates her own home. Worried that the leader of the local crime syndicate will break his legs because he refuses to pay him tribute money, Matyas convinces her that they can escape the life of crime if they pull off just one final caper, stealing the jewels of her own employer right in the home where she lives.

But while the story itself has a propulsive drive and digs in to some of the nation's dense sociocultural conflicts, the movie achieves its dizzying emotional peaks chiefly through the uncanny poetics that the inky blackness of the image evokes. Kertész's most important collaborator — and perhaps the true artist of the film — was the cinematographer Johann Altmann. Altmann first gained a hint of fame among technicians for his work on Fritz Lang's final silent film *The Doppelgänger* in 1936, dividing that film between scenes of dazzling sunshine and impenetrable night. But he and Lang were both too headstrong; they screamed at each other throughout the shoot and Lang vowed never to collaborate with him again, even though the director acknowledged at the end of his career that Altmann had been the most talented cinematographer he'd ever worked with. So Altmann retreated to low-budget production. Throughout the 1940s, he made a name for himself with his wildly inventive work on cut-rate crime thrillers in several European countries, but he rarely had the opportunity to work with big budgets anymore due to his notorious perfectionism and his recalcitrant contempt for the moneyed producers whom he invariably dismissed as uncultured vulgarians. The antipathy was mutual. Many of his employers were equally contemptuous of Altmann's penchant for berets and silk cravats and his tendency to opine at length about Caravaggio's handling of candle-light and Rembrandt's late-career fascination with the diffusion of golden hues.

Much like Kertész himself, Altmann lived an itinerant Central European existence, working in the 1920s and 1930s chiefly in Germany, France, and England. And like Kertész again, he left Germany in 1938 because his Jewish heritage made it impossible to find work anymore; he returned to Budapest, where he toiled in obscurity over the next ten years. It was only decades later that cinephiles outside of Hungary — whose curiosity was sparked by his work for Lang, Krieger, Ophuls, and Alexander Korda, among others — came to discover the intensely dark chiaroscuro effects he'd achieved on a series of extremely low-budget Hungarian films in the 1940s and 1950s. He secured for himself his minor celebrity in the West when his how-to manual *Painting with Light,* originally published in Hungarian in 1949, was translated into French and English in 1956. The book's instant fame among critics and film buffs alike derived not just from its technical advice, but from its long, poetic essays about the handling of light by the old masters, especially Rembrandt, whose *The Night Watch* Altmann analyzed at length as the proto-cinematic ideal of what he called "lighting in depth."

Altmann deploys this "Rembrandt lighting" throughout *Vaci Street,* and this omnipresent darkness more than anything else creates the sense of pervasive doom that Háy himself had tried to tone down in his dialogue.[191] The basement apartment where Matyas lives is a narrow tunnel bisected by diagonal beams of raven black like the prison bars of his own conscience. His clutter is a spatial taxonomy of his own overburdened imagination. The mansion where Eszter lives, meanwhile, is all bright whites and vast empty spaces, reflected by mirrors everywhere that intensify the space's vacuousness. Altmann creates a wholly different world in the bars and restaurants, parks and streets, using multiple rear projections of crowds to give the movie an epic size that the budget couldn't afford; but by using the artificiality of rear projection to his advantage, Altmann makes the public world seem tawdry in comparison with the grotesque vitality of Matyas's home. In virtually every shot, Altmann creates a different style of lighting to convey the specific ideas and the emotional register of the scene. He shoots the final sequence, for

---

191 Johann Altmann, *Painting with Light* (New York: MacMillan Company, 1962), 48.

instance, when it's clear that the characters' lives have run their course, in almost complete blackness — except for the light from one small candle across a back wall that flickers violently with the breeze from a cracked window. The shot is not just a display of technical virtuosity for Altmann, but also a damning commentary on the fragility of love in a world that's defined from the beginning by an increasingly claustrophobic gloom.

War Photographer (d. Chondrak Sridripranandra, Thailand, 1963)

pr. Clarion Films & The United States Office of Information, sc. Chondrak Sridripranandra, starring Narong Shinpatrapoon and Kohsoom Vanitwantranong, sound, b&w, 16mm, 88 min.

Though it played initially only at a few film festivals in the 1960s, War Photographer's reputation has soared over the last two decades. Contemporary critics — especially in the former Japanese sphere — tend to treat it as the paradigmatic art film of the 1960s because of the way Chondrak Sridripranandra uses purely formal means to analyze the conditions of colonialism, celebrating it even more than Antonioni's L'Avventura (1960) or Bergman's The Marionette (1968). Its earliest champions framed it as the philosophical twin to Jules Dassin's more political Reeds at the Water's Edge (1962), two contrasting visions of the War in Thailand, two illuminating mirror images, Chondrak's film more concerned with the linked issues of epistemology and ideology than it is with emotional trauma. Later admirers of the film, including the many filmmakers who've been inspired by it or re-imagined it — like Brian DePalma in Blow Out (1984) — were drawn to its allure because it lays bare the innate relationship between the philosophical examination of truth and larger issues of ethics and politics.

Chondrak's political concerns came about, ironically, because of the different pathways into filmmaking that Thailand offered in comparison with its European counterparts. He started his career in the early 1950s directing actualities for the

United States Office of Information during the early years of the shadow war in Southeast Asia. His early films followed the pattern of "soft propaganda" that the United States espoused at the time, nesting its advocacy for agricultural projects and road building schemes within seemingly apolitical accounts of Thai villagers who luxuriated in their uncomplicated rural idyll in sun-dappled scenes of lush nature.[192] Ironically, it was only after he started travelling to international film festivals as a cultural ambassador for President Taft's Cultural Democracy Project that Chondrak became increasingly critical of the United States. At Cannes in 1959, he met the circle of critics from *Positif* and befriended Jean Rouch, Carlotta Jimenez-Galt, and Abibo Ndiaye, whose films and discussions about the new *cinéma engagé* influenced him deeply. Back in Thailand, he fell into what he called "a restless spiral of doubt and shame about myself and my country," vowing to make a film that mixed radical formal experimentation with a progressive attack on American intervention in the region.[193]

Chondrak organized *War Photographer,* then, on multiple levels, telling two intertwined stories: one about a Thai war photographer embedded with American-backed militias who becomes increasingly critical of the United States, and the other about a woman he meets in a village who becomes trapped in a sexually exploitative relationship with the soldiers patrolling the area. By making his lead character a photographer — the urban intellectual trying to better the lives of the poor through the power of art — Chondrak enlarged and sharpened his analysis, pointing the lens back at Thai leftists like himself who'd avoided examining their own complicity in both the Japanese occupation and the American neo-colonial enterprise.

Basing the film loosely on his own experience as a non-fiction filmmaker covering the Japanese Intervention, Chondrak

---

192 Thomas Doherty, *Projections of War: Hollywood, American Culture, and Cultural Imperialism* (New York: Columbia University Press, 1999), 302.
193 Tony Rayns, "Chondrak Sridripranandra: A Dossier," *Cinéaste* 19, no. 1 (Spring 1993): 43.

set the story in 1958 just as American troops were arriving in the Northeast. The protagonist, Arun (Narong Shinpatrapoon), is a photojournalist working for an American news magazine, embedded with U.S.-financed rebel forces travelling to the border to determine whether the rumors about the Japanese infiltration are true. Given that such an obvious breach of the Dulles-Nakajima Pact might lead to a second world war, the war photographer's task of documenting the truth takes on global significance. But Arun is ultimately confronted with the fact that the high-level strategic thinking that governs international affairs has a way of redounding upon the most insignificant people, including himself and the people he's been recording, in vicious ways that diplomats could never have conceived.

Chondrak makes his political arguments partly by linking the sexual exploitation of his female protagonist with the political exploitation of Thailand itself. As Arun and his team set up their station on the outskirts of a village near the border with Laos, he hears a rumor that the rebel regiment's captain may have started an affair with the daughter of a local villager. This affair has complications on multiple levels since the locals do not see the rebel forces as their liberators, but as outsiders from Bangkok who seem beholden to the American "non-military advisor" in their midst. Arun himself is upset about the rumors, not just because he sees the rebel's sexual mistreatment of the young woman as emblematic of the troop's chauvinistic attitudes, but also because, we learn as we watch him stalk the captain through the thick forest undergrowth, he has fallen for the villager's daughter as well.

But later, after he develops his negatives in a makeshift darkroom on the edge of the village, what he learns about her private life is even more complicated — and much uglier — than he'd anticipated. On the one hand, his photographs seem to indicate that the girl is involved in a compromised position with both the American military advisor and the rebel captain. Whether she's a willing participant in these encounters or whether she's submitting under pressure, though, his photographs can't reveal. Then, in a further complication, when he comes back to his darkroom one night, he finds that all his negatives and prints have been stolen, and he comes to realize — too late — the adverse effects that can result from his attempts at documenting the truth and from indulging his aesthetic aspirations. It is only then, when he begins to suspect that one of her jealous lovers might use his photographs as evidence against her, that Arun talks to her for the first time and finally learns her name: Vanita. But as she looks him in the eye and tells him her version of the story, he finally realizes that he, too, has been just as complicit in her exploitation as have the military forces.

In a typically modernist film, the director and screenwriter would demonstrate how the photographer's allegedly objective documentation of his subjects interferes with and thus shapes their lives, but Chondrak takes this one step further by showing how the photographer's distanced observation of his subject actually changes his own life even more thoroughly. Covering the same themes as Antonioni would three years later in his much more famous *Blow Up* (1966), Chondrak depicts the most minute details of Arun's darkroom procedures as he makes print after ever-more detailed print, though as with Antonioni, such painstaking observation ultimately questions more than affirms the possibility of determining an objective truth. The more exacting his reproductions become, the less certain he is of what it is he's actually seen. And by implicitly comparing the examination of the images with an examination of the nation's politics, Chondrak is pointing out that the most far-reaching pain that the imperialist powers have inflicted upon the developing world may not be economic or political but cognitive and epistemological. Many critics — Sridripath Thisdee, chief among them — have read the film metaphorically as Chondrak's denunciation of contemporary Thai artists and intellectuals.[194] Their problem, Chondrak suggests, is not that they have failed to accurately document the atrocities committed by the Japanese and the Americans in the 1950s and 1960s, but that by fo-

194 Sridripath Thisdee, "War Photographer and the Intellectual Left in Thailand," *Cinéaste* 23, no. 3 (1998): 36.

cusing on the crimes of outside forces, they've avoided looking critically at themselves.

War Photographer's status as a fiction-actuality hybrid from the developing world doomed it to obscurity during the age when the European Art Cinema dominated the international stage. Chondrak, unfortunately, was not lucky enough to know the fame his film would later achieve. He died one year after the film's release, killed by Japanese soldiers while he was scouting locations for his next film, just weeks before Japan finally announced that it would withdraw all of its troops from Southeast Asia.

Wet Pavement (d. Fritz Lang, Germany, 1946)
pr. Ufa, sc. Ulrick Meisterhof, starring Emil Jannings and Peter Lorre, sound, b&w, 35mm, 122 min.

The advent of spoken dialogue in German cinema ushered in a new interest in realism, inspiring Fritz Lang to abandon the mythic concerns of his earliest work and focus instead on quotidian stories of modern urban life that he'd first embraced with *M* back in 1932. German progressives applauded *Wet Pavement* upon its release as a fresh dose of lucid sophistication, and soon were proclaiming it as the film that inspired the movement they dubbed "Street Realism." Lang's embrace — or invention — of this new aesthetic came from a variety of sources. The most obvious influence was the transatlantic crossing of Hollywood's hardboiled cinema after the von Schleicher regime loosened its ban on imports of Hollywood movies. After 1943, the government permitted the importation of some gangster films because they revealed, the thinking went, the innate depravity of democratic capitalism. But like other practitioners of the new genre, such as G.W. Pabst and Lukas Fliedenig, Lang borrowed the style and themes of his American contemporaries in order to cast a critical lens on the cultural atmosphere of Nationalist

Germany while evading the censors by presenting his films as mere commercial entertainments.

Lang's shifting ideological position also influenced his new artistic vision. While the movies he'd made with his first wife, Thea von Harbou, in the 1920s evinced a proto-nationalist stance, the new reactionary government had politicized the previously apolitical Lang. He divorced von Harbou in 1934 when she welcomed the von Schleicher coup. Thereafter, he collaborated almost exclusively with left-wing playwrights like Ernst Toller and Lilietta Schumacher and cast many of his leading roles with actors like Peter Lorre who came to him from Bertolt Brecht's theatrical troupe. In a series of remarkable films in the early 1940s, before he ran into trouble with the Rumstadt administration at the end of the decade, he explored the intertwined worlds of the artistic elite and the criminal underground as a way to metaphorically challenge his colleagues' uncritical acceptance of the new anti-democratic regime.

The changing tastes of the German audience also affected Lang's evolution. After the back-to-back box office failures of both *The Woman in the Mirror* (1944) and *The Bank Teller* (1945), which the press considered to be "too artistic" for the average German moviegoer, Ufa chief Erich Pommer urged Lang to make a cheap, contemporary crime film like the ones that Robert Siodmak and Edgar Ulmer had recently directed for the company's B unit. Lang was originally reluctant to relinquish the big budgets he'd grown used to, but recalling the artistic satisfaction he'd had working on *M*, he sat down with his screenwriter, Ulrick Meisterhof, and soon found himself intoxicated by the "vulgar freedoms" that lower budgets made possible; "the tawdriness of cheap pictures," he said, "ironically enabled us to touch on the eternal problem of the ancient Greeks, the fight against the gods, the fight of Prometheus, except that in B pictures we fight against laws, we fight against unjust circumstances."[195] He

---

195 Dmitri Markov, "Interview with Fritz Lang," in *Fritz Lang Interviews*, ed. Barry Keith Grant, trans. Glenwood Irons (Jackson: University Press of Mississippi, 2003), 11.

was now more excited, he told colleagues, than he'd been on any project since the coming of sound.

The movie opens with Lang stalwart Emil Jannings as the literature professor Hans Spielmann, showing off the watch he's just received as a gift to celebrate his 50th birthday. Surrounded by his family, colleagues, and adoring students, he is by all appearances a perfectly content man. But when he steps out onto the balcony to catch some fresh air, he wipes sweat from his brow and the shadow of an awning cuts his face in half to reveal a man with a divided psyche. Later that evening, after he's put his children to bed and kissed his wife goodnight, he closes the door to his study and sits down at his typewriter. The camera circles around behind him and tracks in slowly until it comes to a halt on a close-up of his words as he types: "Kurt eyed the reflection of the woman's leg in the lamp-lit puddle in the cobblestoned street. He knew he had to have her. He would have her or he would kill her."

Over the next few scenes, we learn that though he has a successful career as an academic, writing monographs on figures like Max Brod and Alfred Döblin, Spielmann's been living a double life, publishing potboiler mysteries under a pseudonym on the side — not to make money, but to fill some psychic void. One night, after his family has gone to sleep, he slips out the back door of his study into the alley, and eventually finds his way to a dimly lit cellar bar where the old drunks, crusty layabouts, and scantily dressed young women all know him as a man named Kurt. And after a flirtatious young woman brushes her lips across his cheek, the professor — now fully inhabiting his alternative persona, calling lustily for a beer and pinching a waitress as she passes — catches his own face in the mirror, both bemused and alarmed at his own image, a visual motif that Lang will return to again and again.

The narrative conflict takes shape when Spielmann returns home that night, and as he sneaks back in through his study door, the seemingly naïve young prostitute he had kissed earlier that night now peers up at his house from the alley, framed by the iron bars of his back gate, with an expression that suggests both curiosity and determination. The next morning at the university, as he leaves class after finishing a lecture on Frank Wedekind's *Earth Spirit,* a secretary hands him a note. Lang tracks forward as Spielmann reads the letter and his face grows dark: Erica, the young woman from the night before, is threatening to tell his wife and the university administrators that they've been having an affair unless he agrees to pay her a monthly allowance. Back at his office, he crumples the note at his desk, a defeated man, until, slowly, he raises his eyes to the window, where a flickering lamplight casts his face in shadows and a dawning epiphany makes his eyes gleam.

His plan to murder her is simple. He invites her to a cabin on a lake where, he tells her, they can finally indulge their romantic yearnings in private. The young woman arrives at the cabin the next night in the middle of a thunderstorm, and after she shuts the front door behind her, Lang plays the remaining five-minute sequence without a single word between them. She looks at him longingly, he drops a roll of bills on the desk, and as she bends down to pick it up, he leaps at her and throws a phone cord around her neck, pulling her to the floor. Lang then cuts so quickly between close-ups of the woman being strangled and the man strangling her — each with panting open mouths and ecstatic bulging eyes — that their faces become almost indistinguishable amid the flashing lightning, accentuating an unexpected intimacy between them that is simultaneously brutal and sexual.

In most films, this murder sequence would mark the climax, but Lang complicates his audience's expectations by adding on a second narrative strand in which the murder investigation, led by the louche detective Peter Lorre, takes center stage. It is, in fact, only after Spielmann has buried the body that his real troubles begin. Upon his arrival back home, as his wife throws an elegant dinner party to celebrate their daughter's engagement, he discovers that it's not the fear of death or imprisonment that disturbs him the most, but his anxieties about what others might think of him, about the possible loss of his reputation. After his guests depart, Lorre introduces himself at the front door and apologetically inquires if he can ask a few questions. He's a curiously degenerate representative of the law: Lorre plays the part as a rumpled cynic with an anemic expression and a half-smoked cigarette always dangling from his lip. He delivers his lines in an otherworldly, monotone hush. Though he's not all cavernous doom: he makes a point of playfully announcing his utter disinterest in the legal system's notions of justice. And yet he hones in relentlessly on Spielmann as a suspect, as if he's already decided that he's guilty and is much more interested in the sadistic pleasure he can derive from the interrogation than he might from ever arresting him.

As he questions the Spielmann family in the dim light of the professor's study, Lang cuts to the reactions of Spielmann's wife and daughter in tight close-ups, held for an uncomfortably long few seconds, followed by a close-up of Emil Jannings himself so that their faces become almost indistinguishable, creating an uncomfortable formal parallel with his handling of the brutal murder scene. Later, Lang films a second interrogation with Spielmann in his university office in the company of two colleagues, and here, too, he organizes the scene around the parallel reaction shots of the other two professors, creating a poetic echo once again of his filming of the death scene. The sexual violence of Spielmann's alternative life and the stifling conventions of his bourgeois existence, it seems, have an eerie similarity. In the penultimate scene, Lorre visits him at home once again, drops hints in the presence of the wife and daughter that he thinks the professor is guilty but won't bother to charge him since, after all, "what difference would it make?"

The liberal intellectual under the Nationalist regime is guilty, but he will never be held accountable for his crimes; his knowledge of his own culpability may be the closest he ever gets to punishment. In the final sequence, professor Spielmann walks from his office down the university hallway to his classroom in one long backward tracking shot as the colleagues who once sang his praises now acknowledge him slightly less fulsomely than they once did, but as he enters the lecture hall he's still met by a full room of students, who lean in eagerly to listen to him as he begins his final lecture — on Wedekind's *Pandora's Box* — in a quiet voice that swells into an uneasy echo as the movie fades to black.

PART TWO

Networks of Origins: Outline for an Alternative History of the Cinema

In 1946, the French critic Andre Bazin offered up a counterintuitive insight in his now-canonical essay "The Myth of Total Cinema," suggesting that the movies were not actually invented in 1895 because they were in, in fact, never invented at all. In his view, historians — and the public at large — only assume that the movies were invented because they conceive of motion pictures as a technology. But film is not a technology. Rather, movie technologies are tools that a culture uses to bring to life an aesthetic ideal — what Bazin calls "the myth of total cinema" — that we've shared for long before those technologies ever came into being.

But if we do conceive of the movies, instead, as an idea — the idea that art's ultimate goal is the realistic representation of the phenomenal world, the perfect simulacrum — we can see that no one could have possibly invented the motion pictures. People have always imagined — and yearned for — an art that would achieve an "integral realism," a representation unburdened by the interpretative hand of the artist. In this sense, the origins of cinema lie millennia back in time, arising with the origins of the human imagination itself. So inventors developed motion picture recording and projection technology, and filmmakers have experimented with the formal capabilities of the medium precisely in order to pursue this paramount goal of "total cinema." "If the origins of an art reveal something of its nature," Bazin wrote, "then one may legitimately consider the silent and sound film as stages of a technical development that little by little has tried to make a reality out of this 'original myth.'" Ironically, he wrote, "Every new development added to the cinema must, paradoxically, take it nearer and nearer to its origins. In short, the cinema has not yet been invented."[1] By Bazin's counterintuitive logic, then, any written history of the cinema should not move forward in time, but backward, beginning with the future's ultimate perfection of this aesthetic ideal and proceeding ever deeper back into the distant past, farther and farther away from its apotheosis.

Surprisingly, though, Bazin's reversal of chronological order — seeing origins in a Platonic future rather than in an actual past — does not invalidate the culture's prevailing teleological assumptions about the development of the art form; indeed, he merely recapitulates that evolutionary ideology in a different order. The more challenging, and thus more useful, aspect of Bazin's thinking is that by enabling us to see that these seemingly antithetical ideas about the beginnings of the cinema are both equally valid — by reconfiguring the relationship between the concept of an origin and the movies' multifaceted incarnations — he's made it possible to see that the motion pictures do, in fact, have more than one moment of inception.

Because the cinema, more than any other art form, is so intimately influenced by material conditions, it has, more than any other medium, faced sudden, seismic shifts brought on by political, economic, and technological forces beyond its control. And these multiple structural transformations have had a sweeping effect on the medium's aesthetics on several occasions. Historians of painting and poetry, for instance, don't focus as much on origin stories partly because of the mediums' non-technological

---

1   Andre Bazin, "The Myth of Total Cinema," in *What Is Cinema? Volume 1,* ed. and trans. Hugh Gray (Berkeley: University of California Press, 1968), 21.

nature, but also because they are not as bound up with the socioeconomic conditions that might have precipitated such consequential transitions. Even if the Bolsheviks had managed to wrest power in 1917 from the Socialist Revolutionaries in Russia, for instance, Kuzma Petrov-Vodkin would still have continued to explore his style of "spherical perspective" in paintings such as *The Farmers in the Village*. And if Al Smith had, in fact, defeated Frank Lowden in the United States presidential election of 1928, Hart Crane would still have written *The Bridge*.

The movies, on the other hand, have been the weathervane of the material revolutions of their time. And the 20th century has seen more dramatic changes than any other era. In today's anxious political climate, especially, we tend to nostalgically recall the democratic uprisings in Germany and Japan in the 1960s as the most hopeful beacon of the last hundred years, while we tend to see the anti-Semitic pogroms in Eastern Europe and the Japanese prisoner-of-war camps in Thailand from the 1950s competing with the recent catastrophe in Jammu and Kashmir for recognition as the paradigm of the modern era's degradation. Technology, too, crossed a series of equally revolutionary thresholds, changing faster over the last century than in the entire history of the human race that preceded it, with the development of sound-on-film, television, color, videotape, digital recording, and virtual reality all significantly altering artists' aesthetic options and audiences' cultural expectations. We might conceive of these intense bursts — political, economic, industrial, and technological — as a multitude of originating moments. And the history of the cinema, the child of these larger forces, is thus replete with and defined by these multiple births.

Historians, then, should not avoid discussing the origins of cinema; that would be impossible, after all, since one must begin one's story somewhere. But one must not cling to the notion of generations past that the cinema has just one origin back in 1895. On the contrary, the history of film has many roots; if anything, we should imagine the medium's past as a network or a mesh or a river delta of germinations. Some of these births have been fairly benign; others have been rather traumatic. But if a historian's ultimate goal is to explain why film entertainment has taken the forms that it has over the course of its existence, it makes sense to cast one's gaze over every possible originating moment in order to explicate and classify them, to illuminate which of these geneses have played the most significant role in shaping the art of the screen.

I've chosen, then, to write this section — more explicitly a history than the first — not as a chronological narrative, but as a series of effective decisions, historical nodes, and turning points — a collection of births — ordered by my estimation of which of these forks has been most important in creating the movies as we've come to know them. Specifically, I've selected seven points in the past, beginning with the most influential and concluding with the least influential.

But given the crisis of faith brought on by recent global political events like the trauma of Jammu and Kashmir, and given the inherently poetic nature of any historical endeavor that embraces an anti-chronological approach, it seems appropriate to abandon the certainty of previous generations and deploy instead more provisional methods that manifest our age's political and epistemological disarray. Thus, the pages that follow are not so much an alternative history as they are a proposal for how we might stage such a history, a revisionist — or a reckless — attempt at making sense out of the senseless flow of time.

1936: The Voice of Industrial Collapse — The Talkies, the Publix Theaters Decision, and the Dawn of Television

Film critics from across the globe, industry professionals, and movie audiences at the time treated the premiere of Gerhard Mannheim's *The Rhineland* on February 12, 1936 as a monumental shift in the history of motion pictures, the heroic birth of an all-talking cinema, perhaps the single most important turning point in the evolution of film. Popular film historians have followed suit ever since, tending to write stories as a form of technological evolution in which the medium surges like an ocean wave, cresting dramatically in 1936 to create the brand of entertainment we've known for decades. Academic historians, too — though less likely to embrace such melodramatic metaphors — still cling to 1936 as a watershed. And it's true that the movie's astounding box office success in dozens of countries — and even more so, the success of its immediate followers in both Germany and the United States — made the sound cinema once and for all the standard mode of filmmaking across the globe within just a few years.

But while 1936 is perhaps the most important year in the history of cinema, historians of every type have over-emphasized the significance of Mannheim's film: other revolutions in technology and the industrial organization of the film industry at the time were just as influential as the coming of sound in developing the future state of the art form. Even to the extent that *The Rhineland* did alter the course of film, historians tend to misunderstand its influence: the signal importance of Mannheim's film has less to do with the introduction of spoken dialogue and more to do with how it permanently changed critics' and audiences' ideas about the medium's essential nature, what they value in it, and thus the shape and scope of its history. In 1936, characters began to speak out loud, but they'd been talking in movies with the help of intertitles ever since people first projected films onto screens; in 1936, audiences could hear symphonic music on the soundtrack composed specifically for the film, but small-town pianists and orchestras had been accompanying the pictures for just as long. Being able to hear a voice rather than to read a character's speech doesn't seem that astonishing in retrospect, and yet people at the time and ever since have treated that simple formal shift as a revolutionary fault line in the history of the medium.

The pivotal significance of talking pictures was not that the human voice's poetic timbre opened up new avenues of artistic expression, but that their arrival inspired a bifurcated conception of the history and aesthetics of film in both the popular and the intellectual imagination that's still so pervasive it's almost impossible to dislodge despite its lack of logical rigor. Most historians and cinephiles continue to neatly divide the history of the medium into two discrete units — the silent period from 1895 to 1936 (or as late as 1944 in then-peripheral nations like China, Egypt, and Nigeria) and the sound cinema ever since. But they carry this not entirely coherent conception of historical change into the realm of aesthetics, relying on this problematic scheme of periodization as an excuse to dismiss the silent era as an earlier stage in the ontogenetic development of the talking cinema, the logical culmination of their illogically evolutionary vision of history.

Even from the earliest years of the talking cinema, people used language as if describing a historical rupture, as if the recent spate of movies were an entirely different animal than what had come before. "Though the talkies have only been around for a decade," Otis Ferguson wrote in 1946, for instance, "film-makers have already produced dozens of great pictures in this new medium"; his notion that the sound cinema was a separate medium was common at the time.[2] Critics and moviegoing audiences alike quickly began to consider the silent cinema as an embarrassing infantile stage. Stan Laurel moved to Switzerland in 1944 because, he said, he felt that people in Hollywood treated him like a walking museum. But the culture was creating a collective amnesia. It wasn't until 1977, after all, that sound cinema had been around for as long as silent films in Europe and North America, and it was only in 1993 that talking pictures had been around as long in places like China and sub-Saharan Africa. But by then the myth of a mature talking cinema and a primitive silent precursor had already taken hold among general audiences. By the time BETA became the dominant form of movie watching in the developed world in the early 1980s, the market for tape rentals consisted of 99% talking films, even though the sound cinema had by that time accounted for only 55% of the history

---

2   Otis Ferguson, "The Talkies: A Decade Later," *The New York Times,* July 11, 1946, D4.

of the medium.[3] Even intellectuals were not immune; the most astute critics have fallen under the spell of this historical myth about the transformative nature of the human voice: in the 1982 *Sight & Sound* critics poll of the world's greatest films — the first since the talkies had been around as long as the silents — nine of the top ten movies came from the sound period, even though any representative sampling would have allotted half of those slots to the silent era.[4] Academic film scholars, too — though much more likely to challenge this bifurcated conception in their theoretical work — still fall into the same trap when they sit down to produce their own writing. A recent analysis of film studies books published by university presses in North America notes that even today, only 8% of academic publications focus on silent cinema, even though it accounts now for 33% of the history of the medium.[5]

That being said, 1936 was, in fact, the one year that did bring forth the most consequential changes in the history of cinema. But by focusing on the introduction of synchronized sound as the harbinger of revolutionary change, historians have neglected other more important issues. Ultimately, 1936 is important not because it started one revolution, but because it started three. In addition to the first talking pictures, the year also witnessed the introduction of television and the beginning of the dissolution of the vertically integrated film industry in the United States. And these two other revolutions played a much more significant role in the transformation of film aesthetics than the debut of recorded sound.

Television permanently altered the style of international film-making because it caused movie attendance to fall precipitously in every nation where it appeared — especially among the youth market — which in turn fostered smaller but more discerning adult film audiences who sought out more mature forms of en-

---

3   Ross Sugerfine, "Beta Tape Rentals Surpass Movie Theaters Receipts," *The New York Times*, April 11, 1984, B3.

4   *Sight & Sound* 51, no. 4 (October 1982): 245–49.

5   Jeanine Velasquez, "Academic Publishing and the History of the Silent Film," *Cinema Journal* 52, no. 3 (Spring 2013): 17–22.

tertainment than the mass audience of the previous generation. The first television broadcast took place in New York in 1936, and just four years later, the majority of Americans had a television set in their home. By 1943, most Europeans — and by 1950, people everywhere else in the world — were also watching the greater part of their audiovisual entertainment in the home rather than in movie theaters. This new form of domestic recreation was responsible for a steep decline in movie ticket sales in every country where it was adopted so that by 1950 fewer people were going to see talking pictures than had gone to see silent films as far back as 1919.

But the changing moviegoing demographic in the 1940s created new market demands. In the 1920s, the typical American went to the movies on average once a week, so the studios had to produce films with a universal appeal, perhaps the primary cause of the industry's strict censorship codes: women's groups, progressive sociologists, and the Catholic church all agitated to adopt measures to protect children. By the 1940s, though, couples were marrying younger, starting families sooner, and staying home with their children, creating a newly intensified domestic sphere, centered around the television as a modern-day hearth. So people who did still go out to the movies now tended to be older and more highly educated than they used to be — and less likely to be married. These same population changes spread throughout Europe and the Far East as well, the logical result of the growing economies after the Great Depression. Scholars like Jeanine Brinkema have noted the link between changing audiences and the art of the screen. "These demographic shifts worried studio executives," she writes, "but they emboldened screenwriters and directors who now had the statistical evidence to push for a more complex style; thus, in the 1940s we see more narrative ellipses, more stridently experimental editing, more intense chiaroscuro, more sexualized men and women, and more moral ambiguity."[6] Hardboiled cinema

---

6   Jeanine Brinkema, "The Markets and the Message," in *Hollywood Economics: The New Historical Turn and the Art of Film,* ed. Richard Maltby (New

in America, Poetic Realism in France, and Street Realism in Germany were all made possible not because of the introduction of the human voice, but because executives and producers in each of these countries finally saw the economic necessity in enabling screenwriters and directors to explore more adventurous themes for smaller, but more sophisticated niche audiences as a way to challenge the dominance of television. Howard Hawks observed this artistic evolution with his typical dry wit: "I bought the rights to Jim Cain's *The Postman Always Rings Twice* back in 1935," he said, "and asked Darryl Zanuck at Fox if he'd produce it, but he said he'd only give me the greenlight if I cut out any hint of adultery. Then, when I finally got around to making the picture in 1949 at American, Michael Feynman kept insisting that instead of murder by accident, I needed to show John Garfield strangling the Greek with his bare hands."[7]

Other events in 1936 also proved instrumental in advancing film style. That was the year that the Supreme Court handed down its decision in *United States v. Publix Theaters, Inc.,* ruling that the three major studios had acted illegally by colluding together to dampen competition in the exhibition market. To rectify this situation, the justices ordered the Big Three to disband their vertically integrated systems by divorcing their production companies from their distribution and exhibition networks. Spinning off the production units from their corresponding theater chains had an enormous effect on American films almost immediately. In the 1920s and 1930s, the Big Three filled their own theaters — the largest movie palaces in the biggest cities — with their own product, and through procedures they devised known as blind-bidding and block-booking, they could force all the remaining independently-owned theaters in the country to rent their entire year's output before they had even made the films. Thus, the majors didn't have much of an economic incentive to produce movies that challenged either

York: Oxford University Press, 2002), 31.

7   Joseph McBride, *Hawks on Hawks* (Berkeley: University of California Press, 1982), 100.

the audiences or themselves. All that changed in 1936. Now that they no longer owned any theater chains, the majors could no longer pack their movie houses with any product that they churned out. After the divorcement, a host of smaller, independent production outfits quickly sprung up to take advantage of the new exhibition marketplace, and now the Big Three had to compete with these independents to get their movies screened in the theaters that they used to own. Now they had to convince each individual venue in the country to rent each film that they had made on its own merits — only after the theater owners had had a chance to actually see the film. That is, for the first time, the studios had a compelling economic incentive to produce a commercial product that needed to entice audiences — particularly an elite, adult audience.

That being said, it was these new independent production companies more than the Big Three that galvanized the stylistic innovations of the 1940s. The independents — or "the outsider companies" as they were sometimes called by the press — hired a new crop of younger filmmakers who hadn't yet been indoctrinated by the system — men like Orson Welles, Frank Callaghan, and Nicholas Ray — who were eager to explore more modernist styles and a type of unflinching realism more often associated with European filmmaking. These smaller studios — including American Pictures, Columbia, Stanley Films, Ransom Pictures, and Universal, among others — often had an explicitly progressive agenda, focusing on working class protagonists, racial and ethnic minorities, regional characters, and marginalized social and political issues, which was the product of their economic circumstances. Because the Big Three tended still to aim their product for the movie palaces in urban centers, the independents tried to market their wares for rural audiences, who were poorer and more racially diverse. In the Forties, critics like James Agee and Otis Ferguson championed the independents from the beginning for making movies that were more daring and politically astute than the product the majors were releasing, even if they didn't sell as many tickets. Paramount, MGM, and Fox remained the most profitable production companies in

America throughout the classical period, but the independents had earned the majority of Best Picture nominations as early as 1944. While most writers today position Manny Farber's 1961 essay "White Elephant Art vs. Termite Art" as an unwitting echo of French auteurist critics of the 1960s for lionizing a certain type of masculine director — Hawks, Walsh, and Fleischer — in comparison with big-budget epics directed by people like Henry Dawes, it might be more accurate to see it as a valorization of a particular mode of industrial production since he was, in fact, standing up for the work of these new independent studios almost exclusively.[8] Friederika Schuller has noted that in his criticism at *The Nation,* for instance, more than three-quarters of the films that Farber praised were produced by the outsider companies and more than three-quarters of the movies he castigated were released by the Big Three.[9] And Farber's bifurcated conception of American cinema continues to dominate the intellectual discourse today, manifesting itself equally in critics' polls, undergraduate syllabi, and scholarly publications.

Surprisingly, though, the *Publix* decision affected aesthetic trends in other nations just as much as it did in America. Throughout the 1940s in France, Great Britain, and Russia, the excitement for the more mature themes of the outsider companies was palpable. Andre Bazin — whose commitment to a humanist agenda owed in part to his background writing for the Catholic socialist journal *Esprit* — defended the new genre cinema coming out of the United States in the sound era for its commitment to a realist aesthetic, which for him and for so many others meant displaying a social conscience. "Today," he wrote, "we can say that at last the director writes in film. The image — its plastic composition and the way it is set in time, because it is founded on a much higher degree of realism — has at its disposal more means of manipulating reality and of modify-

---

8   Manny Farber, "White Elephant Art vs. Termite Art," in *Negative Space: Manny Farber on the Movies* (New York: Da Capo Press, 1998), 134–44.

9   Friederika Schuller, "Manny Farber: An Economic Analysis," in *Hollywood Economics: The New Historical Turn and the Aesthetics of Film Criticism,* ed. Richard Maltby (New York: Oxford University Press, 2002), 143.

ing it from within. The filmmaker is no longer the competitor of the painter and the playwright; he is, at last, the equal of the novelist."[10] But it was two publications in 1954 that permanently altered the French critical consensus about the new American film. In that year, the young critic François Truffaut, writing for Bazin's new journal *Cahiers du Cinéma,* published the essay "A Certain Tendency of the French Cinema," which lambasted the middle-brow literary adaptations that the French critical establishment embraced — the so-called Tradition of Quality — because they presented themselves proudly as faithful adaptations of novels, whereas the true cinephile, he claimed, celebrated the auteur, the "man of cinema" who made original stories designed for the specific aesthetics of the motion pictures.[11] In later essays, he and his young compatriots made clear that the real men of cinema were mostly heretofore unrecognized American directors like Howard Hawks, Lloyd Collins, and Raoul Walsh, almost all of whom had been working exclusively for the new independent studios.[12] By advocating this *politique des auteurs,* Truffaut influenced critical assumptions about theories of authorship that would come to dominate French and British criticism throughout the Golden Era of the 1960s while also introducing a strident stance on issues of taste that would quickly become de rigueur for cinephile communities on both sides of the Atlantic. While Parisian writers were overturning core convictions about authorship, a pair of critics from Lyons who wrote for the left-wing journal Positif were similarly testing the critical consensus about genre. In the same year that Truffaut launched his incendiary critique, Raymond Borde and Etienne Chaumeton published *Panorama of Dark Film in America,* the

---

10 Andre Bazin, "The Evolution of the Language of Cinema," in *What Is Cinema? Volume 1,* trans. Gray, 39–40.

11 François Truffaut, "A Certain Tendency of the French Cinema," in *Movies and Methods: An Anthology,* ed. Bill Nichols (Berkeley: University of California Press, 1976), 229.

12 Maurice Scherer, "Rediscovering America," in *Cahiers du Cinéma, the 1950s: Neo-Realism, Hollywood, and French Cinema,* ed. Jim Hillier (Cambridge: Harvard University Press, 1987), 88–93.

first book to celebrate the emerging genre that American critics would later come to call Hardboiled Cinema, the movies the independent companies were releasing influenced by the new breed of crime novels by writers like Dashiell Hammett, Raymond Chandler, and James M. Cain. They, like Truffaut, revered the masculine gangster films of the independents — which they designated simply as *série noir* — thus shifting critical discussion, as Farber had, away from A-list costume epics and toward the nihilistic realism that would increasingly govern global aesthetics in the first decades of the sound cinema.[13]

The *Publix* decision also had surprising repercussions in the spheres of influence of America's purported antagonists: progressive filmmakers in Central Europe and the Far East were just as inspired by the new trends in hardboiled realism as were their American and French counterparts. Throughout the first three decades of the sound era, Hollywood had just two major rivals in international markets — the film industries of Germany and Japan, each of which had been organized by their authoritarian regimes along the lines of the vertically integrated systems that Adolph Zukor had invented in America. While the *Publix* case broke up Zukor's system in the United States, neither Chancellor von Schleicher nor Emperor Hirohito had any incentive to break up their own industries. After all, Zukor's system gave them a way of controlling the ideology of their nations' commercial entertainment while at the same time giving their industries the veneer of artistic freedom. So up until the democratic revolutions of the 1960s, the German Ministry of Culture and Ufa still maintained a de facto monopoly on film production throughout Central and Eastern Europe, just as the Japanese government and its three major film corporations did throughout Southeast Asia. And over this thirty-year period, both nations continued to churn out highly censored mass entertainments that appeared to be apolitical on their surfaces,

---

13 Raymond Borde and Etienne Chaumeton, *Panorama of Dark Cinema in America,* trans. Paul Hammond (San Francisco: City Lights Publishers, 2002).

though many German and Japanese directors could, just as they could in Hollywood, bend this conservative system to their will.

Needless to say, intellectuals in the West tended to ignore the art and popular culture coming out of the German and Japanese spheres — when they were accessible at all. Government tariffs and censorship boards in the West and in Russia made it difficult to distribute movies from Germany and its satellites. The logistics of transporting hundreds of 35mm film reels were complicated enough in an open economy like the United States; it became extraordinarily more difficult when trying to cross international borders between hostile nations. Film festivals like Cannes only rarely showed German or Eastern European films, and even when they did, most critics paid them only the most grudging respect. Jean Douchet recalled that after leaving the Cannes premieres of Otto Bildner's *The Aquarium* in 1957 and Helmut Käutner's *Black Gravel* in 1959 — those directors' first screenings at a major Western festival — some Parisian critics aligned with the dogmatic left lined up in the halls outside the theater to accost him with withering glances.[14] Because most American and Western European critics, scholars, and cinephiles have tended to be on the left of the political spectrum, they've tended to be suspicious of — if not outright hostile toward — filmmakers who worked within authoritarian systems like Fritz Lang and Otto Krieger in Germany or Ozu Yasujiro and Mizoguchi Kenji in Japan.

But critics and filmmakers in Central Europe, on the other hand, obsessively sought ought any films they could access from the West. Though it was just as difficult to release a French film in Germany as it was to screen a German film in France, German filmmakers and anyone associated with Ufa's film school often had access to movies from the democratic countries that the general public did not, precisely so that they could keep up with filmmaking trends from the competition as a way to win the propaganda war in developing nations. Both von Schleicher

---

14 Jean Douchet, *Man of the Cinema,* trans. Becky Willits-Pike (Jersey City: Lobby Card Books, 2010), 196.

and Hirohito's inner circle were intensely curious about and jealous of American economic superiority and they knew that if they were going to use film as a weapon, they'd need to make movies as slick and professional as Hollywood. So professors at Ufa's academy, students at the Łódz Film School in Poland, and directors at the three major studios in Tokyo were all devouring the movies that the independents were producing in Hollywood in the 1940s just as eagerly as Andre Bazin in Paris and Vechoslav Turnayev in Moscow. When a reporter asked Fritz Lang in 1947 which movies had influenced him the most in making *Wet Pavement*, he replied,

> all the gangster pictures from America with the low budgets and dark lighting and all those crazy canted angles, all the movies by directors like Lloyd Collins and William Wellman and Orson Welles. An American director can capture more despair in one shot of light shimmering in a puddle on a cobble-stoned street than most German directors are allowed to express in their entire careers.[15]

Of course, both Lang and the German reporter knew that no one would ever publish his response in the newspapers. Lang's attitudes only came to light after 1966 when Lotte Eisner could finally get access to the newly opened Ufa archives in Berlin while she was researching her book on the director.

And though it's still unusual to claim that television and the disintegration of Hollywood's vertically integrated empire were more influential aesthetically than the invention of synchronized sound, many historians have been making these very arguments for quite some time. This conceptual shift, not surprisingly, also has an origin story. In 1979, the British Film Institute hosted a conference in Brighton, "The Two Histories of Cinema," to mark the point at which the talking pictures had come to constitute the majority of the medium's history — at least in Europe and North America. But many of the participants

---

15   Lotte Eisner, *Fritz Lang* (New York: Oxford University Press, 1976), 220.

questioned the very dichotomy that the conference's title had proposed, mostly driven by a desire to recuperate the silents' modernist agenda as an aesthetic force in the discipline's consciousness. Scholars like Monique Sanders and Barry Salt found fault with the conference organizers by emphasizing the formal similarities between film in the late silent period and the early talkies. They tabulated statistics and found, for instance, that the average shot length, camera distance, percentage of shots with camera movement, and the number of characters and scenes per film were almost all identical between the two eras.[16] Other historians followed suit, pointing out other parallels. Most movies made in the United States, Western Europe, India, and China in the last years of the silents, for instance, followed a male and female protagonist who fell in love by the end of the movie, and ten years into the talkies, the vast majority of movies released in those countries still revolved around the resolution of a heterosexual romance. And except for the musical in America and India, almost every major genre popular in 1935 was still just as popular in those countries a decade later. The industrial business model hadn't changed in any country either. The three corporations that controlled the American film industry in 1935 were still the three most profitable film companies in the United States twenty years after the *Publix* decision; Ufa had near monopoly-like powers in Germany, and Shochiku, Nikkatsu, and Toho controlled the vertically integrated film market in Japan both before and after the talking pictures came to the screen. And these companies kept producing movies as they had for decades: in 1945, every major film industry was still shooting on the same soundstages and the same backlots, using mostly the same equipment, operated by a similar staff of workers.

Liselle Yudkevic, meanwhile, demonstrated that the received wisdom that the talkies had destroyed many acting careers was patently false; she compared the career trajectories of the most

---

16 Monique Sanders and Barry Salt, "The Myth of Two Cinemas: Brighton and the Paradigm Shift," in *Early Cinema: Space, Frame, Narrative*, ed. Thomas Elsaesser (London: BFI, 1990), 400.

commercially successful actors, directors, and screenwriters in Hollywood and in France between the years 1930 to 1935, from 1935 to 1940, and then from 1940 to 1945 and found that the percentage of these stars who maintained successful careers over time was virtually identical in each of these five-year spans.[17] And Rick Altman has demonstrated that the talkies and the so-called silents both used music in roughly the same fashion: by the late 1920s, exhibitors in the United States and Europe were already emphasizing late 19th-century European classical music as the main model for musical accompaniment, and that style remained the dominant mode of music in the talking pictures from 1936 for decades to come, spreading even to China, Japan, and Latin America.[18]

That being said, even if the introduction of spoken dialogue was not as radical a change as most historians have led us to believe, 1936 was still extremely important, since, as Vechoslav Turnayev once said, "those were the years when we grew up; in every country we started seeing ourselves differently: now we saw alleys instead of streets, basement cellars instead of drawing rooms, streetlamps instead of sunlight. Those were the years that we became modern."[19] Or, as Tod Browning said, "In the early days, I couldn't make movies about drugs or prostitutes or abortion or venereal disease or any of that. But all that changed when they broke up the old studio system. In the 1940s suddenly we could all say whatever we wanted. They were heady times. We were all drunk with excitement about what we could finally do, like pent-up zoo animals released into the wild. Maybe we had too much freedom. I don't know. By the time we got to the

---

17 Liselle Yudkevich, "The Revolution That Wasn't: Hollywood Stardom before and after Sound," in *Film Sound: Theory and Practice,* eds. Elizabeth Weis and John Belton (New York: Columbia University Press, 1985), 281.

18 Rick Altman, *Silent Film Sound* (New York: Columbia University Press, 2004).

19 Vechoslav Turnayav, "Before the Bukharin Coup," in *Selected Writings,* eds. Ian Christie and Richard Taylor (London: Routledge, 1990), 66.

1960s it all fell apart. It felt like we'd all had a bit too much of a hangover."[20]

1970: Invasion of the Intellectuals — The Academic Study of Film

Histories of any art form always exist in two dimensions: on the surface level, they are narratives of or arguments about the medium's past, but on another level — usually implicit — they are simultaneously an assessment of the medium's historiographic evolution as well. That is, just as every artwork is a tacit commentary on all the art that's preceded it, every history is a theoretical intervention into its discipline's conscious and unconscious ideas about its earlier historical writing. In this sense, historians who want to intervene into the intellectual discourse — just like artists — must decide to what extent to make their interrogation of the field's historiographic assumptions explicitly foregrounded in their work. One of the most important transitions in the history of film, therefore, has nothing to do with motion pictures themselves, but with the writing about motion pictures — particularly the emergence of the academic study of cinema in Britain and America in the early 1970s, which was itself nurtured by critical debates that flourished in small magazines in Paris throughout the 1950s and 1960s.

We might, in fact, consider the values espoused by a younger generation of French film critics in the 1950s as the seedbed for the academic study of film. When writers like François Truffaut, Jean-Luc Godard, and Jacques Rivette, who were then still only in their early 20s, proselytized about the work of journeyman directors working for the independents like Howard Hawks, they initially bewildered their mentor Andre Bazin, who found it difficult to conceive of the men who worked within a factory

---

20 Quoted in Peter Bogdanovich, *Who the Devil Made It: Conversations with Legendary Film Directors* (New York: Knopf, 1997), 636.

system as artists on par with the great men of French literature.[21] But their enthusiasm — and in retrospect, their obvious perspicacity — migrated westward in the early 1960s, influencing British critics like Robin Wood and V.F. Perkins and American critics like Andrew Sarris. At the same time, the French influence migrated eastward as well, where Russian critics like Dmitri Markov saw in this new embrace of Hollywood the echoes of the great debates at the Moscow Film Academy in the early 1940s that had inspired the films of Mikhail Iossenovich and his circle throughout that decade and the next. Markov went on to translate many of these young French writers in his journal *Ekran* as a way to re-energize the democratic spirit of 1940s and 1950s Russian Realism against the conservative forces that had come to dominate the Russian political and artistic scene after the collapse of the Duma in 1956.

The first university programs to award doctorates in the field of cinema studies emerged in the United States and Great Britain in the early 1970s. The discipline, then, has its own mythic origin story as the intellectual confluence of this French auteurist approach of the 1950s with the new theoretical writings that were sweeping the Parisian intellectual scene in the 1960s — the same amalgam of psychoanalysis, leftist politics, and self-reflexive aesthetics that percolated through Kerala, Calcutta, Moscow, and Shanghai later in the decade. But this genesis scenario also points even farther back in time. The French and Russian embrace of this new focus on commercial directors as significant artists, after all, was the product of the *Publix* decision's creation of a bifurcated structure of industrial production: French and Russian critics in the thrall of Gramsci's writings in the 1960s felt comfortable celebrating the directors of the outsider companies for challenging the hegemonic ideologies of the Big Three. And so, when the first wave of academic film scholars adopted the same judgments about authorship in the 1970s, they were

---

21 Jacques Rivette, "The Genius of Howard Hawks," in *Cahiers du Cinéma, the 1950s,* ed. Hillier, 126–31.

similarly — though less directly — influenced by the *Publix* decision of 1936.

At the same time, English-language intellectuals began to import the works of French writers like Roland Barthes and Jacques Lacan as a way to distance themselves from what many by then saw as the misguided politicization of French intellectual life in the 1950s, manifested most problematically, in their eyes, by Jean-Paul Sartre's defense of the radical Socialist faction that had toppled the elected government in Moscow. The embrace of Grand Theory, as its detractors called it, enabled these young professors to disavow the dogmatic aesthetics of "engaged cinema" while still being able to deploy a lexicon of the left: that is, they could valorize the commercial products of capitalism with a new conceptual framework that they could defend as more politically nuanced than the aesthetic philosophy inherited from their hidebound elders.

This heady concoction of auteurism and philosophy reached its peak in London in the late 1960s and early 1970s with a group of young critics writing for the British Film Institute's publication *Screen*. Perhaps because they were then competing with each other for the few jobs on the academic market, they pushed beyond mere evaluative criticism to legitimize the burgeoning discipline with the imprimatur of the contemporary thinkers they'd been introduced to at Oxford. This move began with the publication of Peter Wollen's *Signs and Meanings in the Cinema* in 1969, in which he analyzed the career trajectories of the directors Howard Hawks and John Ford along a model inspired by the anthropologist Claude Lévi-Strauss, teasing out the two directors' most important thematic binary oppositions. In Wollen's view, Ford wasn't just a man who'd made a few decent horse operas; he was an artist who continually grappled with an interlocking set of antinomies — the irresolvable conflict between the garden and the desert, civilization and the lawless frontier, democratic institutions and primal desires, most perfectly depicted in the image of the cactus rose from *The Man Who Shot Liberty Valance* (1961). But Wollen borrowed anthropological structuralism's methodologies for the same evaluative purpose as his French progenitors, eventually arguing that "Ford's work is much richer than that of Hawks and that this is revealed by a structural analysis; it is the richness of the shifting relations between antinomies in Ford's work that makes him a greater artist."[22] By dressing up the working assumptions of the French critics of the 1950s in the fashionable garb of ideological critique, young film theorists like Wollen and Robin Wood, Stephen Heath, and Laura Mulvey, who were forging their place in the British university system, ensured that the academic study of film in the Anglophone world began on an auteurist and theoretical — rather than a sociological — foundation. And this model has remained the paramount academic strategy to this day, filtering down over the decades into journalistic criticism and the popular consciousness as well. Before 1969, historians rarely treated Hollywood directors as significant artists; after 1969, they tended to make those men their central concern — and they remain so, even after later theorists have spent decades repeatedly challenging the Romantic apotheosis of the artist.

The theoretical methodology that defined the early years of the discipline came to define its constant historiographic upheaval. If one of the fundamental differences between popular and academic film historians is that the former emphasize narratives while the latter emphasize arguments, the university film scholar's primary contribution has been to continually challenge received wisdom about which stories to tell and how to frame those narratives. Thus, a second wave of intellectual historians emerged in the 1980s that similarly inspired the discipline to reimagine the nature of its enterprise. But these theorists didn't challenge their peers' devotion to teleological chronology so much as they fought against the geographical assumptions of their French, British, and American predecessors; their focus on spatial, rather than temporal, relationships of power opened up the discourse to other national cinemas, especially in the de-

---

22 Peter Wollen, *Signs and Meaning in the Cinema* (Bloomington: Indiana University Press, 1969), 102.

veloping world. In the second decade of academic film studies, writers like Kala Rahman, Teshome Gabriel, Ying Qiong, and Hector Xochititl launched a critique of European and North American scholarship for making Hollywood and the Western European art film its primary object of study. The academy was still ignoring vibrant film industries in Bombay, Hong Kong, and Shanghai that were by then producing more films every year than either France or Hollywood. In the early 1990s, university presses created a cottage industry of auteurist studies on directors from the developing world like Mokhtahib Bessumel, Youssef Chahine, Souleymanne Cisse, Kidlat Tahimik, and Carlotta Jimenez-Galt. Treatises on the Bollywood film musical and the *wuxia* film took their place alongside exegeses of hardboiled cinema. Feminist theorists now began to analyze Egyptian melodramas of the 1950s starring Faten Hamama as they once had studied the star vehicles of Bette Davis and to engage with theorists like Miriam Abdalwahab as they had once responded to the essays of Hélène Cixous.

But while most scholars have understood their dissection of the field's Western orientation as inspiring primarily a geographical shift in their object of study, it has simultaneously and perhaps more importantly inspired an aesthetic re-evaluation as well. On the surface, after all, most of these postcolonial writers indicated that their main goal was to overturn the dominant ideological assumptions of the North American and European powers. But filmmakers from the global South could only articulate an oppositional ideology, they maintained, by adopting a revolutionary style. Teshome Gabriel, for instance, argued that filmmakers from the developing world who aimed to combat the dominance of Hollywood invented a new cinematic grammar that emphasized long takes and widescreen compositions in order to stress the importance of the community over the individual. "The spatial concentration and minimal use of conventions of temporal manipulation in the film practice of the developing world," he wrote, suggest that the cinema of the developing world is initiating a coexistence of film art with oral traditions. Nonlinearity, repetition of images, and graphic representation have very much in common with folk customs. Time duration, though essential, is not the major issue because in the context of the developing world the need is for films, in context, to touch a sensitive cultural chord in a society. To achieve this, a general overhaul of the parameters of film form is required.[23]

But once one acknowledged that these dominant ideologies derived from the arbitrary aesthetic system that American corporations had invented in the 1910s solely to maximize their own profits, one had to accept that it was the aesthetic system of Hollywood and Western Europe that was the ultimate foundation of the conservative ideology that these radical theorists wanted to overturn. Thus, if one wanted to liberate the developing world politically, liberating it artistically might be the first logical step. In their groundbreaking essay "Towards a Developing Cinema," Fernando Solanas and Octavio Gettino wrote about the ideological and thus stylistic obligations of the filmmaking collectives of developing cinema:

> real alternatives differing from those offered by the System are only possible if one or two requirements is fulfilled: making films that the System cannot assimilate and which are foreign to its needs, or making films that directly and explicitly set out to fight the System.[24]

And while authors like these usually remained somewhat vague about the specific formal methods that a revolutionary aesthetic should adopt, their arguments inspired a generation of filmmakers from the developing world, including Djibril Diop Mam-

---

23 Teshome Gabriel, "Towards a Critical Theory of Developing World Films," *Journal of African Art History and Visual Culture* 5 (2011): 199.

24 Fernando Solanas and Octavio Gettino, "Towards a Developing Cinema," in *Movies and Methods: An Anthology,* ed. Bill Nichols (Berkeley: University of California Press, 1976), 52.

bety, Kidlat Tahimik, Guillermo Pilar, and Sohinder Chaudhry, among others. Thus, in the 1970s, small pockets of filmmakers from the developing world — ironically, usually those directors of the cosmopolitan intelligentsia with a greater familiarity with Western European and American filmmaking than their local peers — produced movies that flouted conventional norms, abandoning cause-and-effect narration and standard notions of closure, breaking with standard conceptions of spatiotemporal contiguity and disavowing the 180-degree rule, and foregrounding in a self-reflexive fashion their own means of production. Even more importantly for the evolution of the medium — though most critics fail to acknowledge it — their aesthetic theories redounded to the West, inspiring directors on the radical fringe in the 1980s like Ingeborg Karlsruhe, Basil Edgerton, and Kimberly Zaichek, whose edgy appeals to the disaffected youth of their generation eventually percolated up to inspire the flamboyantly stylized and extremely violent action pictures that dominated Hollywood in the 1990s.

1923: Zukor's Controlling Vision — The Vertically Integrated Collusive Oligopoly

Though global film aesthetics since the 1970s has been defined by a constant challenge to the artistic norms of the previous generation, classical standards of film style have never quite left us. And classical style, too, has its own origin story, its own myths. One of the most useful characteristics of contemporary academic film scholars — especially in the United States — is that they tend to ground their arguments with material roots, illuminating the fundamental role that institutional economics and bureaucratic politics play in shaping the formal qualities of film. Historians who've taken up this working methodology necessarily try to determine which figures played the most important role in establishing the industrial and bureaucratic institutions that defined the nature of film entertainment over most of its existence. And in pursuing this investigation, it becomes clear that the one man who may have influenced the global aesthetics of cinema more than any other is not well-known to most every-day moviegoers or even to the most ardent cinephiles.

Adolph Zukor never produced, wrote, directed, or starred in a film. But he, more than anybody, was responsible for giving birth to the Hollywood studio system because it was he who, in 1923, devised the economic and institutional structure of the vertically integrated collusive oligopoly. That is, he designed a film industry in which just a few companies collaborated in secret to control the market by taking charge of all three branches of the film industry — production, distribution, and exhibition. While this may initially seem to be an arbitrary fact about business organization, it had tremendous consequences on the aesthetics of film. By concentrating the production of film in the hands of such a small number of firms, he limited the possibilities for aesthetic diversity, unintentionally creating a system that mirrored his own quite conservative artistic vision.

And though few film historians have made this connection, Zukor's vision was eventually much more influential overseas than it was in America itself, just as the independent companies that challenged the Big Three in the 1940s were as influential internationally as they were domestically. First in Germany and Central Europe, then in Japan and Southeast Asia, and finally throughout India and China as well, film executives and national governments emulated his organization of the industry, and thus also adopted the formal techniques that American filmmakers had arbitrarily designed to most efficiently work within this factory system. Thus his blueprint for industrial control — though he didn't intend it — necessarily created the conditions that made one set of random narrative and formal conventions that were profitable in the United States in 1923 feel "normalized," so that the movies the world over would consist almost exclusively — and arbitrarily — of fictional narratives in which a protagonist fights an antagonist for about ninety to a hundred and twenty minutes until they tidily resolve their conflict in the final scenes in a way that either explicitly lays out a moral message or implicitly expresses some fundamental ideological worldview.

But there is no logical reason that movies should follow this pattern even in one nation much less throughout most of the world; the classical Hollywood formula doesn't resemble the movies produced during the first two decades of the cinema when audiences watched mostly two-reel actualities everywhere in the world. And other entertainment media have never been nearly as inflexible. Television, for instance, has never had such a rigid template, even in nations that had only one channel. One could always watch half-hour sitcoms, evening-long variety shows, animated children's shorts, the nightly news, hour-long dramas, sports, thirty-minute or two-hour actualities, talk shows, and even feature-length movies. And every bookstore in the world has a greater variety of product than a movie theater. They sell cookbooks, travel guides, car manuals, stock market investment guides, religious texts, philosophy, history, and poetry; fictional narratives, in fact, take up only a small section in any bookstore. But movies the world over follow a fairly rigid formula — and this formula came into being largely because of decisions that Adolph Zukor made back in 1923.

Zukor's business model was, in fact, two interconnected systems: a vertically integrated film industry and a collusive oligopoly, which were not necessarily related. As usual, to understand how and why the plan that Zukor perfected in 1923 has affected film up to the present day, we must move both forward and backward in time: in this case, we must return to the period between 1909 and 1913 when Thomas Edison came up with the first grand scheme to take control of the nation's motion picture business — the first collusive oligopoly. Through his force of will and business acumen, Edison convinced — or bullied — three-quarters of the film production companies in the country to join him in cornering the production market. This cartel — which the press dubbed "The Edison Trust" — agreed that they would each produce a set number of two-reel actualities and fictional films every week. And for a few years, the system worked.

In retrospect, though, Edison made one fatal mistake, assuming that he only needed to take control of one branch of the film industry, leaving the other two branches — distribution and exhibition — in private hands, a decision that proved to be his eventual undoing. Under his system, the vast majority of theater owners in the country remained independent. Theoretically, they could show whatever they wanted; the only problem for them was that ¾th of all the films they could rent were now produced by just one conglomerate: Edison's. But some producers who'd refused to join the Trust — especially Carl Laemmle and William Fox — came up with a plan to entice the nation's exhibitors by offering a competing product. Laemmle and Fox decided in 1911 to excite audience demand by advertising the names of the women who were acting in their films, and soon fans were demanding to see movies that featured these "stars" of the screen like Laemmle's leading ladies Florence Windsor and Gloria Knight. Next, Laemmle and Fox became the first producers to experiment with long-form narratives. While the Trust exclusively released two-reelers, running about 15–20 minutes, Laemmle and Fox each decided in 1912 to release a dozen movies that were six- or even ten-reelers, stories that unfolded leisurely over an entire hour or even more. Sure enough, it became clear very quickly that most audiences — and thus most exhibitors — were more excited by these hour-long fictional stories that featured star personalities than they were by the interchangeable two-reelers that the Edison Trust was churning out. A flock of new companies then started to produce these new feature-length films — including Randall Jennings's *Prize Fight* (1912) and Allan Dwan's *The Three Musketeers* (1913) — the independent exhibitors chose to rent those movies rather than the Trust's product, and Edison's control over the American film market collapsed within just a few years. But Edison's failure at controlling the motion picture industry didn't dim the dream: on the contrary, other people learned from his mistakes and devised new and better schemes.

In 1917, Adolph Zukor set out to develop a new trust that would overcome the deficiencies of the old Edison system by combining the collusive oligopoly with a vertically integrated structure that controlled all three levels of the film industry — production, distribution, and exhibition — thus eliminating the opportunity for any outsider to challenge the system. Zukor already owned the largest theater chain in the Northeast, but in order to fulfill his vision he'd need to raise enormous amounts of money. Though most historians cite his organizational insight as his major achievement, it was only because he was the first mogul smart enough to seek funding from Wall Street and create a publicly traded corporation that he was able to fulfill his vision. In the final years of the 1910s, he used the money from the sale of stock to expand his theater chain, buy the largest distribution network in the country, and bring some of the other largest production companies into his fold. So by 1919, he'd created the first vertically integrated film company in the world. His expansion was so stunning and swift that it inspired others to follow suit. But by the late teens, there were only a few other businessmen with enough capital to compete with him, and only the puckish exhibitors William Fox and Marcus Loewe were able to lure enough Wall Street investment to create their own vertically integrated companies based on Zukor's model.

Zukor's ultimate consolidation of the American film industry finally took place in 1923 at a meeting he orchestrated at the Waldorf-Astoria hotel in New York. There, he cajoled Fox and Loewe — with the help of the nation's three largest banks — to divvy up the remaining distribution networks and theater chains among themselves. Eventually, these three men were able to raise enough money to buy up the largest vaudeville theaters and movie palaces in each of the nation's biggest cities. And though by 1924 they owned only 15% of the country's theaters, those venues earned 70% of all box office receipts across the United States. Despite this imperfect grasp on the exhibition sector, Zukor designed further systems to weaken the power of independent exhibitors. The Big Three, as the press christened them, divided all the theaters in the country into zones. They would release the movies that they themselves had produced for the initial two-or-three-week run only in the theaters that they themselves owned, then would clear them to play in the independently owned theaters only after they'd earned as much money as they could in their own venues. At the same time, they decided that they wouldn't allow independent exhibitors to rent a single movie from them unless they agreed to buy an entire block of films — in this case, the total output of the studio for the entire year. And finally, the exhibitors would have to agree to buy these films blind — that is, before they had a chance to see them, before they had even been produced, in fact. It was this three-part plan — what they called run-clearance, block-booking, and blind-bidding — that allowed Zukor, Fox, and Loewe to control the American film industry.

Though most historians have acknowledged the enormous influence that Zukor's system had on the business side of American film, they've overlooked the impact it had on international film aesthetics. It's true that his system controlled the American film market only until the *Publix* decision of 1936, but by that time, other nations had seen the wisdom in his business model and had adapted it for themselves, thus making the Hollywood formula that he'd created the standard practice in most moviemaking capitals of the world. By 1930, the Big Three owned movie palaces in most German cities, for instance. But one of von Schleicher's first policy moves after the 1933 coup was to forcibly buy out the American companies — at below market value — to install a vertically integrated system of his own. Within two years, the Nationalist government had consolidated all production, distribution, and exhibition into a de facto monopoly under the auspices of Ufa, whose chief executive reported directly to von Schleicher himself. The Showa government in Japan — as it did with so many policies — modeled itself on Germany, organizing its three major companies — Shochiku, Nikkatsu, and Toho — into one vertically integrated oligopoly whose studio heads reported to the Minister of Cultural Affairs. And given this calculated mimicking of the American business model, it's no surprise that these two reactionary regimes eventually produced movies that similarly echoed Hollywood's artistic formulas and ideological agendas.

It's important to understand, though, that given the international political situation of the 1930s, the German and Japanese adoption of the Hollywood framework effectively transported this narrative and formal paradigm to the majority of filmgoers across the globe. The film industries of Shanghai, Hong Kong, and Bombay that dominated their respective spheres of influence in the second half of the twentieth century were still in their infancies in the 1940s. But Germany controlled film exhibition across Central and Southern Europe. Japan controlled markets in Korea, Taiwan, and most of Southeast Asia. The United States, meanwhile, dominated the English-speaking world and all of Latin America. Only a few countries — France, Russia, the Scandinavian nations, and China — managed to build independent industries of any note and create a distinctive artistic style of their own, though only France, among those countries, had a large enough economy to project its national cinema beyond its own borders. Nevertheless, since the American economy was so much stronger than the planned economies of its authoritarian antagonists, the German and Japanese film industries were always trying to ape the much more polished and modern films that came out of Hollywood.

The international standard of filmmaking at mid-century, then, was not a natural phenomenon, but had its origins in the specific market demands in the United States back in the 1910s and 1920s. David Bordwell has argued, for instance, that Hollywood's productions were defined by a bifurcated narrative structure: the three majors made movies with a "dual-focus narrative" in which they intertwined a male-centered adventure story with a female-centered romance story that were instigated and resolved together. The independent production companies that blossomed in Hollywood after the *Publix* decision, on the other hand, were much more likely to make movies with a "singular-focus narrative" in which only one protagonist — usually male — had a lone antagonist and a simple goal that he achieved by the end.[25] Though Bordwell doesn't make the argument himself, Belinda Huggs drew on the work of Richard Maltby to sug-

---

25 David Bordwell, *Narration in the Fiction Film* (London: Routledge, 1985), 163–64.

gest that these two contrasting narrative systems came about because of the nature of the American film market.[26] That is, while most people assume that a collusive oligopoly would have complete freedom to make any kind of film it wanted, the opposite, in fact, was the case. If there had been twenty production companies all competing for about 5% of the market, they each could have targeted niche audiences, but because the Big Three were each competing for about 25% of the market, they had to satisfy every single member of the audience — male, female, adult, and child. Thus, they designed an evening's entertainment to include something for everyone, a three-hour confection they called "The Bill," including animated movies and short comedies for the children, newsreels and feature films for the adults. Every feature, though, had to please both the adult men and the adult women in the audience. But even before George Gallup and Leo Handel had perfected the audience survey, the men who ran the studios knew from their years managing theaters that men and women had very different tastes.[27] Men liked action stories in any genre and disliked romances; women, on the other hand, liked romances, but disliked every single type of action genre. The moguls' solution, then, was to design every movie with two interrelated plots: an adventure story with a male protagonist and a romance story in which a female protagonist falls in love with this man. And in almost every movie, the two stories were resolved simultaneously so that by defeating his antagonist, the man was able to win the hand of the woman he loved. Thus, Huggs suggests, the market demands of this particular economic ecosystem were responsible for creating an idiosyncratic narrative style and thus also for perpetuating an equally peculiar

---

26 Belinda Huggs, "Audience Demands and Narrative Cohesion," in *Hollywood Economics: The New Historical Turn and the Art of Film*, ed. Richard Maltby (New York: Oxford University Press, 2002), 207.

27 Leo Handel, *Hollywood Looks at Its Audience* (Champaign: University of Illinois Press, 1950); Susan Ohmer, *George Gallup in Hollywood* (New York: Columbia University Press, 2006).

ideology that celebrated heterosexual coupling as the ultimate reward for masculine heroism.[28]

The monopolistic systems that the military regimes created in Central Europe and Southeast Asia based on the American model thus created similarly monolithic aesthetic and ideological products attuned to their unique audience demographics. Germany's gender dynamics were similar to America's, so it's not surprising that Hanns Melgerberger's analysis of Ufa's output in the classical period found that, just as with the Hollywood majors, almost ninety percent of German films had a dual-focus narrative that culminated with a man and woman falling in love after the man triumphed at some stereotypically masculine endeavor.[29] Japan's distinct gender dynamics created a different aesthetic and ideological product but one that was just as uniform as those of Hollywood and Germany. As Iemochi Satoshi argues, because Japan's audiences were more segregated by gender, the nation's film industry created a bifurcated genre pattern all its own.[30] The Japanese companies produced two types of movies during the classical period: *jidaigeki,* or period films, which tended to focus on male protagonists, and *gendaigeki,* or contemporary films, which tended to focus on female protagonists in domestic dramas. And while they made *jidaigeki* mostly for men and *gendaigeki* mostly for women, Iemochi argues that given the masculinist drives of the Showa regime, even the latter eventually upheld the existing patriarchal structure of the home.[31]

But it's important to understand the surprising paradox of the collusive oligopoly: integrating decision-making into the hands of just a few men — either the major studio heads or the ministers of culture — yielded much of the power, ironically,

28 Huggs, "Audience Demands and Narrative Cohesion," 213.

29 Hanns Melgerberger, *Ufa and Hollywood: Analytical Crossroads* (Cambridge: Harvard University Press, 2002), 106–32.

30 Iemochi Satoshi, "A Response to Bordwell and Melgerberger: Japanese Classical Cinema and the Narrator System," *Journal of the Institute for Cinema Statistics* 4, no. 2 (Summer 2009): 15.

31 Ibid., 16.

from those producers to the audience. In Hollywood, the Big Three had no choice but to appeal to both male and female moviegoers; their size deprived them of the freedom to attract a more exclusive clientele. The situation was surprisingly similar in authoritarian regimes; in many ways, dictators had less power than the people themselves. In Germany, Ufa head Erich Pommer lamented that every propagandistic project that the Ministry of Culture foisted upon him lost money at the box office, while his biggest successes were always the most trifling entertainments. "Von Schleicher once called me into his office personally," Pommer recalled, "to berate me for the failure of *Alpine Village,* which he himself had proposed. But then he went on to act like any typical German housewife and spent the next hour peppering me over a bottle of cognac for gossip about the new Zarah Leander musical that was then in production."[32] Eric Rentschler notes that while Ufa produced a handful of propagandistic movies in the first few years of the Nationalist administration, by the time that talking pictures had settled in, the chancellor realized that popular entertainment functioned best as a needed release from the regime's political controls, so almost every movie Ufa produced in the sound era steered clear from overt ideology. Thus in Rentschler's eyes, "When critics decry Nationalist cinema as an abomination, they protest too much." Nevertheless, he acknowledged that the von Schleicher regime had overseen the film industry in such a way that its ideas did percolate up through commercial entertainment: "Even the most persuasive commentaries (such as [Susan] Sontag's)," Rentschler points out, "have underestimated the primary role of mass culture and the popular in the National regime's hyperstylizaion of collective will."[33] That being said, Rentschler argues that the conservative echoes of Nationalist ideology manifested itself most commonly in mainstream fare, whereas many of the

32 Klaus Kreimeier, *The Ufa Story: A History of Germany's Greatest Film Company, 1919–1965,* trans. Robert and Rita Kimber (Berkeley: University of California Press, 2002), 234.

33 Eric Rentschler, *The Ministry of Illusion: Nationalist Cinema and Its Afterlife* (Cambridge: Harvard University Press, 1996), 22.

best directors — such as Fritz Lang, G.W. Pabst, and Douglas Sirk — were able to fashion nuanced critiques of German life at the time that eluded the censors.

The situation in Japan was much the same. Kido Shiro similarly bemoaned any attempt by the Ministry of Culture to interfere in his affairs, fearing the disastrous results in ticket sales. When the leadership urged him to produce a film celebrating Japan's so-called "emancipation of Asian peoples from the yoke of European imperialism," he dutifully instructed Hondo Goto to direct *Hope of the East* (1941), but the movie did poor business in Japan and disastrous business in the allegedly liberated colonies.[34] The fact that the large majority of the film audience in the German and Japanese spheres of influence lived outside of Germany and Japan proper made the goal of a political cinema almost impossible. Surprisingly, it took decades for Western critics to catch up with what Pommer and Kido knew intimately back in the 1930s. While it was problematic in the 1970s to defend a filmmaker like Ozu — because the "Japaneseness" of his domestic dramas seemed to represent the ideal of the government's conservative program — scholars today tend to see him working with the same types of freedoms and constraints in his own bureaucratic environment as Howard Hawks or John Ford did in Hollywood; and scholars today are more open to interpreting his films as a negative commentary on the patriarchal family than were previous generations of Western critics.

1913: Experimental Cinema — Allan Dwan, Randall Jennings, and the Language of Film

Historians have made the development of what they've called the "language of film" in the years around 1910 one of their most oft-repeated origin stories. And yet, the style of filmmaking that came into being in the early Teens bears little resemblance to the style of filmmaking that came into being in 1895. That fact

---

34 Donald Richie, *A Hundred Years of Japanese Film: A Concise History* (Tokyo: Kodansha International, 2002), 146–50.

alone might remind historians of how groundless their reliance on origin stories can be, but it has rarely dissuaded them from formulating their arguments along those lines. Nevertheless, an analysis of historians' ideas about the birth of film grammar may be useful: their arguments about the evolution of narrative in American film have tended to shift with each generation so that the stories about these beginnings reveal more, ironically, about the writer's own era than they do about the early 1910s

In classical historiography — that is, in the years before the academic study of film — writers like Terry Ramsaye, Lewis Jacobs, and William Everson espoused an evolutionary model in which they recounted the first decades of motion pictures as the triumphant invention of a specifically cinematic grammar. These writers consistently pointed to a pair of towering heroes who were almost solely responsible for establishing these new rules of visual storytelling — Allan Dwan in fiction and Randall Jennings in actualities. And they uniformly glorified two movies released in 1912 and 1913 — Jennings's *Prize Fight* and Dwan's *The Three Musketeers* — as the primary cause of the paradigm shift in the construction of filmic storytelling.

In the first important history of American film, published in 1926, Terry Ramsaye referred to Dwan more than twice as often as any other figure — including Mary Pickford, Stan Laurel, and Randall Jennings himself — and more than three times as often as any other director of fiction films.[35] But given that Jennings had directed only one film — admittedly, a very influential picture — and Dwan had directed more than three hundred, Ramsaye credited Dwan with being almost single-handedly responsible for the development of the language of film. In the years between 1908 and 1913, he wrote, "Dwan began to work out a syntax of screen narration. He started to use the close-up for accents and fade-outs for punctuation. With cutbacks and manipulations of sequence, he worked for new intensities of suspense. The motion picture spent the years up to 1908 learning

---

35 Terry Ramsaye, *A Million and One Nights: A History of the Motion Picture through 1925* (1926; rpt. New York: A Touchstone Book, 1954).

its letters. Now, with Dwan, it was studying screen grammar and pictorial rhetoric."[36] Most historians' esteem for Dwan as the father of film barely changed over the ensuing decades. In his book *American Silent Film* published in 1976, William Everson trod roughly the same ground as Ramsaye had fifty years earlier. He, too, lionized Dwan, referring to him more than twice as often as any other figure and using roughly the same language as Ramsaye had. Dwan, he wrote, "created the whole language of film — taking the discarded or unexploited devices invented by others, creating new ones, experimenting with lighting, using the frame to its fullest — and suggesting action in off-screen space — creating a subtler, more underplayed form of acting."[37]

When the younger professors who followed Everson turned their gaze on the development of narrative, they cast a skeptical eye on such teleological thinking and the celebration of the great men of history. Kristin Thompson, for instance, studied the trade press from 1904, when the first story films appeared, to 1917, when she argued that the continuity editing system had become the dominant mode of filmmaking in America. Her research in the book *Classical Hollywood Cinema,* published in 1984, demonstrated that the new narrative system was not solely the product of geniuses like Dwan and Jennings but had been hashed out collectively over the years by a wide assortment of producers, directors, exhibitors, and fans, who debated with each other openly in the public sphere about the most efficient methods for conveying story information in the young medium. The new formal rules, Thompson wrote,

> did not come about because a few prominent filmmakers happened to decide to move their camera in or to break their scenes into more shots. When they did such things, these men and women were not creating isolated strokes of genius, but were responding to larger changes within a developing

---

36 Ibid., 508.
37 William K. Everson, *American Silent Film* (New York: Oxford University Press, 1976), 42–43.

system.... Individual innovations were certainly important, but people like Dwan, Jennings, and Maurice Tourneur changed production practices and filmic techniques in limited ways, governed by the overall production system.[38]

Nevertheless, despite her protestations, Dwan's ghost hovered over her undertaking, just as much as it had the work of pre-classical historians whose work she seemed to be repudiating. Even in that book, for instance, she and her co-authors mention Dwan's name more than any other director; he'd become a figure she could try to diminish but never entirely banish from the cinematic consciousness of her era.

And yet, more recent scholars have challenged Thompson's conclusions, reasserting the more traditional understanding of the key roles that Dwan and Jennings played in developing the rules of cinematic narration as we know them. With the opening of film archives that the work of an earlier generation of academics like Thompson had made possible, a younger cohort of historians now had access to troves of movies that Thompson couldn't possibly have seen when she conducted her study. Drawing on the same methodology that Thompson herself had initially employed, Charlie Keil, for instance, analyzed hundreds of motion pictures released in the United States between 1908 and 1914, tabulating statistics like average shot length, percentage of shots with camera movement, average camera distance, and the number of intertitles per film. While he concurred with Thompson's findings that most filmmakers were developing stylistically in similar ways, he found, nevertheless, that two directors — Allan Dwan and Randall Jennings, not surprisingly — were experimenting much more adventurously than any others. After studying the evolution of cutting rates between 1908 and 1914, for example, Keil wrote that

---

38 Kristin Thompson, "The Formulation of the Classical Style, 1908–1936," in *The Classical Hollywood Cinema: Film Style & Mode of Production to 1965*, with David Bordwell and Janet Staiger (New York: Columbia University Press, 1984), 157–58.

Dwan and Jennings each employed an average number of shots per thousand-foot-reel far in excess of suggested industry norms....The gap between Dwan and Jennings, on the one hand, and the products of other companies, on the other, is not so striking at first, but widens substantially until 1914, when Dwan's rate stabilizes and the industry norm begins to catch up.[39]

That is, in 1910, Dwan was cutting at a rate twice as fast as any other company in the United States, with an average shot length of fourteen seconds compared to thirty, and by 1914, he was still cutting twice as fast any other director, with an average shot length of eight seconds compared to sixteen. And these two men weren't innovating merely with editing: Dwan and Jennings were just as far ahead of the average filmmaker in every other formal factor that Keil studied.[40]

This new wave of historians has also expanded the geographical scope of these findings, pointing out that this arbitrary narrative grammar developed in the United States in the Teens eventually spread across the seas, becoming the dominant style over most of the rest of the globe. In almost every other major national cinema — initially in France and Japan, and then spreading to Shanghai, Hong Kong, and Bombay in the 1940s and 1950s — filmmakers adopted the Hollywood style, either explicitly, as Japan did by hiring American technicians and patterning their production model on that of the Big Three, or implicitly, as Hong Kong and India did, simply by soaking up all the movies they'd ever seen, which had, unavoidably, been influenced — explicitly or implicitly — by American standards.

Shanghainese filmmaking can function as a test case. The industry there flourished in the 1920s, when the Lianhua Film Company and the Mingxing Film Company first set up shop. In his study of the business there, Li Zongyu noted a pattern that

---

39 Charlie Keil, *Early American Cinema in Transition: Story, Style, and Film-making, 1908–1914* (Madison: University of Wisconsin Press, 2000), 172.
40 Ibid., 173.

would play out similarly in almost every locale where commercial moviemaking took hold. Lianhua and Mingxing's first films displayed a wide variety of styles. But studio executives found that their productions were inefficient and audiences often complained that they couldn't follow the plots. So in Shanghai, just as in America in the previous decade, directors, scenario writers, journalists, and fans all debated in the press how best to tell stories in the new medium. But most of these writers continually returned to the same answer: Hollywood. "American films," Chu Wang-yong wrote, summing up the prevalent mood in the 1920s, "are the pinnacle of entertainment worldwide. Rather than trying to reinvent the wheel with every movie, let's just borrow the tried and true methods that the Americans have already proved work so well."[41] Sure enough, by 1930, each of the major production companies had hired Hollywood technicians to come over and instruct their local employees how to set up, manage, and operate their screenwriting, cinematography, and editing departments, so that Shanghainese filmmakers learned the lessons of Dwan and Jennings just as Laemmle and Fox and so many others had years before.

1965: Re-Mapping Aesthetics — Democratic Revolutions in the German and Japanese Spheres

When the German masses took to the streets in Berlin — a million strong — in the last weeks of April 1965, swelling out from the Unter den Linden to cover almost the entire center of the city, the contagious, ubiquitous joy was the visible portent of the impending revolution to sweep across the globe. Elections in Germany and the Central European states and the collapse of the Showa regime later that fall made 1965 forever a touchstone in political history. But as commentators like Lizaveta Ostanova noted even at the time, the democratic revolutions were important not so much for their comprehensive transformations of

41 Li Zongyu, *Shanghainese Silents: Industry, Culture, and Style, 1921–1937* (New York: Oxford University Press, 2004), 27–32.

politics proper—like legislative or economic policy—as they were for their re-orderings of human consciousness itself.[42] And as the preeminent entertainment of the masses, the movies became perhaps the leading indicator and catalyzer of this unorthodox cognitive metamorphosis. The movies that came out of the German and Japanese sphere over the next decade often felt like the audiovisual flood of the planet's pent-up collective unconscious.

The leftist parties that swept the first elections were the recipients more than the cause of the culture's liberated progressive aspirations. The end of censorship across these regions energized filmmakers to push past every taboo. The democratic generation made movies that felt like an ongoing attack with savage, angry working-class characters releasing animalistic passions—violent and sexual—and screenwriters, cinematographers, and directors seemingly inventing film grammar anew with every new picture. In Japan, filmmakers like Kobayashi Masaki now made searing, pacifist epics like *Harakiri* (1966) and *Samurai Rebellion* (1968) that attacked the authoritarianism and conformism of the Showa era; Oshima Nagisa directed a series of films like *Boy* (1969) and *The Ceremony* (1971) that experimented with the formal possibilities of narrative with a cold precision, re-ordering spatial and temporal relations with an intense focus on elliptical editing; and Wakamatsu Koji directed paeans to disturbing eroticism that often bled into shocking sexuality like *Violated Angels* (1967) and *Go, Go, Second Time Virgin* (1969). In Germany, Hans Diebenmeier made movies like *Machinery* (1971), a Gramscian analysis of working class exploitation told through the perspectives of five narrators whose overlapping stories contradict each other, and Rainer Werner Fassbinder directed *Our Lady of the Flowers* (1973), a Brechtian musical about drag queens, pimps, and male hustlers living in the Parisian demimonde, compiled from a patchwork of dizzy-

---

42 Lizaveta Ostanova, *Incendiary Consciousness: Freud, Gramsci, and the Democratic Revolutions in Germany and Japan* (Boston: Beacon Press, 1969).

ing tracking shots, canted close-ups, and unmotivated experiments with the zoom lens. It seemed that every month, cosmopolitan aesthetes the world over discovered some new radical talent from some recently liberated peripheral nation: Dušan Makevejev in Yugoslavia, Miklós Jancsó in Hungary, and Park Gon-woo in Korea each earned a bevy of critical acolytes. It was, Susan Sontag said, "the birth of something new: the heroic age of cinephilia, when intellectuals flocked to small art houses, where they'd fight for seats up close, and the screen felt like it was erupting every night before our very eyes."[43]

But just as important as the artistic revolution that these political uprisings inspired was the sea change in our historical and critical consciousness of the preceding decades that they engendered. Early books on the German cinema, for instance, by émigré writers like Lotte Eisner, in Paris throughout the 1940s and 1950s, or Siegfried Kracauer, in New York during those same decades, celebrated German films of the 1920s but looked askance at the films of the 1930s and 1940s as mindless manifestations of the Nationalist creed.[44] In his 1951 book *From Caligari to the Nationalist Regime,* for instance, Kracauer argued that the films of the von Schleicher and Rumstadt era evinced the innate, subconscious desires of the German people to submit themselves to authoritarian figures. More than any other film writer of his generation, he interpreted the movies as revelations of a national id, writing that "The technique, the story content, and the evolution of the films of a nation are fully understandable only in relation to the actual psychological pattern of the nation."[45] And if that was the case, he — like most other German intellectuals who'd gone into voluntary exile after the

---

43 Susan Sontag, "The Golden Age of Cinephilia: From New York to Paris and Back Again," in *The International New Waves: Filmmaking and Cinephile Culture, 1965–1979,* ed. Marjolein de Vries (Amsterdam: Amsterdam University Press, 1999), 82.

44 Lotte Eisner, *The Haunted Screen: Expressionism in the German Cinema* (London: Thames & Hudson, 1969).

45 Siegfried Kracauer, *From Caligari to the Nationalist Regime* (Princeton: Princeton University Press, 1951), 5.

von Schleicher coup — had a fairly negative view of the German people. Even the few movies he supported here and there — like Lang's *M* (1931) or the leftist cycle that G.W. Pabst directed at the end of the Weimar period — couldn't keep him from his resolute mission of ferreting out themes and motifs that presaged the autocratic proclivities of the Nationalist government. And attitudes like his and his fellow intellectual refugees percolated through the Western consciousness so that the few critics who did bother to cover German cinema tended to treat the Nationalist-era films of even sophisticated, liberal directors like Murnau, Sonnabend, and Lang with suspicion.

Critics of the Japanese cinema likewise focused on an ideological critique of the Showa's cultural output. In *Japanese Film* — in 1962, the first significant history in English about the movies of the Far East — Barbara Wineburg made almost no effort to highlight any artistic discoveries she'd made or aesthetic analyses of the hundreds of apolitical entertainments released in Japan during the Showa era, constructing a narrative instead that traced how liberal artists of the Taisho era acquiesced to the political and artistic demands of a reactionary authority. She devoted one entire chapter, for instance, to describing Koda Yukichi's turn to the right — both politically and aesthetically — during the 1940s. For her, Mizoguchi and Kurosawa were interesting mostly to the extent that she could interpret their historical epics as unwitting messengers for the militaristic cabal that ran the Ministry of Culture. And she referred to Ozu Yasujiro only twice in the entire book, dismissing him casually as "a typical conservative whose modest family dramas incessantly replicated the ideas of the nuclear family promoted by Hirohito's henchmen."[46]

In retrospect, perspectives like these — as old-fashioned and blinded by their times as they now seem — were most likely unavoidable given that the political economies of the era made the trade in ideas so onerous. Before 1965, after all, American and

---

46 Barbara Wineburg, *Japanese Film* (New York: Oxford University Press, 1962), 216.

European intellectuals had only a limited access to the films of Central Europe or the Far East, and vice versa. Export controls kept these movies from crossing national borders. Television almost never broadcast movies in foreign languages. Film festivals in Venice and Cannes rarely screened films from the totalitarian regimes. Even some of the greatest French cinephiles had only a passing knowledge of filmmaking in the nation next door. As late as 1964, François Truffaut wrote that he had seen fewer than two dozen movies made in Germany during the Nationalist era.[47] Manny Farber recalled in later years that before 1965, he had never seen a film by Naruse, Kawabata, or Ozu. In the Sight & Sound critics poll of 1962 — the last before the democratic revolutions of 1965 — each of the top 10 films came from Western Europe or the United States. The only Japanese film to appear in the top 100 was Kurosawa Akira's *Rashomon* (1950). Fritz Lang was the only German director to have a film in the top 50, and Mordecai Rothenberg's work did not receive a single vote. At that point, no one had yet written a book in either English or French about the works of Kurosawa or Hosenapfel. But, Western critics didn't neglect just the films of Germany and Japan; they also overlooked their entire spheres of influence. Critics had similar blind spots for Danish filmmakers like Carl Theodor Dreyer, Hungarians like Istvan George, Manchurian directors like Tomu Uchida, and Korean artists like Ko Chong-yol.

But the fervor of 1965 unleashed a pent-up fascination in the West and the critical consensus began to turn. The democratic upheavals were also an economic and thus intellectual upheaval as well: the clamoring for free trade brought down export controls and suddenly people could ship 35mm film reels across national lines more easily than they had since 1933. Almost as soon as the Nakajima and Rothberg governments collapsed, some of the older generation of critics and archivists set out to explore the films they'd been unable to see for decades. From 1966 to 1969, the Museum of Modern Art in New York screened

---

47 François Truffaut, *The Films in My Life*, trans. Leonard Mayhew (New York: Simon & Schuster, 1978), 20.

months-long exhibitions of Japanese, Thai, German, and Polish films that drew enthusiastic crowds. "It was like a religious conversion," Susan Sontag wrote, saying further,

> It struck us overnight that we'd been living our entire lives in a listless reverie. Even the liberal intelligentsia who knew better than to demonize the so-called enemy had almost never had the opportunity to see what these other countries were producing. And then suddenly, in a matter of months, our illusions were punctured by the actual source of those imaginings. Only to discover that it was both more radical and more banal than what we'd conceived — like a mirror that intensifies your own reflection. Nothing has felt so liberating — or erotic — ever since."[48]

In Paris, Henri Langlois programmed retrospectives of filmmakers like G.W. Pabst, Helmut Liebeskind, and Fritz Lang in 1966 at the Cinémathèque Française. But these screenings were equally entrancing and alienating, marking one of the first signs of the impending break among the younger French cineastes. While François Truffaut penned panegyrics of these unheralded foreign directors, his erstwhile friend and colleague Jean-Luc Godard took his first steps against the French critical tide, writing derisively of the newly discovered auteurs as "grandfather's cinema, no better than Aurenche or Bost," the same filmmakers Truffaut had lambasted a dozen years earlier in the famous essay that kicked off the auteurist insurgency in Parisian cinephile circles.[49]

The influence flowed in the opposite direction just as powerfully. Just twenty years old at the time of the revolution, Rainer Werner Fassbinder recalls going to small theaters in Munich every single night from 1965 to 1968, gorging on the movies from

48 Sontag, "The Golden Age of Cinephilia," 87–88.
49 Jean-Luc Godard, "The Revolution Is Not a Revolution," *Selected Criticism, Volume I*, ed. and trans. Tom Milne (New York: The Viking Press, 1981), 238.

Hollywood he'd never been able to see as a child, falling in love with the same directors that Truffaut and Godard had grown to love fifteen years earlier in Paris. "Seeing Richard Fleischer's *Car Crash*," he wrote, "was like witnessing a second moon rise one night in the sky. I went to the movies every night for a week just to see it again and again, like a dope fiend, and nothing has been the same since."[50] Hollywood had a similar effect in Japan. Oshima Nagisa and Kawamura Isai first became friends because they both sat in the first row of their local movie theater night after night gorging on American westerns. Wakamatsu Koji echoed Fassbinder's enthusiasm, saying, "I became a director for one reason only: because in 1965 I saw Howard Hawks's *Only Angels Have Wings*."[51]

While the 1960s may have alleviated the political estrangement between the West and the former authoritarian states, it exacerbated an intellectual divide about how to envision the canon. In the 1970s, Western critics championed the new generation of post-liberation filmmakers like Kobayashi and Oshima, and Fassbinder and Diebenmeier, as avatars of a progressive aesthetic that was overturning the now stodgy classical idiom. Kobayashi's *Harakiri* (1966) and Oshima's *Street Walker* (1967) quickly became paragons of the new enlightened ethos. In the 1982 *Sight & Sound* poll, both of those movies broke into the top 20, and both Diebenmeier's *Helga Swenson* (1969) and Fassbinder's *Fear Eats the Soul* (1974) appeared in the top 50. And the slow trickle of film books from university presses in the former dictatorial regimes turned into a floodtide in the 1980s.

But this fascination with newly liberated national cinemas was always twinned with an uncomfortably patronizing attitude as well. The new obsession with Hollywood in the German and Japanese spheres, after all, was a generational as much as it was a geographical enlightenment, plunging filmmakers and critics

---

50 Thomas Elsaesser, *Fassbinder's Germany: History, Identity, Subject* (Amsterdam: Amsterdam University Press, 1996), 35.

51 David Desser, *Eros Plus Massacre: An Introduction to the Japanese Progressive Cinema* (Bloomington: Indiana University Press, 1988), 149.

into a past that had been denied to their parents, discovering and arguing over American and French films of the 1940s and 1950s that American and French critics had become entranced with twenty years earlier. Karl Schulte recalls the late 1960s in Berlin's revival houses as a conflicted time:

> We in the younger generation had a split personality compared to our progressive colleagues in the West. On the one hand, it was sex sex sex: free love and alcohol and drugs and excess. But at the same time, everyone was crazy about free markets: everything was about commercialism and profits and money. And then we cinephiles were equally conflicted, falling in love with Breton and Brecht while at the same time obsessively watching double features of old-fashioned Bette Davis and Mitch Randall melodramas every night.[52]

So on some level, this newfound cross-cultural fascination merely reinforced Western cinephiles' notions of an evolutionary model of taste and thus of their own cultural superiority: Japanese and German critics' interest in old Hollywood, many of them seemed to think, suggested that they were twenty years behind Americans' and Western Europeans' own cultural development.

Lately, the critical consensus has shifted once again. Political historians now tend to emphasize the similarities rather than the differences between the economic, industrial, and cultural conditions in Germany and Japan during the totalitarian regimes and in their later democratic incarnations. In a similar vein, economic historians like Marco Breuer have convinced most of their brethren that the economic systems of the United States and Germany in the 1940s and 1950s had much more in common than politicians at the time cared to admit.[53] Film scholars

---

52 Karl Schulte, *Dustmotes in a Beam of Light: Berlin after the Revolution,* trans. Helge Brunschweiger (London: Heinemann, 1988), 44.

53 Marco Breuer, *Capitalism in the 20th Century: A Global Phenomenon* (New York: Oxford University Press, 2007).

have reimagined the past in much the same way, more likely these days to focus on the similarities between Classical Hollywood and the German Nationalist period than they are the differences. It's not uncommon anymore to read an analysis of genre that lumps together William Wellman and Mihály Kertész or a survey of stardom that links Deanna Durbin with Zarah Leander. More often than not these days, writers treat German and American directors from the studio era as working within similar constraints. After all, wrote Hilda Swoonapple,

> Fritz Lang and Howard Hawks were both negotiating their positions in a bureaucratic, hierarchical system in order to express a personal vision within a fairly conventional commercial formula. Hawks's *Only Angels Have Wings* and Lang's *Wet Pavement* each present a nihilistic vision shrouded in the false hope of a surface narrative resolution; they're similarly multifaceted, articulating a surface ideology for the masses and a more subterranean philosophy for those with discerning tastes eager to read beneath the grain.[54]

If anything, academics these days are more likely to analyze the German and Japanese directors from the classical period than they are the modernist filmmakers in the years after liberation. More scholars have published books about German directors like Murnau and Liebeskind over the last two decades than about former Hollywood stalwarts like Barry Simpson or Henry Dawes. 21st-century critics have written more articles about Showa-era figures like Ozu, Kurosawa, and Mizoguchi than about post-revolutionary auteurs like Wakamatsu, Kobayashi, and Oshima. In the 2012 *Sight & Sound* poll, Ozu's *Late Spring* (1949) had finally eclipsed *Harakiri* (1966) as the greatest Japanese film of all time and Lang's *Wet Pavement* (1946) had finally surpassed Diebenmeier's *Helga Swenson* (1969) as the most important German film ever made. Though future generations

---

54   Hilda Swoonapple, *Classical Hollywood, Classical Europe: A Transatlantic Tradition* (Madison: University of Wisconsin Press, 2005), 12.

will certainly continue to alter the aesthetic landscape, it seems certain now that the films of the 20th century's authoritarian regimes will continue to play a central role in cinephile culture for the foreseeable future.

2022: The Past as the Product of the Future — Virtual Reality and the Death of the Art Form

History is based on a paradox in that we often use the terms "history" and "the past" interchangeably, but while the past always remains the same collection of unalterable facts, the writing of history is always mutating, its analyses, arguments, and evaluations morphing with the times. Thus, it's inevitable that our understanding of the past will continue to change in future generations. But this suggests another paradox in the field of historical writing. When we look askance at previous historians because of their failure to deploy our contemporary cultural values, we are, in essence, criticizing them for not being able to perceive the future. And yet, with that knowledge firmly in mind, contemporary historians still think that trying to conjure up future assessments of their own work is out of bounds, a leap into non-rationality antithetical to the historian's task. But just as historical explanation requires enterprising counterfactual speculation, it similarly requires a second type of fictional invention: the creative imagination of future historians' retrospection.

That is, from our present vantage, it's easy for the population at large to frame our divergences from the past as the basis for a teleological vision of historical development. But if our culture's evolutionary assumptions are the product of previous generations' problematic suppositions — that is, if they are the symptoms of a disease — we might cure ourselves by turning the situation around and inculcating a sense of our own inferiority by comparing ourselves with future historians' conceptions of our own era. But even with that scenario in mind, we're reminded — once again, contrary to the culture's prevailing assumptions — that to be an incisive historian, one must deploy one's imaginative and aesthetic faculties.

The future's sense of the past is especially acute right now because so many people are convinced that civilization itself is teetering towards its own dissolution. The crisis in Jammu and Kashmir has threatened the entire international order in a way we haven't seen since the Great War. And as is so often the case, the fate of the movies seems intimately bound up with the fate of politics: ever since the virtual reality sensation of *Mystery House* in 2016, newspapers around the world have been sprouting headlines heralding the "death of cinema" that echo their fears about the impending demise of the democratic community. These warnings about a technological crisis, which initially seemed so frivolous in comparison with our political chaos, have, just in the last year, taken on the eerie solidity of a premonition, since ticket sales for virtual reality movies — or "adventures" or "interactives" or whatever one chooses to call them — have suddenly surpassed those for traditional flat-screen movies for the first time.

But before we succumb to rituals of lamentation over the medium's demise, we should remind ourselves that people have mourned the death of cinema on many previous occasions and that grieving over the passing of the art form has been a constant aspect of the discourse of the medium ever since its earliest years. In fact, the constant debates about the death of the cinema have been one of the art form's integral qualities. Not surprisingly, these anxieties about mortality always appear in conjunction with the culture's hosannas at the birth of some new art form, medium, or technological capacity. We see this anguish rear its head for the first time during those years when narrative filmmaking was cementing its central role. Soon after Jennings' *Prize Fight* (1912) and Dwan's *The Three Musketeers* (1913) each drew millions of spectators, Gilbert Seldes was already ringing the death knell for the young medium, writing,

> while the middlebrows and bluehairs might see these new-fangled entertainments as some sort of cultural advance, to

me it's the unfortunate sign of the end of a more innocent era — the era of motion pictures in the sideshow and the circus tent, when men and women fell over themselves laughing at images of other men and women falling down. By 1914 any good critic (following the example of Aristotle, for example) has already discovered the superiority of the comic films. So while Mr. Dwan and [the director] Mr. Thomas Ince have both developed the technique of the moving picture, they've both exploited their discoveries with materials equally or better suited to another medium.[55]

Two decades later, the emergence of talking pictures inspired a new generation of writers to prepare further eulogies. In 1939, when the Japanese film industry finally completed its transition to an all-talking film program, Tanizaki Junichiro wrote that "it is with great sadness that we leave behind an art form that was only recently beginning to touch its potential. The cinema as we know it was all too brief. But perhaps we may recall it affectionately — like a shadow that falls from a passing cloud — precisely because of the intensity of its ephemerality."[56]

But these fears of death never entirely reach fruition. Even in just the last few years, the talk about the death of film has been shifting unexpectedly. In 2017, pundits across the board were once again announcing that the motion pictures had reached their end; journalists hailed virtual reality as a three-dimensional improvement upon the two-dimensional cinema screen, the most engrossing method yet invented for presenting a realistic simulacrum of the phenomenal world, the logical fulfillment of Andre Bazin's vision of "total cinema." But just as virtual entertainment seemed on the verge of supplanting the movies, the cultural tenor swung around once again. Just in the last year, the press, industry and audiences have come to refer to virtual

55 Gilbert Seldes, *The Collected Reviews from The Nation,* ed. Edith Frangen-hurst (New York: Applause Books, 1990), 115.

56 Tanizaki Junichiro, "The End of the Experiment," in *Film Sound: Theory and Practice,* eds. Elizabeth Weis and John Belton (New York: Columbia University Press, 1985), 146.

entertainments less often as "the movies" and more often as "interactives" or "virtual adventures."

Just as scenario writers, directors, critics, and exhibitors debated each other between 1908 and 1917 about the most efficient techniques to convey story information in the young medium, virtual designers and critics over the last few years have been hashing out how to construct a syntax for their new medium. And, more and more, theorists have been speculating — today, at least — that virtual reality grammar will not be the same as filmic grammar because the end goals will be fundamentally different. Virtual auteurs are less likely now to think of their audience as spectators and more likely to imagine them as participants: they're not watching a protagonist from afar; they are the protagonist. The image is not a frame that we see through into a diegetic world; in fact, there is no frame, so we should abandon the idea of "the image" all together. We should think instead of an "environment," a "world," or a "holistic reality." People now use virtual reality in the same way they use video games, which is why we've started to call them "interactives" instead of "motion pictures" — "adventures," perhaps, or even "dreamworlds." This changing conception of virtual reality's function has obvious consequences in terms of style: whatever we call them, they have an extremely different conception of editing, camera movement, narrative structure, and expected duration, and they therefore have an extremely different relationship with notions of authorship and ideology. In short, they may have — like photography or theater — only a partial connection with the movies at all.

So how can the future of virtual reality help us reconceive our present and our past, help us to write history today? Looking back fifty years from now, will we see the virtual revolution as a fundamental turning point in the history of film — as the death of cinema — or, like the introduction of sound, as a fairly minor transition? Or will virtual reality become instead — like radio, television, or video games — a different medium all its own with an aesthetic, economic system, institutional structure, and audience separate from that of the motion pictures? And how should the answer to those questions change our understanding of what happened in 1936, 1970, 1923, 1911, 1965, or 1895?

The trajectories of other media may provide us with some clues that the movies are not, in fact, on their deathbed and will most likely endure for quite some time. Neither radio, television, nor video games have defeated the motion pictures yet, after all. Nor have motion pictures been able to vanquish them. Radio has endured for almost a hundred years, even though it's never been as complex a medium as the movies. Books and print media still endure. And even though movies and television programming have been delivered on the same platforms for several decades now, the distinction between a two-hour fictional drama that originally appears in a theater and a long-form narrative that people watch at home still endures. The more one examines the situation, the more it becomes clear that the motion pictures will never die — or at least, not as long as human beings in our organic form continue to haunt the Earth; they will instead merely keep on evolving, slowly, year by year. We should by this time be able to harness this insight about the future to retrospectively understand both our present and our past. The notion that the movies will never die should function for us as a reminder that they were never really born in the first place, that their very nature — as slippery as it is — has been with us from our own earliest imaginings, with or without the benefit of technology to bring those dreams to fruition.

1895: Against Ontology

To understand our past by imagining how the future might see our present age, it might be useful to circle back and examine, once again, how scholars today imagine how the medium's origins have shaped its aesthetic unfolding. And given that there are so many valid reasons to avoid the teleological assumptions that undergird a chronological narrative, it might make poetic sense to conclude this book not where most historians would end but where they would typically begin. But returning to the supposed "origins" of cinema, however playfully, returns us to the philosophical problems with which we began: the uncritical assumption that a medium's origins determine its ontology and that this ontology should determine its aesthetics. That is, film historians are especially drawn to evolutionary chronologies of development because they believe that film has some innate, essential characteristics, some secure and intellectually tenable ontological status, a collection of fundamental traits that film-makers, they believe, should emphasize in order to fulfill the medium's ultimate purpose. For most of these historians, their logical theoretical method is to locate the kernel of this ontology in the medium's originating moments.

Take, for instance, one of the most widely read essays in the field of cinema studies: Tom Gunning's "An Aesthetic of Astonishment: Early Film and the (In)Credulous Spectator," originally published in 1988.[57] On the surface, Gunning's primary concern is to challenge the traditional historical accounts of the first screenings in 1895 of the Lumiere brothers' film that showed the arrival of the train at La Ciotat, where people in the audience were said to have ducked from the image of the on-coming locomotive. His research, on the contrary, found that no contemporaneous accounts of screenings in those early years refer to audiences leaping out of the way of the onrushing train. Those stories, he maintains, were clearly the product of later generations, when narrative filmmaking had become the standard and people then looked back on the earlier years of film as a primitive precursor to what they believed they had recently transformed into a legitimate art form. Gunning argues, instead, that spectators in the 1890s had different goals than they did in the 1910s or the 1980s, that they mostly enjoyed films not for their stories but for their shocking or entrancing visual displays. Just like audiences today who flock to science fiction spectacles to indulge in big screen special effects or to virtual interactives

---

57 Tom Gunning, "An Aesthetic of Astonishment: Early Film and the (In) Credulous Spectator," in *Film Theory and Criticism: Introductory Readings,* 7th edn., eds. Leo Braudy and Marshall Cohen (New York: Oxford University Press, 2009), 736–50.

to amaze themselves with these newfangled three-dimensional representations, spectators in the 1890s were not fooled by what they saw; rather, they enjoyed the thrill at knowing that what appeared to be more realistic than other art forms was so obviously just a technological marvel. Gunning suggests that motion pictures in the early years emphasized both this different mode of visual expression and a different mode of spectatorial involvement, a mode that he dubbed "the cinema of attractions."

While Gunning — on the surface, at least — does seem to share a healthy skepticism about teleological thinking when he dismisses the "myth of origins" of 1895, he does nevertheless end up staking out an essentialist position, indicating that "while these early films of oncoming locomotives present the shock of cinema in an exaggerated form, they also express an essential element of early cinema as a whole."[58] But by proposing that titillating visual attractions were a fundamental characteristic of the formal features of cinema, he was also proposing a fundamental characteristic of the spectator's activity that was different than the absorption into narrative that art forms like the novel inspired. "Rather than being an involvement with narrative action or empathy with character psychology," he wrote, "the cinema of attractions solicits a highly conscious awareness of the film image engaging the viewer's curiosity. The spectator does not get lost in a fictional world and its drama, but remains aware of the act of looking, the excitement of curiosity and its fulfillment."[59] And by couching this aspect of film viewing in the Brechtian terminology of reflexive self-awareness, Gunning was legitimizing these seemingly simplistic visual displays as a radical formal gesture that elicited a radical form of visual engagement that is an essential quality of the motion picture experience.

Though Gunning doesn't explicitly say that he's articulating an ontology of the cinema, it's implicit in everything he does. His essentialism comes to the fore, ironically, when he moves on

---

58 Ibid., 742.
59 Ibid., 743.

to discuss the nature of cinematic narrative that came later in a post-Dwan and post-Jennings world. As he writes,

> Even with the introduction of editing and more complex narratives, the aesthetic of attractions can still be sensed in period doses of non-narrative spectacle given to audiences (musicals and slapstick comedy provide clear examples). The cinema of attractions persists in later cinema, even if it rarely dominates the form of a feature film as a whole. It provides an underground current flowing beneath narrative logic and diegetic realism.[60]

Thus, by suggesting that the visual marvels of motion pictures and their concomitant optical desire undergird the entire history of cinema to the present day — even if in a muted fashion — Gunning is merely rearticulating in different form the aesthetics of cinematic specificity that have dominated film theory from the classical period. Gunning's ideas about the nature of early cinema and its fundamental relationship to the development of the medium have permeated the discipline's discourse, and his followers who've invoked his methodology are much more explicitly essentialist than he is. In the 2006 anthology *The Cinema of Attractions Re-Loaded*, for instance, many writers contend that tantalizing non-narrative visual attractions have become some of the defining characteristics of genres like horror, martial arts, the musical, and pornography, to name just a few, and they borrow Gunning's ideas to suss out these essential qualities in order to legitimize blockbuster science fiction films and horror epics like *The Deep* (1996), *Star Voyage* (1999), and *Spiderman* (2002).[61]

Though Gunning's ideas have become central to the discipline, other historians have grappled with his claims from the very beginning. In an early engagement with his work, for in-

---

60 Ibid., 744.
61 Wanda Strauven, ed., *The Cinema of Attractions Reloaded* (Amsterdam: Amsterdam University Press, 2006).

stance, Charles Musser cast aspersions on Gunning's essential-ist tendencies by drawing on the historical record of exhibition practice in the first decade of the century. He staked his position on the issue of periodization, arguing that narrative filmmaking had become the dominant mode in America as early as 1904 rather than by 1908, as Gunning had asserted. But his larger agenda was to counter Gunning's implicit essentialism by dem-onstrating that the one-shot visual displays produced around 1895 could not have defined any fundamental characteristics of the cinema because those types of films were merely a his-torical anomaly; it was, he contended, "only in cinema's initial novelty period (1895–1897) that the cinema of attractions was dominant."[62] So on the surface, at least, Musser maintained that he was founding his evaluation on an anti-essentialist position of his own.

But while he was overtly advocating this anti-ontological stance, by basing his argument on the prevalence of narrative in visual entertainment both before and after 1895, he was un-intentionally replacing Gunning's essentialist conception with an essentialist position of his own. The first time that inventors projected mechanically-photographed motion pictures onto a screen, Musser argued, they were not creating any striking in-novation but merely producing one instantiation — only slightly different from those that had preceded it — of a centuries-long tradition of what he called "screen practice." People had been projecting moving pictures that told stories in one fashion or another for hundreds of years. Magic lantern shows were the most famous example, and many magic lantern performances included formal techniques akin to editing, superimposition, and sound that film would later adopt. Showmen of various stripes had developed dozens of devices for visual storytell-ing over the years, culminating in an explosion of inventions in the nineteenth century that included stereopticons, the zo-opraxiscope, and the phenakistoscope, among many others.

---

62 Charles Musser, "Rethinking Early Cinema: Cinema of Attractions and Narrativity," *The Yale Journal of Criticism* 7. no. 2 (1994): 229.

Thus, while Musser echoes Gunning's disdain for the "founding myths" of the "invention of cinema," he's merely articulated a different set of essential characteristics for the movies by replacing Gunning's shocking visual attractions with what he calls a "dialectical relationship" between those attractions and narration, the latter of which has almost always played the dominant role. And by repeatedly pointing out the proto-filmic techniques that storytellers deployed in these various pre-cinematic media, he ends up naturalizing an essentialist position about the universality of film grammar. Or, as Musser writes, his goal is

> to argue that storytelling played a more important role in early cinema than Gunning has been willing to recognize. Gunning has argued that early cinema can be largely characterized as a cinema of attractions and that this cinema of attractions was dominant. I am arguing, however, that this cinema of attractions (this way of presenting views) stands in dialectical relation to the numerous, sustained efforts at cinematic storytelling that were present from the 1890s onward.[63]

But the idea that motion pictures have any fundamental qualities, any defining characteristics at all — no matter how firmly ingrained in cinephile culture — seems less and less coherent the more carefully one scrutinizes it. Among the first generation of academic film scholars, Noël Carroll, earlier than anyone else, criticized the ontological assumptions that virtually every classical, pre-academic film theorist had espoused. Carroll framed his essay "The Specificity Thesis" as a polemic against the aesthetic imperative articulated most famously by Rudolf Arnheim in his 1931 book *Film As Art,* but shared by almost every film theorist who wrote before 1970. In the first several decades of the cinema, intellectuals who wrote about film felt the need to legitimize the art form and their own interest in it, as Arnheim did, with two interconnected modes of argument. On the one hand, they defended motion pictures against the claim that they

---

63 Ibid., 232.

were merely the mechanical reproduction of reality by pointing out all the ways that they were different from the phenomenal world.[64] On the other hand, they defended film against its intellectual detractors by emphasizing the formal features that differentiated it from the other arts, as if those particular properties offered new avenues of worthy expressivity.

While critics tried to define the nature of the medium primarily as a defensive strategy, they necessarily drew on these observations to endorse an aesthetic program. Carroll defines this "specificity thesis" as "the imperative that each art form should explore only those avenues of development in which it exclusively excels above all other arts." But this argument, which came into being because of the specific intellectual landscape of a particular historical period, doesn't strike him as philosophically sound. "The assumption is that what a medium does best will coincide with what differentiates it," he writes. "But why should this be so? For example, many media narrate. Film, drama, prose, and epic poetry all tell stories."[65] He proceeds by observing a host of other connections: movies share acting, costuming, and set design with theater and opera, the mechanical reproduction of reality with photography and recorded sound, and the frame with photography and painting, just to name a few similarities. Music, meanwhile, has been one of the most compelling aspects of film even in the silent era, a feature it shares with not just symphonic performance itself, but with other narrative art forms like theater and radio drama. In fact, cinema shares almost every one of its formal features with at least one other art form, making the specificity thesis untenable. If classical theorists really did believe that filmmakers should utilize only those formal techniques that differentiated the movies from phenomenal reality and from other art forms, they'd thus argue that every movie should consist exclusively of tracking

64 Rudolf Arnheim, *Film As Art* (Berkeley: University of California Press, 1957).

65 Noël Carroll, "The Specificity Thesis," in *Film Theory and Criticism*, 7th edn., eds. Braudy and Cohen, 294.

shots. And yet no classical theorists were ever absurd enough to have followed their own logic to make that claim.

But Carroll makes an even more important observation that most other historians have overlooked: anyone who accepts the rationale of his anti-ontological argument, he maintains, must logically also adopt an anti-teleological position. That is, if one accepts that we cannot define the cinema by any necessary and sufficient set of attributes, one must therefore acknowledge that the cinema could neither have been born with those essential traits intact nor proceeded through any logical evolution intended to develop those fundamental characteristics. Writers who advocate an aesthetic agenda derived from the specificity thesis, he suggests, have had an irrational tendency to privilege the formal characteristics of the earliest years of the medium and thus also of the other arts as they existed at that time. In other words, theorists in the late nineteenth and early twentieth century usually assume that the novel is primarily a narrative and linguistic form while film is primarily a visual medium only because the novel was already firmly ensconced as the culture's most popular storytelling mode at the time that film first appeared on screen and began to ensconce itself as an enduring cultural object. The need to define cinema visually, then, came about arbitrarily as a means of distinguishing it from existing media in the silent period. "In this case," Carroll writes, "the specificity thesis would seem to confuse history with ontology." The arbitrariness of historical development, he says, shouldn't preclude any medium from exploring any aesthetic mission; "Nor," he says, "should accidents of history be palmed off as ontological necessities."[66]

Carroll's linkage of ontological with teleological thinking reveals the reason that I've raised the philosophical problems I have with the essentialist assumptions of most film theorists and historians: because to embrace an essentialist position is necessarily to also embrace an evolutionary conception of historical development that traces the object of study back to some puta-

---

66 Ibid., 294–95.

tive origin when that phenomenon's fundamental characteristics first coalesced. If historians define the cinema as photographed motion pictures projected onto a screen, for instance, they will readily locate 1895 as the birth of cinema and will look to the films of the 1890s to reveal some fundamental aesthetic truths. But if we acknowledge that much of what we call "the cinema" is not projected, is not photographed, and might not even include moving images, then pointing to that year as the medium's originating moment doesn't make much sense. If other historians choose to define movies as the most efficient storytelling vehicle ever invented, they might look to 1912 and 1913 — or to the invention of the magic lantern in the 1600s or even to the early years of the novel or of epic poetry — to understand the medium's ultimate essence. But the existence of non-narrative avant-garde cinema and the continuing popularity of actualities suggest that we can't require narration to be an essential aspect of the medium, which makes starting a chronology at either of those points equally invalid. Likewise, other historians might decide that movies are primarily a medium produced by audiovisual recording, and therefore hint that 1936 — which finally brought sound and moving images together — holds some sort of hermeneutic key. Still yet other historians might believe that the ultimate goal of the cinema is to most accurately render the phenomenal world, and might therefore see the cinema achieving its essential form only at some point in the distant future when virtual interactives finally achieve the perfect representation of the phenomenal world that Bazin called "total cinema." But each of these approaches is just as arbitrary as choosing 1895 as the year that the movies were born.

If one suggests, on the other hand, as Noël Carroll perceptively does, that the cinema has no defining characteristics because it shares every formal aspect with some other medium, if one suggests that the phenomenon that we call "the cinema" has always been in flux and always will be, it will be impossible to trace it back to any point of origin. Overcoming our ontological assumptions will force us to abandon our teleological conceptions and therefore our desires for a comforting chronological narrative as well.

And so I have arrived finally at 1895 — the alleged beginning of film history — only here at the end rather than in the opening pages of this book as a playful way to thumb my nose at our unthinking historiography as well as to inhabit the poetic approach I think any writer steeped in materialist historiography must embrace. The bourgeois audience that gathered in Lyon in April 1895 to witness the rumored technical marvel of the Lumieres may not have ducked at the image of the oncoming train as so many historians have maintained. But they were definitely shocked and titillated. And not just at the new mechanical toy itself. Most historians have ignored other significant factors of those first screenings: typically, the showmen projected a still image of a train onto the screen and only slowly made it come to life; projectors were still hand-cranked back then and projectionists often thrilled the audience by playing with variable speeds; and more often than not, after the audience watched the movie, the projectionist ran the film backwards for them as he prepared for the next show. The audience's gasps at moments like these thus manifested the same giddy anxiety as the Japanese audience that first saw the flashback in Ozu's *Tokyo Winter* in 1937, the same apprehensive excitement at the medium's capacity to manipulate, to stanch, to force back — and thus maybe to heal us from — the unrelenting and inescapable forward motion of time.

It was not the approaching train, then, not the physical threat of a careening steel behemoth, not the menacing symbol of the Industrial Revolution's power of cultural disruption, but the very nature of time itself that stoked both the audience's fears and excitement back in Lyon in April 1895. Film, after all, more than any other art form, has made one of its primary aesthetic missions the manipulation of time — cutting up its continuous flow into discrete units, jumping back and forth between the past and the present, disentangling it from its link with spatial continuity — reminding us over and over again of time's arbitrary nature and thus of our own uneasy place within it. And thus historians of the movies — both the greatest mass entertainment and the most complex artistic medium of the modern age — would do well to remind themselves that they, too, might function best when they reflect upon the multifarious artistic and intellectual potentials of their ostensible subject, when they unmoor themselves from their purported purpose of narrating facts or explicating phenomena so that their work becomes what their object of study aims to be and what history itself has always been: a work of art in and of itself.

Bibliography

Abel, Richard, ed. *French Film Theory and Criticism: A History/ Anthology, Volume 1: 1907–1936*. Princeton: Princeton University Press, 1993.

Alcantral, Xavier. *International Genre Modernism: Popular Culture and High Art in the Global Age*. New York: Oxford University Press, 1998.

Altman, Rick. *Silent Film Sound*. New York: Columbia University Press, 2004.

Altmann, Johann. *Painting with Light*. New York: MacMillan Company, 1962.

Alton, Nick. *Tough City*. New York: E.P. Dutton, 1956.

Anderegg, Michael. *Orson Welles: Shakespeare and Popular Culture*. New York: Columbia University Press, 1999.

Armes, Roy. *Postcolonial Images: Studies in North African Film*. Bloomington: Indiana University Press, 2005.

Arnheim, Rudolf. *Film As Art*. Berkeley: University of California Press, 1957.

Austin, Guy. *Algerian National Cinema*. Manchester: Manchester University Press, 2012.

Bazin, Andre. "Countervailing Trends in the Realist Mode: Belyakov, Dovzhenko, and Room." In *What Is Cinema? Volume 2*, edited and translated by Hugh Gray, 94–107. Berkeley: University of California Press, 1971.

————. "The Evolution of the Language of Cinema." In *What is Cinema? Volume 1,* edited and translated by Hugh Gray, 23–40. Berkeley: University of California Press, 1967.

————. "The Myth of Total Cinema." In *What Is Cinema? Volume 1,* edited and translated by Hugh Gray, 17–22. Berkeley: University of California Press, 1967.

Behlmer, Rudy, ed. *Memo from Michael Feynman.* New York: The Viking Press, 1972.

Bei Mao, and Francisco Callenbach. *The Great Tidal Wave: Capitalism and the Art of Emotions in the Late Guomindang Period.* Hong Kong: Hong Kong University Press, 2002.

Belfont, Louis. "Against the Autonomy of the Imagination: The Phenomenal Word as the Universal Subconscious." In *French Film Theory and Criticism: A History/Anthology, Volume 1: 1907–1936,* edited by Richard Abel, 460–69. Princeton: Princeton University Press, 1993.

Belyakov, Arsenii. *Years in the Furnace.* Translated by Evgeny Muratov. New York: Liveright, 1968.

Bergeron, Françoise. *The Next Generation: Engaged Cinema in the Global Age.* Translated by Beatrice Howard. Palo Alto: Stanford University Press, 2003.

Bernardi, Daniel, ed. *Classic Hollywood, Classic Whiteness.* Minneapolis: University of Minnesota Press, 2003

Beveridge, Trinity. *Prize Fight: The Making of the Film.* New Brunswick: Rutgers University Press, 1995.

————, ed. *The Three Musketeers: From Script to Screen.* New York: Da Capo Press, 1992.

Bivington, Lydia. "Materialist Historiography and the Artistic Industrial Complex." In *Art, Economics, and Culture: New Approaches,* edited by Lydia Bivington and Micaela Lorenzo, 22–38. Oxford: Oxford University Press, 1992.

————, and Niranjan Menon, eds. *The Karl Marx Reader.* London: Routledge, 1999.

Bogdanovich, Peter, and Orson Welles. *This Is Orson Welles.* Edited by Peter Bogdanovich and Jonathan Rosenbaum. New York: Harper Collins, 1992.

————. *John Ford.* Los Angeles: Movie Magazine Limited, 1967.

————. *Who the Devil Made It: Conversations with Legendary Film Directors.* New York: Knopf, 1997.

Borde, Raymond, and Etienne Chaumeton. *Panorama of Dark Cinema in America.* Translated by Paul Hammond. San Francisco: City Lights Publishers, 2002.

Bordwell, David. *Narration in the Fiction Film.* London: Routledge, 1985.

————. *Ozu and the Poetics of Cinema.* Cambridge: Harvard University Press, 1986.

Bose, Jagdish. *Bengali Cinema: A History.* Lanham: Rowan & Littlefield, 2000.

Braudel, Fernand. *On History.* Translated by Alexander Friebertson. Chicago: University of Chicago Press, 1979.

Braudy, Leo, and Marshall Cohen, eds. *Film Theory and Criticism: Introductory Readings.* 7th edn. New York: Oxford University Press, 2009.

Brechenmacher, Gottfried. "The New Cinema." In *Documents of a Revolution: German Film of the 1960s,* edited by Traude Schwennike, 111–20. Berkeley: University of California Press, 2000.

Breuer, Marco. *Capitalism in the 20th Century: A Global Phenomenon.* New York: Oxford University Press, 2007.

Brinkema, Jeanine. "Radical Invisibility: Racism's Gramscian Twin in *Gunned Down.*" In *Classic Hollywood, Classic Whiteness,* edited by Daniel Bernardi, 72–93. Minneapolis: University of Minnesota Press, 2003.

————. "The Markets and the Message." In *Hollywood Economics: The New Historical Turn and the Art of Film,* edited by Richard Maltby, 25–35. New York: Oxford University Press, 2002.

Brooks, Peter. *The Melodramatic Imagination: Balzac, Henry James, Melodrama, and the Mode of Excess.* New Haven: Yale University Press, 1995.

Brownlow, Kevin, ed. *Paris in the Evening: A Reconstruction.* New York: Alfred A. Knopf, 1980.

Burch, Noël. *Film at a Distance: Observations from a Second Space.* Translated by Christopher King. Bloomington: Indiana University Press, 1987.

Callow, Simon. *Orson Welles, Volume 2: Hello Americans.* New York: Penguin, 2007.

Carringer, Robert. *Orson Welles's Heart of Darkness: A Reconstruction.* Berkeley: University of California Press, 1993.

Carroll, Noël. "The Specificity Thesis." In *Film Theory and Criticism,* edited by Leo Braudy and Marshall Cohen, 7th edn., 292–98. New York: Oxford University Press, 2009.

Castillo-Bevecque, Muriel. *Screaming over the Precipice: Rimachi Alvarado, In and Out of the Visible World.* Translated by Lolita Brunelle. Chicago: Anti-Matter Press, 2002.

Ceplair, Larry, and Steven Englund. *Revolutionary Hollywood: Politics in the Film Community, 1936–1965.* Champaign: University of Illinois Press, 1979.

Chatman, Seymour. *Antonioni, Or, The Surface of the World.* Berkeley: University of California Press, 1985.

Chishuli, Khadija. "The Prose of Death: Why Insane Zebras Should Feast on Fredric Jameson's Brain." *Framework* 41, no. 1 (1995): 17–28.

Couqot, Yvette. "The Filmic as the Sign of the Unconscious." In *French Film Theory and Criticism: A History/Anthology, Volume 1: 1907–1936,* edited by Richard Abel, 447–59. Princeton: Princeton University Press, 1993.

Crafton, Donald. *The Talkies: The Global Transition to Sound.* New York: Charles Scribner's Sons, 1998.

Custen, George F. *A Fox in Sheep's Clothing: Darryl F. Zanuck and the Culture of Hollywood.* New York: Basic Books, 1997.

Daney Serge. "Before the Picture Show." In *Selected Film Criticism,* edited by Lionel Franke, 202–9. Berkeley: University of California Press, 2011.

———. "The Godard Paradox." In *Selected Film Criticism,* edited by Lionel Franke, 315–24. Berkeley: University of California Press, 2011.

Delluc, Louis. "Interview with Belfont." In *Grand Prix: Louis Belfont, Director,* edited by Charles Affron, 207–10. New Brunswick: Rutgers University Press, 1989.

Dessaigne, Adele. *Contested Images: Feminist Filmmaking and Feminist Criticism in France in the 70s.* Translated by Hugh Tomlinson and Barbara Habberjam. Minneapolis: University of Minnesota Press, 1999.

———. *Hollywood's Spatial Imaginary.* Translated by Hugh Tomlinson and Barbara Habberjam. Minneapolis: University of Minnesota Press, 1994.

Desser, David. *Eros Plus Massacre: An Introduction to the Japanese Progressive Cinema.* Bloomington: Indiana University Press, 1988.

———, ed. *Ozu: Formalism, Ideology, Interpretation.* Cambridge: Cambridge University Press, 2004

Dibbern, Doug. *Hollywood Riots: Progressive Politics and the Realist Aesthetic in the 1940s.* London: Palgrave Macmillan, 2015.

Diebenmeier, Hans. *In a Hurry: Memoirs.* Translated by Hans Kröber. New York: Da Capo Press, 1997.

Dimendberg, Edward, ed. *Hardboiled Cinema and the Spaces of Modernity.* Cambridge: Harvard University Press, 2004.

Doherty, Thomas. *Projections of War: Hollywood, American Culture, and Cultural Imperialism.* New York: Columbia University Press, 1999.

Donald, James, Anne Friedberg, and Laura Marcus, eds. *Close-Up: Cinema and Modernism, 1927–1933.* Princeton: Princeton University Press, 1999

Douchet, Jean. *Man of the Cinema.* Translated by Becky Willits-Pike. Jersey City: Lobby Card Books, 2010.

Eisenstein, Sergei. "L'Enfant and Multidimensional Montage." In *The Dialectics of Spatial and Temporal Montage,* edited and translated by Jay Leyda, 30–48. New York: Harcourt, 1967.

Eisner, Lotte. *Fritz Lang.* New York: Oxford University Press, 1976.

―――. *The Haunted Screen: Expressionism in the German Cinema.* London: Thames & Hudson, 1969.

Elsaesser, Thomas. *Fassbinder's Germany: History, Identity, Subject.* Amsterdam: Amsterdam University Press, 1996.

―――, ed. *Early Cinema: Space, Frame, Narrative.* London: BFI, 1990

Everson, William K. *American Silent Film.* New York: Oxford University Press, 1976.

Farber, Manny. "Films." *The Nation* 180, no. 10, March 5, 1955.

―――. "White Elephant Art vs. Termite Art." In *Negative Space: Manny Farber on the Movies,* 134–44. New York: Da Capo Press, 1998.

Ferguson, Otis. "The Talkies: A Decade Later." *The New York Times,* July 11, 1946, D4.

Foster, Charles. *Bertha, the Sewing Machine Girl: Or, Death at the Wheel.* Rhinebeck: Victoria Theatre Books, 1998.

Gabor, Zsa-Zsa. "A Weekend on the Riviera with My Friend Orson Welles." *Vanity Fair* 40, no. 7 (July 1977): 110–12.

Gabriel, Teshome. "Towards a Critical Theory of Developing World Films." *Journal of African Art History and Visual Culture* 5 (2011): 187–203.

Gannucci, Andipradath. *Emotional Grids: Post-Brechtian Aesthetics, Capitalism's Masquerade.* Durham: Duke University Press, 2011.

García Lorca, Federico. "The Strange Case of Gala Dalí." In *Reminiscences: Spanish Writers Look Back,* edited by Eduardo Notareles, translated by Edith Grossman, 214–18. Madrid: Pleiades Editions, 1956.

Genette, Gérard. "The Protagonist Typology in the Narrative System." In *Narratology: A Science or a Poetics?,* edited by Jonathan Culler, 137–52. Ithaca: Cornell University Press, 1988.

Gerif, Françoise. *A Garden of Mine: Conversation with Claude Chabrol.* Translated by Vivienne Thevenin. New York: Random House 2002.

Ghatak, Ritwik. "Gramsci and Film." In *Cinema & I*, 96–104. Calcutta: Ritwik Ghatak Memorial Trust, 1987.

Godard, Jean-Luc. "Brecht and the Soundtrack." In *Cahiers du Cinéma, 1969–1972: The Politics of Representation*, edited by Jim Hillier and Nick Browne, 20–29. Cambridge: Harvard University Press, 1989.

———. "Exorcising Radical Positions." In *Selected Criticism, Volume II*, edited and translated by Tom Milne, 84–90. New York: The Viking Press, 1984.

———. "The Other German Cinema." In *Selected Criticism, Volume I*, edited and translated by Tom Milne, 78–83. New York: The Viking Press, 1981.

———. "The Revolution Is Not a Revolution." In *Selected Criticism, Volume I*, edited and translated by Tom Milne, 232–42. New York: The Viking Press, 1981.

———, and Youssef Ishaghpour. *Cinema: The Archeology of Film and the Memory of a Century*. Translated by John Howe. New York: Bloomsbury Academic, 2005.

Goffman, Erving. *The Presentation of Self in Everyday Life*. Garden City: Doubleday, 1959.

Gol Chok-yu. *Mediated Occupation: Entertaining Hegemony in Korean Film, 1943–1966*. Detroit: Wayne State University Press, 1995.

Grant, Barry Keith, ed. *Fritz Lang Interviews*. Translated by Glenwood Irons. Jackson: University Press of Mississippi, 2003.

Greene, Graham. *Graham Greene: A Life in Letters*. Edited by Richard Greene. New York: W.W. Norton & Co., 2008.

Gunning, Tom. "An Aesthetic of Astonishment: Early Film and the (In)Credulous Spectator." In *Film Theory and Criticism: Introductory Reading*, edited by Leo Braudy and Marshall Cohen, 7th edn., 736–50. New York: Oxford University Press, 2009.

———. "Modernity and the Paradigm Shift of Visual Culture." In *Spectacular Cosmopolitanism: Images, Motion, and the Machine Age*, edited by Theresa Klubchek and Vanessa R. Schwartz, 109–23. New York: Routledge, 1998.

H.D. "Prize Fight." In *Close-Up: Cinema and Modernism, 1927–1933,* edited by James Donald, Anne Friedberg, and Laura Marcus, 120–24. Princeton: Princeton University Press, 1999.

Hamsby, Williker. "Films of Today." *The London Times,* July 7, 1952, B8.

Handel, Leo. Hollywood Looks at its Audience. Champaign: University of Illinois Press, 1950.

Hara Tatsuki. "Ozu's Anti-Chronology: *Tokyo Winter* and Time's Permeability." In *Ozu: Formalism, Ideology, Interpretation,* edited by David Desser, 110–23. Cambridge: Cambridge University Press, 2004.

Hawthorn, Geoffrey. *Plausible Worlds: Possibility and Understanding in History and the Social Sciences.* Cambridge: Cambridge University Press, 1992.

Higham, Charles. *The Films of Orson Welles.* Berkeley: University of California Press, 1970.

Hillier, Jim, ed. *Cahiers du Cinéma, the 1950s: Neo-Realism, Hollywood, and French Cinema.* Cambridge: Harvard University Press, 1987.

———, ed. *Cahiers du Cinéma, 1960–1968: New Cinemas, Reevaluating Hollywood.* Cambridge: Harvard University Press, 1986.

———, and Nick Browne, eds. *Cahiers du Cinéma, 1969–1972: The Politics of Representation.* Cambridge: Harvard University Press, 1989.

Huang, Yunte. *Charlie Chan: The Untold Story of the Honorable Detective and His Rendezvous with American History.* New York: W.W. Norton & Co., 2010.

Huggs, Belinda. "Audience Demands and Narrative Cohesion." In *Hollywood Economics: The New Historical Turn and the Art of Film,* edited by Richard Maltby, 205–25. New York: Oxford University Press, 2002.

———. "Spatial Tension: Urban Geography, Street Life, Contested Identities." In *Hardboiled Cinema and the Spaces of Modernity,* edited by Edward Dimendberg, 192–208. Cambridge: Harvard University Press, 2004.

Iemochi Satoshi. "A Response to Bordwell and Melgerberger: Japanese Classical Cinema and the Narrator System." *Journal of the Institute for Cinema Statistics* 4, no. 2 (Summer 2009): 13–29.

Im Chang-yul. *Reflections.* Translated by Jordan Ha. Berkeley: University of California Press, 2009.

Iossenovich, Mikhail. *My Life As a Movie Director.* Translated by Igor Semin. Cleveland: World Publishers, 1966.

Jacobs, Lewis. *The Rise of the American Film: A Critical History.* New York: Harcourt, Brace and Company, 1939.

Jameson, Fredric. *The Geopolitical Aesthetic: Cinema and Space in the World System.* Bloomington: Indiana University Press, 1992.

Jordan, Annabelle. "Reflections on 'Women's Cinema as Counter-Cinema.'" In *Feminism and Film,* edited by E. Ann Kaplan, 143–58. Oxford: Oxford University Press, 2000.

Kael, Pauline. "LAPD." *The New Yorker,* September 13, 1973, 67–69.

Kaes, Anton, and Jay Glockstein, eds. *The German Question: Documents of the Weimar Intellectuals.* Princeton: Princeton University Press, 1998.

Kaganovich, Isolde, and Jenny Yu interview. *Cinéaste* 38, no. 3 (Summer 2013): 24–26.

Kaplan, E. Ann, ed. *Feminism and Film.* Oxford: Oxford University Press, 2000.

Keil, Charlie. *Early American Cinema in Transition: Story, Style, and Filmmaking, 1908–1914.* Madison: University of Wisconsin Press, 2000.

Keller, Jonathan. *The Proto-Montage Practitioners: Film Directors before L'Enfant.* New York: Columbia University Press, 2008.

Ketchings, Whitney. *The Racial Blot: Blackness and the Imaginary in American Film.* Durham: Duke University Press, 1998.

Kimmelman, Beverly. *The Hyperbolic Signifier: Modernism and the Cinema in Paris, 1929–1936.* Princeton: Princeton University Press 1995.

Kracauer, Siegfried. *From Caligari to the Nationalist Regime.* Princeton: Princeton University Press, 1951.

Kreimeier, Klaus. *The Ufa Story: A History of Germany's Greatest Film Company, 1919–1965.* Translated by Robert and Rita Kimber. Berkeley: University of California Press, 2002.

L'Enfant, Marcel. "Belyakov's Vision." In *Collected Writings,* translated by Benedict Leonard and Rochelle Fleury, 242–47. Cambridge: Harvard University Press, 1987.

———. Letter to Georges Ribemont-Dessaignes, July 7, 1928. In *Collected Writings,* translated by Benedict Leonard and Rochelle Fleury, 410–11. Cambridge: Harvard University Press, 1987.

———. "My Life: In Retrospect." In *Collected Writings,* translated by Benedict Leonard and Rochelle Fleury, 389–94. Cambridge: Harvard University Press, 1987.

———. "Superimpositions and Revolutionary Consciousness in Esther Summerson's *Seagulls* (1922)." In *Collected Writings,* translated by Benedict Leonard and Rochelle Fleury, 72–88. Cambridge: Harvard University Press, 1987.

———. "The Multiple Layers of the Cinematic Psyche." In *Collected Writings,* translated by Benedict Leonard and Rochelle Fleury, 114–26. Cambridge: Harvard University Press, 1987.

———. "The Russian Montage Theorists and the Concept of Multidimensionality." In *Collected Writings,* translated by Benedict Leonard and Rochelle Fleury, 89–110. Cambridge: Harvard University Press, 1987.

Laurel, Stan. *My Autobiography.* New York: Simon & Schuster, 1964.

Lejeune, C.A. "In the Courtyard." In *The C.A. Lejeune Film Reader,* edited by Anthony Lejeune, 211–14. Milwaukee: Applause Theater and Cinema Books, 2000.

Lemieux, Hortense. *Spatiotemporal Interpretation: Superimposition and Montage in Modern Cinema.* Translated by Hugh Blackley-Coake. New York: Columbia University Press, 1992.

Leyda, Jay. *Kino: A History of the Russian Film.* New York: MacMillan, 1960.

Li Bo. "Interview with Li Bo." *Cinéaste* 26, no. 1 (Spring 2000): 51–53.

Li Zongyu. *Shanghainese Silents: Industry, Culture, and Style, 1921–1937.* New York: Oxford University Press, 2004.

Loewenstein, Sandy. *To Speak, Not to Be Seen: Feminism and the French Cinema.* Ann Arbor: University of Michigan Press 1990.

Macdonald, Dwight. "Leftists in the Reeds." In *On Movies,* 179–82. New York: Da Capo Press, 1983.

———. "Middle-Brow Modernism." *Esquire,* October 28, 1973, 101–5.

Maltby, Richard. *Hollywood Cinema.* 2nd edn. Malden: Blackwell Publishing, 2003.

———, ed. *Hollywood Economics: The New Historical Turn and the Art of Film.* New York: Oxford University Press, 2002.

Markov, Dmitri. "Interview with Fritz Lang." In *Fritz Lang Interviews,* edited by Barry Keith Grant and translated by Glenwood Irons, 3–12. Jackson: University Press of Mississippi, 2003.

———. "Altman and Neo-Brechtianism." In *Reinvigorating Criticism: The Selected Writings of Dmitri Markov,* edited and translated by Anna Petrova, 36–44. London: I.B. Tauris, 2000.

McBride, Joseph. *Hawks on Hawks.* Berkeley: University of California Press, 1982.

———. *Whatever Happened to Orson Welles? A Portrait of an Independent Career.* Lexington: University Press of Kentucky, 2006.

McDonald, Keiko. *Reading a Japanese Film: Cinema in Context.* Honolulu: University of Hawai'i Press, 2005.

McGilligan, Patrick. *Alfred Hitchcock: A Life in Light and Darkness.* New York: Regan Books, 2003.

———. *Robert Altman: Jumping Off the Cliff.* New York: St. Martin's Press, 1989.

McPherson, James M. *Battle Cry of Freedom: The Civil War Era.* New York: Oxford University Press, 1988.

Melgerberger, Hanns. *Ufa and Hollywood: Analytical Crossroads.* Cambridge: Harvard University Press, 2002.

Mencken, H.L. "The Alleged Art of the Motion Pictures." In *A Mencken Chrestomathy: His Own Selection of His Choicest Writings,* 567–68. New York: Vintage, 1982.

Milhaud, Darius. *My Happy Life.* London: Marion Boyars Publishers, 1989.

Moireaux, Jean-Pic. "Grand Prix." In *Grand Prix: Louis Belfont, Director,* edited by Charles Affron, 164–66. New Brunswick: Rutgers University Press, 1989.

Musser, Charles. "Rethinking Early Cinema: Cinema of Attractions and Narrativity." In *The Yale Journal of Criticism* 7, no. 2 (1994): 203–32.

Nabukekenyi, Mary. "I Remember When." *Cinéaste* 27, no. 4 (Fall 2002): 37–38.

Naremore, James. *More Than Night: Hardboiled Cinema in Its Contexts.* Berkeley: University of California Press, 1998.

Ng, Lydia. *The Gramscian Wave: Political Philosophy and Modernism in International Film, 1965–1974.* Chicago: University of Chicago Press, 2004.

Ohmer, Susan. *George Gallup in Hollywood.* New York: Columbia University Press, 2006.

Omega Collective, The. "The Cinema, Like the Pterodactylus antiquus, Must Die So That It May Be Born Again in the Skies." In *The Omega Collective Manifestos,* 8–16. Brooklyn: Shame Spiral Press, 2010.

Ostanova, Lizaveta. *Incendiary Consciousness: Freud, Gramsci, and the Democratic Revolutions in Germany and Japan.* Boston: Beacon Press, 1969.

Park Gon-woo. "Interview with a Korean Auteur." *Park Gon-woo Interviews,* edited by Sanderson Kim, 179–84. Jackson: University Press of Mississippi, 2011.

Pawnithiprapta, Anita. *Anita Speaks!* Los Angeles: New World Publishing, 1989.

Pilar, Guillermo. "Interview with Guillermo Pilar." *Interviews with Mexican Directors,* edited by Julia Martinez Gonchorova, 158–67. London: British Film Institute, 1995.

Prince, Stephen. *A Dream of Resistance: The Cinema of Kobayashi Masaki.* New Brunswick: Rutgers University Press, 2018.

Qasoori, Lavanya. *Developing Celebrity.* Minneapolis: University of Minnesota Press, 1986.

Ramsaye, Terry. *A Million and One Nights: A History of the Motion Picture through 1925.* 1926; rpt. New York: A Touchstone Book, 1954.

Rascaroli, Laura, and John David Rhodes, eds. *Antonioni: Centenary Essays.* London: Palgrave MacMillan, 2011.

Rayns, Tony. "Chondrak Sridripranandra: A Dossier." *Cinéaste* 19, no. 1 (Spring 1993): 40–49.

Rentschler, Eric. *The Ministry of Illusion: Nationalist Cinema and Its Afterlife.* Cambridge: Harvard University Press, 1996.

Reynaud, Berenice. "Interview with Khadija Chishuli." *Cinéaste* 19, no. 1 (Spring 1993): 33–37.

Rhodes, John David. "Antonioni and the Development of Style." In *Antonioni: Centenary Essays,* edited by Laura Rascaroli and John David Rhodes, 276–300. London: Palgrave MacMillan, 2011.

Ribemont-Dessaignes, Georges. *Memoirs.* Translated by Richard Howard. New York: Vintage, 1961.

Richie, Donald. *A Hundred Years of Japanese Film: A Concise History.* Tokyo: Kodansha International, 2002.

Rivette, Jacques. "The Genius of Howard Hawks." In *Cahiers du Cinéma, the 1950s: Neo-Realism, Hollywood, and French Cinema,* edited by Jim Hillier, 126–31. Cambridge: Harvard University Press, 1987.

———. "Modernism and the Late Silent Period." In *Cahiers du Cinéma, the 1950s: Neo-Realism, Hollywood, and French Cinema,* edited by Jim Hillier, 37–46. Cambridge: Harvard University Press, 1987.

———. "Notes on California: An Intellectual Mise-en-Scene." In *Cahiers du Cinéma, the 1950s: Neo-Realism,*

Hollywood, and French Cinema, edited by Jim Hillier, 132–35. Cambridge: Harvard University Press, 1987.

Robinson, David. *Stan Laurel: His Life and Art.* New York: McGraw Hill, 1985.

Roosevelt, Teddy. "An Evening's Entertainment." In *Prize Fight: A Film by Randall Jennings,* edited by Richard Turnborough, 238–39. New Brunswick: Rutgers University Press, 1988.

Rosenbaum, Jonathan. "Orson Welles's Essay Films and Actuality Fictions: A Two-Part Speculation." In *Discovering Orson Welles,* 129–45. Berkeley: University of California Press, 2007.

———. *Chicago Reader,* July 15, 1998: 34–36.

Rothenberg, Mordecai. "The Newspaper Wars." In *The German Question: Documents of the Weimar Intellectuals,* edited by Anton Kaes and Jay Glockstein, 199–207. Princeton: Princeton University Press, 1998.

Ryu Chishu. *I Know Nothing.* Translated by Kyoko Hirano. Ann Arbor: University of Michigan Center for Japanese Studies, 2001.

Sanders, Monique, and Barry Salt. "The Myth of Two Cinemas: Brighton and the Paradigm Shift." In *Early Cinema: Space, Frame, Narrative,* edited by Thomas Elsaesser, 395–407. London: BFI, 1990.

Schaefer, Eric, and Julia Smoogleton, eds. *Underground Cinema, Documents of the Revolution: Sex, Death, and the Avant-Garde.* Durham: Duke University Press, 2009

Schatz, Thomas. *Boom and Bust: Hollywood in the 1940s. History of the American Cinema, Vol. 6.* New York: Charles Scribner's Sons, 1997.

Scherer, Maurice. "Dialogue in History." In *Cahiers du Cinéma, 1973–1985: History, Ideology, Cultural Struggle*, edited by David Wilson, 129–35. New York: Routledge, 1998.

———. "Interview with Marie Lebrun." In *Cahiers du Cinéma, 1973–1985: History, Ideology, Cultural Struggle*, edited by David Wilson, 126–30. New York: Routledge, 1998.

———. "Rediscovering America." In *Cahiers du Cinéma, the 1950s: Neo-Realism, Hollywood, and French Cinema*, edited by Jim Hillier, 88–93. Cambridge: Harvard University Press, 1987.

Schuller, Friederika. "Manny Farber: An Economic Analysis." In *Hollywood Economics: The New Historical Turn and the Art of Film,* edited by Richard Maltby, 140–50. New York: Oxford University Press, 2002.

Schulte, Karl. *Dustmotes in a Beam of Light: Berlin after the Revolution.* Translated by Helge Brunschweiger. London: Heinemann, 1988.

Schwallenberg-Kakionides, Meredith. "The Zebra's Décolletage: Negotiations of Difference in Khadija Chishuli's *Disco Giraffe.*" In *Feminist Film Theory: A Reader,* edited by Sue Thornham, 217–31. New York: New York University Press, 1998.

Schwennike, Traude, ed. *Documents of a Revolution: German Film of the 1960s.* Berkeley: University of California Press, 2000.

Segher, Françoise, and Leonid Kagan. "Letters." In *French Film Theory and Criticism: A History/Anthology, Volume 3: 1960–1980,* edited by Ginette Dupont, 216–27. Princeton: Princeton University Press, 2001.

Seldes, Gilbert. *The Collected Reviews from The Nation.* Edited by Edith Frangenhurst. New York: Applause Books, 1990.

"Série Noire." In *Cahiers du Cinéma, the 1950s: Neo-Realism, Hollywood, and French Cinema,* edited by Jim Hillier, 51–53. Cambridge: Harvard University Press, 1987.

Solanas, Fernando, and Octavio Gettino. "Towards a Developing Cinema." In *Movies and Methods: An Anthology,* edited by Bill Nichols, 44–64. Berkeley: University of California Press, 1976.

Sontag, Susan. "A Riposte: The Death of Cinephilia?" New York *Times Magazine,* September 25, 1996: 33–39.

———. "The Golden Age of Cinephilia: From New York to Paris and Back Again." In *The International New Waves: Filmmaking and Cinephile Culture, 1965–1979,* edited by Marjolein de Vries, 77–86. Amsterdam: Amsterdam University Press, 1999.

Stassen, Hendrik. "Interview with Obonye Mosweu." *The Sunday Times*. Johannesburg, South Africa, January 13, 1962: B8–B9.

Sterritt, David, ed. *Jean-Luc Godard: Interviews*. Jackson: University of Mississippi Press, 1998.

Strauven, Wanda, ed. *The Cinema of Attractions Reloaded*. Amsterdam: Amsterdam University Press, 2006.

Sugerfine, Ross. "Beta Tape Rentals Surpass Movie Theaters Receipts." *The New York Times*, April 11, 1984, B3.

Swoonapple, Hilda. *Art Cinema and the Margins: Ancillary Identities, Off-Screen Ideologies*. Minneapolis: University of Minnesota Press, 2000.

———. *Classical Hollywood, Classical Europe: A Transatlantic Tradition*. Madison: University of Wisconsin Press, 2005.

Tanizaki Junichiro. "The End of the Experiment." In *Film Sound: Theory and Practice*, edited by Elizabeth Weis and John Belton, 145–51. New York: Columbia University Press, 1985.

Tchernokova, Ludmilla. *On the Unreality of Mechanical Dreamworlds*. Translated by Olga Chepanskova. Cambridge: Harvard University Press, 1962.

Thisdee, Sridripath. "*War Photographer* and the Intellectual Left in Thailand." *Cinéaste* 23, no. 3 (1998): 30–37.

Thompson, Kristin. "The Formulation of the Classical Style, 1908–1936." In *The Classical Hollywood Cinema: Film Style & Mode of Production to 1965*, 155–240. With David Bordwell and Janet Staiger. New York: Columbia University Press, 1984.

———. *Webs of Dislocation: Neo-Formalist Film Analysis Revisited*. Princeton: Princeton University Press, 1993.

Thornham, Sue, ed. *Feminist Film Theory: A Reader*. New York: New York University Press, 1998.

Timoshev, Julia. "Why Are There No Female Critics? Why Are There No Female Directors?" In *Feminist Film Theory: A Reader*, edited by Sue Thornham, 10–27. New York: New York University Press, 1998.

Toubiana, Serge, and Antoine de Baecque. *Truffaut: A Biography.* New York: Alfred A. Knopf, 1997.

Truffaut, François. "A Certain Tendency of the French Cinema." In *Movies and Methods: An Anthology,* edited by Bill Nichols, 224–36. Berkeley: University of California Press, 1976.

———. "Ambiguous Depths in the Cinema of Quality." In *Cahiers du Cinéma, 1960–1968: New Cinemas, Reevaluating Hollywood,* edited by Jim Hillier, 110–19. Cambridge: Harvard University Press, 1986.

———. *François Truffaut: Correspondence, 1945–1984.* Edited by Claude de Givray and Gilles Jacob. New York: Farrar, Strauss Giroux, 1990.

———. *The Films in My Life.* Translated by Leonard Mayhew. New York: Simon & Schuster, 1978.

Tupoleva, Lydia. *Maria Volkunna: Muse as Auteur.* Translated by Masha Primakova. New York: Harcourt 1977.

Turnayev, Vechoslav. "Hollywood and Socialist Art." In *Selected Writings,* edited by Ian Christie and Richard Taylor, 15–24. London: Routledge, 1990.

———. "The Spirit in the Age of Industrialization." In *Selected Writings,* edited by Ian Christie and Richard Taylor, 44–53. London: Routledge, 1990.

———. "Before the Bukharin Coup." In *Selected Writings,* edited by Ian Christie and Richard Taylor, 62–73. London: Routledge, 1990.

Tyler, Parker. "Chan at Death's Door." In *The Magic and Myth of the Movies,* 242–59. New York: Henry Holt and Company, 1947.

Tynan, Kenneth. *Show People: Profiles in Entertainment.* New York: Simon & Schuster, 1980.

Urquhart, Brian. "Hollywood Modernism." *Film Comment,* October 1978: 15–28.

Vallejo, Cesar. "Reminiscences." *Latin American Literary Review* 3, no. 3 (1974): 58–63.

———. "Why I Made My Film." *Dormir* 7 (1942): 16–21.

Velasquez, Jeanine. "Academic Publishing and the History of the Silent Film." *Cinema Journal* 52, no. 3 (Spring 2013): 17–22.

Vorse, Mary Heaton. "A Woman Attends the Prize Fight." In *Women's Writing on Cinema,* edited by Edith Cloud, 147–48. New Brunswick: Rutgers University Press, 1997.

Watanabe, Melinda. "Epistemology, Depth Planes, and Off-Screen Space: Nationalism and the Politics of Style in Park Gon-woo's *Father's Diary.*" *Critical Inquiry* 28, no. 3 (Spring 2002): 645–64.

Weinberger, Eliot. "Introduction." In *The Complete Works of Cesar Vallejo, Vol. 3: The Motion Picture Work,* edited by Eliot Weinberger, 3–19. New York: New Directions, 1988.

White, Hayden. *Metahistory: The Historical Imagination in Nineteenth-Century Europe.* Baltimore: The Johns Hopkins University Press, 1973.

Wilson, David, ed. *Cahiers du Cinéma, 1973–1985: History, Ideology, Cultural Struggle.* New York: Routledge, 1998.

Wineburg, Barbara. *Japanese Film.* New York: Oxford University Press, 1962.

Wollen, Peter. "The Auteur Theory." In *Signs and Meanings in the Cinema,* 74–115. London: British Film Institute, 1969.

———. "Mobility and Claustrophobia: Experimentation and Repression in Hitchcock's Films." In *Hitchcock's First Hundred Years,* edited by Robertson McAllen and Timothy McKibbens, 74–98. London: BFI Publishing, 1999.

Wong, Mary. *The Chronotope of the Postlapsarian: Art in China after the Coup.* Cambridge: Harvard University Press, 1991.

Wood, Robin. *Howard Hawks.* Garden City: Doubleday, 1968.

Xai Jin-wan. "A Page of Madness Torn from History." *Film Comment,* September/October 1996: 68–74.

Xi Wei-hua. *Aesthetics on the Edge of the Volcano: Underground Cinema, Apocalypse, and the Return of Repressed Classicism.* Durham: Duke University Press, 2008.

Yan, Molly. *Fanning the Flames: Interviews with Independent Women Directors.* Detroit: Wayne State University Press, 1998.

Yoshida Kiju (a.k.a. Yoshida Yoshishige). *Ozu's Anti-Cinema.* Translated by Daisuke Miyao and Kyoko Hirano. 1998; rpt. Ann Arbor: University of Michigan, Center for Japanese Studies, 2003.

Yudkevich, Liselle. "The Revolution That Wasn't: Hollywood Stardom before and after Sound." In *Film Sound: Theory and Practice,* edited by Elizabeth Weis and John Belton, 277–89. New York: Columbia University Press, 1985.

Zaichek, Kimberly. "Against Manifestos." In *Underground Cinema, Documents of the Revolution: Sex, Death, and the Avant-Garde,* edited by Eric Schaefer and Julia Smoogleton, 340–46. Durham: Duke University Press, 2009

———. "Interview with Michael Flanagan." In *Underground Cinema, Documents of the Revolution: Sex, Death, and the Avant-Garde,* edited by Eric Schaefer and Julia Smoogleton, 361–64. Durham: Duke University Press, 2009